Happy Homes

and the Hearts That Make Them

Happy Homes

and

The Hearts That Make Them.

—or—

Thrifty People and Why They Thrive.

By

Samuel Smiles,

AUTHOR OF "SELF-HELP," "LIFE OF THE STEPHENSONS," "THE HUGUENOTS," "CHARACTER," "THRIFT," "DUTY," ETC.

Carefully Revised, with Additional Matter,
—by—
Chas. A. Gaskell, A. M.

WAKING LION PRESS

ISBN 978-1-4341-0351-2

The views expressed in this book are the responsibility of the author and do not necessarily represent the position of the publisher. The reader alone is responsible for the use of any ideas or information provided by this book.

Published by Waking Lion Press, an imprint of The Editorium

Any additions to original text (publisher's preface, editor's notes, etc.) © 2012 by The Editorium. All rights reserved. Printed in the United States of America.

Waking Lion Press™, the Waking Lion Press logo, and The Editorium™ are trademarks of The Editorium, LLC

The Editorium, LLC
West Valley City, UT 84128-3917
wakinglionpress.com
wakinglion@editorium.com

Contents

Foreword		vii
1	The Art of Living; or Making the Most of Life	1
2	Healthy Homes	16
3	Influence of Character	28
4	Home Power	44
5	Companionship and Example	62
6	Work	77
7	Helping One's Self	89
8	Leaders of Industry—Inventors and Producers	102
9	Application and Perseverance	121
10	Helps and Opportunities—Scientific Pursuits	132
11	Energy and Will	149
12	Self—Culture—Facilities and Difficulties	161
13	Workers in Art	182
14	Men of Business	196
15	Money—Its Use and Abuse	205
16	Habits of Thrift	219
17	Methods of Economy	230

18	Courage	246
19	Self-Control	261
20	Duty—Truthfulness	272
21	Temper	282
22	Manner—Art	290
23	Companionship of Books	301
24	Companionship in Marriage	309
25	Example—Models	324
26	Character—the True Gentleman	332
27	The Discipline of Experience	343

Foreword

PROBABLY NO BOOKS *of the same general type* were ever written that have so much interested and inspired to worthy action the various classes to whom they were addressed, as have the productions of Samuel Smiles. Though written for the people of Great Britain, and containing numerous paragraphs not at all adapted to American readers, yet the large proportion of matter is of such general application, embracing, as it does, so vast a range of experience and testimony, that they have already reached a large sale, not only among all classes of English speaking people, but also among the people of Continental Europe. Many books of their class have been produced in this country, much of the matter of which has been unscrupulously garbled from the various volumes of Mr. Smiles. It has been our purpose, in the preparation of this book, to place within the reach of our people all of this author's ethical works, including those most recently published, carefully sifting from them such matter as has been thought to be of local or purely Anglican application, or to be least interesting and beneficial to American readers. Mr. Smiles' more lengthy and detailed biographical sketches become tiresome to many. The omission of such, and in some cases the substitution of lessons from the lives of certain of our own countrymen, while not subtracting from its interest with the few, will certainly add greatly to that with which the larger circle of readers peruse it. These changes and additions have made necessary an entirely new index, the laborious preparation of which none can appreciate but those who have had work of this character to do.

The marked interest which attaches to Mr. Smiles' productions is chiefly due to his happy use of biography. Readers who tire of extended biographical histories find here groups of the wise and distinguished of earth, each giving testimony to the various principles the author wishes to inculcate. This method of applying the accumulated experience and testimony of the past to illustrate and enforce principles, although by no means new, is certainly a most effective method of impressing truth. The interest excited by the novel arises solely from our interest in the lives and struggles of men and women. They are interesting biographies. But much more interest should attach to lives actually lived and conquests actually made, provided they are produced with equal care.

The home is the epitome of society and government. The application of these principles to every member of the home—the importance of their inculcation in the home where character is chiefly molded—and the value of such lessons in making every home what it may be and should be, has dictated the title, "Happy Homes, and the Hearts that Make Them."

—Chas. A. Gaskell.

Chapter 1

The Art of Living; or Making the Most of Life

"Everyone is the son of his own work." —Cervantes.

THE ART OF LIVING deserves a place among the fine arts. Like literature, it may be ranked with the humanities. It is the art of turning the means of living to the best account—of making the best of everything. It is the art of extracting from life its highest enjoyment, and through it, of reaching its highest results.

To live happily, the exercise of no small degree of art is required. Like poetry and painting, the art of living comes chiefly by nature; but all can cultivate and develop it. It can be fostered by parents and teachers, and perfected by self-culture. Without intelligence it cannot exist.

Happiness is not, like a large and beautiful gem, so uncommon and rare that all search for it is vain, all efforts to obtain it hopeless; but it consists of a series of smaller and commoner gems, grouped and set together, forming a pleasing and graceful whole. Happiness consists in the enjoyment of little pleasures scattered along the common path of life, which in the eager search for some great and exciting joy, we are apt to overlook. It finds delight in the performance of common duties, faithfully and honorably fulfilled.

The art of living is abundantly exemplified in actual life. Take two men of equal means, one of whom knows the art of living, and the other not. The one has the seeing eye and the intelligent mind. Nature is ever new to him, and full of beauty. He can live in the present, rehearse the past, or anticipate the glory of the future. With him life has a deep meaning, and requires the performance of duties which are satisfactory to his conscience, and are therefore pleasurable. He improves himself; acts upon his age, helps to elevate the depressed classes, and is active in every good work. His hand is never tired, his mind is never weary. He goes through life joyfully, helping others to its enjoyment. Intelligence, ever expanding, gives him every day fresh insight into men and things. He lays down his life full of honor and blessing, and his greatest monument is the good deeds he has done, and the beneficent example he has set before his fellow-creatures.

The other has comparatively little pleasure in life. He has scarcely reached manhood ere he has exhausted its enjoyments. Money has done everything that it could for him, yet he feels life to be vacant and cheerless. Traveling does him no good, because, for him, history has no meaning. He is only alive to the impositions of innkeepers and couriers, and the disagreeableness of traveling for days amidst great mountains, among peasants and sheep, cramped up in a carriage. Picture galleries he feels to be a bore, and he looks into them because other people do. When he grows old, and has run the round of fashionable dissipations, and there is nothing left which he can relish, life becomes a masquerade, in which he recognizes only knaves, hypocrites and flatterers. Though he does not enjoy life, yet he is terrified to leave it. Then the curtain falls. With all his wealth, life has been to him a failure, for he has not known the art of living, without which life cannot be enjoyed.

It is not wealth that gives the true zest to life, but reflection, appreciation, taste, culture. Above all, the seeing eye and the feeling heart are indispensable. With these, the humblest lot may be made blessed. Labor and toil may be associated with the highest thoughts and the purest tastes. The lot of labor may thus become elevated and ennobled. Montaigne observes that "all moral philosophy is as applicable to a vulgar and private life as to the most splendid. Every man carries the entire form of the human condition within him."

Even in material comfort, good taste is the real economist, as well as an enhancer of joy. Scarcely have you passed the door-step of your friend's house, when you can detect whether taste presides within it or not. There is an air of neatness, order, arrangement, grace, and refinement that gives a thrill of pleasure, though you can not define it or explain how it is. There is a flower in the window, or a picture against the wall, that marks the home of taste. A bird sings at the windowsill, books lie about, and the furniture, though common, is, tidy, suitable, and, it may be, even elegant.

The art of living extends to all the economies of the household. It selects wholesome food, and serves it with taste. There is no profusion; the fare may be very humble, but it has a savor about it; everything is so clean and neat, the water so sparkles in the glass, that you do not desire richer viands or a more exciting beverage.

Look into another house, and you will see profusion enough, without either taste or order. The expenditure is larger, and yet you do not feel "at home" there. The atmosphere seems to be full of discomfort. Books, hats, shawls, and stockings in course of repair, are strewed about. Two or three chairs are loaded with goods. The rooms are in confusion. No matter how much money is spent, it does not mend matters. Taste is wanting, for the manager of the household has not yet learned the art of living.

You see the same contrast in cottage-life. The lot of poverty is sweetened by taste. It selects the healthiest, most open neighborhood, where the air is pure and the streets are clean. You see at a glance, by the sanded door-step, and the window-panes without a speck—perhaps blooming roses or geraniums shining through them—that the tenant within, however poor, knows the art of making the best of his lot. How different from the foul cottage-dwellings you see elsewhere, with the dirty children playing in the gutters, the slattern-like women lounging by the door-step, and the air of sullen poverty that seems to pervade the place! And yet the weekly income in the former home may be no greater, perhaps even less, than in the other.

How is it that of two men working in the same field or in the same shop, one is merry as a lark; always cheerful, well-clad, and as clean as his work will allow him to be; comes out on Sunday mornings in his best suit to go to church with his family; is never without a penny in his purse, and has something besides in the savings-bank; is a reader of books and a subscriber to a newspaper, besides taking in some literary journal for family reading; while the other man, with equal or even superior weekly wages, comes to work in the mornings sour and sad; is always full of grumbling; is badly clad and badly shod; is never seen out of his house on Sundays till about mid-day, when he appears in his shirtsleeves, his face unwashed, his hair unkempt, his eyes bleared and blood-shot; his children left to run about the gutters, with no one, apparently, to care for them; is always at his last coin, except on Saturday night, and then he has a long score of borrowings to repay; belongs to no club, has nothing saved, but lives literally from hand to mouth; reads none, thinks none, but only toils, eats, drinks, and sleeps—why is it that there is so remarkable a difference between these two men?

Simply for this reason: that the one has the intelligence and the art to extract joy and happiness from life; to be happy himself, and to make those about him happy; whereas the other has not cultivated his intelligence, and knows nothing whatever of the art of either making himself or his family happy. With the one, life is a scene of loving, helping, and sympathizing; of carefulness, forethought, and calculation; of reflection, action and duty; with the other, it is only a rough scramble for meat and drink; duty is not thought of, reflection is banished, prudent forethought is never for a moment entertained.

But look to the result: the former is respected by his fellow-workmen and beloved by his family; he is an example of well-being and well-doing to all who are within reach of his influence; whereas the other is as unreflective and miserable as nature will allow him to, be; he is shunned by good men; his family are afraid at the sound of his footsteps, his wife perhaps trembling at his approach; he dies without leaving any regrets behind him, except, it may be, on the part of his family, who are left to be maintained by the charity of the public, or by the pittance doled out by friends and relatives.

For these reasons, it is worth every man's while to study the important art of living happily. Even the poorest man may by this means extract an increased amount of joy and blessing from life. The world need not be a "vale of tears," unless we ourselves will it to be so. We have the command, to a great extent, over our own lot. At all events, our mind is our own possession; we can cherish happy thoughts there; we can regulate and control our tempers and dispositions to a considerable extent, we can educate ourselves, and bring out the better part of our nature, which in most men is allowed to sleep a deep sleep; we can read good books, cherish pure thoughts, and lead lives of peace, temperance and virtue, so as to secure the respect of good men, and transmit the blessing of a faithful example to our successors.

The art of living is best exhibited in the home. The first condition of a happy home, where good influences prevail over bad ones, is comfort. Where there are carking cares, querulousness, untidiness, slovenliness, and dirt, there can be little comfort either for man or woman. The husband who has been working all day expects to have something as a compensation for his toil. The least that his wife can do for him is to make his house snug, clean and tidy against his home-coming at eve. That is the truest economy, the best housekeeping, the worthiest domestic management, which makes the home so pleasant and agreeable that a man feels, when approaching it, that he is about to enter a sanctuary; and that when there, there is no ale-house attraction that can draw him away from it.

We are not satisfied merely with a home. It must be comfortable. The most wretched, indeed, are those who have no homes—the homeless! but not less wretched are those whose homes are without comfort—those of whom Charles Lamb once said, "The homes of the very poor are no homes." It is comfort, then, that is the soul of the home—its essential principle, its vital element.

Comfort does not merely mean warmth, good furniture, good eating and drinking. It means something higher than this. It means cleanliness, pure air, order, frugality; in a word, house-thrift and domestic government. Comfort is the soil in which the human being grows, not only physically, but morally. Comfort lies, indeed, at the root of many virtues.

Wealth is not necessary for comfort. Luxury requires wealth, but not comfort. A poor man's home, moderately supplied with the necessaries of life, presided over by a cleanly, frugal housewife, may contain all the elements of comfortable living. Want of comfort is for the most part caused, not so much by the absence of sufficient means as by the absence of the requisite knowledge of domestic management.

Comfort, it must be admitted, is in a great measure *relative*. What is comfort to one man would be misery to another. Even the commonest mechanic of this day would consider it miserable to live after the style of the nobles a few centuries ago—to sleep on straw beds, and live in rooms littered with rushes. William the Conqueror had neither a shirt to his back nor a pane of glass to his windows. Queen Elizabeth was one of the first to wear stockings. All the queens before her were stockingless.

Comfort depends as much on persons as on "things." It is out of the character and temper of those who govern homes that the feeling of comfort arises, much more than out of handsome furniture, heated rooms, or household luxuries and conveniences.

Comfortable people are kindly-tempered. Good temper may be set down as an invariable condition of comfort. There must be peace, mutual forbearance, mutual help, and disposition to make the best of everything. "Better is a dinner of herbs where love is, than a stalled ox and hatred therewith."

Comfortable people are persons of common sense, discretion, prudence, and economy. They have a natural affinity for honesty and justice, goodness and truth. They do not run into debt, for that is a species of dishonesty. They live within their means, and lay by something for a rainy day. They provide for the things of their own household, yet they are not wanting in hospitality and benevolence on fitting occasions. And what they do is done without ostentation.

Comfortable people do everything in order. They are systematic, steady, sober, industrious. They dress comfortably. They adapt themselves to the season—neither shivering in winter, nor perspiring in summer. They do not toil after a "fashionable appearance." They spend more on warm stockings than on gold rings, and prefer healthy, good bedding to gaudy window curtains.

The organization of the home depends, for the most part, upon woman. She is necessarily the manager of every family and household. How much, therefore, must depend upon her intelligent co-operation! Man's life revolves round woman. She is the sun of his social system. She is the queen of domestic life. The comfort of every home mainly depends upon her—upon her character, her temper, her power of organization, and her business management. A man may be economical, but unless there be economy at home, his frugality will be comparatively useless. "A man cannot thrive," the proverb says, "unless his wife let him."

House-thrift is homely, but beneficent. Though unseen of the world, it makes many people happy. It works upon individuals, and by elevating them, it elevates society itself. It is, in fact, a recipe of infallible efficacy for conferring the greatest possible happiness upon the greatest possible number. Without it, legislation, benevolence and philanthropy are mere palliatives; sometimes worse than useless, because they hold out hopes which are for the most part disappointed.

How happy does a man go forth to his labor or his business, and how doubly happy does he return from it, when he knows that his means are carefully husbanded and wisely applied by a judicious and well-managing wife! Such a woman is not only a power in her own house, but her example goes forth among her neighbors, and she stands before them as a model and a pattern. The habits of her children are formed after her habits; her actual life becomes the model after which they unconsciously mold themselves; for example always speaks more eloquently than words; it is instruction in action—wisdom at work.

First among woman's qualities is the intelligent use of her hands and fingers. Everyone knows how useful, how indispensable to the comfort of a household, is the tidy, managing, handy woman. Pestalozzi, with his usual sagacity, has observed that half the education of a woman comes through her fingers. There are wisdom and virtue at her finger-ends. But intellect must also accompany thrift, they must go hand-in-hand. A woman must not only be clever with her fingers, but possessed of the power of organizing household work.

Accordingly, to manage a household efficiently, there must be method. Without this, work can not be got through satisfactorily, either in offices, workshops, or households. By arranging work properly, by doing everything at the right time, with a view to the economy of labor, a large amount of business can be accomplished. Muddle flies before method, and confusion disappears. There is also a method in spending—in laying out money—which is as valuable to the housewife as method is in accomplishing her work. Money slips through the fingers of some people like quicksilver. We have already seen that many men are spendthrifts. But many women are the same, at least they do not know how to expend their husbands' earnings to the best advantage. You observe things very much out of place—frills and ruffles and ill-darned stockings, fine bonnets and clouted shoes, silk gowns and dirty petticoats, while the husband goes about ragged and torn, with scarcely a clean thing about him.

Industry is, of course, essential. This is the soul of business. But without method, industry will be less productive. Industry may sometimes look like confusion, but the methodical and industrious woman gets through her work in a quiet, steady style—without fuss, or noise, or dust-clouds.

Prudence is another important household qualification. Prudence comes from cultivated judgment, it means practical wisdom. It has reference to fitness, to propriety. It judges of the right thing to be clone, and of the right way of doing it. It calculates the means, order, time, and method of doing. Prudence learns much from experience, quickened by knowledge.

Punctuality is another eminently household qualification. How many grumblings would be avoided in domestic life by a little more attention being paid to this virtue. Late breakfasts and late dinners, "too late" for church and market, "cleanings" out of time, and "washings" protracted till midnight, bills put off with a "call again tomorrow," engagements and promises unfulfilled—what a host of little nuisances spring to mind at thought of the unpunctual housewife. The unpunctual woman, like the unpunctual man, becomes disliked, because she consumes our time, interferes with our plans, causes uneasy feelings, and virtually tells us that we are not of sufficient importance to cause her to be more punctual. To the business man time is money, and to the business woman it is more—it is peace, comfort, and domestic prosperity.

Perseverance is another good household habit. Lay down a good plan, and adhere to it. Do not be turned from it without a sufficient reason. Follow it diligently and faithfully, and it will yield fruits in good season. If the plan be a prudent one, based on practical wisdom, all things will gravitate toward it, and a mutual dependence will gradually be established among all the parts of the domestic system.

We might furnish numerous practical illustrations of the truth of these remarks, but our space will not permit, and we must leave the reader to supply them from his or her own experience.

There are many other illustrations which might be adduced of the art of making life happy. The management of the temper is an art full of beneficent results. By kindness, cheerfulness, and forbearance we can be happy almost at will, and at the same time spread happiness about us on every side. We can encourage happy thoughts in ourselves and others. We can be sober in habit. What can a wife and her children think of an intemperate husband and father? We can be sober in language, and shun cursing and swearing—the most useless, unmeaning, and brutal of vulgarities. Nothing can be so silly and unmeaning—not to say shocking, repulsive, and sinful—as the oaths so common in the mouths of vulgar swearers. They are profanation without purpose; impiety without provocation; blasphemy without excuse.

This leads us to remark, in passing, that in this country we are not sufficiently instructed in the art of good manners. We are rather rude and sometimes unapproachable. Manners do *not* make the man, as the proverb alleges; but manners make the man much more agreeable. A man may be noble in his heart, true in his dealings, virtuous in his conduct, and yet unmannerly. Suavity of disposition and gentleness of manners give the finish to the true gentleman.

By good manners we do not mean etiquette. This is only a conventional set of rules adopted by what is called "good society"; and many of the rules of etiquette are of the essence of rudeness. Etiquette does not permit genteel people to recognize in the streets a man with a shabby coat, though he be their brother. Etiquette is a liar in its "not at home"—ordered to be told by servants to callers at inconvenient seasons.

Good manners include many requisites; but they chiefly consist in politeness, courtesy, and kindness. They cannot be taught by rule, but they may be taught by example. It has been said that politeness is the art of showing men, by external signs, the internal regard we have for them. But a man may be perfectly polite to another without necessarily having any regard for him. Good manners are neither more nor less than beautiful behavior. It has been well said that "a beautiful form is better than a beautiful face, and a beautiful behavior is better than a beautiful form; it gives a higher pleasure than statues or pictures; it is the finest of the fine arts."

Manner is the ornament of action; indeed, a good action without a good manner of doing it is stripped of half its value. A poor fellow gets into difficulties, and solicits help of a friend. He obtains it, but it is with a "There—take that; but I don't like lending." The help is given with a kind of kick, and is scarcely accepted as a favor. The manner of the giving long rankles in the mind of the acceptor. Thus good manners mean kind manners, benevolence being the preponderating element in all kinds of pleasant intercourse between human beings.

A story is told of a poor soldier having one day called at the shop of a hair-dresser, who was busy with his customers, and asked relief, stating that he had staid beyond his leave of absence, and unless he could get a lift on the coach, fatigue and severe punishment awaited him. The hair-dresser listened to his story respectfully, and gave him a guinea. "God bless you, sir!" exclaimed the soldier, astonished at the amount, "how can I repay you? I have nothing in the world but this"—pulling out a dirty piece of paper from his pocket; "it is a recipe for making blacking; it is the best that was ever seen. Many a half-guinea I have had for it from the officers, and many bottles I have sold. May you be able to get something for it to repay you for your kindness to the poor soldier!" Oddly enough, that dirty piece of paper proved worth half a million of money to the hair-dresser. It was no less than the recipe for the famous Day & Martin's blacking; the hair-dresser being the late wealthy Mr. Day, whose manufactory is one of the notabilities of the metropolis.

Good manners have been supposed to be a peculiar mark of gentility, and that the individual exhibiting them has been born in some upper class of society. But the poorest classes may exhibit good manners toward each other, as well as the richest. One may be polite and kind toward others, without a penny in the purse. Politeness goes very far, yet it costs nothing; it is the cheapest of commodities. But we want to be taught good manners as well as other things. Some happy natures are "to the manor born." But the bulk of men need to be taught manners, and this can only be efficiently done in youth.

We have said that working-men might study good manners with advantage. Why should they not respect themselves and each other? It is by their demeanor toward each other—in other words, by their manners—that self-respect and mutual respect are indicated. We have been struck by the habitual politeness of even the poorest classes on the Continent. The workman lifts his cap and respectfully salutes his fellow-workman in passing. There is no sacrifice of manliness in this, but rather grace and dignity. The working-man, in respecting his fellow, respects himself and his order. There is kindness in the act of recognition, as well as in the manner in which it is denoted.

We might learn much from the French people in this matter. They are not only polite to each other, but they have a great respect for property. Some may be disposed to doubt this, after the recent destruction of buildings in Paris. But the Communists must be regarded as altogether exceptional people; and to understand the French character, we must look to the body of the population scattered throughout France. There we find property much more respected by the people than among ourselves. Even the beggar respects the fruit by the roadside, although there is nobody to protect it. The reason of this is, that France is a nation of small proprietors; that property is much more generally diffused and exposed; and parents of even the lowest class educate their children in carefulness of and fidelity to the property of others.

This respect for property is also accompanied with respect for the feelings of others, which constitutes what is called good manners. This is carefully inculcated in the children of all ranks in France. They are very rarely rude. They are civil to strangers. They are civil to each other. Mr. Laing, in his "Notes of a Traveler," makes these remarks, "This reference to the feelings of others in all that we do is a moral habit of great value when it is generally diffused, and enters into the home-training of every family. It is an education both of the parent and child in morals, carried on through the medium of external manners. . . . It is a fine distinction of the French national character, and of social economy, that practical morality is more generally taught through manners, among and by the people themselves than in any country in Europe."

The same kindly feeling might be observed throughout the entire social intercourse of working-men with each other. There is not a moment in their lives in which the opportunity does not occur for exhibiting good manners—in the workshop, in the street, and at home. Provided there be a wish to please others by kind looks and ways, the habit of combining good manners with every action will soon be formed. It is not merely the pleasure a man gives to others by being kind to them: he receives tenfold more pleasure himself. The man who gets up and offers his chair to a woman, or to an old man—trivial though the act may seem—is rewarded by his own heart, and a thrill of pleasure runs through him the moment he has performed the kindness.

Work-people need to practice good manners toward each other the more, because they are under the necessity of constantly living with each other and among each other. They are in constant contact with their fellow-workmen, whereas the richer classes need not mix with men unless they choose, and then they can select whom they like. The working-man's happiness depends much more upon the kind looks, words, and acts of those immediately about him than the rich man's does. It is so in the workshop, and it is the same at home. There the workman cannot retire into his study, but must sit among his family, by the side of his wife, with his children about him. And he must either live kindly with them—performing kind and obliging acts toward his family, or he must see, suffer, and endure the intolerable misery of reciprocal unkindness.

Admitted that there are difficulties in the way of working-men cultivating the art of good manners; that their circumstances are often very limited, and their position unfavorable—yet no man is so poor but that he can be civil and kind if he choose; and to be civil and kind is the very essence of good manners. Even in the most adverse circumstances, a man may try to do his best. If he do—if he speak and act courteously and kindly to all—the result will be so satisfactory, so self-rewarding, that he cannot but be stimulated to persevere in the same course. He will diffuse pleasure about him in the home, make friends of his work-fellows, and be regarded with increased kindness and respect by every right-minded employer. The civil workman will exercise increased power among his class, and gradually induce them to imitate him by his persistent steadiness, civility and kindness.

Thus Benjamin Franklin, when a workman, reformed the habits of an entire workshop.

Then, besides the general pleasure arising from the exercise of good manners, there is a great deal of healthful and innocent pleasure to be derived from amusements of various kinds. One cannot be always working, eating and sleeping. There must be time for relaxation, time for mental pleasures, time for bodily exercise.

There is a profound meaning in the word "amusement"; much more than most people are disposed to admit. In fact, amusement is an important part of education. It is a mistake to suppose that the boy or the man who plays at some outdoor game is wasting his time. Amusement of any kind is not wasting time, but economizing life.

Relax and exercise frequently, if you would enjoy good health. If you do not relax, and take no exercise, the results will soon appear in bodily ailments which always accompany sedentary occupations. "The students," says Lord Derby, "who think they have not time for bodily exercise will, sooner or later, find time for illness."

There are people in the world who would, if they had the power, hang the heavens about with crape, throw a shroud over the beautiful and life-giving bosom of the planet, pick the bright stars from the sky, veil the sun with clouds, pluck the silver moon from her place in the firmament, shut up our gardens and fields, and all the flowers with which they are bedecked, and doom the world to an atmosphere of gloom and cheerlessness. There is no reason or morality in this, and there is still less religion.

Temperance reformers have not sufficiently considered how much the drinking habits of the country are the consequences of gross tastes, and of the too limited opportunities which exist in this country for obtaining access to amusements of an innocent and improving tendency. The workman's tastes have been allowed to remain uncultivated; present wants engross his thoughts; the gratification of his appetites is his highest pleasure, and when he relaxes, it is to indulge immoderately in beer or whisky. The Germans were at one time the drunkenest of nations. They are now among the soberest. "As drunken as a German boor," was a common proverb. How have they been weaned from drink? Principally by education and music.

Music has a most humanizing effect. The cultivation of the art has a most favorable influence upon public morals. It furnishes a source of pleasure in every family. It gives home a new attraction. It makes social intercourse more cheerful. Father Mathew followed up his temperance movement by a singing movement. He promoted the establishment of musical clubs all over Ireland, for he felt that, as he had taken the people's whisky from them, he must give them some wholesome stimulus in its stead. He gave them music. Singing-classes were established to refine the taste, soften the manners, and humanize the mass of the Irish people. But we fear that the example set by Father Mathew has already been forgotten.

"What a fulness of enjoyment," says Channing, "has our Creator placed within our reach, by surrounding us with an atmosphere which may be shaped into sweet sounds! And yet this goodness is almost lost upon us, through want of culture of the organ by which this provision is to be enjoyed."

How much would the general cultivation of the gift of music improve us as a people! Children ought to learn it in schools, as they do in Germany. The voice of music would then be heard in every household. Our old English glees would no longer be forgotten. Men and women might sing in the intervals of their work, as the Germans do in going to and coming from their work. The work would not be worse done, because it was done amidst music and cheerfulness. The breath of society would be sweetened, and pleasure would be linked with labor.

Why not have some elegance in even the humblest home? We must of course have cleanliness, which is the special elegance of the poor. But why not have pleasant and delightful things to look upon? There is no reason why the humbler classes should not surround themselves with the evidences of beauty and comfort in all their shapes, and thus do homage alike to the gifts of God and the labors of man. The taste for the beautiful is one of the best and most useful endowments. It is one of the handmaids of civilization. Beauty and elegance do not necessarily belong to the homes of the rich. They are, or ought to be, all-pervading. Beauty in all things—in nature, in art, in science, in literature, in social and domestic life.

How beautiful and yet how cheap are flowers! Not exotics, but what are called common flowers. A rose, for instance, is among the most beautiful of the smiles of nature. The "laughing flowers," exclaims the poet. But there is more than gayety in blooming flowers, though it takes a wise man to see the beauty, the love, and the adaptation of which they are full.

What should we think of one who had *invented* flowers, supposing that, before him, flowers were unknown? would he not be regarded as the opener-up of a paradise of new delight? Should we not hail the inventor as a genius, as a god? And yet these lovely offsprings of the earth have been speaking to man from the first dawn of his existence until now, telling him of the goodness and wisdom of the creative power, which bid the earth bring forth, not only that which was useful as food, but also flowers, the bright consummate flowers to clothe it in beauty and joy!

Bring one of the commonest field-flowers into a room, place it on a table or chimney-piece, and you seem to have brought a ray of sunshine into the place. There is a cheerfulness about flowers. What a delight are they to the drooping invalid! They are a sweet enjoyment, coming as messengers from the country, and seeming to say, "come and see where we grow and let your heart be glad in our presence."

Have a flower in the room, by all means! It will cost only a trifle if your ambition is moderate, and the gratification it gives will be beyond price. If you can have a flower for your window, so much the better. What can be more delicious than the sun's light streaming through flowers—through the midst of crimson fuchsias or scarlet geraniums? To look out into the light through flowers—is not that poetry? And to break the force of the sunbeams by the tender resistance of green leaves? If you can train a nasturtium round the window, or some sweet pease, then you will have the most beautiful frame you can invent for the picture without, whether it be the busy crowd, or a distant landscape, or trees with their lights and shades, or the changes of the passing clouds. Any one may thus look through flowers for the price of an old song. And what pure taste and refinement does it not indicate on the part of the cultivator!

A flower in the window sweetens the air, makes the room look graceful, gives the sun's light a new charm, rejoices the eye, and links nature with beauty. The flower is a companion that will never say a cross thing to any one, but will always look beautiful and smiling. Do not despise it because it is cheap, and because every, body may have the luxury as well as yourself. Common things are cheap, but common things are invariably the most valuable. Could we only have fresh air or sunshine by purchase, what luxuries they would be considered. But they are free to all, and we think little of their blessings.

There is indeed much in nature that we do not yet half enjoy, because we shut our avenues of sensation and feeling. We are satisfied with the matter of fact, and look not for the spirit of fact which is above it. If we opened our minds to enjoyment, we might find tranquil pleasures spread about us on every side. We might live with the angels that visit us on every sunbeam, and sit with the fairies who wait on every flower. We want more loving knowledge to enable us to enjoy life, and we require to cultivate the art of making the most of the common means and appliances of enjoyment which lie about us on every side.

A snug and clean home, no matter how tiny it be, so that it be wholesome. Windows into which the sun can shine cheerily, a few good books (and who need be without a few good books in these days of universal cheapness?)—no duns at the door, and the cupboard well supplied, and with flowers in your room! There is none so poor as not to have about him these elements of pleasure.

But why not, besides the beauty of nature, have a taste for the beauty of art? Why not hang up a picture in the room? Ingenious methods have been discovered—some of them quite recently—for almost infinitely multiplying works of art, by means of wood-engravings, lithographs, photographs and autotypes, which render it possible for every person to furnish his rooms with beautiful pictures. Skill and science have thus brought art within reach of the poorest.

Any picture, print or engraving that represents a noble thought, that depicts a heroic act, or that brings a bit of nature from the fields or the streets into our room, is a teacher, a means of education, and a help to self culture. It serves to make the home more pleasant and attractive. It sweetens domestic life, and sheds a grace and beauty about it. It draws the gazer away from mere consideration of self, and increases his store of delightful association with the world without as well as with the world within.

The portrait of a great man, for instance, helps us to read his life. It invests him with a personal interest. Looking at his features, we feel as if we knew him better, and were more closely related to him. Such a portrait, hung up before us daily, at our meals and during our leisure hours, unconsciously serves to lift us up and sustain us. It is a link that in some way binds us to a higher and nobler nature.

It is not necessary that a picture should be high-priced in order to be beautiful and good. We have seen things for which hundreds of guineas have been paid that have not one-hundredth part of the meaning or beauty that is to be found in Linton's wood-cut of Raffaelle's "Madonna," which may be had for twopence. The head reminds one of the observation made by Hazlitt upon a picture, that it seems as if an unhandsome act would be impossible in its presence. It embodies the ideas of mother's love, womanly beauty and earnest piety. As some one said of the picture, "it looks as if a bit of heaven were in the room."

Picture-fanciers pay not so much for the merit as for the age and rarity of their works. The poorest may have the *seeing eye* for beauty, while the rich man may be blind to it. The cheapest engraving may communicate the sense of beauty to the artisan, while the thousand guinea picture may fail to communicate to the millionaire anything—excepting, perhaps, the notion that he has got possession of a work which the means of other people cannot compass.

Does the picture give you pleasure on looking at it? That is one good test of its worth. You may grow tired of it. Your taste may outgrow it and demand something better, just as the reader may grow out of Montgomery's poetry into Milton's. Then you will take down the daub, and put up a picture with a higher idea in its place. There may thus be a steady progress of art made upon the room walls. If the pictures can be put in frames, so much the better, but if they cannot, no matter. Up with them! We know that Owen Jones says it is not good taste to hang prints upon walls; he would merely hang room-papers there. But Owen Jones may not be infallible, and here we think he is wrong. To our eyes a room always looks unfurnished, no matter how costly and numerous the tables, chairs and ottomans, unless there be pictures upon the walls.

It ought to be, and no doubt it is, a great stimulus to artists to know that their works are now distributed in prints and engravings, to decorate and beautify the homes of the people. The wood-cutter, the lithographer, and the engraver are the popular interpreters of the great artist. Thus Turner's pictures are not confined to the wealthy possessors of the original works, but may be diffused through all homes by the Millers, and Brandards, and Wilmotts, who have engraved them. Thus Landseer finds entrance, through wood-cuts and mezzotints, into every dwelling. Thus Cruikshank preaches temperance, and Ary Sheffer purity and piety. The engraver is the medium by which art in the palace is conveyed into the humblest homes in the kingdom.

The art of living may be displayed in many ways. It may be summed up in the words, "Make the best of everything." Nothing is beneath its care, even common and little things it turns to account. It gives a brightness and grace to the home, and invests nature with new charms. Through it we enjoy the rich man's parks and woods, as if they were our own. We inhale the common air, and bask under the universal sunshine: We glory in the grass, the passing clouds, and the flowers. We love the common earth, and hear joyful voices through all nature. It extends to every kind of social intercourse. It engenders cheerful good will and loving sincerity. By its help we make others happy, and ourselves blessed. We elevate our being and ennoble our lot. We rise above the groveling creatures of earth, and aspire to the infinite. And thus we link time to eternity, where the true art of living has its final consummation.

Chapter 2

Healthy Homes

"The best security for civilization is the dwelling." —B. Disraeli.

"Cleanliness is the elegance of the poor." —English Proverb.

"Virtue never dwelt long with filth." —Count Rumford.

HEALTH IS SAID to be wealth. Indeed, all wealth is valueless without health. Every man who lives by labor, whether of mind or body, regards health as one of the most valuable of possessions. Without it, life would be unenjoyable. The human system has been so framed as to render enjoyment one of the principal ends of physical life. The whole arrangement, structure, and functions of the human system are beautifully adapted for that purpose.

Happiness is the rule of healthy existence; pain and misery are its exceptional conditions. Nor is pain altogether an evil; it is rather a salutary warning. It tells us that we have transgressed some rule, violated some law, disobeyed some physical obligation. It is a monitor which warns us to amend our state of living. It virtually says, "Return to Nature, observe her laws, and be restored to happiness." Thus, paradoxical though it may seem, pain is one of the conditions of the physical well-being of man; as death, according to Dr. Thomas Brown, is one of the conditions of the enjoyment of life.

To enjoy physical happiness, therefore, the natural laws must be complied with. To discover and observe these laws, man has been endowed with the gift of reason. Does he fail to exercise this gift—does he neglect to comply with the law of his being—then pain and disease are the necessary consequence.

Man violates the laws of nature in his own person, and he suffers accordingly. He is idle, and overfeeds himself; he is punished by gout, indigestion, or apoplexy. He drinks too much; he becomes bloated, trembling, and weak; his appetite falls off, his strength declines, his constitution decays, and he falls a victim to the numerous diseases which haunt the steps of the drunkard.

Society suffers in the same way. It leaves districts undrained and streets uncleaned. Masses of the population are allowed to live crowded together in unwholesome dens, half poisoned by the mephitic air of the neighborhood. Then a fever breaks out, or a cholera, or a plague. Disease spreads from the miserable abodes of the poor into the comfortable homes of the rich, carrying death and devastation before it. The misery and suffering incurred in such cases are nothing less than willful, inasmuch as the knowledge necessary to avert them is within the reach of all.

Wherever any number of persons live together, the atmosphere becomes poisoned, unless means be provided for its constant change and renovation. If there be not sufficient ventilation, the air becomes charged with carbonic acid, principally the product of respiration. Whatever the body discharges, becomes poison to the body if introduced again through the lungs. Hence the immense importance of pure air. A deficiency of food may be considerably less injurious than a deficiency of pure air. Every person above fourteen years of age requires about six hundred cubic feet of shut-up space to breathe in during the twenty-four hours. If he sleeps in a room of smaller dimensions, he will suffer more or less, and gradually approach the condition of being smothered.

Shut up a mouse in a glass receiver, and it will gradually die by rebreathing its own breath. Shut up a man in a confined space, and he will die in the same way. The English soldiers expired in the Black Hole of Calcutta because they wanted pure air. Thus about half the children born in some manufacturing towns die before they are five years old, principally because they want pure air. Humboldt tells of a sailor who was dying of fever in the close hold of a ship. His comrades brought him out of the hold to die in the open air. Instead of dying, he revived, and eventually got well. He was cured by the pure air.

The first method of raising a man above the life of an animal is to provide him with a healthy home. The home is, after all, the best school for the world. Children grow up into men and women there; they imbibe their best and their worst morality there; and their morals and intelligence are in a great measure well or ill trained there. Men can only be really and truly humanized and civilized through the institution of the home. Domestic purity and moral life are in the good home, and individual defilement and moral death in the bad one.

The school-master has really very little to do with the formation of the characters of children. These are formed in the home by the father and mother—by brothers, sisters, and companions. It does not matter how complete may be the education given in schools. It may include the whole range of knowledge; yet if the scholar is under the necessity of daily returning to a home which is indecent, vicious, and miserable, all this learning will prove of comparatively little value. Character and disposition are the result of home training; and if these are, through bad physical and moral conditions, deteriorated and destroyed, the intellectual culture acquired in the school may prove an instrumentality for evil rather than for good.

The home should not be considered merely as an eating and sleeping place; but as a place where self-respect may be preserved, and comforts secured, and domestic pleasures enjoyed. Three-fourths of the petty vices which degrade society, and swell into crimes which disgrace it, would shrink before the influence of self-respect. To be a place of happiness, exercising beneficial influences upon its members, and especially upon the children growing up within it, the home must be pervaded by the spirit of comfort, cleanliness, affection, and intelligence. And in order to secure this, the presence of a well-ordered, industrious and educated woman is indispensable. So much depends upon the woman, that we might almost pronounce the happiness or unhappiness of the home to be woman's work. No nation can advance except through the improvement of the nation's homes; and they can only be improved through the instrumentality of women. They must *know* how to make homes comfortable; and before they can know, they must have been taught.

Women, must, therefore, have sufficient training to fit them for their duties in real life. Their education should be conducted throughout with a view to their future position as wives, mothers, and housewives. But among all classes, even the highest, the education of girls is rarely conducted with this object. Among the working-people, the girls are sent out to work; among tile higher classes, they are sent out to learn a few flashy accomplishments; and men are left to pick from them, very often with little judgment, the future wives and mothers.

Men themselves attach little or no importance to the intelligence or industrial skill of women; and they only discover their value when they find their homes stupid and cheerless. Men are caught by the glance of a bright eye, by a pair of cherry cheeks, by a handsome figure; and when they "fall in love," as the phrase goes, they never bethink them of whether the "loved one" can mend a shirt or cook a pudding. And yet the most sentimental of husbands must come down from his "ecstatics" so soon as the knot is tied, and then he soon enough finds out that the clever hands of a woman are worth far more than her bright glances; and if the shirt and pudding qualifications be absent, then woe to the unhappy man, and woe also to the unhappy woman! If the substantial element of physical comfort be absent from the home, it soon becomes hateful; the wife, notwithstanding all her good looks, is neglected; and the public-house separates those whom the law and the church have joined together.

Men are really desperately ignorant respecting the home department. If they thought for a moment of its importance, they would not be so ready to rush into premature housekeeping. Ignorant men select equally ignorant women for their wives; and these introduce into the world families of children whom they are utterly incompetent to train as rational or domestic beings. The home is no home, but a mere lodging, and often a very comfortless one.

We speak not merely of the poorest laborers, but of the best-paid workmen in the large manufacturing towns. Men earning from ten to fifteen dollars a week—or more than the average pay of dry goods and grocers' clerks—though spending considerable amounts on beer, will often grudge so small a part of their income as two dollars per week to provide decent homes for themselves and their children. What is the consequence? They degrade themselves and their families. They crowd together, in foul neighborhoods, into dwellings possessing no element of health and decency; where even the small rental which they pay is in excess of the accommodation they receive. The results are inevitable—loss of self-respect, degradation of intelligence, failure of physical health, and premature death. Even the highest-minded philosopher, placed in such a situation, would gradually gravitate toward brutality. A healthy home presided over by a thrifty, cleanly woman, may be the abode of comfort, of virtue and of happiness. It may be the scene of every ennobling relation in family life. It may be endeared to a man by many delightful memories—by the affectionate voices of his wife, his children and his neighbors. Such a home will be regarded, not as a mere nest of common instinct, but as a training ground for young immortals, a sanctuary for the heart, a refuge from storms, a sweet resting-place after labor, a consolation in sorrow, a pride in success, and a joy at all times.

Sanitary science may be summed up in the one word—cleanliness. Pure water and pure air are its essentials. Wherever there is impurity, it must be washed away and got rid of. Thus sanitary science is one of the simplest and most intelligible of all the branches of human knowledge. Perhaps it is because of this that, like most common things, it has continued to receive so little attention. Many still think that it requires no science at all to ventilate a chamber, to clean out a drain, and to keep house and person free from uncleanliness.

Sanitary science may be regarded as an unsavory subject. It deals with dirt and its expulsion—from the skin, from the house, from the street, from the city. It is comprised in the words, "Wherever there is dirt, get rid of it instantly, and with cleanliness let there be a copious supply of pure water and of pure air for the purpose of human health."

Take, for instance, an unhealthy street, or block of streets in a large town. There you find typhoid fever constantly present. Cleanse and sewer the streets, supply it with pure air and pure water, and fever is forthwith banished. Is not this a much more satisfactory result than the application of drugs? Fifty thousand persons, says Mr. Lee, annually fall victims to typhoid fever in New England, originated by causes which are preventable. The result is the same as if these fifty thousand persons were annually taken out of their wretched dwellings and put to death! We are shocked by the news of murder—by the loss of a single life by physical causes! And yet we hear, almost without a shudder, of the reiterated statement of the loss of tens of thousands of lives yearly from physical causes in daily operation. The annual slaughter from preventable causes of typhoid fever is double the amount of what was suffered by the allied armies at the battle of Waterloo! By neglect of the ascertained conditions of healthful living, the great mass of the people lose nearly half the natural period of their lives. "Typhoid," says a physician, "is a curse which man inflicts upon himself by the neglect of sanitary arrangements."

The connection is close and intimate between physical and moral health, between domestic well-being and public happiness. The destructive influence of an unwholesome dwelling propagates a moral typhoid worse than a plague itself. Where the body is enfeebled by the depressing influence of vitiated air and bodily defilement, the mind, almost of necessity, takes the same low, unhealthy tone. Self-respect is lost; a stupid, inert, languid feeling overpowers the system, the character becomes depraved, and too often— eager to snatch even a momentary enjoyment, to feel the blood bounding in the veins—the miserable victim flies to the demon of strong drink for relief, hence, misery, infamy, shame, crime and wretchedness.

Mere improvement of towns, as respects drainage, sewerage, paving, water-supply, and abolition of cellar dwellings, will effect comparatively little, unless we can succeed in carrying-the improvement further—namely, into the houses of the people themselves. A well-devised system of sanitary measures may insure external cleanliness; may provide that the soil on which the streets of houses are built shall be relieved of all superfluous moisture, and that all animal and vegetable refuse shall be promptly removed— so that the air circulating through the streets and floating from them into the houses of the inhabitants, shall not be laden with poisonous miasmata, the source of disease, suffering and untimely death. Cellar dwellings may be prohibited, and certain regulations as to the buildings hereafter to be erected may also be enforced. But here municipal authority stops; it can go no further; it cannot penetrate into the home, and it is not necessary that it should do so.

The individual efforts of the community themselves are therefore needed, and any legislative enactments which dispensed with these would probably be an evil. The Government does not build the houses in which the people dwell. These are provided by employers and by capitalists, small and large. It is necessary, therefore, to enlist these interests in the cause of sanitary improvement, in order to insure success. Individual capitalists have already done much to provide wholesome houses for their working-people, and have found their account in so doing by their increased health, as well as in their moral improvement in all ways. Capitalists imbued with a benevolent and philanthropic spirit can thus spread blessings far arid wide. And were a few enterprising builders in every town to take up this question practically, and provide a class of houses for laborers, with suitable accommodation—provided with arrangements for ventilation, cleanliness, and separation of the sexes, such as health and comfort require—they would really be conferring an amount of benefit on the community at large, and at the same time, we believe, upon themselves, which it would not be easy to overestimate.

But there also needs the active co-operation of the dwellers in poor men's homes themselves. They, too, must join cordially in the sanitary movement; otherwise comparatively little good can be effected. You may provide an efficient water-supply, yet if the housewife will not use the water as it ought to be used, if she be lazy and dirty, the house will be foul and comfortless still. You may provide for ventilation, yet if offensive matters be not removed, and doors and windows are kept closed, the pure outer air will be excluded, and, the house will still smell musty and unwholesome. In any case, there must be a cleanly woman to superintend the affairs of the house; and she cannot be made so by act of congress. The sanitary commissioners cannot, by any "notification," convert the slatternly shrew into a tidy housewife, nor the disorderly drunkard into an industrious, home-loving husband. There must, therefore, be individual effort on the part of the housewife in every working-man's home. As a recent writer on home reform observes: "We must begin by insisting that, however much of the physical and moral evils of the working-classes may be justly attributable to their dwellings, it is too often the case that more ought, in truth, to be attributed to themselves; for, surely, the inmate depends less on the house than the house on the inmate, as mind has more power over matter than matter over mind. Let the dwelling be ever so poor and incommodious, yet a family with decent and cleanly habits will contrive to make the best of it, and will take care that there shall be nothing offensive in it which they have power to remove. Whereas a model house, fitted up with every convenience and comfort which modern science can supply, will, if occupied by persons of intemperate and uncleanly habits, speedily become a disgrace and a nuisance. A sober, industrious, and cleanly couple will impart an air of decency and respectability to the poorest dwelling; while the spendthrift, the drunkard, or the gambler will convert a palace into a scene of discomfort and disgust. Since, therefore, so much depends on the character and conduct of the parties themselves, it is right that they should feel their responsibility in this matter, and that they should know and attend to the various points connected with the improvement of their own homes."

Homes are the manufactories of men; and as the homes are, so will the men be. Mind will be degraded by the physical influences around it, decency will be destroyed by constant contact with impurity and defilement, and coarseness of manners, habits, and tastes will become inevitable. You cannot rear a kindly nature, sensitive against evil, careful of properties, and desirous of moral and intellectual improvement, amidst the darkness, dampness, disorder, and discomfort which unhappily characterize so large a portion of the dwellings of the poor in our large towns; and until we can, by some means or other, improve their domestic accommodation, their low moral and social condition must be regarded as inevitable.

We want not only a better class of dwellings, but we require the people to be so educated as to appreciate them. A certain landlord took his tenantry out of their mud-huts, and removed them into comfortable dwellings which he had built for their accommodation. When he returned to his estate, he was greatly disappointed. The houses were as untidy and uncomfortable as before. The pig was still under the bed, and the hens over it. The concrete floor was as dirty as the mud one had been. The panes of the windows were broken, and the garden was full of weeds. The landlord wrote to a friend in despair. The friend replied, "You have begun at the wrong end. You ought to have taught them the value of cleanliness, thriftiness, and comfort." To begin at the beginning, therefore, we must teach the people the necessity of cleanliness, its virtues, and its wholesomeness; for which purpose it is requisite that they should be intelligent, capable of understanding ideas conveyed in words, able to discern, able to read, able to think. In short, the people, as children, must first have been to school, and properly taught there; whereas we have allowed the majority of the working people to grow up untaught, nearly half of them unable to read and write; and then we expect them to display the virtues, prudence, judgment, and forethought of well-educated beings.

It is of the first importance to teach people cleanly habits. This can be done without teaching them either reading or writing. Cleanliness is more than wholesomeness. It furnishes an atmosphere of self-respect, and influences the moral condition of the entire household. It is the best exponent of the spirit of Thrift. It is to the economy of the household what hygiene is to the human body. It should preside at every detail of domestic service. It indicates comfort and wellbeing. It is among the distinctive attributes of civilization, and marks the progress of nations.

We need scarcely refer to the moral as well as the physical beauty of cleanliness—cleanliness which indicates self-respect, and is the root of many fine virtues, and especially of purity, delicacy, and decency. We might even go further, and say that purity of thought and feeling results from habitual purity of body; for the mind and heart of man are, to a very great extent, influenced by external conditions and circumstances; and habit and custom, as regards outward things, stamp themselves deeply on the whole character, alike upon the moral feelings and the intellectual powers.

Moses was the most practical of sanitary reformers. Among the Eastern nations generally, cleanliness is a part of religion. They esteem it not only as next to godliness, but as a part of godliness itself. They connect the idea of internal sanctity with that of external purification. They feel that it would be an insult to the Maker they worship to come into his presence covered with impurity. Hence the Mohammedans devote almost as much care to the erection of baths as to that of mosques; and alongside the place of worship is usually found the place of cleansing, so that the faithful may have the ready means of purification previous to their act of worship.

The common well-being of men, women and children depends upon attention to what at first may appear comparatively trivial matters. And unless these small matters be attended to, comfort in person, mind and feeling is absolutely impossible. The physical satisfaction of a child, for example, depends upon attention to its feeding, clothing and washing. These are the commonest of common things, and yet they are of the most essential importance. If the child is not properly fed and clothed, it will grow up feeble and ill-conditioned. And as the child is, so will the man be.

Grown people cannot be comfortable without regular attention to these matters. Everyone needs, and ought to have, comfort at home; and comfort is the united product of cleanliness, thrift, regularity, industry—in short, a continuous performance of duties, each in itself apparently trivial. The cooking of a potato, the baking of a loaf, the mending of a shirt, the darning of a pair of stockings, the making of a bed, the scrubbing of a floor, the washing and dressing of a baby, are all matters of no great moment, but a woman ought to know how to do all these before the management of a household, however poor, is entrusted to her.

"Why," asked Lord Ashburton in a lecture to the students of the Wolvesey training-schools, "was one mother of a family a better economist than another? Why could one live in abundance where another starved? Why, in similar dwellings, were the children of one parent healthy, of another puny and ailing? Why could this laborer do with ease a task that would kill his fellow? It was not luck or chance that decided those differences; it was the patient observation of nature that suggested to some gifted minds rules for their guidance which had escaped the heedlessness of others."

It is not so much, however, the patient observation of nature, as good training in the home and in the school, that enables some women to accomplish so much more than others in the development of human beings and the promotion of human comfort. And to do this efficiently, women as well as men require to be instructed as to the nature of the objects upon which they work.

Take one branch of science as an illustration—the physiological. In this science we hold that every woman should receive some instruction. And why? Because, if the laws of physiology were understood by women, children would grow up into better, healthier, happier and probably wiser men and women. Children are subject to certain physiological laws, the observance of which is necessary for their health and comfort. Is it not reasonable, therefore, to expect that women should know something of the laws, and of their operation? If they are ignorant of them, they will be liable to commit all sorts of blunders, productive of suffering, disease and death. To what are we to attribute the frightful mortality of children in most of our large towns, where one-half of all that are born perish before they reach their fifth year? If women, as well as men, knew something of the laws of healthy living, about the nature of the atmosphere, how its free action upon the blood is necessary to health, of the laws of ventilation, cleanliness, and nutrition—we cannot but think that the moral, not less than the physical, condition of the human beings committed to their charge would be greatly improved and promoted.

Were anything like a proper attention given to common things, there would not be such an amount of discomfort, disease and mortality among the young. But we accustom people to act as if there were no such provisions as natural laws. If we violate them, we do not escape the consequences because we have been ignorant of their mode of operation. We have been provided with intelligence that we might *know* them, and if society keep its members blind and ignorant, the evil consequences will be inevitably reaped. Thus tens of thousands perish for lack of knowledge of even the smallest and yet most necessary conditions of right living.

Much might be said in favor of household management, and especially in favor of improved cookery. Ill-cooked meals are a source of discomfort in many families. Bad cooking is waste—waste of money and loss of comfort. Whom God has joined in matrimony, ill-cooked joints and ill-boiled potatoes have very often put asunder. Among the "common things" which educators should teach the rising generation, this ought certainly not to be overlooked. It is the most common and yet most neglected of the branches of female education.

The greater part of human labor is occupied in the direct production of the materials for human food. The farming classes and their laborers devote themselves to the planting, rearing and reaping of oats and other cereals, and the grazing farmer to the production of cattle and sheep, for the maintenance of the population at large. All these articles—corn, beef, mutton and such-like—are handed over to the female half of the human species to be converted into food, for the sustenance of themselves, their husbands, and their families. How do they use their power? Can they cook? Have they been taught to cook? Is it not a fact that, in this country, cooking is one of the lost or undiscovered arts?

Thousands of artisans and laborers are deprived of half the actual nutriment of their food, and continue half starved, because their wives are utterly ignorant of the art of cooking. They are yet in entire darkness as to the economizing of food, and the means of rendering it palatable and digestible.

Great would be the gain to the community if cookery were made an ordinary branch of female education. To the poor the gain would be incalculable. "Among the prizes which the Bountifuls of both sexes are fond of bestowing in the country, we should like to see some offered for the best boiled potato, the best grilled mutton-chop, and the best seasoned soup, or broth. In writing of a well boiled potato, we are aware that we shall incur the contempt of many for attaching importance to a thing they suppose to be so common. But the fact is that their contempt arises, as is often the origin of contempt, from their ignorance, there being not one person in a hundred who has ever seen and tasted that great rarity, a well boiled potato."

In short, we want common sense in cookery, as in most other things. Food should be used, and not abused. Much of it is now absolutely wasted—wasted for want of a little art in cooking it. Food is not only wasted by bad cooking, but much of it is thrown away which Frenchwomen would convert into something savory and digestible. Health, morals and family enjoyments are all connected with the question of cookery. Above all, it is the handmaid of thrift. It makes the most and the best of the bounties of God. It wastes nothing, but turns everything to account. Every woman ought to be accomplished in an art which confers so much comfort, health and wealth upon the members of her household.

Many intelligent, high-minded ladies, who have felt disgusted at the idleness to which "society" condemns them, have of late years undertaken the work of visiting the poor and of nursing—a noble work. But there is another school of usefulness which stands open to them. Let them study the art of common cookery, and diffuse the knowledge of it among the people. They will thus do an immense amount of good, and bring down the blessings of many a half-hungered husband upon their benevolent heads. Women of the poorer classes require much help from those who are better educated, or who have been placed in better circumstances than themselves. The greater number of them marry young, and suddenly enter upon a life for which they have not received the slightest preparation. They know nothing of cookery, of sewing, of clothes-mending, or of economical ways of spending their husbands' money. Hence, slatternly and untidy habits, and uncomfortable homes, from which the husband is often glad to seek refuge in the nearest public house. The following story, told by Joseph Corbett, a Birmingham operative, before a Parliamentary committee, holds true of many working-people in the manufacturing districts:

"My mother," he said, "worked in a manufactory from a very early age. She was clever and industrious, and, moreover, she had the reputation of being virtuous. She was regarded as an excellent match for the working-man. She was married early. She became the mother of eleven children; I am the eldest. To the best of her ability she performed the important duties of a wife and mother. But she was lamentably deficient in domestic knowledge. In that most important of all human instructions—how to make the home and the fireside to possess a charm for her husband and children—she had never received one single lesson. As the family increased, so everything like comfort disappeared altogether. The power to make home cheerful and comfortable was never given to her. She knew not the value of cherishing in my father's mind a love of domestic objects. Not one moment's happiness did I ever see under my father's roof. All this dismal state of things I can distinctly trace to the entire and perfect absence of all training and instruction to my mother. He became intemperate, and his intemperance made her destitute. She made many efforts to abstain from shop work, but her pecuniary necessities forced her back into the shop. The family was large, and every moment was required at home. I have known her, after the close of a hard day's work, sit up nearly all night for several nights together, washing and mending clothes. My father could have no comfort there. These domestic obligations, which in a well-regulated house would be done so as not to provoke the husband, were to my father a sort of annoyance; and he, from an ignorant and mistaken notion, sought comfort in an ale-house. My mother's ignorance of household duties, my father's consequent irritability and intemperance, the frightful poverty, the constant quarrelling, the pernicious example to my brothers and sisters, the bad effect upon the future conduct of my brothers—one and all of us being forced out to work so young that our feeble earnings would produce only one shilling a week—cold and hunger, and the innumerable sufferings of my childhood crowd upon my mind and overpower me. They keep alive a deep anxiety for the emancipation of thousands of families who are in a similar state of horrible misery. My own experience tells me that the instruction of the females in the work of a house, in teaching them to produce cheerfulness and comfort at the fireside, would prevent a great amount of misery and crime. There would be fewer drunken husbands and disobedient children. Female education is disgracefully neglected. I attach more importance to it than to anything else; for woman imparts the first impression to the young susceptible mind; she moulds the child from which is formed the future man."

Chapter 3

Influence of Character

"The prosperity of a country depends, not on the abundance of its revenues, nor on the strength of its fortifications, nor on the beauty of its public buildings; but it consists in the number of its cultivated citizens, in its men of education, enlightenment, and character; here are to be found its true interest, its chief strength, its real power." —Martin Luther.

CHARACTER IS ONE of the greatest motive powers in the world. In its noblest embodiments, it exemplifies human nature in its highest forms, for it exhibits man at his best.

Men of genuine excellence, in every station of life—men of industry, of integrity, of high principle, of sterling honesty of purpose—command the spontaneous homage of mankind. It is natural to believe in such men, to have confidence in them, and to imitate them. All that is good in the world is upheld by them, and without their presence in it the world would not be worth living in.

Although genius always commands admiration, character most secures respect. The former is more the product of brain-power, the latter of heart-power; and in the long run it is the heart that rules in life. Men of genius stand to society in the relation of its intellect, as men of character of its conscience; and while the former are admired, the latter are followed.

Great men are always exceptional men; and greatness itself is but comparative. Indeed, the range of most men in life is so limited, that very few have the opportunity of being great. But each man can act his part honestly and honorably, and to the best of his ability. He can use his gifts and not abuse them. He can strive to make the best of life. He can be true, just, honest, and faithful, even in small things. In a word, he can do his duty in that sphere in which Providence has placed him.

Commonplace though it may appear, this doing of one's duty embodies the highest ideal of life and character. There may be nothing heroic about it; but the common lot of men is not heroic. And though the abiding sense of duty upholds man in his highest attitudes, it also equally sustains him in the transaction of the ordinary affairs of every-day existence. Man's life is "centred in the sphere of common duties." The most influential of all the virtues are those which are the most in request for daily use. They wear the best, and last the longest. Superfine virtues, which are above the standard of common men, may only be sources of temptation and danger. Burke has truly said that "the human system which rests for its basis on the heroic virtues is sure to have a superstructure of weakness or of profligacy."

When Dr. Abbot, drew the character of his deceased friend Thomas Sackville, he did not dwell upon his merits as a statesman, or his genius as a poet, but upon his virtues as a man in relation to the ordinary duties of life. "How many rare things were in him!" said he. "Who more loving unto his wife?—Who more kind unto his children?—Who more fast unto his friend?—Who more moderate unto his enemy?—Who more true to his word?" Indeed, we can always better understand and appreciate a man's real character by the manner in which he conducts himself towards those who are the most nearly related to him, and by his transaction of the seemingly commonplace details of daily duty, than by his public exhibition of himself as an author, an orator, or a statesman.

At the same time, while duty, for the most part, applies to the conduct of affairs in common life by the average of common men, it is also a sustaining power to men of the very highest standard of character. They may not have either money, or property, or learning, or power; and yet they may be strong in heart and rich in spirit—honest, truthful, dutiful. And whoever strives to do his duty faithfully is fulfilling the purpose for which he was created, and building up in himself the principles of a manly character. There are many persons of whom it may be said that they have no other possession in the world but their character, and yet they stand as firmly upon it as any crowned king.

Intellectual culture has no necessary relation to purity or excellence of character. In the New Testament, appeals are constantly made to the heart of man and to "the spirit we are of," while allusions to the intellect are of very rare occurrence. "A handful of good life," says George Herbert, "is worth a bushel of learning." Not that learning is to be despised, but that it must be allied to goodness. Intellectual capacity is sometimes found associated with the meanest moral character—with abject servility to those in high places, and arrogance to those of low estate. A man may be accomplished in art, literature, and science, and yet, in honesty, virtue, truthfulness, and the spirit of duty, be entitled to take rank after many a poor and illiterate peasant.

"You insist," wrote Perthes to a friend, "on respect for learned men. I say, Amen! But at the same time, don't forget that largeness of mind, depth of thought, appreciation of the lofty, experience of the world, delicacy of manner, tact and energy in action, love of truth, honesty, and amiability—that all these may be wanting in a man who may yet be very learned."

When some one, in Sir Walter Scott's hearing, made a remark as to the value of literary talents and accomplishments, as if they were above all things to be esteemed and honored, he observed, "God help us! what a poor world this would be if that were the true doctrine! I have read books enough, and observed and conversed with enough of eminent and splendidly-cultured minds, too, in my time; but I assure you, I have heard higher sentiments from the lips of poor *uneducated* men and women, when exerting the spirit of severe yet gentle heroism under difficulties and afflictions, or speaking their simple thoughts as to circumstances in the lot of friends and neighbors, than I ever yet met with out of the Bible. We shall never learn to feel and respect our real calling and destiny, unless we have taught ourselves to consider every thing as moonshine, compared with the education of the heart."

Still less has wealth any necessary connection with elevation of character. On the contrary, it is much more frequently the cause of its corruption and degradation. Wealth and corruption, luxury and vice, have very close affinities to each other. Wealth in the hands of men of weak purpose, of deficient self-control, or of ill-regulated passions, is only a temptation and a snare—the source, it may be, of infinite mischief to themselves, and often to others.

On the contrary, a condition of comparative poverty is compatible with character in its highest form. A man may possess only his industry, his frugality, his integrity, and yet stand high in the rank of true manhood. The advice which Burns's father gave him was the best:

> "He bade me act a manly part, though I had ne'er a farthing,
> For without an honest manly heart no man was worth regarding."

One of the purest and noblest characters the writer ever knew was a laboring-man in a northern county, who brought up his family respectably on an income never amounting to more than ten shillings a week. Though possessed of only the rudiments of common education, obtained at an ordinary parish school, he was a man full of wisdom and thoughtfulness. His library consisted of the Bible, "Flavel," and "Boston"—books which, excepting the first, probably few readers have ever heard of. This good man might have sat for the portrait of Wordsworth's well-known "Wanderer." When he had lived his modest life of work and worship, and finally went to his rest, he left behind him a reputation for practical wisdom, for genuine goodness, and for helpfulness in every good work, which greater and richer men might have envied.

When Luther died, he left behind him, as set forth in his will, "no ready money, no treasure of coin of any description." He was so poor at one part of his life, that he was under the necessity of earning his bread by turning, gardening, and clock-making. Yet, at the very time when he was thus working with his hands, he was moulding the character of his country; and he was morally stronger, and vastly more honored and followed, than all the princes of Germany.

Character is property. It is the noblest of possessions. It is an estate in the general good-will and respect of men; and they who invest in it—though they may not become rich in this world's goods—will find their reward in esteem and reputation fairly and honorably won. And it is right that in life good qualities should tell—that industry, virtue, and goodness should rank the highest—and that the really best men should be foremost.

Simple honesty of purpose in a man goes a long way in life, if founded on a just estimate of himself and a steady obedience to the rule he knows and feels to be right. It holds a man straight, gives him strength and sustenance, and forms a mainspring of vigorous action. "No man," once said Sir Benjamin Rudyard, "is bound to be rich or great—no, nor to be wise; but every man is bound to be honest." But the purpose, besides being honest, must be inspired by sound principles, and pursued with undeviating adherence to truth, integrity, and uprightness. Without principles, a man is like a ship without rudder or compass, left to drift hither and thither with every wind that blows. He is as one without law, or rule, or order, or government. "Moral principles," says Hume, "are social and universal. They form, in a manner, the *party* of humankind against vice and disorder, its common enemy."

Epictetus once received a visit from a certain magnificent orator going to Rome on a lawsuit, who wished to learn from the Stoic something of his philosophy. Epictetus received his visitor coolly, not believing in his sincerity. "You will only criticise my style," said he; "not really wishing to learn principles."—"Well, but," said the orator, "if I attend to that sort of thing, I shall be a mere pauper, like you, with no plate, nor equipage, nor land."—"I don't *want* such things," replied Epictetus; "and besides, you are poorer than I am, after all. Patron or no patron, what care I? You *do* care. I am richer than you. I don't care what Caesar thinks of me. *I* flatter no one. This is what I have, instead of your gold and silver plate. You have silver vessels, but earthenware reasons, principles, appetites. My mind to me a kingdom is, and it furnishes me with abundant and happy occupation in lieu of your restless idleness. All your possessions seem small to you; mine seem great to me. Your desire is insatiate—mine is satisfied."

Talent is by no means rare in the world; nor is even genius. But can the talent be trusted? Can the genius? Not unless based on truthfulness—on veracity. It is this quality more than any other that commands the esteem and respect, and secures the confidence of others. Truthfulness is at the foundation of all personal excellence. It exhibits itself in conduct. It is rectitude—truth in action, and shines through every word and deed. It means reliableness, and convinces other men that it can be trusted. And a man is already of consequence in the world when it is known that he can be relied on—that when he says he knows a thing, he does know it; that when he says he will do a thing, he can do, and does do it. Thus reliableness becomes a passport to the general esteem and confidence of mankind.

In the affairs of life or of business, it is not intellect that tells so much as character—not brain so much as heart—not genius so much as self-control, patience, and discipline regulated by judgment. Hence there is no better provision for the uses of either private or public life, than a fair share of ordinary good sense guided by rectitude. Good sense, disciplined by experience and inspired by goodness, issues in practical wisdom. Indeed, goodness in a measure implies wisdom—the highest wisdom—the union of the worldly with the spiritual. "The correspondences of wisdom and goodness," says Sir Henry Taylor, "are manifold; and that they will accompany each other is to be inferred, not only because men's wisdom makes them good, but because their goodness makes them wise."

It is because of this controlling power of character in life that we often see men exercise an amount of influence apparently out of all proportion to their intellectual endowments. They appear to act by means of some latent power, some reserved force, which acts secretly, by mere presence. As Burke said of a powerful nobleman of the last century, "his virtues were his means." The secret is, that the aims of such men are felt to be pure and noble, and they act upon others with a constraining power.

Though the reputation of men of genuine character may be of slow growth, their true qualities can not be wholly concealed. They may be misrepresented by some and misunderstood by others; misfortune and adversity may, for a time, overtake them, but with patience and endurance, they will eventually inspire the respect and command the confidence which they really deserve.

It has been said of Sheridan that, had he possessed reliableness of character, he might have ruled the world; whereas, for want of it, his splendid gifts were comparatively useless. He dazzled and amused, but was without weight or influence in life or politics. Even the poor pantomimist of Drury

Lane felt himself his superior. Thus, when Delpini one day pressed the manager for arrears of salary, Sheridan sharply reproved him, telling him he had forgotten his station. "No, indeed, Monsieur Sheridan, I have net," retorted Delpini; "I know the difference between us perfectly well. In birth, parentage and education you are superior to me, but in life, character and behavior I am superior to you."

Unlike Sheridan, Burke, his countryman, was a great man of character. He was thirty-five before he gained a seat in Parliament, yet he found time to carve his name deep in the political history of England. He was a man of great gifts, and of transcendent force of character. Yet he had a weakness, which proved a serious defect—it was his want of temper; his genius was sacrificed to his irritability. And without this apparently minor gift of temper, the most splendid endowments may be comparatively valueless to their possessor.

Character is formed by a variety of minute circumstances, more or less under the regulation and control of the individual. Not a day passes without its discipline, whether for good or for evil. There is no act, however trivial, but has its train of consequences, as there is no hair so small but casts its shadow. It was a wise saying of Mrs. Schimmelpenninck's mother, never to give way to what is little; or by that little, however you may despise it, you will be practically governed.

Every action, every thought, every feeling, contributes to the education of the temper, the habits, and understanding, and exercises an inevitable influence upon all the acts of our future life. Thus character is undergoing constant change, for better or for worse—either being elevated on the one hand, or degraded on the other. "There is no fault nor folly of my life," says Mr. Ruskin, "that does not rise up against me, and take away my joy, and shorten my power of possession, of sight, of understanding. And every past effort of my life, every gleam of rightness or good in it, is with me now, to help me in my grasp of this art and its vision." Says Lewes in his life of Goethe: "Instead of saying that man is the creature of circumstance, it would be nearer the mark to say that man is the architect of circumstance. It is character which builds an existence out of circumstance. Our strength is measured by our plastic power. From the same materials one man builds palaces, another hovels: one warehouses, another villas. Bricks and mortar are mortar and bricks, until the architect can make them something else. Thus it is that in the same family, in the same circumstances, one man rears a stately edifice, while his brother, vacillating and incompetent, lives forever amid ruins: the block of granite which was an obstacle on the pathway of the weak, becomes a stepping-stone on the pathway of the strong."

The mechanical law, that action and reaction are equal, holds true also in morals. Good deeds act and react on the doers of them; and so do evil. Not only so: they produce like effects, by the influence of example, on those who are the subjects of them. But man is not the creature, so much as he is the creator, of circumstances; and, by the exercise of his free-will, he can direct his actions so that they shall be productive of good rather than evil. "Nothing can work me damage but myself," said St. Bernard; "the harm that I sustain I carry about with me; and I am never a real sufferer but by my own fault."

The best sort of character, however, can not be formed without effort. There needs the exercise of constant self-watchfulness, self-discipline, and self-control. There may be much faltering, stumbling, and temporary defeat; difficulties and temptations manifold to be battled with and overcome; but if the spirit be strong and the heart be upright, no one need despair of ultimate success. The very effort to advance—to arrive at a higher standard of character than we have reached—is inspiring and invigorating; and even though we may fall short of it, we can not fail to be improved by every honest effort made in an upward direction.

And with the light of great examples to guide us—representatives of humanity in its best forms—everyone is not only justified, but bound in duty to aim at reaching the highest standard of character; not to become the richest in means, but in spirit; not the greatest in worldly positions, but in true honor; not the most intellectual, but the most virtuous; not the most powerful and influential, but the most truthful, upright and honest.

Character exhibits itself in conduct, guided and inspired by principle, integrity and practical wisdom. In its highest form, it is the individual will acting energetically under the influence of religion, morality and reason. It chooses its way considerately, and pursues it steadfastly; esteeming duty above reputation, and the approval of conscience more than the world's praise. While respecting the personality of others, it preserves its own individuality and independence, and has the courage to be morally honest, though it may be unpopular, trusting tranquilly to time and experience for recognition.

Although the force of example will always exercise great influence upon the formation of character, the self-originating and sustaining force of one's own spirit must be the main-stay. This alone can hold up the life, and give individual independence and energy. "Unless man can erect himself above himself"; said Daniel, a poet of the Elizabethan era, "how poor a thing is man!" Without a certain degree of practical efficient force, compounded of will, which is the root, and wisdom, which is the stem of character, life will be indefinite and purposeless—like a body of stagnant water, instead of a running stream doing useful work and keeping the machinery of a district in motion.

When the elements of character are brought into action by determinate will and influenced by high purpose, man enters upon and courageously perseveres in the path of duty, at whatever cost of Worldly interest, he may be said to approach the summit of his being. He then exhibits character in its most intrepid form, and embodies the highest idea of manliness. The acts of such a man become repeated in the life and action of others. His very words live and become actions. Thus every word of Luther's rang through Germany like a trumpet. As Richter said of him, "his Words were half-battles." And thus Luther's life became transfused into the life of his country, and still lives in the character of modern Germany.

It was truly said of Sheridan—who, with all his improvidence, was generous, and never gave pain—that

> "His wit in the combat, as gentle as bright,
> Never carried a heart-stain away on its blade."

Such also was the character of Fox, who commanded the affection and service of others by his uniform heartiness and sympathy. He was a man who could always be most easily touched on the side of his honor. Thus the story is told of a tradesman calling upon him one day for the payment of a promissory note which he presented. Fox was engaged at the time counting out gold. The tradesman asked to be paid from the money before him. "No," said Fox, "I owe this money to Sheridan; it is a debt of honor; if any accident happened to me, he would have nothing to show." "Then," said the tradesman, "I change *my* debt into one of honor"; and he tore up the note. Fox was conquered by the act; he thanked the man for his confidence, and paid him, saying, "Then Sheridan must wait; yours is the debt of older standing."

The man of character is conscientious. He puts his conscience into his work, into his words, into his every action. When Cromwell asked the Parliament for soldiers in lieu of the decayed serving-men, who filled the Commonwealth's army, he required that they should be men "who made some conscience of what they did"; and such were the men of which his celebrated regiment of "Ironsides" was composed.

The man of character is also reverential. The possession of this quality marks the noblest and highest type of manhood and womanhood; reverence for things consecrated by the homage of generations—for high objects, pure thoughts, and noble aims—for the great men of former times, and the high-minded workers among our contemporaries. Reverence is alike indispensable to the happiness of individuals, of families, and of nations. Without it there can be no trust, no faith, no confidence, either in man or God—neither social peace nor social progress. For reverence is but another word for religion, which binds men to each other, and all to God.

Energy of will—self-originating force—is the soul of every great character. Where it is, there is life; where it is not, there is faintness, helplessness, and despondency. "The strong man and the water-fall," says the proverb, "channel their own path." The energetic leader of noble spirit not only wins a way for himself, but carries others with him. His every act has a personal significance, indicating vigor, independence, and self-reliance, and unconsciously commands respect, admiration, and homage. Such intrepidity of character was possessed by Luther, Cromwell, Washington, Pitt, Wellington, and all great leaders of men.

"I am convinced," said Mr. Gladstone, in describing the qualities of the late Lord Palmerston in the House of Commons, shortly after his death—"I am convinced that it was the force of will, a sense of duty, and a determination not to give in, that enabled him to make himself a model for all of us who yet remain and follow him, with feeble and unequal steps, in the discharge of our duties; it was that force of will that in point of fact did not so much struggle against the infirmities of old age, but actually repelled them and kept them at a distance. And one other quality there is, at least, that may be noticed without the smallest risk of stirring in any breast a painful emotion. It is this, that Lord Palmerston had a nature incapable of enduring anger or any sentiment of wrath. This freedom from wrathful sentiment was not the result of painful effort, but the spontaneous fruit of the mind. It was a noble gift of his original nature—a gift which beyond all others it was delightful to observe, delightful also to remember in connection with him who has left us, and with whom we have no longer to do, except in endeavoring to profit by his example wherever it can lead us in the path of duty and of right, and of bestowing on him those tributes of admiration and affection which he deserves at our hands."

The great leader attracts to himself men of kindred character, drawing them towards him as the loadstone draws iron. Thus, Sir John Moore early distinguished the three brothers Napier from the crowd of officers by whom he was surrounded, and they, on their part, repaid him by their passionate admiration. They were captivated by his courtesy, his bravery, and his lofty disinterestedness; and he became the model whom they resolved to imitate, and, if possible, to emulate. "Moore's influence," says the biographer of Sir William Napier, "had a signal effect in forming and maturing their characters; and it is no small glory to have been the hero of those three men, while his early discovery of their mental and moral qualities is a proof of Moore's own penetration and judgment of character."

There is a contagiousness in every example of energetic conduct. The brave man is an inspiration to the weak, and compels them, as it were, to follow him. Thus Napier relates that at the combat of Vera, when the Spanish centre was broken and in flight, a young officer, named Havelock, sprang forward, and, waving his hat, called upon the Spaniards within sight to follow him. Putting spurs to his horse, he leaped the abattis which protected the French front, and went headlong against them. The Spaniards were electrified; in a moment they dashed after him, cheering for *"El chico blanco!"* (the fair boy), and with one shock they broke through the French and sent them flying down hill.

And so it is in ordinary life. The good and the great draw others after them; they lighten and lift up all who are within reach of their influence. They are as so many living centres of beneficent activity. Let a man of energetic and upright character be appointed to a position of trust and authority, and all who serve under him become, as it were, conscious of an increase of power. When Chatham was appointed minister, his personal influence was at once felt through all the ramifications of office. Every sailor who served under Nelson, and knew he was in command, shared the inspiration of the hero.

When Washington consented to act as commander-in-chief, it was felt as if the strength of the American forces had been more than doubled. Many years later, in 1798, when Washington, grown old, had withdrawn from public life and was living in retirement at Mount Vernon, and when it seemed probable that France would declare war against the United States, President Adams wrote to him, saying, "We must have your name, if you will permit us to use it; there will be more efficacy in it than in many an army." Such was the esteem in which the great President's noble character and eminent abilities were held by his countrymen! When the dissolution of the Union at one time seemed imminent, and Washington wished to retire into private life, Jefferson wrote to him, urging his continuance in office. "The confidence of the whole Union," he said, "centres in you. Your being at the helm will be more than an answer to every argument which can be used to alarm and lead the people in any quarter into violence and secession. . . . There is sometimes an eminence of character on which society has such peculiar claims as to control the predilection of the individual for a particular walk of happiness, and restrain him to that alone arising from the present and future benedictions of mankind. This seems to be your condition, and the law imposed on you by Providence in forming your character and fashioning the events on which it was to operate; and it is to motives like these, and not to personal anxieties of mine or others, who have no right to call on you for sacrifices, that I appeal from your former determination, and urge a revisal of it, on the ground of change in the aspect of things."

An incident is related by the historian of the Peninsular War, illustrative of the personal influence exercised by a great commander over his followers. The British army lay at Sauroren, before which Soult was advancing, prepared to attack in force. Wellington was absent, and his arrival was anxiously looked for. Suddenly a single horseman was seen riding up the mountain alone. It was the duke, about to join his troops. One of Campbell's Portuguese battalions first descried him, and raised a joyful cry; then the shrill clamor, caught up by the next regiment, soon swelled as it ran along the line into that appalling shout which the British soldier is wont to give upon the edge of battle, and which no enemy ever heard unmoved. Suddenly he stopped at a conspicuous point, for he desired both armies should know he was there, and a double spy who was present pointed out Soult, who was so near that his features could be distinguished. Attentively Wellington fixed his eyes on that formidable man, and, as if speaking to himself, he said: "Yonder is a great commander; but he is cautious, and will delay his attack to ascertain the cause of those cheers; that will give time for the Sixth Division to arrive, and I shall beat him," which he did.

In some cases, personal character acts by a kind of talismanic influence, as if certain men were the organs of a sort of supernatural force. "If I but stamp on the ground in Italy," said Pompey, "an army will appear." At the voice of Peter the Hermit, as described by the historian, "Europe arose and precipitated itself upon Asia." It was said of the Caliph Omar that his walking-stick struck more terror into those who saw it than another man's sword. The very names of some men are like the sound of a trumpet. When the Douglas lay mortally wounded on the field of Otter-burn, he ordered his name to be shouted still louder than before, saying there was a tradition in his family that a dead Douglas should win a battle. His followers, inspired by the sound, gathered fresh courage, rallied and conquered; and thus, in the words of the Scottish poet:

"The Douglas dead, his name hath won the field."

There have been some men whose greatest conquests have been achieved after they themselves were dead. "Never," says Michelet, "was Caesar more alive, more powerful, more terrible, than when his old and worn-out body, his withered corpse, lay pierced with blows; he appeared then purified, redeemed—that which he had been, despite his many stains—the man of humanity." Never did the great character of William of Orange, surnamed the Silent, exercise greater power over his countrymen than after his assassination at Delft by the emissary of the Jesuits. On the very day of his murder the Estates of Holland resolved "to maintain the good cause, with

God's help, to the uttermost, without sparing gold or blood"; and they kept their word.

Character embodied in thought and deed, is of the nature of immortality. The solitary thought of a great thinker will dwell in the minds of men for centuries, until at length it works itself into their daily life and practice. It lives on through the ages, speaking as a voice from the dead, and influencing minds living thousands of years apart. Thus, Moses and David and Solomon, Plato and Socrates and Xenophon, Seneca and Cicero and Epictetus, still speak to us as from their tombs. They still arrest the attention, and exercise an influence upon character, though their thoughts be conveyed in languages unspoken by them, and in their time unknown. Theodore Parker has said that a single man like Socrates was worth more to a country than many such States as South Carolina that if that State went out of the world today, she would not have done so much for the world as Socrates. Erasmus so reverenced the character of Socrates that he said, when he considered his life and doctrines, he was inclined to put him in the calendar of saints, and to exclaim, Holy Socrates, pray for us!

Great workers and great thinkers are the true makers of history, which is but continuous humanity influenced by men of character—by great leaders, kings, priests, philosophers, statesmen, and patriots—the true aristocracy of man. Indeed, Mr. Carlyle has broadly stated that Universal History is, at bottom, but the history of Great Men. They certainly mark and designate the epochs of national life. Their influence is active, as well as reactive. Though their mind is, in a measure, the product of their age, the public mind is also, to a great extent, their creation. Their individual action identifies the cause—the institution. They think great thoughts, cast them abroad, and the thoughts make events. Thus the early Reformers initiated the Reformation, and with it the liberation of modern thought. Emerson has said that every institution is to be regarded as but the lengthened shadow of some great man; as Islamism of Mohammed, Puritanism of Calvin, Jesuitism of Loyola, Quakerism of Fox, Methodism of Wesley, Abolitionism of Clarkson.

Great men stamp their mind upon their age and nation—as Luther did upon modern Germany, and Knox upon Scotland. And if there be one man more than another that stamped his mind on modern Italy, it was Dante. During the long centuries of Italian depredation his burning words were as a watch-fire and a beacon to all true men. He was the herald of his nation's liberty—braving persecution, exile and death, for the love of it. He was always the most national of the Italian poets, the most loved, the most read. From the time of his death all educated Italians had his best passages by heart; and the sentiments they enshrined inspired their lives, and eventually influenced the history of their nation. "The Italians," wrote Byron in

1821, "talk Dante, write Dante, and think and dream Dante, at this moment, to an excess which would be ridiculous, but that he deserves their admiration."

Washington left behind him, as one of the greatest treasures of his country, the example of a stainless life—of a great, honest, pure and noble character—a model for the nation to form themselves by in all time to come. And in the case of Washington, as in so many other great leaders of men, his greatness did not so much consist in his intellect, his skill and his genius, as in his honor, his integrity, his truthfulness, his high and controlling sense of duty—in a word, in his genuine nobility of character.

Men such as these are the true life-blood of the country to which they belong. They elevate and uphold it, fortify and ennoble it, and shed a glory over it by the example of life and character which they have bequeathed. "The names and memories of great men," says an able writer, "are the dowry of a nation. Widowhood, overthrow, desertion, even slavery, cannot take away from her this sacred inheritance. . . . Whenever national life begins to quicken . . . the dead heroes rise in the memory of men, and appear to the living to stand by in solemn spectatorship and approval. No country can be lost which feels herself overlooked by such glorious witnesses. They are the salt of the earth, in death as well as in life. What they did once, their descendants have still and always a right to do after them; and their example lives in their country, a continual stimulant and encouragement for him who has the soul to adopt it."

But it is not great men only that have to be taken into account in estimating the qualities of a nation, but the character that pervades the great body of the people. When Washington Irving visited Abbotsford, Sir Walter Scott introduced him to many of his friends and favorites, not only among the neighboring farmers, but the laboring peasantry. "I wish to show you," said Scott, "some of our really excellent plain Scotch people. The character of a nation is not to be learnt from its fine folks, its fine gentlemen and ladies; such you meet everywhere, and they are everywhere the same." While statesmen, philosophers and divines represent the thinking power of society, the men who found industries and carve out new careers, as well as the common body of working-people, from whom the national strength and spirit are from time to time recruited, must necessarily furnish the vital force and constitute the real backbone of every nation.

Nations have their character to maintain as well as individuals, and under constitutional governments, where all classes more or less participate in the exercise of political power—the national character will necessarily depend more upon the moral qualities of the many than of the few. And the same qualities which determine the character of individuals also determine the character of nations. Unless they are high-minded, truthful, honest, virtuous, and courageous, they will be held in light esteem by other nations, and be without weight in the world. To have character they must needs also be reverential, disciplined, self-controlling, and devoted to duty. The nation that has no higher god than pleasure, or even dollars or calico, must needs be in a poor way. It were better to revert to Homer's gods than be devoted to these for the heathen deities at least imagined human virtues, and were something to look up to.

As for institutions, however good in themselves, they will avail but little in maintaining the standard of national character. It is the individual men, and the spirit which actuates them, that determine the moral standing and stability of nations. Government, in the long run, is usually no better than the people governed. Where the mass is sound in conscience, morals and habits, the nation will be ruled honestly and nobly. But where they are corrupt, self-seeking and dishonest in heart, bound neither by truth nor by law, the rule of rogues and wire-pullers becomes inevitable.

The only true barrier against the despotism of public opinion, whether it be of the many or of the few, is enlightened individual freedom and purity of personal character. Without these there can be no vigorous manhood, no true liberty in a nation. Political rights, however broadly framed, will not elevate a people individually depraved. Indeed, the more complete a system of popular suffrage, and the more perfect its protection, the more completely will the real character of a people be reflected, as by a mirror, in their laws and government. Political morality can never have any solid existence on a basis of individual immorality. Even freedom, exercised by a debased people, would come to be regarded as a nuisance, and liberty of the press but a vent for licentiousness and moral abomination.

Nations, like individuals, derive support and strength from the feeling that they belong to an illustrious race, that they are the heirs of their greatness, and ought to be the perpetuators of their glory. It is of momentous importance that a nation should have a great past to look back upon. It steadies the life of the present, elevates and upholds it, and lightens and lifts it up, by the memory of the great deeds, the noble sufferings, and the valorous achievements of the men of old. The life of nations, as of men, is a great treasury of experience, which, wisely used, issues in social progress and improvement; or, misused, issues in dreams, delusions, and failure. Like men, nations are purified and strengthened by trials. Some of the most glorious chapters in their history are those containing the record of the sufferings by means of which their character has been developed. Love of liberty and patriotic feeling may have done much, but trial and suffering nobly borne more than all. A great deal of what passes by the name of patriotism in these days consists of the merest bigotry and narrow-mindedness; exhibiting itself in national prejudice, national conceit, and national hatred. It does not show itself in deeds, but in boastings—in howlings, gesticulations, and shrieking helplessly for help—in flying flags and singing songs—and in perpetual grinding at long-dead grievances and long-remedied wrongs. To be infested by *such* a patriotism as this is perhaps among the greatest curses that can befall any country.

But as there is an ignoble, so is there a noble patriotism—the patriotism that invigorates and elevates a country by noble work—that does its duty truthfully and manfully—that lives an honest, sober, and upright life, and strives to make the best use of the opportunities for improvement that present themselves on every side; and at the same time a patriotism that cherishes the memory and example of the great men of old, who, by their sufferings in the cause of religion or of freedom, have won for themselves a deathless glory, and for their nation those privileges of free life and free political institutions of which they are the inheritors and possessors.

Nations are not to be judged by their size any more than individuals:

"It is not growing like a tree
In bulk, cloth make Man better be."

For a nation to be great, it need not necessarily be large, though size is often confounded with greatness. A nation may be very large in point of territory and population, and yet be devoid of true greatness. The people of Israel were a small people, yet what a great life they developed, and how powerful the influence they have exercised on the destinies of mankind! Greece was not big; the entire population of Attica was less than that of Illinois. Athens was less populous than New York; and yet how great it was in art, in literature, in philosophy, and in patriotism! A public orator lately spoke with contempt of the Battle of Marathon, because only 192 men perished on the side of the Athenians, whereas by improved mechanism and destructive chemicals, some 50,000 men or more may now be destroyed within a few hours. Yet the Battle of Marathon, and the heroism displayed in it, will probably continue to be remembered when the gigantic butcheries of modern times have been forgotten.

But it was the fatal weakness of Athens that its citizens had no true family or home life, while its freemen were greatly outnumbered by its slaves. Its public men were loose, if not corrupt, in morals. Its women, even the most accomplished, were unchaste. Hence its fall became inevitable, and was even more sudden than its rise.

In like manner, the decline and fall of Rome was attributable to the general corruption of its people, and to their engrossing love of pleasure and idleness—work, in the latter days of Rome, being regarded only as fit for slaves. Its citizens ceased to pride themselves on the virtues of character of their great forefathers; and the empire fell because it did not deserve to live. And so the nations that are idle and luxurious—that "will rather lose a pound of blood," as old Burton says, "in a single combat, than a drop of sweat in any honest labor" must inevitably die out, and laborious, energetic nations take their place.

When Louis XIV asked Colbert how it was that, ruling so great and populous a country as France, he had been unable to conquer so small a country as Holland, the minister replied: "Because, sire, the greatness of a country does not depend upon the extent of its territory, but on the character of its people. It is because of the industry, the frugality, and the energy of the Dutch that your majesty has found them so difficult to overcome."

It is also related of Spinola and Richardet, the ambassadors sent by the King of Spain to negotiate a treaty at the Hague in 1608, that one day they saw some eight or ten persons land from a little boat, and, sitting down upon the grass, proceed to make a meal of bread-and-cheese and beer. "Who are those travelers?" asked the ambassadors of a peasant. "These are our worshipful masters, the deputies from the States," was his reply. Spinola at once whispered to his companion, "We must make peace: these are not men to be conquered."

In fine, stability of institutions must depend upon stability of character. Any number of depraved units can not form a great nation. The people may seem to be highly civilized, and yet be ready to fall to pieces at the first touch of adversity. Without integrity of individual character, they can have no real strength, cohesion or soundness. They may be rich, polite, and artistic, and yet hovering on the brink of ruin. If living for themselves only, and with no end but pleasure—each little self his own little god—such a nation is doomed, and its decay is inevitable.

Where national character ceases to be upheld, a nation may be regarded as next to lost. Where it ceases to esteem and to practice the virtues of truthfulness, honesty, integrity, and justice, it does not deserve to live. And when the time arrives in any country when wealth has so corrupted, or pleasure so depraved, or faction so infatuated the people, that honor, order, obedience, virtue, and loyalty have seemingly become things of the past; then, amidst the darkness, when honest men—if, haply, there be such left—are groping about and feeling for each other's hands, their only remaining hope will be in the restoration and elevation of Individual Character; for by that alone can a nation be saved; and if character be irrecoverably lost, then indeed there will be nothing left worth saving.

Chapter 4

Home Power

"Live as long as you may, the first twenty years is the longest half of your life." —Southey.

HOME IS THE FIRST and most important school of character. It is there that every human being receives his best moral training, or his worst; for it is there that he imbibes those principles of conduct which endure through manhood, and cease only with life.

It is a common saying that "Manners make the man," and there is a second, that "Mind makes the man"; but truer than either is a third, that "Home makes the man." For the home-training includes not only manners and mind, but character. It is mainly in the home that the heart is opened, the habits are formed, the intellect is awakened, and character moulded for good or for evil.

From that source, be it pure or impure, issue the principles and maxims that govern society. Law itself is but the reflex of homes. The tiniest bits of opinion sown in the minds of children in private life, afterwards issue forth to the world, and become its public opinion; for nations are gathered out of nurseries, and they who hold the leading-strings of children may even exercise a greater power than those who wield the reins of government.

It is in the order of nature that domestic life should be preparatory to social, and that the mind and character should first be formed in the home. There the individuals who afterwards form society are dealt with in detail, and fashioned one by one. From the family they enter life, and advance from boyhood to citizenship. Thus the home may be regarded as the most influential school of civilization. For, after all, civilization mainly resolves itself into a question of individual training, and according as the respective members of society are well or ill trained in youth, so will the community which they constitute be more or less humanized and civilized.

The training of any man, even the wisest, cannot fail to be powerfully influenced by the moral surroundings of his early years. He comes into the world helpless, and absolutely dependent upon those about him for nurture and culture. From the very first breath that he draws, his education begins. When a mother once asked a clergyman when she should begin the education of her child, then four years old, he replied: "Madam, if you have not begun already, you have lost those four years. From the first smile that gleams upon an infant's cheek, your opportunity begins."

However apparently trivial the influences which contribute to form the character of the child, they endure through life. The child's character is the nucleus of the man's; all after-education is but superposition; the form of the crystal remains the same. Thus the saying of the poet holds true in a large degree, "The child is father of the man"; or, as Milton puts it, "The childhood shows the man, as morning shows the day." Those impulses to conduct which last the longest and are rooted the deepest, always have their origin near our birth. It is then that the germs of virtues or vices, of feelings or sentiments, are first implanted which determine the character for life.

The child is, as it were, laid at the gate of a new world, and opens his eyes upon things all of which are full of novelty and wonderment. At first it is enough for him to gaze, but by-and-by he begins to see, to observe, to compare, to learn, to store up impressions and ideas, and under wise guidance the progress which he makes is really wonderful. Lord Brougham has observed that between the ages of eighteen and thirty months, a child learns more of the material world, of his own powers, of the nature of other bodies, and even of his own mind and other minds, than he acquires in all the rest of his life. The knowledge which a child accumulates, and the ideas generated in his mind, during this period, are so important, that if we could imagine them to be afterwards obliterated, all the learning of a senior wrangler at Cambridge, or a first-classman at Oxford, would be as nothing to it, and would literally not enable its object to prolong his existence for a week.

It is in childhood that the mind is most open to impressions, and ready to be kindled by the first spark that falls into it. Ideas are then caught quickly and retained. Thus Scott is said to have received his first bent towards ballad literature from his mother's and grandmother's recitations in his hearing, before he himself had learned to read. Childhood is like a mirror, which reflects in after life the images first presented to it. The first thing continues forever with the child. The first joy, the first sorrow, the first success, the first failure, the first achievement, the first misadventure, paint the foreground of his life.

All this while, too, the training of his character is in progress—of the temper, the will and the habits—on which so much of the happiness of human beings in after-life depends. Although man is endowed with a certain self-acting, self-helping power of contributing to his own development, independent of surrounding circumstances, and of reacting upon the life around him, the bias given to his moral character in early life is of immense importance. Place even the highest-minded philosopher in the midst of daily discomfort, immorality and vileness, and he will insensibly gravitate towards brutality. How much more susceptible is the impressionable and helpless child amidst such surroundings! It is not possible to rear a kindly nature, sensitive to evil, pure in mind and heart, amidst coarseness, discomfort, and impurity.

Thus homes, which are the nurseries of children who grow up into men and women, will be good or bad, according to the power that governs them. Where the spirit of love and duty pervades the home—where head and heart bear rule wisely there—where the daily life is honest and virtuous—where the government is sensible, kind, and loving, then may we expect from such a home an issue of healthy, useful, and happy beings, capable, as they gain the requisite strength, of following the footsteps of their parents, of walking uprightly, governing themselves wisely, and contributing to the welfare of those about them.

On the other hand, if surrounded by ignorance, coarseness, and selfishness, they will unconsciously assume the same character, and grow up to adult years rude, uncultivated, and all the more dangerous to society if placed amidst the manifold temptations of what is called civilized life. "Give your child to be educated by a slave," said an ancient Greek, "and, instead of one slave, you will then have two."

The child can not help imitating what he sees. Every thing is to him a model—of manner, of gesture, of speech, of habit, of character. "For the child," says Richter, "the most important era of life is that of childhood, when he begins to color and mould himself by companionship with others. Every new educator effects less than his predecessor; until at last, if we regard all life as an educational institution, a circumnavigator of the world is less influenced by all the nations he has seen than by his nurse." Models are, therefore, of every importance in moulding the nature of the child; and if we would have fine characters, we must necessarily present before them fine models. Now, the model most constantly before every child's eye is the mother.

One good mother, said George Herbert, is worth a hundred schoolmasters. In the home she is "load-stone to all hearts, a loadstar to all eyes." Imitation of her is constant—imitation, which Bacon likens to a "globe of precepts." But example is far more than precept. It is instruction in action. It is teaching without words, often exemplifying more than tongue can teach.

In the face of bad example, the best of precepts are of but little avail. The example is followed, not the precepts. Indeed, precept at variance with practice is worse than useless, inasmuch as it only serves to teach the most cowardly of vices—hypocrisy. Even children are judges of consistency, and the lessons of the parent who says one thing and does the opposite, are quickly seen through. The teaching of the friar was not worth much who preached the virtue of honesty with a stolen goose in his sleeve.

By imitation of acts, the character becomes slowly and imperceptibly, but at length decidedly formed. The several acts may seem in themselves trivial; but so are the continuous acts of daily life. Like snow-flakes, they fall unperceived; each flake added to the pile produces no sensible change, and yet the accumulation of snow-flakes makes the avalanche. So do repeated acts, one following another, at length become consolidated in habit, determine the action of the human being for good or for evil, and, in a word, form the character.

It is because the mother, far more than the father, influences the action and conduct of the child, that her good example is of so much greater importance in the home. It is easy to understand how this should be so. The home is the woman's domain—her kingdom, where she exercises entire control. Her power over the little subjects she rules there is absolute. They look up to her for every thing. She is the example and model constantly before their eyes, whom they unconsciously observe and imitate.

Cowley, speaking of the influence of early example, and ideas early implanted in the mind, compares them to letters cut in the bark of a young tree, which grow and widen with age. The impressions then made, howsoever slight they may seem, are never effaced. The ideas then implanted in the mind are like seeds dropped into the ground, which lie there and germinate for a time, afterwards springing up in acts and thoughts and habits. Thus the mother lives again in her children. They unconsciously mould themselves after her manner, her speech, her conduct, and her method of life. Her habits become theirs; and her character is visibly repeated in them.

This maternal love is the visible providence of our race. Its influence is constant and universal. It begins with the education of the human being at the outstart of life, and is prolonged by virtue of the powerful influence which every good mother exercises over her children through life. When launched into the world, each to take part in its labors, anxieties, and trials, they still turn to their mother for consolation, if not for counsel, in their time of trouble and difficulty. The pure and good thoughts she has implanted in their minds when children continue to grow up into good acts long after she is dead; and when there is nothing but a memory of her left, her children rise up and call her blessed.

It is not saying too much to aver that the happiness or misery, the enlightenment or ignorance, the civilization or barbarism of the world, depends in a very high degree upon the exercise of woman's power within her special kingdom of home. Indeed, Emerson says, broadly and truly, that "a sufficient measure of civilization is the influence of good women." Posterity may be said to lie before us in the person of the child in the mother's lap. What that child will eventually become, mainly depends upon the training and example which he has received from his first and most influential educator.

Woman, above all other educators, educates humanly. Man is the brain, but woman is the heart of humanity; he its judgment, she its feeling; he its strength, she its grace, ornament, and solace. Even the understanding of the best woman seems to work mainly through her affections. And thus, though man may direct the intellect, woman cultivates the feelings, which mainly determine the character. While he fills the memory, she occupies the heart. She makes us love what he can only make us believe, and it is chiefly through her that we are enabled to arrive at virtue.

The respective influences of the father and the mother on the training and developing of character are remarkably illustrated in the life of St. Augustine. While Augustine's father, a poor freeman of Thagaste, proud of his son's abilities, endeavored to furnish his mind with the highest learning of the schools, and was extolled by his neighbors for the sacrifices he made with that object "beyond the ability of his means"—his mother, Monica, on the other hand, sought to lead her son's mind in the direction of the highest good, and with pious care counselled him, entreated him, advised him to chastity, and, amidst much anguish and tribulation, because of his wicked life, never ceased to pray for him until her prayers were heard and answered. Thus her love at last triumphed, and the patience and goodness of the mother were rewarded, not only by the conversion of her gifted son, but also of her husband. Later in life, and after her husband's death, Monica, drawn by her affection, followed her son to Milan to watch over him, and there she died, when he was in his thirty-third year. But it was in the earlier period of his life that her example and instruction made the deepest impression upon his mind, and determined his future character.

There are many similar instances of early impressions made upon a child's mind, springing up into good acts late in life, after an intervening period of selfishness and vice. Parents may do all that they can to develop an upright and virtuous character in their children, and apparently in vain. It seems like bread cast upon the waters and lost. And yet sometimes it happens that long after the parents have gone to their rest—it may be twenty years or more—the good precept, the good example set before their sons and daughters in childhood, at length springs up and bears fruit.

One of the most remarkable of such instances was that of the Reverend John Newton, of Olney, the friend of Cowper, the poet. It was long subsequent to the death of both his parents, and after leading a vicious life as a youth and as a seaman, that he became suddenly awakened to a sense of his depravity, and then it was that the lessons which his mother had given him when a child sprang up vividly in his memory. Her voice came to him as it were from the dead, and led him gently back to virtue and goodness.

Another instance is that of John Randolph, the American statesman, who once said: "I should have been an atheist if it had not been for one recollection—and that was the memory of the time when my departed mother used to take my little hand in hers and cause me on my knees to say, 'Our Father who art in heaven!'"

But such instances must, on the whole, be regarded as exceptional. As the character is biased in early life, so it generally remains, gradually assuming its permanent form as manhood is reached. "Live as long as you may," said Southey, "the first twenty years are the longest half of your life," and they are by far the most pregnant in consequences. When the worn-out slanderer and voluptuary, Dr. Wolcot, lay on his death bed, one of his friends asked if he could do anything to gratify him. "Yes," said the dying man, eagerly, "give me back my youth." Give him but that, and he would repent—he would reform. But it was all too late! His life had become bound arid enthralled by the chains of habit.

Gretry, the musical composer, thought so highly of the importance of woman as an educator of character, that he described a good mother as "Nature's masterpiece." And he was right: for good mothers, far more than fathers, tend to the perpetual renovation of mankind, creating as they do the moral atmosphere of the home, which is the nutriment of man's moral being, as the physical atmosphere is of his corporeal frame. By good temper, suavity and kindness, directed by intelligence, woman surrounds the indwellers with a pervading atmosphere of cheerfulness, contentment, and peace, suitable for the growth of the purest as of the manliest natures.

The poorest dwelling, presided over by a virtuous, thrifty, cheerful, and cleanly woman, may thus be the abode of comfort, virtue and happiness; it may be the scene of every ennobling relation in family life; it may be endeared to a man by many delightful associations; furnishing a sanctuary for the heart, a refuge from the storms of life, a sweet resting-place after labor, a consolation in misfortune, a pride in prosperity, and a joy at all times.

The good home is thus the best of schools, not only in youth, but in age. There young and old best learn cheerfulness, patience, self-control, and the spirit of service and of duty. Izaak Walton, speaking of George Herbert's mother, says she governed her family with judicious care, not rigidly or sourly, "but with such a sweetness and compliance with the recreations and pleasures of youth, as did incline them to spend much of their time in her company, which was to her great content."

The home is the true school of courtesy, of which woman is always the best practical instructor. Philanthropy radiates from the home as from a centre. "To love the little platoon we belong to in society," said Burke, "is the germ of all public affections." The wisest and the best have not been ashamed to own it to be their greatest joy and happiness to sit "behind the heads of children" in the inviolable circle of home. A life of purity and duty there is not the least effectual preparative for a life of public work and duty; and the man who loves his home will not the less fondly love and serve his country.

But while homes, which are the nurseries of character, may be the best of schools, they may also be the worst. Between childhood and manhood how incalculable is the mischief which ignorance in the home has the power to cause! Between the drawing of the first breath and the last, how vast is the moral suffering and disease occasioned by incompetent mothers and nurses! Commit a child to the care of a worthless, ignorant woman, and no culture in after-life will remedy the evil you have done. Let the mother be idle, vicious, and a slattern; let her home be pervaded by caviling, petulance, and discontent, and it will become a dwelling of misery—a place to fly from, rather than to fly to; and the children whose misfortune it is to be brought up there will be morally dwarfed and deformed—the cause of misery to themselves as well as to others.

Napoleon Bonaparte was accustomed to say that "the future good or bad conduct of a child depended entirely on the mother." He himself attributed his rise in life in a great measure to the training of his will, his energy, and his self-control, by his mother at home. "Nobody had any command over him," says one of his biographers, "except his mother, who found means, by a mixture of tenderness, severity, and justice, to make him love, respect, and obey her; from her he learnt the virtue of obedience."

A curious illustration of the dependence of the character of children on that of the mother incidentally occurs in one of Mr. Tufnell's school reports. The truth, he observes, is so well established that it has even been made subservient to mercantile calculation. "I was informed," he says, "in a large factory, where many children were employed, that the managers before they engaged a boy always inquired into the mother's character, and if that was satisfactory they were tolerably certain that her children would conduct themselves creditably. *No attention was paid to the character of the father.*"

It has also been observed that in cases where the father has turned out badly—become a drunkard, and "gone to the dogs"—provided the mother is prudent and sensible, the family will be kept together, and the children probably make their way honorably in life; whereas in cases of the opposite sort, where the mother turns out badly, no matter how well-conducted the father may be, the instances of after-success in life on the part of the children are comparatively rare.

The greater part of the influence exercised by women on the formation of character necessarily remains unknown. They accomplish their best works in the quiet seclusion of the home and the family, by sustained effort and patient perseverance in the path of duty. Their greatest triumphs, because private and domestic, are rarely recorded; and it is not often, even in the biographies of distinguished men, that we hear of the share which their mothers have had in the formation of their character, and in giving them a bias towards goodness. Yet are they not on that account without their reward. The influence they have exercised, though unrecorded, lives after them, and goes on propagating itself in consequences forever.

We do not so often hear of great women, as we do of great men. It is of good women that we mostly hear; and it is probable that, by determining the character of men and women for good, they are doing even greater work than if they were to paint great pictures, write great books, or compose great operas. "It is quite true," said Joseph de Maistre, "that women have produced no masterpieces. They have written no 'Iliad,' nor 'Jerusalem Delivered,' nor 'Hamlet,' nor 'Phaedre,' nor 'Paradise Lost,' nor 'Tartuffe'; they have designed no Church of St. Peter's, composed no 'Messiah,' carved no 'Apollo Belvedere,' painted no 'Last Judgment'; they have invented neither algebra, nor telescopes, nor steam-engines; but they have done something far greater and better than all this, for it is at their knees that upright and virtuous men and women have been trained—the most excellent productions in the world."

De Maistre, in his letters and writings, speaks of his own mother with immense love and reverence. Her noble character made all other women venerable in his eyes. He described her as his "sublime mother—an angel to whom God had lent a body for a brief season." To her he attributed the bent of his character, and all his bias towards good; and when he had grown to mature years, while acting as ambassador at the Court of St. Petersburg, he referred to her noble example and precepts as the ruling influence in his life.

One of the most charming features in the character of Samuel Johnson, notwithstanding his rough and shaggy exterior, was the tenderness with which he invariably spoke of his mother—a woman of strong understanding, who firmly implanted in his mind, as he himself acknowledges, his first impressions of religion. He was accustomed, even in the time of his greatest difficulties, to contribute largely, out of his slender means, to her comfort;

and one of his last acts of filial duty was to write "Rasselas" for the purpose of paying her little debts and defraying her funeral charges.

George Washington was only eleven years of age—the eldest of five children—when his father died, leaving his mother a widow. She was a woman of rare excellence, full of resources, a good woman of business, an excellent manager, and possessed of much strength of character. She had her children to educate and bring up, a large household to govern, and extensive estates to manage, all of which she accomplished with complete 'success. Her good sense, assiduity, tenderness, industry and vigilance enabled her to overcome every obstacle, and, as the richest reward of her solicitude and toil, she had the happiness to see all her children come forward with a fair promise into life, filling the spheres allotted to them in a manner equally honorable to themselves, and to the parent who had been the only guide of their principles, conduct and habits.

The biographer of Cromwell says little about the Protector's father, but dwells upon the character of his mother, whom he describes as a woman of rare vigor and decision of purpose: "A woman," he says, "possessed of the glorious faculty of self-help when other assistance failed her, ready for the demands of fortune in its extremest adverse turn, of spirit and energy equal to her mildness and patience, who, with the labor of her own hands, gave dowries to five daughters sufficient to marry them into families as honorable but more wealthy than their own, whose single pride was honesty, and whose passion was love, who preserved in the gorgeous palace at Whitehall the simple tastes that distinguished her in the old brewery at Huntingdon, and whose only care, amidst all her splendor, was for the safety of her son in his dangerous eminence."

We have spoken of the mother of Napoleon Bonaparte as a woman of great force of character. Not less so was the mother of the Duke of Wellington, whom her son strikingly resembled in features, person and character, while his father was principally distinguished as a musical composer and performer. But, strange to say, Wellington's mother mistook him for a dunce, and for some reason or other, he was not such a favorite as her other children, until his great deeds in after-life constrained her to be proud of him.

The Napiers were blessed in both parents, but especially in their mother, Lady Sarah Lennox, who early sought to inspire their sons' minds with elevating thoughts, admiration of noble deeds, and a chivalrous spirit, which became embodied in their lives, and continued to sustain them, until death, in the path of duty and of honor.

Among statesmen, lawyers and divines, we find marked mention made of the mothers of Lord Chancellors Bacon, Erskine and Brougham, all women of great ability, and in the case of the first, of great learning; as well as of the mothers of Canning, Curran and President Adams, of Herbert, Paley and Wesley. Lord Brougham speaks in terms almost approaching reverence of his grandmother, the sister of Professor Robertson, as having been mainly instrumental in instilling into his mind a strong desire for information, and the first principles of that persevering energy in the pursuit of every kind of knowledge which formed his prominent characteristic throughout life.

Canning's mother was an Irish woman of great natural ability, for whom her gifted son entertained the greatest love and respect to the close of his career. She was a woman of no ordinary intellectual power. "Indeed," says Canning's biographer, "were we not otherwise assured of the fact from direct sources, it would be impossible to contemplate his profound and touching devotion to her without being led to conclude that the object of such unchanging attachment must have been possessed of rare and commanding qualities. She was esteemed by the circle in which she lived as a woman of great mental energy. Her conversation was animated and vigorous, and marked by a distinct originality of manner and a choice of topics fresh and striking, and out of the commonplace routine. To persons who were but slightly acquainted with her, the energy of her manner had even something of the air of eccentricity."

Curran speaks with great affection of his mother, as a woman of strong original understanding, to whose wise counsel, consistent piety, and lessons of honorable ambition, which she diligently enforced on the minds of her children, he himself principally attributed his success in life. "The only inheritance," he used to say, "that I could boast of from my poor father was the very scanty one of an unattractive face and person, like his own, and if the world has ever attributed to me something more valuable than face or person, or than earthly wealth, it was that another and a dearer parent gave her child a portion from the treasure of her mind."

When ex-President Adams was present at the examination of a girls' school at Boston, he was presented by the pupils with an address which deeply affected him, and in acknowledging it, he took the opportunity of referring to the lasting influence which womanly training and association had exercised upon his own life and character. "As a child," he said, "I enjoyed perhaps the greatest of blessings that can be bestowed on man—that of a mother who was anxious and capable to form the characters of her children rightly. From her I derived whatever instruction (religious especially, and moral) has pervaded a long life—I will not say perfectly, or as it ought to be, but I will say, because it is only justice to the memory of her I revere, that in the course of that life, whatever imperfection there has been, or deviation from what she taught me, the fault is mine and not hers."

The Wesleys were peculiarly linked to their parents by natural piety, though the mother, rather than the father, influenced their minds and developed their characters. The father was a man of strong will, but occasionally harsh and tyrannical in his dealings with his family, while the mother, with much strength of understanding and ardent love of truth, was gentle, persuasive, affectionate and simple. She was the teacher and cheerful companion of her children, who gradually became moulded by her example. It was through the bias given by her to her sons' minds in religious matters that they acquired the tendency which, even in early years, drew to them the name of Methodist. In a letter to her son, Samuel Wesley, when a scholar at Westminster in 1709, she said: "I would advise you as much as possible to throw your business into a certain *method*, by which means you will learn to improve every precious moment, and find an unspeakable facility in the performance of your respective duties." This method she went on to describe, exhorting her son "in all things to act upon principle"; and the society which the brothers, John and Charles, afterward founded at Oxford is supposed to have been in a great measure the result of her exhortations.

In the case of poets, literary men, and artists, the influence of the mother's feeling and taste has doubtless had great effect in directing the genius of their sons; and we find this especially illustrated in the lives of Gray, Thomson, Scott, Southey, Bulwer, Schiller, and Goethe. Gray inherited, almost complete, his kind and loving nature from his mother, while his father was harsh and unamiable. Gray was, in fact, a feminine man—shy, reserved, and wanting in energy—but thoroughly irreproachable in life and character. The poet's mother maintained the family after her unworthy husband had deserted her; and, at her death, Gray placed on her grave, an epitaph describing her as "the careful, tender mother of many children, one of whom alone had the misfortune to survive her." The poet himself was, at his own desire, interred beside her worshipped grave.

Goethe, like Schiller, owed the bias of his mind and character to his mother, who was a woman of extraordinary gifts. She was full of joyous, flowing mother-wit, and possessed in a high degree the art of stimulating young and active minds, instructing them in the science of life out of the treasures of her abundant experience. After a lengthened interview with her, an enthusiastic traveler said, "Now do I understand how Goethe has become the man he is." Goethe himself affectionately cherished her memory. "She was worthy of life!" he once said of her; and when he visited Frankfort, he sought out every individual who had been kind to his mother, and thanked them all.

It was Ary Scheffer's mother—whose beautiful features the painter so loved to reproduce in his pictures of Beatrice, St. Monica, and others of his works—that encouraged his study of art, and by great self-denial provided him with the means of pursuing it. While living at Dordrecht, in Holland, she first sent him to Lille to study, and afterwards to Paris; and her letters to him, while absent, were always full of sound motherly advice, and affectionate womanly sympathy. "If you could but see me," she wrote on one occasion, "kissing your picture, then, after a while, taking it up again, and, with a tear in my eye, calling you my beloved son, you would comprehend what it costs me to use sometimes the stern language of authority, and to occasion to you moments of pain. . . . Work diligently—be, above all, modest and humble; and when you find yourself excelling others, then compare what you have done with Nature itself, or with the ideal of your own mind, and you will be secured, by the contrast which will be apparent, against the effects of pride and presumption."

Long years after, when Ary Scheffer was himself a grandfather, he remembered with affection the advice of his mother, and repeated it to his children. And thus the vital power of good example lives on from generation to generation, keeping the world ever fresh and young. Writing to his daughter, Madame Marjolin, in 1846, his departed mother's advice recurred to him, and he said: "The word *work*—fix it well in your memory, dear child; your grandmother seldom had it out of hers. The truth is, that through our lives nothing brings any good fruit except what is earned by either the work of the hands or by the exertion of one's self-denial. Sacrifices must, in short, be ever going on if we would obtain any comfort or happiness. Now that I am no longer young, I declare that few passages in my life afford me so much satisfaction as those in which I made sacrifices or denied myself enjoyments."

"The Forbidden" is the motto of the wise man. Self-denial is the quality of which Jesus Christ set us the example.

The French historian Michelet makes the following touching reference to his mother in the Preface to one of his most popular books, the subject of much embittered controversy at the time at which it appeared:

"While writing all this, I have had in my mind a woman whose strong and serious mind would not have failed to support me in these contentions. I lost her thirty years ago (I was a child then)—nevertheless, ever living in my memory, she follows me from age to age.

"She suffered with me in my poverty, and was not allowed to share my better fortune. When young, I made her sad, and now I can not console her. I know not even where her bones are: I was too poor then to buy earth to bury her!

"And yet I owe her much. I feel deeply that I am the son of woman. Every instant, in my ideas and words (not to mention my features and gestures), I find again my mother in myself. It is my mother's blood which gives me the sympathy I feel for by-gone ages, and the tender remembrance of all those who are now no more.

"What return, then, could I, who am myself advancing towards old age, make her for the many things I owe her? One, for which she would have thanked me—this protest in favor of women and mothers."

But while a mother may greatly influence the poetic or artistic mind of her son for good, she may also influence it for evil. Thus the characteristics of Lord Byron the waywardness of his impulses, his defiance of restraint, the bitterness of his hate, and the precipitancy of his resentments—were traceable in no small degree to the adverse influences exercised upon his mind from his birth by his capricious, violent and headstrong mother. She even taunted her son with his personal deformity; and it was no unfrequent occurrence, in the violent quarrels which occurred between them, for her to take up the poker or tongs and hurl them after him as he fled from her presence. It was this unnatural treatment that gave a morbid turn to Byron's after-life; and, care-worn, unhappy, great, and yet weak, as he was, he carried about with him the mother's poison which he had sucked in his infancy.

In like manner, though in a different way, the character of Mrs. Foote, the actor's mother, was curiously repeated in the life of her joyous, jovial-hearted son. Though she had been heiress to a large fortune, she soon spent it all, and was at length imprisoned for debt. In this condition she wrote to Sam, who had been allowing her a hundred a year out of the proceeds of his acting: "Dear Sam, I am in prison for debt; come and assist your loving mother, E. Foote." To which her son characteristically replied—"Dear mother, so am I; which prevents his duty being paid to his loving mother by her affectionate son, Sam Foote."

We have spoken of the mother of Washington as an excellent woman of business; and to possess such a quality as capacity for business is not only compatible with true womanliness, but is in a measure essential to the comfort and well-being of every properly-governed family. Habits of business do not relate to trade merely, but apply to all the practical affairs of life—to every thing that has to be arranged, or be organized, to be provided for, to be done. And in all those respects the management of a family and of a household is as much a matter of business as the management of a shop or of a counting-house. It requires method, accuracy, organization, industry, economy, discipline, tact, knowledge, and capacity for adapting means to ends. All this is of the essence of business; and hence business habits are as necessary to be cultivated by women who would succeed in the affairs of home—in other words, who would make home happy—as by men in the affairs of trade, of commerce, or of manufacture.

The idea has, however, heretofore prevailed, that women have no concern with such matters, and that business habits and qualifications relate to men only. Take, for instance, the knowledge of figures. Mr. Bright has said of boys, "Teach a boy arithmetic thoroughly, and he is a made man." And why?—Because it teaches him method, accuracy, value, proportions, relations. But how many girls are taught arithmetic well?—Very few indeed. And what is the consequence? When the girl becomes a wife, if she knows nothing of figures, and is innocent of addition and multiplication, she can keep no record of income and expenditure, and there will probably be a succession of mistakes committed which may be prolific in domestic contention. The woman, not being up to her business—that is, the management of her domestic affairs in conformity with the simple principles of arithmetic—will, through sheer ignorance, be apt to commit extravagances, though unintentional, which may be most injurious to her family peace and comfort.

Method, which is the soul of business, is also of essential importance in the home. Work can only be got through by method. Method demands punctuality, another eminently business quality. The unpunctual woman, like the unpunctual man, occasions dislike, because she consumes and wastes time, and provokes the reflection that we are not of sufficient importance to make her more prompt. To the business man, time is money; but to the business woman, method is more—it is peace, comfort, and domestic prosperity.

Prudence is another important business quality in women, as in men. Prudence is practical wisdom, and conies of the cultivated judgment. It has reference in all things to fitness, to propriety; judging wisely of the right thing to be done, and the right way of doing it. It calculates the means, order, time, and method of doing. Prudence learns from experience, quickened by knowledge.

For these, among other reasons, habits of business are necessary to be cultivated by all women, in order to their being efficient helpers in the world's daily life and work. Furthermore, to direct the power of the home aright, women, as the nurses, trainers, and educators of children, need all the help and strength that mental culture can give them.

Mere instinctive love is not sufficient. Instinct, which preserves the lower creatures, needs no training; but human intelligence, which is in constant request in a family, needs to be educated. The physical health of the rising generation is entrusted to woman by Providence; and it is in the physical nature that the moral and mental nature lies enshrined. It is only by acting in accordance with the natural laws, which, before she can follow, woman must needs understand, that the blessings of health of body, and health of mind and morals, can be secured at home. Without a knowledge of such laws, the mother's love too often finds its recompense only in a child's coffin. That about one-third of all the children born in this country die under five years of age, can only be attributable to ignorance of the natural laws, ignorance of the human constitution, and ignorance of the uses of pure air, pure water, and of the art of preparing and administering wholesome food. There is no such mortality among the lower animals.

Woman was not meant to be either an unthinking drudge, or the merely pretty ornament of man's leisure. She exists for herself as well as for others; and the serious and responsible duties she is called upon to perform in life require the cultivated head as well as the sympathizing heart. Her highest mission is not to be fulfilled by the mastery of fleeting accomplishments, on which so much useful time is now wasted; for, though accomplishments may enhance the charms of youth and beauty, of themselves sufficiently charming, they will be found of very little use in the affairs of real life.

The highest praise which the ancient Romans could express of a noble matron was that she sat at home and spun. In our own time it has been said that chemistry enough to keep the pot boiling, and geography enough to know the different rooms in her house, was science enough for any woman; while Byron, whose sympathies for woman were of a very imperfect kind, professed that he would limit her library to a Bible and a cookery-book. But this view of woman's character and culture is as absurdly narrow and unintelligent, on the one hand, as the opposite view, now so much in vogue, is extravagant and unnatural on the other—that woman ought to be educated so as to be as much as possible the equal of man; undistinguishable from him except in sex; equal to him in rights and votes; and his competitor in all that makes life a fierce and selfish struggle for place and power and money.

Speaking generally, the training and discipline that are most suitable for the one sex in early life are also the most suitable for the other; and the education and culture that fill the mind of the man will prove equally wholesome for the woman. Indeed, all the arguments -which have yet been advanced in favor of the higher education of men plead equally strongly in favor of the higher education of women. In all the departments of home, intelligence will add to woman's usefulness and efficiency. It will give her thought and forethought, enable her to anticipate and provide for the contingencies of life, suggest improved methods of management, and give her strength in every way. In disciplined mental power she will find a stronger and safer protection against deception and imposture than in mere innocent and unsuspecting ignorance; in moral and religious culture she will secure sources of influence more powerful and enduring than in physical attractions; and in due self-reliance and self-dependence she will discover the truest sources of domestic comfort and happiness.

But while the mind and character of women ought to be cultivated with a view to their own well-being, they ought not the less to be educated liberally with a view to the happiness of others. Men themselves can not be sound in mind or morals if women be the reverse; and if, as we hold to be the case, the moral condition of a people mainly depends upon the education of the home, then the education of women is to be regarded as a matter of national importance. Not only does the moral character but the mental strength of man find its best safeguard and support in the moral purity and mental cultivation of woman; but the more completely the powers of both are developed, the more harmonious and well-ordered will society be—the more safe and certain its elevation and advancement.

When, about fifty years since, the first Napoleon said that the great want of France was mothers, he meant, in other words, that the French people needed the education of homes, presided over by good, virtuous, intelligent women. Indeed, the first French Revolution presented one of the most striking illustrations of the social mischiefs resulting from a neglect of the purifying influence of women. When that great national outbreak occurred, society was impenetrated with vice and profligacy. Morals, religion, virtue, -were swamped by sensualism. The character of woman had become depraved. Conjugal fidelity was disregarded; maternity was held in reproach; family and home were alike corrupted. Domestic purity no longer bound society together. France was motherless; the children broke loose; and the Revolution burst forth, "amidst the yells and the fierce violence of women."

But the terrible lesson was disregarded, and again and again France has grievously suffered from the want of that discipline, obedience, self-control and self-respect which can only be truly learnt at home. It is said that the Third Napoleon attributed the recent powerlessness of France, which left her helpless and bleeding at the feet of her conquerors, to the frivolity and lack of principle of the people, as well as to their love of pleasure, which, however, it must be confessed, he himself did not a little to foster. It would thus seem that the discipline which France still needs to learn, if she would be good and great, is that indicated by the first Napoleon—home education by good mothers.

The influence of woman is the same everywhere. Her condition influences the morals, manners and character of the people in all countries. Where she is debased, society is debased; where she is morally pure and enlightened, society will be proportionately elevated.

Hence, to instruct woman is to instruct man; to elevate her character is to raise his own; to enlarge her mental freedom is to extend and secure that of the whole community. For nations are but the outcomes of homes, and peoples of mothers. But while it is certain that the character of a nation will be elevated by the enlightenment and refinement of woman, it is much more than doubtful whether any advantage is to be derived from her entering into competition with man in the rough work of business and politics. Women can no more do men's special work in the world than men can do women's. And wherever woman has been withdrawn from her home and family to enter upon other work, the result has been socially disastrous. Indeed, the efforts of some of the best philanthropists have of late years been devoted to withdrawing women from toiling alongside of men in coal-pits, factories, nail-shops and brick-yards.

It is still not uncommon in the North for the husbands to be idle at home, while the mothers and daughters are working in the factory, the result being in many cases, an entire subversion of family order, of domestic discipline, and of home rule. And for many years past, in Paris, that state of things has been reached which some women desire to effect among ourselves. The women there mainly attend to business while the men lounge about the boulevards. But the result has only been homelessness, degeneracy and family and social decay.

Nor is there any reason to believe that the elevation and improvement of women are to be secured by investing them with political power. There are, however, in these days, many believers in the potentiality of "votes," who anticipate some indefinite good from the "enfranchisement" of women. It is not necessary here to enter upon the discussion of this question. But it may be sufficient to state that the power which women do not possess politically is far more than compensated by that which they exercise in private life—by their training in the home those who, whether as men or as, women, do all the manly as well as womenly work of the world. The Radical Bentham has said that man, even if he would, cannot keep power from woman, for that she already governs the world "with the whole power of a despot," though the power that she mainly governs by is love; and to form the character of the whole human race, is certainly a power far greater than that which women could ever hope to exercise as voters for members of parliament, or even as law-makers.

There is, however, one special department of woman's work demanding the earnest attention of all true female reformers, though it is one which has hitherto been unaccountably neglected. We mean the better economizing and preparation of human food, the waste of which at present, for want of the most ordinary culinary knowledge, is little short of scandalous. If that man is to be regarded as a benefactor of his species who makes two stalks of corn to grow where only one grew before, not less is she to be regarded as a public benefactor who economizes and turns to the best practical account the food-products of human skill and labor. The improved use of even our existing supply would be equivalent to an immediate extension of the cultivable acreage of our country—not to speak of the increase in health, economy and domestic comfort. Were our female reformers only to turn their energies in this direction with effect, they would earn the gratitude of all households, and be esteemed as among the greatest of all practical philanthropists.

Chapter 5

Companionship and Example

"Keep good company, and you shall be of the number." —George Herbert.

THE NATURAL EDUCATION of the home is prolonged far into life—indeed, it never entirely ceases. But the time arrives, in the progress of years, when the home ceases to exercise an exclusive influence on the formation of character, and it is succeeded by the more artificial education of the school, and the companionship of friends and comrades, which continue to mould the character by the powerful influence of example.

Men, young and old—but the young more than the old—cannot help imitating those with whom they associate. It was a saying of George Herbert's mother, intended for the guidance of her sons, "that as our bodies take a nourishment suitable to the meat on which we feed, so do our souls as insensibly take in virtue or vice by the example or conversation of good or bad company."

Indeed, it is impossible that association with those about us should not produce a powerful influence in the formation of character. For men are by nature imitators, and all persons are more or less impressed by the speech, the manners, the gait, the gestures, and the very habits of thinking of their companions. "Is example nothing?" said Burke. "It is everything. Example is the school of mankind, and they will learn at no other." Burke's grand motto, which he wrote for the tablet of the Marquis of Rockingham, is worth repeating. It was, "Remember, resemble, persevere."

Imitation is for the most part so unconscious that its effects are almost unheeded, but its influence is not the less permanent on that account. It is only when an impressive nature is placed in contact with an impressionable one that the alteration in the character becomes recognizable. Yet even the weakest natures exercise some influence upon those about them. The approximation of feeling, thought and habit is constant, and the action of example unceasing.

Emerson has observed that even old couples, or persons who have been house-mates for a course of years, grow gradually like each other; so that, if they were to live long enough, we should scarcely be able to know them apart. But if this be true of the old, how much more true is it of the young, whose plastic natures are so much more soft and impressionable, and ready to take the stamp of the life and conversation of those about them!

"There has been," observed Sir Charles Bell in one of his letters, "a good deal said about education, but they appear to me to put out of sight *example*, which is all-in-all. My best education was the example set me by my brothers. There was, in all the members of the family, a reliance on self, a true independence, and by imitation I obtained it."

It is in the nature of things that the circumstances which contribute to form the character should exercise their principal influence during the period of growth. As years advance, example and imitation become custom, and gradually consolidate into habit, which is of so much potency that, almost before we know it, we have in a measure yielded up to it our personal freedom.

It is related of Plato, that on one occasion he reproved a boy for playing at some foolish game. "Thou reprovest me," said the boy, "for a very little thing." "But custom," replied Plato, "is not a little thing." Bad custom, consolidated into habit, is such a tyrant that men sometimes cling to vices even while they curse them. They have become the slaves of habits whose power they are impotent to resist. Hence Locke has said that to create and maintain that vigor of mind which is able to contest the empire of habit may be regarded as one of the chief ends of moral discipline.

Though much of the education of character by example is spontaneous and unconscious, the young need not necessarily be the passive followers or imitators of those about them. Their own conduct, far more than the conduct of their companions, tends to fix the purpose and form the principles of their life. Each possesses in himself a power of will and of free activity, which, if courageously exercised, will enable him to make his own individual selection of friends and associates. It is only through weakness of purpose that young people as well as old, become the slaves of their inclinations, or give themselves up to a servile imitation of others.

It is a common saying that men are known by the company they keep. The sober do not naturally associate with the drunken, the refined with the coarse, the decent with the dissolute. To associate with depraved persons argues a low taste and vicious tendencies, and to frequent their society leads to inevitable degradation of character. "The conversation of such persons," says Seneca, "is very injurious, for even if it does not immediate harm, it leaves its seeds in the mind, and follows us when we have gone from the speakers—a plague sure to spring up in future resurrection."

If young men are wisely influenced and directed, and conscientiously exert their own free energies, they will seek the society of those better than themselves, and strive to imitate their example. In companionship with the good, growing natures will always find their best nourishment, while companionship with the bad will only be fruitful in mischief. There are persons whom to know is to love, honor and admire, and others whom to know is to shun and despise. Live with persons of elevated characters, and you will feel lifted and lighted up in them. "Live with wolves," says the Spanish proverb, "and you will learn to howl."

Intercourse with even commonplace, selfish persons, may prove most injurious, by inducing a dry, dull, reserved and selfish condition of mind, more or less inimical to true manliness and breadth of character. The mind soon learns to run in small grooves, the heart grows narrow and contracted, and the moral nature becomes weak, irresolute and accommodating, which is fatal to all generous ambition or real excellence.

On the other hand, associations with persons wiser, better and more experienced than ourselves, is always more or less inspiring and invigorating. They enhance our own knowledge of life. We correct our estimates by theirs, and become partners in their wisdom. We enlarge our field of observation through their eyes, profit by their experience, and learn not only from what they have enjoyed, but—which is still more instructive—from what they have suffered. If they are stronger than ourselves, we become participators in their strength. Hence companionship with the wise and energetic never fails to have a most valuable influence on the formation of character, increasing our resources, strengthening our resolves, elevating our aims, and enabling us to exercise greater dexterity and ability in our own affairs, as well as more effective helpfulness of others.

"I have often deeply regretted in myself," says Mrs. Schimmelpenninck, "the great loss I have experienced from the solitude of my early habits. We need no worse companion than our unregenerate selves, and, by living alone, a person not only becomes wholly ignorant of the means of helping his fellow-creatures, but is without the perception of those wants which most need help. Association with others, when not on so large a scale as to make hours of retirement impossible, may be considered as furnishing to an individual a rich multiplied experience; and sympathy so drawn forth, though, unlike charity, it begins abroad, never fails to bring rich treasures home. Association with others is useful also in strengthening the character, and in enabling us, while we never lose sight of our main object, to thread our way wisely and well."

An entirely new direction may be given to the life of a young man by a happy suggestion, a timely hint, or the kindly advice of an honest friend. Thus the life of Henry Martyn, the Indian missionary, seems to have been singularly influenced by a friendship which he formed, when a boy, at Truro Grammar School. Martyn himself was of feeble frame, and of a delicate, nervous temperament. Wanting in animal spirits, he took but little pleasure in school sports; and being of a somewhat petulant temper, the bigger boys took pleasure in provoking him, and some of them in bullying him. One of the bigger boys, however, conceiving a friendship for Martyn, took him under his protection, stood between him and his persecutors, and not only fought his battles for him, but helped him with his lessons. Though Martyn was rather a backward pupil, his father was desirous that he should have the advantage of a college education, and at the age of about fifteen he sent him to Oxford to try for a Corpus scholarship, in which he failed. Ile remained for two years more at the Truro Gramm a; School, and then went to Cambridge, where he was entered at St. John's College. Whom should he find already settled there as a student but his old champion of the Truro Grammar School? Their friendship was renewed; and the elder student from that time forward acted as the Mentor of the younger one. Martyn was fitful in his studies, excitable and petulant, and occasionally subject to fits of almost uncontrollable rage. His big friend, on the other hand, was a steady, patient, hard-working fellow; and he never ceased to watch over, to guide, and to advise for good his irritable fellow-student. He kept Martyn out of the way of evil company, advised him to work hard, "not for the praise of men, but for the glory of God"; and so successfully assisted him in his studies, that at the following Christmas examination he was the first of his year. Yet Martyn's kind friend and Mentor never achieved any distinction himself; he passed away into obscurity, leading, most probably, a useful though an unknown career; his greatest wish in life having been to shape the character of his friend, to inspire his soul with the love of truth, and to prepare him for the noble work, on which he shortly after entered, of an Indian missionary.

A somewhat similar incident is said to have occurred in the college career of Dr. Paley. When a student at Christ's College, Cambridge, he was distinguished for his shrewdness as well as his clumsiness, and he was at the same time the favorite and the butt of his companions. Though his natural abilities were great, he was thoughtless, idle, and a spendthrift; and at the commencement of his third year he had made comparatively little progress. After one of his usual night-dissipations, a friend stood by his bedside on the following morning. "Paley," said he, "I have not been able to sleep for thinking about you. I have been thinking what a fool you are! *I* have the means of dissipation, and can afford to be idle; *you* are poor, and cannot afford it. I could do nothing, probably, even were I to try: *you* are capable of doing any thing. I have lain awake all night thinking about your folly, and I have now came solemnly to warn you. Indeed, if you persist in your indolence, and go on in this way, I must renounce your society altogether."

It is said that Paley was so powerfully affected by this admonition, that from that moment he became an altered man. He formed an entirely new plan of life, and diligently persevered in it. He became one of the most industrious of students. One by one he distanced his competitors, and at the end of the year he came out senior wrangler. What he afterwards accomplished as an author and a divine is sufficiently well known.

No one recognized more fully the influence of personal example on the young than did Dr. Arnold. It was the great lever with which he worked in striving to elevate the character of his school. He made it his principal object, first to put a right spirit into the leading boys by attracting their good and noble feelings; and then to make them instrumental in propagating the same spirit among the rest, by the influence of imitation, example, and admiration. He endeavored to make all feel that they were fellow-workers with himself, and sharers with him in the moral responsibility for the good government of the place. One of the first effects of this high-minded system of management was, that it inspired the boys with strength and self respect. They felt that they were trusted. There were, of course, wayward pupils at Rugby, as there are at all schools; and these it was the master's duty to watch, to prevent their bad example contaminating others. On one occasion, he said to an assistant-master: "Do you see those two boys walking together? I never saw them together before. You should make an especial point of observing the company they keep: nothing so tells the changes in a boy's character."

Dr. Arnold's own example was an inspiration, as is that of every great teacher. In his presence, young men learned to respect themselves, and out of the root of self-respect there grew up the manly virtues. "His very presence," says his biographer, "seemed to create a new spring of health and vigor within them, and to give to life an interest and elevation which remained with them long after they had left him; and dwelt so habitually in their thoughts as a living image, that, when death had taken him away, the bond appeared to be still unbroken, and the sense of separation almost lost in the still deeper sense of a life and a 'union indestructible.'" And thus it was that Dr. Arnold trained a host of manly and noble characters, who spread the influence of his example ire all parts of the world.

So also was it said of Dugald Stewart, that he breathed the love of virtue into whole congregations of pupils. "To me," says the late Lord Cockburn, "his lectures were like the opening of the heavens. I felt that I had a soul. His noble views, unfolded in glorious sentences, elevated me into a higher world.... They changed my whole nature."

Character tells in all conditions of life. The man of good character in a workshop will give the tone to his fellows, and elevate their entire aspirations. Thus Franklin, while a workman in London, is said to have reformed the manners of an entire workshop. So the man of bad character and debased energy will unconsciously lower and degrade his fellows. Captain John Brown, the "marching-on Brown," once said to Emerson, that "for a settler in a new country, one good believing man is worth a hundred, nay, worth a thousand men without character." His example is so contagious that all other men are directly and beneficially influenced by him, and he insensibly elevates and lifts them up to his own standard of energetic activity.

Communication with the good is invariably productive of good. The good character is diffusive in his influence. "I was common clay till roses were planted in me," says some aromatic earth in the Eastern fable. Like begets like, and good makes good. "It is astonishing," says Canon Moseley, "how much good goodness makes. Nothing that is good is alone, nor anything bad; it makes others good or others bad—and that other, and so on, like a stone thrown into a pond, which makes circles that make other wider ones, and then others, till the last reaches the shore.... Almost all the good that is in the world has, I suppose, thus come down to us traditionally from remote times, and often unknown centres of good." So Mr. Ruskin says, "That which is born of evil begets evil; and that which is born of valor and honor teaches valor and honor."

Hence it is that the life of every man is a daily inculcation of good or bad example to others. The life of a good man is at the same time the most eloquent lesson of virtue and the most severe reproof of vice. Dr. Hooker describes the life of a pious clergyman of his acquaintance as "visible rhetoric," convincing even the most godless of the beauty of goodness. And so the good George Herbert said, on entering upon the duties of his parish: "Above all I will be sure to live well, because the virtuous life of a clergyman is the most powerful eloquence, to persuade all who see it to reverence and love, and at least to desire to live like him. And this I will do," he added, "because I know we live in an age that hath more need of good examples than precepts." It was a fine saying of the same good priest, when reproached with doing an act of kindness to a poor man considered beneath the dignity of his office—that the thought of such actions "would prove music to him at midnight." Izaak Walton speaks of a letter written by George Herbert to

Bishop Andrews about a holy life, which the latter "put into his bosom," and, after showing it to his scholars, "did always return it to the place where he first lodged it, and continued it so, near his heart, till the last day of his life."

Great is the power of goodness to charm and to command. The man inspired by it is the true kind of man, drawing all hearts after him. When General Nicholson lay wounded on his death-bed before Delhi, he dictated this last message to his equally noble and gallant friend, Sir Herbert Edwards: "Tell him," said he, "I should have been a better man if I had continued to live with him, and our heavy public duties had not prevented *my* seeing more of him privately. I was always the better for a residence with him and his wife, however short. Give my love to them both."

There are men in whose presence we feel as if we breathed a spiritual ozone, refreshing and invigorating, like inhaling mountain air, or enjoying a bath of sunshine. The power of Sir Thomas More's gentle nature was so great that it subdued the bad at the same time that it inspired the good. Lord Brooke said of his deceased friend, Sir Philip Sidney, that "his wit and understanding beat upon his heart, to make himself and others, not in word or opinion, but in life and action, good and great."

The very sight of a great and good man is often an inspiration to the young, who cannot help admiring and loving the gentle, the brave, the truthful, the magnanimous! Chateaubriand saw Washington only once, but it inspired him for life. After describing the interview, he says: "Washington sank into the tomb before any little celebrity had attached to my name. I passed before him as the most unknown of beings. He was in all his glory—I in the depth of my obscurity. My name probably dwelt not a whole day in his memory. Happy, however, was I that his looks were cast upon me. I have felt warmed for it all the rest of my life. There is a virtue even in the looks of a great man."

When Niebuhr died, his friend, Frederick Perthes, said of him: "What a contemporary! The terror of all bad and base men, the stay of all the sterling and honest, the friend and helper of youth." Perthes said on another occasion: "It does a wrestling man good to be constantly surrounded by tried wrestlers; evil thoughts are put to flight when the eye falls on the portrait of one in whose living presence one would have blushed to own them." A Catholic money-lender, when about to cheat, was wont to draw a veil over the picture of his favorite saint. So Hazlitt has said of the portrait of a beautiful female, that it seemed as if an unhandsome action would be impossible in its presence. "It does one good to look upon his manly, honest face," said a poor German woman, pointing to a portrait of the great reformer hung upon the wall of her humble dwelling.

Even the portrait of a noble or a good man, hung up in a room, is companionship after a sort. It gives us a closer personal interest in him. Looking at the features, we feel as if we knew him better, and were more nearly related to him. It is a link that connects us with a higher and better nature than our own. And though we may be far from reaching the standard of our hero, we are, to a certain extent, sustained and fortified by his depicted presence constantly before us.

Fox was proud to acknowledge how much he owed to the example and conversation of Burke. On one occasion he said of him, that "if he was to put all the political information he had gained from books, all that he had learned from science, or that the knowledge of the world and its affairs taught him into one scale, and the improvement he had derived from Mr. Burke's conversation and instruction into the other, the latter would preponderate."

Professor Tyndall speaks of Faraday's friendship as energy and inspiration. After spending an evening with him, he wrote: "His work excites admiration, but contact with him warms and elevates the heart. Here, surely, is a strong man. I love strength, but let me not forget the example of its union with modesty, tenderness, and sweetness, in the character of Faraday."

Even the gentlest natures are powerful to influence the character of others for good. Thus Wordsworth seems to have been especially impressed by the character of his sister Dorothy, who exercised upon his mind and heart a lasting influence. He describes her as the blessing of his boyhood as well as of his manhood. Though two years younger than himself, her tenderness and sweetness contributed greatly to mould his nature, and open his mind to the influences of poetry:

> "She gave me eyes, she gave me ears,
> And humble cares, and delicate fears;
> A heart, the fountain of sweet tears,
> And love, and thought, and joy."

Thus the gentlest natures are enabled, by the power of affection and intelligence, to mould the characters of men destined to influence and elevate their race through all time.

Sir William Napier attributed the early direction of his character first to the impress made upon it by his mother, when a boy, and afterwards to the noble example of his commander, Sir John Moore, when a man. Moore early detected the qualities of the young officer; and he was one of those to whom the general addressed the encouragement, "Well done, my majors!" at Corunna. Writing home to his mother, and describing the little court by which Moore was surrounded, he wrote, "Where shall we find such a king?" It was to his personal affection for his chief that the world is mainly indebted to Sir William Napier for his great book, "The History of the Peninsular War." But he was stimulated to write the book by the advice of another friend, the late Lord Langdale, while one day walking with him across the fields on which Belgravia is now built. "It was Lord Langdale," he says, "who first kindled the fire within me." And of Sir William Napier himself, his biographer truly says, that "no thinking person could ever come in contact with him, without being strongly impressed with the genius of the man."

The career of the late Dr. Marshall Hall was a lifelong illustration of the influence of character in forming character. Many eminent men still living trace their success in life to his suggestions and assistance, without which several valuable lines of study and investigation might not have been entered on, at least at so early a period. He would say to young men about him, "Take up a subject and pursue it well, and you can not fail to succeed." And often he would throw out a new idea to a young friend, saying, "I make you a present of it; there is fortune in it, if you pursue it with energy."

Energy of character has always a power to evoke energy in others. It acts through sympathy, one of the most influential of human agencies. The zealous, energetic man unconsciously carries others along with him. His example is contagious, and compels imitation. He exercises a sort of electric power, which sends a thrill through every fibre, flows into the nature of those—about him, and makes them give out sparks of fire.

Dr. Arnold's biographer, speaking of the power of this kind exercised by him over young men, says: "It was not so much an enthusiastic admiration for true genius, or learning, or eloquence, which stirred within them; it was a sympathetic thrill, caught from a spirit that was earnestly at work in the world—whose work was healthy, sustained, and constantly carried forward in the fear of God—a work that was founded on a deep sense of its duty and its value."

Such a power, exercised by men of genius, evokes courage, enthusiasm, and devotion. It is this intense admiration for individuals—such as one can not conceive entertained for a multitude—which has in all times produced heroes and martyrs. It is thus that the mastery of character makes itself felt, it acts by inspiration, quickening and vivifying the natures subject to its influence.

Great minds are rich in radiating force, not only exerting power, but communicating and even creating it. Thus Dante raised and drew after him a host of great spirits—Petrarch, Boccacio, Tasso, and many more. From him Milton learned to bear the stings of evil tongues and the contumely of evil days; and long years after, Byron, thinking of Dante under the pine-trees of Ravenna, was incited to attune his harp to loftier strains than he had ever attempted before. Dante inspired the greatest painters of Italy—Giotto, Orcagna, Michael Angelo, and Raphael. So Ariosto and Titian mutually inspired one another, and lighted up each other's glory.

Great and good men draw others after them, exciting the spontaneous admiration of mankind. This admiration of noble character elevates the mind, and tends to redeem it from the bondage of self, one of the greatest stumbling-blocks to moral improvement. The recollection of men who have signalized themselves by great thoughts or great deeds seems as if to create for the time a purer atmosphere around us, and we feel as if our aims and purposes were unconsciously elevated.

"Tell me whom you admire," said Sainte-Beuve, "and I will tell you what you are, at least as regards your talents, tastes and character." Do you admire mean men?—your own nature is mean. Do you admire rich men?—you are of the earth, earthy. Do you admire men of title?—you are a toad-eater, or a tuft-hunter. Do you admire honest, brave and manly men?—you are yourself of an honest, brave and manly spirit.

It was a fine trait in the character of Prince Albert that he was always so ready to express generous admiration of the good deeds of others. "He had the greatest delight," says the ablest delineator of his character, "in anybody else saying a fine saying, or doing a great deed. He would rejoice over it, and talk about it for days, and whether it was a thing nobly said or done by a little child, or by a veteran statesman, it gave him equal pleasure. He delighted in humanity doing well on any occasion and in any manner."

"No quality," said Dr. Johnson, "will get a man more friends than a sincere admiration of the qualities of others. It indicates generosity of nature, frankness, cordiality and cheerful recognition of merit." It was to the sincere—it might almost be said the reverential—admiration of Johnson by Boswell, that we owe one of the best biographies ever written. One is disposed to think that there must have been some genuine good qualities in Boswell to have been attracted by such a man as Johnson, and to have kept faithful to his worship in spite of rebuffs and snubbings innumerable. Macaulay speaks of Boswell as an altogether contemptible Person—as a coxcomb and a bore—weak, vain, pushing, curious, garrulous, and without wit, humor, or eloquence. But Carlyle is doubtless more just in his characterization of the biographer, in whom—vain and foolish though he was in many respects—he sees a man penetrated by the old reverent feeling of discipleship, full of love and admiration for true wisdom and excellence. Without such qualities, Carlyle insists, the "Life of Johnson" never could have been written. "Boswell wrote a good book," he says, "because he had a heart and an eye to discern wisdom, and an utterance to render it forth, because of his free insight, his lively talent, and, above all, of his love and childlike open-mindedness."

Most young men of generous mind have their heroes, especially if they be book-readers. Thus Allen Cunningham, when a mason's apprentice in Nithsdale, walked all the way to Edinburgh for the sole purpose of seeing Sir Walter Scott as he passed along the street. We unconsciously admire the enthusiasm of the lad, and respect the impulse which impelled him to make the journey. It is related of Sir Joshua Reynolds, that, when a boy of ten, he thrust his hand through intervening rows of people to touch the Pope, as if there were a sort of virtue in the contact. At a much later period, the painter Haydon was proud to see and to touch Reynolds when on a visit to his native place. Rogers, the poet, used to tell of his ardent desire, when a boy, to see Dr. Johnson, but when his hand was on the knocker of the house in Bolt Court, his courage failed him, and he turned away. So the late Isaac Disraeli, when a youth, called at Bolt Court for the same purpose, and though he *had* the courage to knock, to his dismay he was informed by the servant that the great lexicographer had breathed his last only a few hours before.

On the contrary, small and ungenerous minds cannot admire heartily. To their own great misfortune, they cannot recognize, much less reverence, great men and great things. The mean nature admires meanly. The toad's highest idea of beauty is his toadess. The small snob's highest idea of manhood is the great snob. The slave dealer values a man according to his muscles. When a Guinea trader was told by Sir Godfrey Kneller, in the presence of Pope, that he saw before him two of the greatest men in the world, he replied: "I don't know how great you may be, but I don't like your looks. I have often bought a man much better than both of you together, all bones and muscles, for ten guineas!" Although Rochefoucauld, in one of his maxims, says that there is something that is not altogether disagreeable to us in the misfortunes of even our best friends, it is only the small and essentially mean nature that finds pleasure in the disappointment, and annoyance at the success of others. There are, unhappily for themselves, persons so constituted that they have not the heart to be generous. The most disagreeable of all people are those who "sit in the seat of the scorner." Persons of this sort often come to regard the success of others, even in a good work, as a kind of personal offense. They cannot bear to hear another praised, especially if he belong to their own art, or calling, or profession. They will pardon a man's failures, but cannot forgive his doing a thing better than they can do. And where they have themselves failed, they are found to be the most merciless of detractors.

The mean mind occupies itself with sneering, carping and fault-finding, and is ready to scoff at everything but impudent effrontery or successful vice. The greatest consolation of such persons are the defects of men of character. "If the wise erred not," says George Herbert, "it would go hard with fools." Yet, though wise men may learn of fools by avoiding their errors, fools rarely profit by the example which wise men set them. A German writer has said that it is a miserable temper that cares only to discover the blemishes in the character of great men or great periods. Let us rather judge them with the charity of Bolingbroke, who, when reminded of one of the alleged weaknesses of Marlborough, observed, "He was so great a man that I forgot he had that defect."

Admiration of great men, living or dead, naturally evokes imitation of them in a greater or less degree. While a mere youth, the mind of Themistocles was fired by the great deeds of his contemporaries, and he longed to distinguish himself in the service of his country. When the battle of Marathon had been fought, he fell into a state of melancholy; and when asked by his friends as to the cause, he replied "that the trophies of Miltiades would not suffer him to sleep." A few years later, we find him at the head of the Athenian army, defeating the Persian fleet of Xerxes in the battles of Artemisium and Salamis—his country gratefully acknowledging that it had been saved through his wisdom and valor.

It is related of Thucydides that, when a boy, he burst into tears on hearing Herodotus read his history, and the impression made upon his mind was such as to determine the bent of his own genius. And Demosthenes was so fired on one occasion by the eloquence of Callistratus, that the ambition was roused within him of becoming an orator himself. Yet Demosthenes was physically weak, had a feeble voice, indistinct articulation, and shortness of breath—defects which he was only enabled to overcome by diligent study and invincible determination. But with all his practice, he never became a ready speaker; all his orations, especially the most famous of them, exhibiting indications of careful elaboration—the art and industry of the orator being visible in almost every sentence. Similar illustrations of character imitating character, and moulding itself by the style and manner and genius of great men, are to be found pervading all history. Warriors, statesmen, orators, patriots, poets and artists—all have been, more or less unconsciously, nurtured by the lives and actions of others living before them or presented for their imitation.

Great men have evoked the admiration of kings, popes and emperors. Francis de Medicis never spoke to Michael Angelo without uncovering, and Julius III made him sit by his side while a dozen cardinals were standing. Charles V made way for Titian, and one day, when the brush dropped from the painter's hand, Charles stooped and picked it up, saying, "you deserve to be served by an emperor." Leo X threatened with excommunication whoever should print and sell the poems of Ariosto without the author's consent. The same pope attended the death-bed of Raphael, as Francis I did that of Leonardo da Vinci.

Though Haydn once archly observed that he was loved and esteemed by everybody except professors of music, yet all the greatest musicians were unusually ready to recognize each other's greatness. Haydn himself seems to have been entirely free from petty jealousy. His admiration of the famous Porpora was such that he resolved to gain admission to his house and serve him as a valet. Having made the acquaintance of the family with whom Porpora lived, he was allowed to officiate in that capacity. Early each morning he took care to brush the veteran's coat, polish his shoes, and put his rusty wig in order. At first Porpora growled at the intruder, but his asperity soon softened, and eventually melted into affection. He quickly discovered his valet's genius, and, by his instructions, directed it into the line in which Haydn eventually acquired so much distinction.

Haydn himself was enthusiastic in his admiration of Handel. "He is the father of us all," he said on one occasion. Scarlatti followed Handel in admiration all over Italy, and, when his name was mentioned, he crossed himself in token of veneration. Mozart's recognition of the great composer was not less hearty. "When he chooses," said he, "Handel strikes like the thunderbolt." Beethoven hailed him as "the monarch of the musical kingdom." When Beethoven was dying, one of his friends sent him a present of Handel's works, in forty volumes. They were brought into his chamber, and, gazing on them with reanimated eye, he exclaimed, pointing at them with his finger, "There—there is the truth!"

Haydn not only recognized the genius of the great men who had passed away, but of his young contemporaries, Mozart and Beethoven. Small men may be envious of their fellows, but really great men seek out and love each other. Of Mozart, Haydn wrote: "I only wish I could impress on every friend of music, and on great men in particular, the same depth of musical sympathy, and profound appreciation of Mozart's inimitable music, that I myself feel and enjoy; then nations would vie with each other to possess such a jewel within their frontiers. Prague ought not only to strive to retain this precious man, but also to remunerate him; for without this the history of a great genius is sad indeed. . . . It enrages me to think that the unparalleled Mozart is not yet engaged by some imperial or royal court. Forgive My excitement; but I love the man so dearly!"

Mozart was equally generous in his recognition of the merits of Haydn. "Sir," said he to a critic, speaking of the latter, "if you and I were both melted down together, we should not furnish materials for one Haydn." And when

Mozart first heard Beethoven, he observed: "Listen to that young man; be assured that he will yet make a great name in the world."

Buffon set Newton above all other philosophers, and admired him so highly that he had always his portrait before him while he sat at work. So Schiller looked up to Shakespeare, whom he studied reverently and zealously for years, until he became capable of comprehending nature at first hand, and then his admiration became even more ardent than before.

Pitt was Canning's master and hero, whom he followed and admired with attachment and devotion. "To one man, while he lived," said Canning, "I was devoted with all my heart and all my soul. Since the death of Mr. Pitt I acknowledge no leader; my political allegiance lies buried in his grave."

The first acquaintance with a great work of art has usually proved an important event in every young artist's life. When Correggio first gazed on Raphael's "Saint Cecilia," he felt within himself an awakened power, and exclaimed, "And I too am a painter!" So Constable used to look back on his first sight of Claude's picture of "Hagar" as forming an epoch in his career. Sir George Beaumont's admiration of the same picture was such that he always took it with him in his carriage when he traveled from home.

The example set by the great and good do not die; they continue to live and speak to all the generations that succeed them. It was very impressively observed by Mr. Disraeli, in the House of Commons, shortly after the death of Mr. Cobden:

"There is this consolation remaining to us, when we remember our unequalled and irreparable losses, that those great men are not altogether lost to us—that their words will often be quoted in this house, that their examples will often be referred to and appealed to, and that even their expressions will form part of our discussions and debates. There are now, I may say, some members of Parliament who, though they may not be present, are still members of this House—who are independent of dissolutions, of the caprices of constituencies, and even of the course of time. I think that Mr. Cobden was one of those men."

It is the great lesson of biography to teach what man can be and can do at his best. It may thus give each man renewed strength and confidence. The humblest, in sight of even the greatest, may admire, and hope, and take courage. These great brothers of ours in blood and lineage, who live a universal life, still speak to us from their graves, and beckon us on in the paths which they have trod. Their example is still with us, to guide, to influence and to direct us. For nobility of character is a perpetual bequest, living from age to age, and constantly tending to reproduce its like.

"The sage," say the Chinese, "is the instructor of a hundred ages. When the manners of Loo are heard of; the stupid become intelligent, and the wavering determined." Thus the acted life of a good man continues to be a gospel of freedom and emancipation to all who succeed him:

> "To live in hearts we leave behind,
> Is not to die."

The golden words that good men have uttered, the examples they have set, live through all time; they pass into the thoughts and hearts of their successors, help them on the road of life, and often console them in the hour of death. "And the most miserable or most painful of deaths," said Henry Marten, the Commonwealth man, who died in prison, "is as nothing compared with the memory of a well-spent life, and great alone is he who has earned the glorious privilege of bequeathing such a lesson and example to his successors!"

Chapter 6

Work

"Lost, yesterday, somewhere between sunrise and sunset, two golden hours, each set with sixty diamond minutes. No reward is offered, for they are gone forever." —Horace Mann.

"Let every man be occupied, and occupied in the highest employment of which his nature is capable, and die with the consciousness that he has done his best." —Sydney Smith.

WORK IS ONE of the best educators of practical character. It evokes and disciplines obedience, self-control, attention, application, and perseverance; giving a man deftness and skill in his special calling, and aptitude and dexterity in dealing with the affairs of ordinary life.

Work is the law of our being—the living principle that carries men and nations onward. The greater number of men have to work with their hands, as a matter of necessity, in order to live, but all must work in one way or another, if they would enjoy life as it ought to be enjoyed.

Labor may be a burden and a chastisement, but it is also an honor and a glory. Without it nothing can be accomplished. All that is great in man comes through work, and civilization is its product. Were labor abolished, the race of Adam would be at once stricken by moral death. It is idleness that is the curse of man, not labor. Idleness eats the heart out of men as of nations, and consumes them as rust does iron.

In describing the earlier social condition of Italy, when the ordinary occupations of rural life were considered compatible with the highest civic dignity, Pliny speaks of the triumphant generals and their men returning contentedly to the plough. In those days the lands were tilled by the hands even of generals, the soil exulting beneath the ploughshare crowned with laurels, and guided by a husbandman graced with triumphs. It was only after slaves became extensively employed in all departments of industry that labor came to be regarded as dishonorable and servile. And so soon as indolence and luxury became the characteristics of the -ruling classes of Rome, the downfall of the empire, sooner or later, was inevitable.

There is, perhaps, no tendency of our nature that has to be more carefully guarded against than indolence. When Mr. Gurney asked an intelligent foreigner who had travelled over the greater part of the world, whether he had observed any one quality which, more than another, could be regarded as a universal characteristic of our species, his answer was, in broken English, "Me tink dat all men *love lazy.*" It is characteristic of the savage as of the despot. It is natural to men to endeavor to enjoy the products of labor without its toils. Indeed, so universal is this desire, that James Mill has argued that it was to prevent its indulgence at the expense of society at large, that the expedient of government was originally invented. Indolence is equally degrading to individuals as to nations. Sloth never made its mark in the world, and never will. Sloth never climbed a hill, nor overcame a difficulty that it could avoid. Indolence always failed in life, and always will. It is in the nature of things that it should not succeed in any thing. It is a burden, an encumbrance, and a nuisance—always useless, complaining, melancholy, and miserable.

Burton, in his quaint and curious book—the only one, Johnson says, that ever took him out of bed two hours sooner than he wished to rise—describes the causes of Melancholy as hinging mainly on Idleness. "Idleness," he says, "is the bane of body and mind, the nurse of naughtiness, the chief mother of all mischief, one of the seven deadly sins, the devil's cushion, his pillow and chief reposal. . . . An idle dog will be mangy; and how shall an idle person escape? Idleness of the mind is much worse than that of the body: wit, without employment, is a disease—the rust of the soul, a plague, a hell itself. As in a standing pool, worms and filthy creepers increase, so do evil and corrupt thoughts in an idle person; the soul is contaminated. . . . Thus much I dare boldly say: he or she that is idle, be they of what condition they will, never so rich, so well allied, fortunate, happy—let them have all things in abundance and felicity that heart can wish and desire, all contentment—so long as he, or she, or they, are idle, they shall never be pleased, never well in body or mind, but weary still, sickly still, vexed still, loathing still, weeping, sighing, grieving, suspecting, offended with the world with every object, wishing themselves gone or dead, or else carried away with some foolish phantasie or other."

The indolent, however, are not wholly indolent. Though the body may shirk labor, the brain is not idle. If it do not grow corn, it will grow thistles, which will be found springing up all along the idle man's course in life. The ghosts of indolence rise up in the dark, ever staring the recreant in the face, and tormenting him:

> "The gods are just, and of our pleasant vices,
> Make instruments to scourge us."

"Dost thou love life?" said Franklin. "Then do not squander time for that is the stuff it is made of." True happiness is never found in torpor of the faculties, but in their action and useful employment. It is indolence that exhausts, not action, in which there is life, health, and pleasure. The spirits may be exhausted and wearied by employment, but they are utterly wasted by idleness. Hence a wise physician was accustomed to regard occupation as one of his most valuable remedial measures. "Nothing is so injurious," said Dr. Marshall Hall, "as unoccupied time." An archbishop of Mayence used to say that "the human heart is like a mill-stone: if you put wheat under it, it grinds the wheat into flour; if you put no wheat, it grinds on, but then 'tis itself it wears away."

It has been truly said that to desire to possess without being burdened with the trouble of acquiring is as much a sign of weakness, as to recognize that every thing worth having is only to be got by paying its price is the prime secret of practical strength. Even leisure can not be enjoyed unless it is won by effort. If it have not been earned by work, the price has not been paid for it.

There must be work before and work behind, with leisure to fall back upon; but the leisure, without the work, can no more be enjoyed than a surfeit. Life must needs be disgusting alike to the idle rich man as to the idle poor man, who has no work to do, or, having work, will not do it. The words found tattooed on the right arm of a sentimental beggar of forty, undergoing his eighth imprisonment in the jail of Bourges in France, might be adopted as the motto of all idlers: "The past has deceived me; the present torments me; the future terrifies me."

The duty of industry applies to all classes and conditions of society. All have their work to do in their respective conditions of life—the rich as well as the poor. The gentleman by birth and education, however richly he may be endowed with worldly possessions, can not but feel that he is in duty bound to contribute his quota of endeavor towards the general well-being in which he shares. He can not be satisfied with being fed, clad, and maintained by the labor of others, without making some suitable return to the society that upholds him. An honest, high-minded man would revolt at the idea of sitting down to and enjoying a feast, and then going away without paying his share of the reckoning. To be idle and useless is neither an honor nor a privilege; and though persons of small natures may be content merely to consume—men of average endowment, of manly aspirations, and of honest purpose, will feel such a condition to be incompatible with real honor and true dignity.

"I don't believe," said Lord Stanley at Glasgow, "that an unemployed man, however amiable and otherwise respectable, ever was, or ever can be, really happy. As work is our life, show me what *you* can do, and I will show you what you are. I have spoken of love of one's work as the best preventive of merely low and vicious tastes. I will go further, and say that it is the best preservative against petty anxieties, and the annoyances that arise out of indulged self-love. Men have thought before now that they could take refuge from trouble and vexation by sheltering themselves, as it were, in a world of their own. The experiment has often been tried, and always with one result. You can not escape from anxiety and labor—it is the destiny of humanity. Those who shirk from facing trouble find that trouble comes to them. The indolent may contrive that he shall have less than his share of the world's work to do, but Nature, proportioning the instinct to the work, contrives that the little shall be much and hard to him. The man who has only himself to please, finds; sooner or later, and probably sooner than later, that he has got a very hard master; and the excessive weakness which shrinks from responsibility has its own punishment too, for where great interests are excluded little matters become great, and the same wear and tear of mind that might have been at least usefully and healthfully expended on the real business of life, is often wasted in petty and imaginary vexations, such as breed and multiply in the unoccupied brain."

Even on the lowest ground—that of personal enjoyment—constant useful occupation is necessary. He who labors not can not enjoy the reward of labor. "We sleep sound," said Sir Walter Scott, "and our waking hours are happy, when they are employed; and a little sense of toil is necessary to the enjoyment of leisure, even when earned by study and sanctioned by the discharge of duty."

It is true there are men who die of overwork; but many more die of selfishness, indulgence, and idleness. Where men break down by overwork, it is most commonly from want of duly ordering their lives, and neglect of the ordinary conditions of physical health. Lord Stanley was probably right when he said, in his address to the Glasgow students above mentioned, that he doubted whether hard work, "steadily and regularly carried on, ever yet hurt any body."

Then, again, length of *years* is no proper test of length of life. A man's life is to be measured by what he does in it, and what he feels in it. The more useful work the man doe's, and the more he thinks and feels, the more he readily lives. The idle, useless man, no matter to what extent his life may be prolonged, merely vegetates.

The early teachers of Christianity ennobled the lot of toil by their example. "He that will not work," said St. Paul, "neither shall he eat"; and he glorified himself in that he had labored with his hands, and had not been chargeable to any man. When St. Boniface landed in Britain, he came with a gospel in one hand and a carpenter's rule in the other; and from England he afterwards passed over into Germany, carrying thither the art of building. Luther also, in the midst of a multitude of other employments, worked diligently for a living, earning his bread by gardening, building, turning, and even clock-making.

It was characteristic of Napoleon, when visiting a work of mechanical excellence, to pay great respect to the inventor, and, on taking his leave, to salute him with a low bow. Once, at St. Helena, when walking with Mrs. Balcombe, some servants came along, carrying a load. The lady, in an angry tone, ordered them out of the way, on which Napoleon interposed, saying, "Respect the burden, madam." Even the drudgery of the general humblest laborer contributes towards the wellbeing of society; and it was a wise saying of a Chinese emperor that, "if there was a man who did not work, or a woman that was idle, somebody must suffer cold or hunger in the empire."

The habit of constant useful occupation is as essential for the happiness and well-being of women as of man. Without it women are apt to sink into a state of listless *ennui* and uselessness, accompanied by sick-headache and attacks of "nerves." Caroline Perthes carefully warned her married daughter Louisa to beware of giving way to such listlessness. "I, myself," she said, "when the children are gone out for a half-holiday, sometimes feel as stupid and dull as an owl by daylight; but one must not yield to this, which happens more or less to all young wives. The best relief is *work*, engaged in with interest and diligence. Work, then, constantly and diligently, at something or other; for idleness is the devil's snare for small and great, as your grandfather says, and he says true."

Constant useful occupation is thus wholesome, not only for the body, but for the mind. While the slothful man drags himself indolently through life, and the better part of his nature sleeps a deep sleep, if not morally and spiritually dead, the energetic man is a source of activity and enjoyment to all who come within reach of his influence. Even any ordinary drudgery is better than idleness. Fuller says of Sir Francis Drake, who was early sent to sea, and kept close to his work by his master, that such "pains and patience in his youth knit the joints of his soul, and made them more solid and compact." Schiller used to say that he considered it a great advantage to be employed in the discharge of some daily mechanical duty—some regular routine of work, that rendered steady application necessary.

Thousands can bear testimony to the truth of the saying of Greuze, the French painter, that work is one of the great secrets of happiness. Casaubon was once induced by the entreaties of his friends to take a few days' entire rest, but he returned to his work with the remark, that it was easier to bear illness doing something than doing nothing.

When Charles Lamb was released for life from his daily drudgery of desk work at the India Office, he felt himself the happiest of men. "I would not go back to my prison," he said to a friend, "ten years longer for ten thousand pounds." He also wrote in the same ecstatic mood to Bernard Barton. "I have scarce steadiness of head to compose a letter," he said; "I am free! free as air! I will live another fifty years. . . . Would I could sell you some of my leisure! Positively the best thing a man can do is—nothing; and next to that, perhaps, Good Works." Two years, two long and tedious years, passed, and Charles Lamb's feelings had undergone an entire change. He now discovered that official, even humdrum work—"the appointed round, the daily task"—had been good for him, though he knew it not. Time had formerly been his friend; it had now become his enemy. To Bernard Barton he again wrote: "I assure you, no work is worse than overwork; the mind preys on itself—the most unwholesome of food. I have ceased to care for almost anything. Never did the waters of heaven pour down upon a forlorner head. What I can do, and overdo, is to walk. I am a sanguinary murderer of time. But the oracle is silent."

No man could be more sensible of the practical importance of industry than Sir Walter Scott, who was himself one of the most laborious and indefatigable of men. Indeed, Lockhart says of him that, taking all ages and countries together, the rare example of tireless energy, in union with serene self-possession of mind and manner, such as Scott's, must be sought for in the roll of great sovereigns or great captains, rather than in that of literary genius. Scott himself was most anxious to impress upon the minds of his own children the importance of industry as a means of usefulness and happiness in the world. To his son Charles, when at school, he wrote: "I cannot too much impress upon your mind that *labor* is the condition which God has imposed on us in every station of life; there is nothing worth having that can be had without it, from the bread which the peasant wins with the sweat of his brow, to the sports by which the rich man must get rid of his *ennui*. . . . As for knowledge, it can no more be planted in the human mind without labor than a field of wheat can be produced without the previous use of a plow. There is, indeed, the great difference that chance or circumstances may so cause it that another shall reap what the farmer sows; but no man can be deprived, whether by accident or misfortune, of the fruits of his own studies, and liberal and extended acquisitions of knowledge which he makes are all for his own use. Labor, therefore, my dear boy, and improve the time. In youth our steps are light, and our minds are ductile, and knowledge is easily laid up, but if we neglect our spring, our summers will be useless and contemptible, our harvest will be chaff, and the winter of our old age unrespected and desolate."

Southey was as laborious a worker as Scott. Indeed, work might almost be said to form part of his religion, He was only nineteen when he wrote these words: "Nineteen years! certainly a fourth part of my life, and yet I have been of no service to society. The clown who scares crows for twopence a day is a more useful man; he preserves the bread which I eat in idleness." And yet Southey had not been idle as a boy—on the contrary, he had been a most diligent student. He had not only read largely in English literature, but was well acquainted, through translations, with Tasso, Ariosto, Homer and Ovid. He felt, however, as if his life had been purposeless, and he determined to do something. He began, and from that time forward he pursued an unremitting career of literary labor down to the close of his life—"daily progressing in learning," to use his own words—"not so learned as he is poor, not so poor as proud, not so proud as happy."

The memoirs of men who have thrown their opportunities away would constitute a painful but memorable volume for the world's instruction. "No strong man, in good health," says Ebenezer Eliot, "can be neglected if he be true to himself. For the benefit of the young, I wish we had a correct account of the number of persons who fail of success in a thousand who resolutely strive to do well. I do not think it exceeds one percent." Men grudge success, but it is only the last term of what looked like a series of failures. They failed at first, then again and again, but at last their difficulties vanished, and success was achieved.

The desire to possess, without being burdened with the trouble of acquiring, is a great sign of weakness and laziness. Everything that is worth enjoying or possessing can only be got by the pleasure of working. This is the great secret of practical strength. "One may very distinctly prefer industry to indolence, the healthful exercise of all one's faculties to allowing them to rest unused in drowsy torpor, In the long run we shall probably find that the exercise of the faculties has of itself been the source of a more genuine happiness than has followed the actual attainment of what the exercise was directed to procure."

"The weakest living creature," says Carlyle, "by concentrating his powers on a single object, can accomplish something; whereas the strongest, by dispersing his over many, may fail to accomplish anything."

Have we difficulties to contend with? Then work through them. No exorcism charms like labor. Idleness of mind and body resembles rust. It wears more than work. "I would rather work out than rust out," said a noble worker. Schiller said that he found the greatest happiness in life to consist in the performance of some mechanical duty.

It is because application to business teaches method most effectually, that it is so useful as an educator of character. The highest working qualities are best trained by active and sympathetic contact with others in the affairs of daily life. It does not matter whether the business relates to the management of a household or of a nation. Indeed, as we have endeavored to show in a preceding chapter, the able housewife must necessarily be an efficient woman of business. She must regulate and control the details of her home, keep her expenditure within her means, arrange everything according to plan and system, and wisely manage and govern those subject to her rule. Efficient domestic management implies industry, application, method, moral discipline, forethought, prudence, practical ability, insight into character, and power of organization, all of which are required in the efficient management of business of whatever sort.

Business qualities have, indeed, a very large field of action. They mean aptitude for affairs, competency to deal successfully with the practical work of life—whether the spur of action lie in domestic management, in the conduct of a profession, in trade or commerce, in social organization, or in political government. And the training which gives efficiency in dealing with these various affairs is, of all others, the most useful in practical life. Moreover, it is the best discipline of character; for it involves the exercise of diligence, attention, self-denial, judgment, tact, knowledge of and sympathy with others.

Like other great captains, Wellington had an almost boundless capacity for work. He drew up the heads of a Dublin Police Bill (being still the Secretary for Ireland) when tossing off the mouth of the Mondego, with Junot and the French army waiting for him on the shore. So Caesar, another of the greatest commanders, is said to have written an essay on Latin Rhetoric while crossing the Alps at the head of his army. And Wallenstein, when at the head of 60,000 men, and in the midst of a campaign, with the enemy before him, dictated from headquarters the medical treatment of his poultry-yard.

Washington, also, was an indefatigable man of business. From his boyhood he diligently trained himself in habits of application, of study, and of methodical work. His manuscript school-books, which are still preserved, show that, as early as the age of thirteen, he occupied himself voluntarily in copying out such things as forms of receipts, notes of hand, bills of exchange, bonds, indentures, leases, land-warrants, and other dry documents, all written out with great care. And the habits which he thus early acquired were, in a great measure, the foundation of those admirable business qualities which he afterwards successfully brought to bear in the affairs of government.

Most of the early English writers were men of affairs, trained to business; for no literary class as yet existed, excepting it might be the priesthood. Chaucer, the father of English poetry, was first a soldier, and afterwards a comptroller of petty customs. The office was no sinecure either, for he had to write up all the records with his own hand; and when he had done his reckonings "at the custom-house, he returned with delight to his favorite studies at home—poring over his books until his eyes were dazed and dull.

Indeed, habits of business, instead of unfitting a cultivated mind for scientific or literary pursuits, are often the best training for them. Voltaire insisted with truth that the real spirit of business and literature are the same; the perfection of each being the union of energy and thoughtfulness, of cultivated intelligence and practical wisdom, of the active and contemplative essence—a union commended by Lord Bacon as the concentrated excellence of man's nature. It has been said that even the man of genius can write nothing worth reading in relation to human affairs, unless he has been in some way or other connected with the serious every-day business of life.

Hence it has happened that many of the best books extant have been written by men of business, with whom literature was a pastime rather than a profession. Gifford, the editor of the "Quarterly," who knew the drudgery of writing for a living, once observed that "a single hour of composition, won from the business of the day, is worth more than the whole day's toil of him who works at the trade of literature; in the one case, the spirit comes joyfully to refresh itself, like a hart to the water-brooks; in the other, it pursues its miserable way, panting and jaded, with the dogs and hunger of necessity behind."

Samuel Richardson successfully combined literature with business—writing his novels in his back shop in Salisbury court, Fleet Street, and selling them over the counter in his front shop. William Hutton, of Birmingham, also successfully combined the occupations of bookselling and authorship. He says, in his Autobiography, that a man may live half a century and not be acquainted with his own character. He did not know that he was an antiquarian until the world informed him of it, from having read his "History of Birmingham," and then, he said, he could see it himself. Benjamin Franklin was alike eminent as a printer and bookseller—an author, a philosopher, and a statesman.

Montaigne has said of true philosophers that "if they were great in science, they were yet much greater in action; . . . and whenever they have been put upon the proof, they have been seen to fly to so high a pitch, as made it very well appear their souls were strangely elevated and enriched with the knowledge of things." Thales, speaking against the pains and care men put themselves to become rich, was answered by one in the company that he did like the fox, who found fault with what he could not obtain. Thereupon Thales had a mind, for the jest's sake, to show them the contrary; and having upon this occasion for once made a muster of all his wits, wholly to employ them in the service of profit, he set a traffic on foot, which in one year brought him in so great riches, that the most experienced in that trade could hardly in their whole lives, with all their industry, have raked so much together.

Niebuhr, the historian, was distinguished for his energy and success as a man of business. He proved so efficient as secretary and accountant to the African consulate, to which he had been appointed by the Danish Government, that he was afterwards selected as one of the commissioners to manage the national finances; and he quitted that office to undertake the joint directorship of a bank at Berlin. It was in the midst of his business occupations that he found time to study Roman history, to master the Arabic, Russian, and other Slavonic languages, and to build up the great reputation as an author by which he is now chiefly remembered.

Men of trained working faculty so contract the habit of labor that idleness becomes intolerable to them; and when driven by circumstances from their own special line of occupation, they find refuge in other pursuits. The diligent man is quick to find employment for his leisure; and he is able to make leisure when the idle man finds none. "He hath no leisure," says George Herbert, "who useth it not." "The most active or busy man that has been or can be," says Bacon, "has many vacant times of leisure, except he be either tedious and of no dispatch, or lightly and unworthily ambitious to meddle with things that may be better done by others." Thus many great things have been done during such "vacant times of leisure," by men to whom industry had become a second nature, and who found it easier to work than to be idle.

One of the most able and laborious of our recent statesmen—with whom literature was a hobby as well as a pursuit—was the late Sir George Cornewall Lewis. He was an excellent man of business—diligent, exact, and painstaking. He filled by turns the offices of president of the poor-law board—the machinery of which he created—chancellor of the exchequer, home secretary, and secretary at war; and in each he achieved the reputation of a thoroughly successful administrator. In the intervals of his official labors he occupied himself with inquiries into a wide range of subjects—history, politics, philology, anthropology, and antiquarianism. His works on

"The Astronomy of the Ancients," and "Essays on the Formation of the Romanic Languages," might have been written by the profoundest of German scholars. He took especial delight in pursuing the abstruser branches of learning, and found in them his chief pleasure and recreation. Lord Palmerston sometimes remonstrated with him, telling him he was "taking too much out of himself" by laying aside official papers after office hours in order to study books; Palmerston himself declaring that he had no time to read books—that the reading of manuscript was quite enough for him.

Doubtless Sir George Lewis rode his hobby too hard, and, but for his devotion to study, his useful life would probably have been prolonged. Whether in or out of office, he read, wrote, and studied. He relinquished the editorship of the "Edinburgh Review" to become chancellor of the exchequer; and when no longer occupied in preparing budgets, he proceeded to copy out a mass of Greek manuscripts at the British Museum. He took particular delight in pursuing any difficult inquiry in classical antiquity. One of the odd subjects with which he occupied himself was an examination into the truth of reported cases of longevity, which, according to his custom, he doubted or disbelieved. This subject wits uppermost in his mind while pursuing his canvass of Herefordshire in 1852. On applying to a voter one day for his support, he was met by a decided refusal. "I am sorry," was the candidate's reply, "that you can't give me your vote; but perhaps you can tell me whether any body in your parish has died at an extraordinary age!"

A fair measure of work is good for mind as well as body. Man is an intelligence sustained and preserved by bodily organs, and their active exercise is necessary to the enjoyment of health. It is not work, but overwork, that is hurtful; and it is not hard work that is injurious so much as monotonous work, fagging work, hopeless work. All hopeful work is healthful; and to be usefully and hopefully employed is one of the great secrets of happiness. Brain-work, in moderation, is no more wearing than any other kind of work. Duly regulated, it is as promotive of health as bodily exercise; and, where due attention is paid to the physical system, it seems difficult to put more upon a man than he can bear. Merely to eat and drink and sleep one's way idly through life is vastly more injurious. The wear-and-tear of rust is even faster than the tear-and-wear of work.

But overwork is always bad economy. It is, in fact, great waste, especially if conjoined with worry. Indeed, worry kills far more than work does. It frets, it excites, it consumes the body—as sand and grit, which occasion excessive friction, wear out the wheels of a machine. Overwork and worry have both to be guarded against. For over-brain-work is strain-work; and it is exhausting and destructive according as it is in excess of nature. And the brain-worker may exhaust and overbalance his mind by excess, just as the athlete may overstrain his muscles and break his back by attempting feats beyond the strength of his physical system.

Chapter 7

Helping One's Self

*"The worth of a State, in the long run, is the worth
of the individuals Composing it." —J. S. Mill.*

"We put too much faith in systems, and look too little to men." —B. Disraeli.

"HEAVEN HELPS THOSE who help themselves" is a well-tried maxim, embodying in a small compass the results of vast human experience. The spirit of self-help is the root of all genuine growth in the individual; and, exhibited in the lives of many, it constitutes the true source of national vigor and strength. Help from without is often enfeebling in its effects, but help from within invariably invigorates. Whatever is done *for* men or classes, to a certain extent takes away the stimulus and necessity of doing for themselves; and where men are subjected to over-guidance and over-government, the inevitable tendency is to render them comparatively helpless.

Even the best institutions can give a man no active help. Perhaps the most they can do is to leave him free to develop himself and improve his individual condition. But, in all times, men have been prone to believe that their happiness and well-being were to be secured by means of institutions rather than by their own conduct. Hence the value of legislation as an agent in human advancement has usually been much over-estimated. To constitute the millionth part of a Legislature, by voting for one or two men once in three or five years, however conscientiously this duty may be performed, can exercise but little active influence upon any man's life and character. Moreover, it is every day becoming more clearly understood, that the function of Government is negative and restrictive, rather than positive and active; being resolvable principally into protection—protection of life, liberty, and property. Laws, wisely administered, will secure men in the enjoyment of the fruits of their labor, whether of mind or body, at a comparatively small personal sacrifice; but no laws, however stringent, can make the idle industrious, the thriftless provident, or the drunken sober. Such reforms can only be effected by means of individual action, economy, and self-denial; by better habits, rather than by greater rights.

The Government of a nation itself is usually found to be but the reflex of the individuals composing it. The Government that is ahead of the people will inevitably be dragged down to their level, as the Government that is behind them will, in the long run, be dragged up. In the order of nature, the collective character of a nation will as surely find its befitting results in its law and government as water finds its own level. The noble people will be nobly ruled, and the ignorant and corrupt ignobly. Indeed, all experience serves to prove that the worth and strength of a State depend far less upon the form of its institutions than upon the character of its men. For the nation is only an aggregate of individual conditions, and civilization itself is but a question of the personal improvement of the men, women, and children of whom society is composed.

National progress is the sum of individual, industry, energy, and uprightness, as national decay is of individual idleness, selfishness, and vice. What we are accustomed to decry, as great social evils, will, for the most part, be found to be but the outgrowth of man's own perverted life; and, though we may endeavor to cut them down and extirpate them by means of Law, they will only spring up again, with fresh luxuriance, in some other form, unless the conditions of personal life and character are radically improved. If this view be correct, then it follows that the highest patriotism and philanthropy consist, not so much in altering laws and modifying institutions, as in helping and stimulating men to elevate and improve themselves by their own free and independent individual action.

It may be of comparatively little consequence how a man is governed from without, whilst everything depends upon how he governs himself from within. The greatest slave is not he who is ruled by a despot, great though that evil be, but he who is the thrall of his own moral ignorance, selfishness and vice. Nations who are thus enslaved at heart cannot be freed by any mere changes of masters or of institutions, and so long as the fatal delusion prevails, that liberty solely depends upon and consists in government, so long will such changes, no matter at what cost they may be effected, have as little practical and lasting result as the shifting of the figures in a phantasmagoria. The solid foundations of liberty must rest upon individual character, which is also the only sure guaranty for social security and national progress. John Stuart Mill truly observes that "even despotism does not produce its worst effects so long as individuality exists under it, and whatever crushes individuality *is* despotism, by whatever name it be called."

Old fallacies as to human progress are constantly turning up. Some call for Caesars, others for nationalities, and others for acts of Parliament. We are to wait for Caesars, and when they are found, "happy the people Who recognize and follow them." This doctrine shortly means everything *for* the people, nothing *by* them, a doctrine which, if taken as a guide, must, by destroying the Tree conscience of a community, speedily prepare the way for any form of despotism. Casarism is human idolatry in its worst form—a worship of mere power, as degrading in its effects as the worship of mere wealth would be. A far healthier doctrine to inculcate among the nations would be that of self-help; and so soon as it is thoroughly understood and carried into action, Casarism will be no more.

All nations have been made what they are by the thinking and the working of many generations of men. Patient and persevering laborers in all ranks and conditions of life, cultivators of the soil and explorers of the mine, inventors and discoverers, manufacturers, mechanics and artisans, poets, philosophers and politicians, all have contributed towards the grand result, one generation building upon another's labors, and carrying them forward to still higher stages. This constant succession of noble workers—the artisans of civilization—has served to create order out of chaos in industry, science and art, and the living race has thus, in the course of nature, become the inheritor of the rich estate provided by the skill and industry of our forefathers, which is placed in our hands to cultivate and to hand down, not only unimpaired but improved, to our successors.

James Watt was one of the most industrious of men, and the story of his life proves, what all experience confirms, that it is not the man of the greatest natural vigor and capacity who achieves the highest results, but he who employs his powers with the greatest industry and the most carefully disciplined skill—the skill that comes by labor, application and experience. Many men in his time knew far more than Watt, but none labored so assiduously as he did to turn all that he did know to useful practical purposes. He was, above all things, most persevering in the pursuit of facts. He cultivated carefully that habit of active attention on which all the higher working qualities of the mind mainly depend. Indeed, Mr. Edgeworth entertained the opinion that the difference of intellect in men depends more upon the early cultivation of this *habit of attention,* than upon any great disparity between the powers of one individual and another.

Even when a boy, Watt found science in his toys. The quadrants lying about his father's carpenter's shop led him to the study of optics and astronomy; his ill health induced him to pry into the secrets of physiology; and his solitary walks through the country attracted him to the study of botany and history. While carrying on the business of a mathematical-instrument maker, he received an order to build an organ, and, though without an ear for music, he undertook the study of harmonics, and successfully constructed the instrument. And, in like manner, when the little model of Newcomen's steam engine, belonging to the University of Glasgow, was placed in his hands to repair, he forthwith set himself to learn all that was then known about heat, evaporation and condensation—at the same time plodding his way in mechanics and the science of construction—the results of which he at length embodied in his condensing steam engine.

For ten years he went on contriving and inventing—with little hope to cheer him, and with few friends to encourage him. He went on, meanwhile, earning bread for his family by making and selling quadrants, making and mending fiddles, flutes and musical instruments, measuring mason-work, surveying roads, superintending the construction of canals, or doing anything that turned up and offered a prospect of honest gain. At length Watt found a fit partner in another eminent leader of industry—Matthew Boulton, of Birmingham, a skillful, energetic and far-seeing man, who vigorously undertook the enterprise of introducing the condensing engine into general use as a working power; and the success of both is now matter of history.

The instances of men, in this and other countries, by dint of persevering application and energy, have raised themselves from the humblest ranks of industry to eminent positions of usefulness and influence in society, are so numerous that they have long ceased to be regarded as exceptional. Looking at some of the more remarkable, it might almost be said that early encounter with difficulty and adverse circumstances was the necessary and indispensable condition of success. The British House of Commons and the United States Congress have always contained a considerable number of such self-raised men—fitting representatives of the industrial character of the people, and it is to the credit of our Legislatures that they have been welcomed and honored there.

Men, who like Lincoln and Garfield, have risen from the humblest condition to great renown, are by no means exceptional in the great Republic of the West, where worth rather than birth forms the basis for promotion and influence. James A. Garfield was a typical American. Born in poverty and obscurity, he struggled forward and upward against a sea of obstacles, and won his way by such gentleness of demeanor, coupled with such patience and courage, that he seems not to have provoked the enmity of any man. Mr. Garfield had a hard time of it as a boy. He toiled hard on the farm early and late in summer, and worked at the carpenter's bench in winter. The best of it was that he liked work. He had an absorbing ambition to get an education, and the only road open to this end seemed that of manual labor. Ready money was hard to get in those days. The Ohio canal ran not far from where he lived, and, finding that the boatmen got their pay in cash and earned better wages than he could make at farming or carpentry, he hired out as a driver on the towpath, and soon got up to the dignity of holding the helm of a boat. Then he determined to ship as a sailor on the lakes, but an attack of fever and ague interfered with his plans. He was ill three months, and when he recovered he decided to go to school. His mother had saved a small sum of money, which she gave him, together with a few cooking utensils and a stock of provisions. He hired a small room and cooked his own food to make his expenses as light as possible. He paid his own way after that, never calling on his mother for any more assistance. By working at the carpenter's bench mornings and evenings and vacation times, and teaching country schools during the winter, he managed to attend the Academy during the spring and fall terms and to save a little money towards going to college. He had excellent health, a robust frame and a capital memory, and the attempt to combine mental and physical work did not hurt him.

When he was 23 years of age he concluded he had got about all there was to be had in the obscure crossroads academy. He calculated he had saved about half enough money to get through college, provided he could begin, as he hoped, with the Junior year. He got a life-insurance policy, and assigned it to a gentleman as security for a loan to make up the amount he lacked. In the Fall of 1854 he entered the Junior Class of Williams College, Massachusetts, and graduated in 1856, with the metaphysical honors of his class.

When Garfield returned to Ohio it was natural that he should soon gravitate to the struggling little college at Hiram, Portage County, near his boyhood's home. Hp became Professor of Latin and Greek, and threw himself, with the energy and industry which were leading traits in his character, into the work of building up the institution. Before he had been two years in his professorship he was appointed President of the college. Hiram is a lonesome country village, three miles from a railroad, built upon a high hill, overlooking twenty miles of cheese-making country to the southward. It contains fifty or sixty houses clustered around the green, in the centre of which stands the homely red-brick college structure. Plain living and high thinking was the order of things at Hiram College in those days. The teachers were poor, but there was a great deal of hard, faithful study done, and many ambitious plans formed. The young President taught, lectured, and preached, and all the time studied as diligently as any acolyte in the temple of knowledge.

During his professorship Garfield married Miss Lucretia Rudolph, daughter of a farmer in the neighborhood, whose acquaintance he had made while at the academy, where she was also a pupil. She was a quiet, thoughtful girl, of singularly sweet and refined disposition, fond of study and reading, possessing a warm heart and a mind with the capacity of steady growth. The marriage was a love affair on both sides, and has been a thoroughly happy one. Much of General Garfield's subsequent success in life may be attributed to the never failing sympathy and intellectual companionship of his wile and the stimulus of a loving home circle. The young couple bought a neat little cottage fronting on the college campus, and began their wedded life poor and in debt, but with brave hearts.

In 1859 the college President was elected to the State Senate, from the counties of Portage and Summit. He did not resign his Presidency, because he looked upon a few months in the Legislature as an episode not likely to change the course of his life. But the war came to alter his plans. During the winter of 1861 he was active in the passage of measures for arming the State militia, and his eloquence and energy made him a conspicuous leader of the Union party. Early in the summer of 1861 he was elected Colonel of an infantry regiment raised in Northern Ohio, many of the soldiers in which had been students at Hiram. He took the field in Eastern Kentucky, was soon put in command of a brigade, and, by making one of the hardest marches ever made by recruits, surprised and routed the Rebel forces, under Humphrey Marshal, at Piketon.

From Eastern Kentucky General Garfield was transferred to Louisville, and from that place hastened to join the army of General Buel, which he reached with his brigade in time to participate in the second day's fighting at Pittsburg Landing. He took part in the siege of Corinth and in the operations along the Memphis and Charleston Railroad.

In January, 1863, he was appointed Chief of Staff of the Army of the Cumberland, and bore a prominent share in all the campaigns in Middle Tennessee in the spring and summer of that year. His last conspicuous military service was at the battle of Chickamauga. For his conduct in that battle he was promoted to a Major-Generalship.

The Congressional district in which Garfield lived was the one long made famous by Joshua R. Giddings. His supporters nominated him while he was in the field, without asking his consent. That was in 1862. When he heard of the nomination Garfield reflected that it would be fifteen months before the Congress would meet to which he would be elected, and believing; as did everyone else, that the war could not possibly last a year longer, concluded to accept. He often expressed regret that he did not help to fight the war through, and said that he never would have left the army to go to Congress had he foreseen that the struggle would continue beyond the year 1863. He continued his military service up to the time Congress met.

On entering Congress, in December, 1863, Gen. Garfield was placed upon the Committee on Military Affairs with Schenck and Farnsworth, who were also fresh from the field. He took an active part in the debates of the House, and won a recognition which few new members succeed in gaining. He was not popular among his fellow members during his first term. They thought him something of a pedant because he sometimes showed his scholarship in his speeches, and they were jealous of his prominence. His solid attainments and able social qualities enabled him to overcome this prejudice during his second term, and he became on terms of close friendship with the best men in both Houses. His committee service during his second term was on the Ways and Means, which was quite to his taste, for it gave him an opportunity to prosecute the studies in finance and political economy which he had always felt a fondness for. He was a hard worker and a great reader in those days, going home with his arms full of books from the Congressional Library and sitting up late nights to read them. It was then that he laid the foundations of the convictions on the subject of National finance which he since held so firmly amid all the storms of political agitation.

In the fortieth Congress Gen. Garfield was chairman of the Committee on Military Affairs. In the forty-first he was given the chairmanship of Banking and Currency, which he liked much better, because it was in the line of his financial studies. His next promotion was to the chairmanship of the Appropriation Committee, which he held until the Democrats came into power in the House in 1875. His chief work on that committee was a steady and judicious reduction of the expenses of the Government. In all the political struggles in Congress he bore a leading part, his clear, vigorous, and moderate style of argument making him one of the most effective debaters in either House.

When James G. Blaine went to the Senate, in 1877, the mantle of Republican leadership in the House was by common consent placed upon Garfield. In January, 1880, Gen. Garfield was elected to the Senate. He received the unanimous vote of the Republican caucus, an honor never before given to any man of any party in the State of Ohio.

Of his industry and studious habits a great deal might be said, but a single illustration will have to suffice here. Once during the busiest part of a very busy session at Washington a visitor found him in his library, behind a big barricade of books. This was no unusual sight, but when the caller glanced at the volumes he saw that they were all different editions of Horace, or books relating to that poet. "I find that I am overworked, and need recreation," said the General. "Now, my theory is that the best way to rest the mind is not to let it be idle, but to put it at something quite outside of the ordinary line of its employment. So I am resting by learning all the Congressional Library can show about Horace and the various editions and translations of his poems."

The circumstances of Gen. Garfield's nomination for the Presidency, at Chicago, are thus told by one of his many biographers: There were some indications as the thirtieth ballot progressed on Tuesday, June 8, that the lesser candidates were giving way. The next ballot demonstrated that the Grant lines could not be broken, and the Blaine lines were at this time wavering. It was apparent the Convention was on the edge of a break. The next ballot, which was finished by half-past 12, was without exciting event. The close of the thirty-fourth was marked with some excitement growing out of a break to Garfield, Wisconsin casting for him sixteen votes. This was the beginning of the end. To make up this number, Washburne, Blaine, and Sherman were drawn upon. When the result was declared, Gen. Garfield arose and addressed the Chair. The Chairman inquired for what purpose the gentleman rose. "To a question of order," said Garfield.

"The gentleman will state it," said the Chair.

"I challenge," said Mr. Garfield, "the correctness of the announcement that contains votes for me. No man has a right, without the consent of the person voted for, to have his name announced and voted for in this Convention. Such consent I have not given."

This was overruled by the Chairman amidst laughter against Garfield, who had made the point on the vote cast for him by Wisconsin.

Then the thirty-fifth ballot was taken. It was apparent that the Blaine men had broken up.

The thirty-sixth ballot was taken amidst breathless excitement. It proved to be the last. It resulted: Grant, 306; Blaine, 42; Sherman, 3; Washburne, 6; Garfield, 399.

The late Mr. Fox was accustomed to introduce his recollections of past times with the words, "when I was working as a weaver-boy at Norwich"; and there are other members of Parliament, still living, whose origin has been equally humble. Mr. Lindsay, the well known ship-owner, once told the simple story of his life to the electors of Weymouth, in answer to an attack upon him by his political opponents. He had been left an orphan at fourteen, and when he left Glasgow for Liverpool, to push his way in the world, not being able to pay the usual fare, the captain of the steamer agreed to take his labor in exchange, and the boy worked his passage by trimming the coals in the coal-hole. At Liverpool he remained for seven weeks before he could obtain employment, during which time he lived in sheds and fared hardly, until at last he found shelter on board a West Indiaman. He entered as a boy, and before he was nineteen, by steady good conduct, had risen to the command of a ship. At twenty-three he retired from the sea, and settled on shore, after which his progress was rapid; "he had prospered," he said, "by steady industry, by constant work, and by ever keeping in view the great principle of doing to others as you would be done by."

Among like men of the same class may be ranked the late Richard Cobden, whose start in life was equally humble. The son of a small farmer at Midhurst, in Sussex, he was sent at an early age to London, and employed as a boy in a warehouse in the city. He was diligent, well conducted, and eager for information. His master, a man of the old school, warned him against too much reading; but the boy went on in his own course, storing his mind with the wealth found in books. He was promoted from one position of trust to another, became a traveler for his house, secured a large connection, and eventually started in business as a calico-printer at Manchester. Taking an interest in public questions, more especially in popular education, his attention was gradually drawn to the subject of the Corn Laws, to the repeal of which he may be said to have devoted his fortune and his life. It may be mentioned, as a curious fact, that the first speech he delivered in public was a total failure. But he had great perseverance, application and energy, and, with persistency and practice, he became at length one of the most persuasive and effective of public speakers, extorting the disinterested eulogy of even Sir Robert Peel himself. A French Ambassador has eloquently said of Mr. Cobden, that he was "a living proof of what merit, perseverance, and labor can accomplish; one of the most complete examples of those men who, sprung from the humblest ranks of society, raise themselves to the highest rank in public estimation, by the effect of their own worth and of their personal services; finally, one of the rarest examples of the solid qualities inherent in the English character."

In all these cases strenuous individual application was the price paid for distinction—excellence of any sort being invariably placed beyond the reach of indolence. It is the diligent hand and head alone that maketh rich—in self-culture, growth in wisdom, and in business. Even when men are born to wealth and high social position, any solid reputation which they may individually achieve can only be attained by energetic application; for, though an inheritance of acres may be bequeathed, an inheritance of knowledge and wisdom can not. The wealthy man may pay others for doing his work for him, but it is impossible to get his thinking clone for him by another, or to purchase any kind of self-culture. Indeed, the doctrine that excellence in any pursuit is only to be achieved by laborious application, holds as true in the case of the man of wealth as that of Drew and Gifford, whose only school was a cobbler's stall, or Hugh Miller, whose only college was a Cromarty stone quarry.

Riches and ease, it is perfectly clear, are not necessary for man's highest culture, else had not the world been so largely indebted in all times to those who have sprung from the humbler ranks. An easy or luxurious existence does not train men to effort or encounter with difficulty, nor does it awaken that consciousness of power which is so necessary for energetic and effective action in life. Indeed, so far from poverty being a misfortune, it may, by vigorous self-help, be converted even into a blessing, rousing a man to that struggle with the world in which, though some may purchase ease by degradation, the right-minded and true-hearted find strength, confidence, and triumph. Bacon says, "Men seem neither to understand their riches nor their strength: of the former they believe greater things than they should; of the latter much less. Self-reliance and self-denial will teach a man to drink out of his own cistern, and eat his own sweet bread, and to learn and labor truly to get his living, and carefully to expend the good things committed to his trust."

A very impressive example of the success to which a system of self-help, vigorously pursued, invariably leads, is presented in the life of our renowned contemporary, Thomas A. Edison. His parents were poor, and he received not more than two months of regular schooling, but was taught in the elementary branches by his mother. He had a passion for reading, and before he was 12 years old he had read Gibbons' "Rome," Hume's "England," and the "Penny Cyclopedia." He also read some books on chemistry in early life, and so strong was his thirst for knowledge that at one time he resolved to read every book in the public library of Detroit. In execution of his purpose he read Newton's "Principia," Ure's scientific dictionaries, Burton's "Anatomy of Melancholy," and other important works. He early became a newsboy on the Grand Trunk railway, opposite Detroit. This position gave him the opportunity of reading many miscellaneous books. He became much interested in chemistry, and put up a laboratory in one of the cars; but his enthusiastic efforts in this direction were soon brought to an end by an unfortunate explosion which came near setting the train on fire, and which led the conductor to throw the apparatus and chemicals out of the car. Not content with selling papers, Edison next bought some old type and began to print, on the cars, a little paper called the *Grand Trunk Herald*. While acting as newsboy he got acquainted with the telegraph operators along the line and became ambitious to be an operator himself. The station master at Mount Clemens Station offered to give him the necessary instruction, and for five months the young newsboy returned to this point after his day's work and received nightly instruction in telegraphy. At the end of this time he was qualified to accept a position in the telegraph office at Port Huron. While at Adrian, Mich., discharging his duties as operator, he spent much time in repairing instruments and at other mechanical employments, for which he had made a small workshop and furnished it with tools. He soon went to Indianapolis, where he invented an automatic repeater, by which a message might be transferred from one wire to another without the aid of an operator. Going in turn to Cincinnati, Memphis, Louisville and New Orleans, he returned to Cincinnati in 1867, where, at the age of twenty, he became absorbed in projects of invention. He had now become one of the most expert operators in the service, and was soon put into the leading position in the Boston office. Here he fitted up a small shop and continued his experiments. In 1870 he went to Rochester, N. Y., to test between that city and Boston the practicability of his invention of the duplex telegraph, but the experiment did not prove successful.

He next entered the service of the Gold Indicator company in New York, of which he was soon made superintendent. Here he introduced improved apparatus, and invented the gold printer and other devices. About this time he established in Newark, N. J., a factory for the purpose of making the machines and apparatus he had invented. About three hundred men were employed in this establishment, but the demands made on his time by the business left him so little opportunity for pursuing his experiments and making inventions that he abandoned the enterprise, and in 1876 established a shop for experimenting, at Menlo Park, a small station on the Pennsylvania railroad, about twenty-four miles from New York.

Although Mr. Edison is still a very young man, his inventions are exceedingly numerous. He has taken out several hundred patents. The most wonderful and famous of these are the carbon telephone and the phonograph. His micro-tasimeter, designed for detecting very slight variations of temperature, was successfully used during the total eclipse of the sun in July, 1878, to demonstrate the existence of heat in the Corona. The aerophone, which has not yet been perfected, is a contrivance for amplifying sound. Its purpose is to increase the loudness of words spoken without imparing the distinctness of articulation.

The phonometer is an instrument for measuring the mechanical force of sound waves produced by the human voice. Mr. Edison's experiments upon the electric light are likely soon to result in a complete revolution in our present methods of illumination. He has already discovered a means for subdividing the electric current indefinitely, so as to make the light practicable for small areas.

He has also invented an harmonic engine, with which he proposes to use compressed air as a motor for propelling sewing machines, and other light machinery. It is said to be in advance of other electric engines, and through its agency, electricity may yet be utilized as a motive power. Among Mr. Edison's other important inventions are the electric pen for multiplying copies of letters or drawings, and the quadruplex system of telegraphy by which four communications may be sent in opposite directions over one wire at the same time. Both these latter inventions are now extensively used.

Mr. Prescott says of him: "The great number and variety of subjects to which Mr. Edison has given his attention is scarcely less surprising than the marked success with which his labors have been crowned. Electricity alone, although receiving the most attention, has furnished but a single field for his versatile powers. His path has been through extended portions of physics and chemistry, and is clearly marked by characteristic inventions in these vast domains."

"Without doubt, Mr. Edison is more than usually endowed with what the world terms genius. His intellectual powers are of no ordinary kind, but it should be clearly understood that his great success is the result, not so much of the divine gift of genius alone, as of his ceaseless activity and indomitable perseverance under all circumstances; these are unquestionably the most remarkable characteristics of his nature and the real elements of his success. The author can state from personal knowledge what is now becoming more generally known regarding Mr. Edison's extraordinary propensities for work. Very few, if favored with like powers of endurance, would be willing to apply themselves so assiduously. During the earlier experiments with the quadruplex system of telegraphy, which took place under his own supervision, and which required a vast amount of time and application for its perfection, it was a very common thing to find Mr. Edison working through the entire night, his only rest being such as a brief interval of sleep just before day might afford, taken in the experimenting rooms. Night after night he has worked in this manner, and been found in the morning with nothing but his coat for a pillow, and the table or desk for his couch."

The indefatigable industry of Lord Brougham became almost proverbial. His public labors extended over a period of upwards of sixty years, during which he ranged over many fields—of law, literature, politics, and science—and achieved distinction in them all. How he contrived it, has been to many a mystery. Once, when Sir Samuel Romilly was requested to undertake some new work, he excused himself by saying that he had no time; "but," he added, "go with it to that fellow Brougham; he seems to have time for every thing." The secret of it was, that he never left a minute unemployed; withal he possessed a constitution of iron. When arrived at an age at which most men would have retired from the world to enjoy their hard-earned leisure, perhaps to doze away their time in an easy-chair, Lord Brougham commenced and prosecuted a series of elaborate investigations as to the laws of Light, and he submitted the results to the most scientific audiences that Paris and London could muster. About the same time, he was passing through the press his admirable sketches of the "Men of Science and Literature of the Reign of George III," and taking his full share of the law business and the political discussions in the House of Lords. Sydney Smith once recommended him to confine himself to only the transaction of so much business as three strong men could get through. But such was Brougham's love of work—long become a habit—that no amount of application seems to have been too great for him; and such was his love of excellence, that it has been said of him that if his station in life had been only that of a shoeblack he would never have rested satisfied until he had become the best shoeblack in England.

Mr. Disraeli affords a similar instance of the power of industry and application in working out an eminent public career. His "Wondrous Tale of Alroy" and "Revolutionary Epic" were laughed at, and regarded as indications of literary lunacy. But he worked on in other directions, and his "Coningsby," "Sybil," and "Tancred," proved the sterling stuff of which he was made. As an orator, too, his first appearance in the House of Commons was a failure. It was spoken of as more screaming than an Adelphi farce. Though composed in a grand and ambitious strain, every sentence was hailed with "loud laughter." "Hamlet" played as a comedy were nothing to it. But he concluded with a sentence which embodied a prophecy. Writhing under the laughter with which his studied eloquence had been received, he exclaimed, "I have begun several times many things, and have succeeded in them at last. I will sit down now, but the time will come when you will hear me." The time did come; and how Disraeli succeeded in at length commanding the attention of the first assembly of gentlemen in the world, affords a striking illustration of what energy and determination will do, for Disraeli earned his position by dint of patient industry. He did not, as many young men do, having once failed, retire dejected, to mope and whine in a corner, but diligently set himself to work. He carefully unlearnt his faults, studied the character of his audience, practised sedulously the art of speech, and industriously filled his mind with the elements of parliamentary knowledge. He worked patiently for success; and it came, but slowly; then the House laughed with him, instead of at him. The recollection of his early failure was effaced, and by general consent he was at length admitted to be one of the most finished and effective of parliamentary speakers.

Chapter 8

Leaders of Industry—Inventors and Producers

"Who best can suffer best can do." —Milton.

*"Deduct all that men of the humbler classes have done for England in the way of inventions only, and see where she would have been but for them."
—Arthur Helps.*

ONE OF THE MOST strongly marked features of the English speaking people is their spirit of industry, standing out prominent and distinct in their past history, and as strikingly characteristic of them now as at any former period. It is this spirit, which has laid the foundations and built up the industrial greatness of our country. This vigorous growth of the nation has been mainly the result of the free energy of individuals, and it has been contingent upon the number of hands and minds from time to time actively employed within it, whether as cultivators of the soil, producers of articles of utility, contrivers of tools and machines, writers of books, or creators of works of art. And while this spirit of active industry has been the vital principle of the nation, it has also been its saving and remedial one, counteracting from time to time the effects of errors in our laws and imperfections in our constitution.

    The career of industry which the nation has pursued, has also proved its best education. As steady application to work is the healthiest training for every individual, so is it the best discipline of a state. Honorable industry travels the same road with duty; and Providence has closely linked both with happiness. The gods, says the poet, have placed labor and toil on the way leading to the Elysian fields. Certain it is that no bread eaten by man is so sweet as that earned by his own labor, whether bodily or mental. By labor the earth has been subdued, and man redeemed from barbarism; nor has a single step in civilization been made without it. Labor is not only a necessity and a duty, but a blessing: only the idler feels it to be a curse. The duty of work is written on the thews and muscles of the limbs, the mechanism of the hand, the nerves and lobes of the brain—the sum of whose healthy action is satisfaction and enjoyment. In the school of labor is taught the best practical wisdom.

It so happens that the history of Pottery furnishes some of the most remarkable instances of patient industry and perseverance to be found in the whole range of biography.

Though the art of making common vessels of clay was known to most of the ancient nations, that of manufacturing enamelled earthenware was much less common. It was, however, practiced by the ancient Etruscans, specimens of whose ware are still to be found in antiquarian collections. But it became a lost art, and was only recovered at a comparatively recent date. The Etruscan ware was very valuable in ancient times, a vase being worth its weight in gold in the time of Augustus.

The reviver or re-discoverer of the art of enamelling in Italy was Luca della Robbia, a Florentine sculptor. Vasari describes him as a man of great perseverance, working with his chisel all day and practicing drawing during the greater part of the night. He pursued the latter art with so much assiduity, that, when working late, to prevent his feet from freezing with the cold, he was accustomed to provide himself with a basket of shavings, in which he placed them, to keep himself warm and enable him to proceed with his drawings. "Nor," says Vasari, "am I in the least astonished at this, since no man ever becomes distinguished in any art whatsoever, who does not early begin to acquire the power of supporting heat, cold, hunger, thirst, and other discomforts; whereas, those persons deceive themselves altogether who suppose that, when taking their ease and surrounded by all the enjoyments of the world, they may still attain to honorable distinction—for it is not by sleeping, but by waking, watching, and laboring continually, that proficiency is attained and reputation acquired."

But Luca, notwithstanding all his application and industry, did not succeed in earning enough money by sculpture to enable him to live by the art, and the idea occurred to him that he might, nevertheless, be able to pursue his modelling in some material more facile and less dear than marble. Hence it was that he began to make his models in clay, and to endeavor, by experiment, so to coat and bake the clay as to render those models durable. After many trials he at length discovered a method of covering the clay with a material which, when exposed to the intense heat of a furnace, became converted into an almost imperishable enamel. He afterwards made the further discovery of a method of imparting color to the enamel, thus greatly adding to its beauty.

The fame of Luca's work extended throughout Europe, and specimens of his art became widely diffused. Many of them were sent into France and Spain, where they were greatly prized. At that time coarse brown jars were almost the only articles of earthenware produced in France; and this continued to be the case, with comparatively small improvement, until the time of Palissy—a man who toiled and fought against stupendous difficulties with a heroism that sheds a glow almost of romance over the events of his chequered life.

Bernard Palissy is supposed to have been born in the south of France, about the year 1510. His father was probably a worker in glass, to which trade Bernard was brought up. His parents were poor people—too poor to give him the benefit of any school education. "I had no other books," said he, afterwards, "than heaven and earth, which are open to all." He learned, however, the art of glass-painting, to which he added that of drawing, and afterwards reading and writing.

When about eighteen years old, the glass trade becoming decayed, Palissy left his father's house, with his wallet on his back, and went out into the world to search whether there was any place in it for him. He first traveled towards Gascony, working at his trade where he could find employment, and occasionally occupying part of his time in land-measuring. Then he traveled northwards, sojourning for various periods at different places in France, Flanders, and Lower Germany.

Thus Palissy occupied about ten more years of his life, after which he married, and ceased from his wanderings, settling down to practice glass-painting and land-measuring at the small town of Saintes. There children were born to him, and, not only his responsibilities, but his expenses increased, while, do what he could, his earnings remained too small for his needs. It was, therefore, necessary for him to bestir himself. Probably he felt capable of better things than drudging in an employment so precarious as glass-painting, and hence he was induced to turn his attention to the kindred art of painting and enamelling earthenware. Yet, on this subject he was wholly ignorant, for he had never seen earth baked before he began his operations. He had, therefore, everything to learn by himself, without any helper, but he was full of hope, eager to learn, of unbounded perseverance and inexhaustible patience.

It was the sight of an elegant cup of Italian manufacture—most probably one of Luca della Robbia's—which first set Palissy thinking about the new art. A circumstance so apparently insignificant would have produced no effect upon an ordinary mind, or even upon Palissy himself at an ordinary time; but, occurring, as it did, when he was meditating a change of ailing, he at once became inflamed with the desire of imitating it. The sight of this cup disturbed his whole existence, and the determination to discover the enamel with which it was glazed thenceforward possessed him like a passion. Had he been a single man he might have traveled into Italy in search of the secret; but he was bound to his wife and his children, and could not leave them; so he remained by their side, groping in the dark, in the hope of finding out the process of making and enamelling earthenware.

At first he could merely guess the materials of which the enamel was composed, and he proceeded to try all manner of experiments to ascertain what they really were. He pounded all the substances which he supposed were likely to produce it. Then he bought common earthen pots, broke them into pieces, and, spreading his compounds over them, subjected them to the heat of a furnace which he erected for the purpose of baking them. His experiments failed, and the results were broken pots and a waste of fuel, drugs, time, and labor. Women do not readily sympathize with experiments whose only tangible effect is to dissipate the means of buying clothes and food for their children; and Palissy's wife, however dutiful in other respects, could not be reconciled to the purchase of more earthen pots, which seemed to her to be bought only to be broken. Yet she must needs submit, for Palissy had become thoroughly possessed by the determination to master the secret of the enamel, and would not let it alone.

For many successive months and years Palissy pursued his experiments. The first furnace having proved a failure, he proceeded to erect another out of doors. There he burnt more wood, spoiled more drugs and pots, and lost more time, until poverty stared him and his family in the face. "Thus," said he, "I fooled away several years, with sorrow and sighs, because I could not at all arrive at my intention." In the intervals of his experiments he occasionally worked at his former callings—painting on glass, drawing portraits, and measuring land; but his earnings from these sources were very small. At length he was no longer able to carry on his experiments in his own furnace because of the heavy cost of fuel; but he bought more potsherds, broke them up as before into three or four hundred pieces; and, covering them with chemicals, carried them to a tile-work a league and a half distant from Saintes, there to be baked in an ordinary furnace. After the operation he went to see the pieces taken out, and, to his dismay, the whole of the experiments were failures. But, though disappointed, he was not yet defeated, for he determined on the very spot to "begin afresh."

His business as a land-measurer called him away for a brief season from the pursuit of his experiments. In conformity with an edict of the State, it became necessary to survey the salt-marshes in the neighborhood of Saintes for the purpose of levying the land-tax. Palissy was employed to make this survey, and prepare the requisite map. The work occupied him some time, and he was doubtless well paid for it; but no sooner was it completed than he proceeded, with redoubled zeal, to follow up his old investigations "in the track of the enamels." He began by breaking three dozen new earthen pots, the pieces of which he covered with different materials which he had compounded, and then took them to a neighboring glass-furnace to be baked. The results gave him a glimmer of hope. The greater heat of the glass-furnace had melted some of the compounds, but though Palissy searched diligently for the white enamel he could find none.

For two more years he went on experimenting without any satisfactory result, until the proceeds of his survey of the salt-marshes having become nearly spent, he was reduced to poverty again. But he resolved to make a last great effort; and he began by breaking more pots than ever. More than three hundred pieces of pottery covered with his compounds were sent to the glass-furnace, and thither he himself went to watch the results of the baking. Four hours passed, during which he watched, and then the furnace was opened. The material on one only of the three hundred pieces of potsherd had melted, and it was taken out to cool. As it hardened it grew white—white and polished! The piece of potsherd was covered with white enamel, described by Palissy as "singularly beautiful!" And beautiful it must no doubt have been in his eyes after all his weary waiting. He ran home with it to his wife, feeling himself, as he expressed it, quite a new creature. But the prize was not yet won—far from it. The partial success of this intended last effort merely had the effect of luring him on to a succession of further experiments and failures.

In order that he might complete the invention, which he now believed to be at hand, he resolved to build for himself a glass-furnace near his dwelling, where he might carry on his operations in secret. He proceeded to build the furnace with his own hands, carrying the bricks from the brick-field upon his back. He was bricklayer, laborer and all. From seven to eight more months passed. At last the furnace was built and ready for use. Palissy had in the mean time fashioned a number of vessels of clay in readiness for the laying on of the enamel. After being subjected to a preliminary process of baking, they were covered with the enamel compound, and again placed in the furnace for the grand crucial experiment. Although his means were nearly exhausted, Palissy had been for some time accumulating a great store of fuel for the final effort, and he thought it was enough. At last the fire was lit, and the operation proceeded. All day he sat by the furnace, feeding it with fuel. He sat there watching and feeding all through the long night. But the enamel did not melt. The sun rose upon his labors. His wife brought him a portion of the scanty morning meal—for he would not stir from the furnace, into which he continued from time to time to heave more fuel. The second day passed, and still the enamel did not melt. The sun set and another night passed. The pale, haggard, unshorn, baffled, yet not beaten Palissy sat by his furnace eagerly looking for the melting of the enamel. A third day and night passed—a fourth, a fifth, and even a sixth—yes, for six long days and nights did the unconquerable Palissy watch and toil, fighting against hope; and still the enamel would not melt.

It then occurred to him that there might be some defect in the materials for the enamel—perhaps something wanting in the flux; so he set to work to pound and compound fresh materials for a new experiment. Thus two or three more weeks passed. But how to buy more pots? For those which he had made with his own hands for the purpose of the first experiment were by long baking irretrievably spoiled for the purposes of a second. His money was now all spent; but he could borrow. His character was still good, though his wife and the neighbors thought him foolishly wasting his means in futile experiments. Nevertheless he succeeded. He borrowed sufficient from a friend to enable him to buy more fuel and more pots, and he was again ready for a further experiment. The pots were covered with the new compound, placed in the furnace, and the fire was again lit.

It was the last and most desperate experiment of the whole. The fire blazed up; the heat became intense; but still the enamel did not melt. The fuel began to run short! How to keep up the fire? There were the garden palings; these would burn. They must be sacrificed rather than that the great experiment should fail. The garden palings were pulled up and cast into the furnace. They were burnt in vain! The enamel had not yet melted. Ten minutes more heat might do it. Fuel must be had at whatever cost. There remained the household furniture and shelving. A crashing noise was heard in the house, and amidst the screams of his wife and children, who now feared Palissy's reason was giving way, the tables were seized, broken up and heaved into the furnace. The enamel had not melted yet! There remained the shelving. Another noise of the wrenching of timber was heard within the house, and the shelves were torn down and hurled after the furniture into the fire. Wife and children then rushed from the house, and went frantically through the town, calling out that poor Palissy had gone mad, and was breaking up his very furniture for firewood.

For an entire month his shirt had not been off his back, and he was utterly worn out—wasted with toil, anxiety, watching and want of food. He was in debt, and seemed on the verge of ruin. But he had at length mastered the secret, for the last great burst of heat had melted the enamel. The common brown household jars, when taken out of the furnace after it had become cool, were found covered with a white glaze. For this he could endure reproach, contumely and scorn, and wait patiently for the opportunity of putting his discovery into practice as better days came round.

Palissy next hired a potter to make some earthen vessels after the designs which he furnished, while he himself proceeded to model some medallions in clay for the purpose of enamelling them. But how to maintain himself and his family until the wares were made and ready for sale? Fortunately there remained one man in Saintes who still believed in the integrity, if not in the judgment, of Palissy—an inn-keeper, who agreed to feed and lodge him for six months, while he went on with his manufacture. As for the working potter whom he had hired, Palissy soon found that he could not pay him the stipulated wages. Having already stripped his dwelling, he could but strip himself; and he accordingly parted with some of his clothes to the potter, in part payment of the wages which he owed him.

Palissy next erected an improved furnace, but he was so unfortunate as to build part of the inside with flints. When it was heated these flints cracked and burst, and the spinculx were scattered over the pieces of pottery, sticking to them. Though the enamel came out right, the work was irretrievably spoilt, and thus six more months' labor was lost. Persons were found willing to buy the articles at a low price, notwithstanding the injury they had sustained; but Palissy would not sell them, considering that to have done so would be to "decry and abase his honor"; and so he broke in pieces the entire batch. "Nevertheless," says he, "hope continued to inspire me, and I held on manfully; sometimes, when visitors called, I entertained them with pleasantry, while I was really sad at heart."

At this stage of his affairs Palissy became melancholy and almost hopeless, and seems to have all but broken down. He wandered gloomily about the fields near Saintes, his clothes hanging in tatters, and himself worn to a skeleton. In a curious passage in his writings he describes how that the calves of his legs had disappeared, and were no longer able with the help of garters to hold up his stockings, which fell about his heels when he walked. The family continued to reproach him for his recklessness, and his neighbors cried shame upon him for his obstinate folly. So he returned for a time to his former calling; and after a year's diligent labor, during which he earned bread for his household, and somewhat recovered his character among his neighbors, he again resumed his darling enterprise. But, though he had already spent about ten years in the search for the enamel, it cost him nearly eight more years of experimental plodding before he perfected his invention. He gradually learnt dexterity and certainty of result by experience, gathering practical knowledge out of many failures. Every mishap was a fresh lesson to him, teaching him something new about the nature of enamels, the qualities of argillaceous earths, the tempering of clays, and the construction and management of furnaces.

At last, after about sixteen years labor, Palissy took heart, and called himself Potter. These sixteen years had been his term of apprenticeship to the art, during which he had wholly to teach himself, beginning at the very beginning. He was now able to sell his wares, and thereby maintain his family in comfort. But he never rested satisfied with what he had accomplished. He proceeded from one step of improvement to another, always aiming at the greatest perfection possible. He studied natural objects for patterns, and with such success that the great Bution spoke of him as "so great a naturalist as Nature only can produce." His ornamental pieces are now regarded as rare gems, and sell at almost fabulous prices. The ornaments on them are, for the most part, accurate models from life, of wild animals, lizards, and plants, found in the fields about Saintes, and tastefully combined as ornaments into the texture of a plate or a vase.

We have not, however, come to an end of the sufferings of Palissy, respecting which a few words remain to be said. Being a Protestant, at a time when religious persecution waxed hot in the south of France, and expressing his views without fear, he was regarded as a dangerous heretic. His enemies having informed against him, his house at Saintes was entered by the officers of "justice," and his workshop was thrown open to the rabble, who entered and smashed his pottery, while he himself was hurried off by night and cast into a dungeon at Bordeaux, to wait his turn at the stake or the scaffold. He was condemned to be burnt, but a powerful noble, the Constable de Montmorency, interposed to save his life—not because he had any special regard for Palissy or his religion, but because no other artist could be found capable of executing the enamelled pavement for his magnificent dwelling, then in course of erection at Ecouen, near Paris. He was liberated, and returned to his home at Saintes, only to find it devastated and broken up. His workshop was open to the sky, and his works lay in ruins. Shaking the dust of Saintes from his feet he left the place never to return to it, and removed to Paris to carry on the works ordered of him by the Constable and the Queen-Mother.

Besides carrying on the manufacture of pottery, with the aid of his two sons, Palissy, during the latter part of his life, wrote and published several books on the potter's art, with a view to the instruction of his countrymen, and in order that they might avoid the many mistakes which he himself had made. He also wrote on agriculture, on fortification, and natural history, on which latter subject he even delivered lectures to a limited number of persons. He waged war against astrology, alchemy, witchcraft, and like impostures. This stirred up against him many enemies, who pointed the finger at him as a heretic, and he was again arrested for his religion and imprisoned in the Bastille. He was now an old man of seventy-eight, trembling on the verge of the grave, but his spirit was as brave as ever. He was threatened with death unless he recanted; but he was as obstinate in holding to his religion as he had been in hunting out the secret of the enamel. The king, Henry III, even went to see him in prison to induce him to abjure his faith. "My good man," said the King, "you have now served my mother and myself for forty-five years. We have put up with your adhering to your religion amidst fires and massacres: now I am so pressed by the Guise party as well as by my own people, that I am constrained to leave you in the hands of your enemies, and tomorrow you will be burnt unless you become converted." "Sire," answered the unconquerable old man, "I am ready to give my life for the glory of God. You have said many times that you have pity on me; and now I have pity on you, who have pronounced the words *I am constrained!* It is not spoken like a king; it is what you, and those who constrain you, can never effect upon me, for I know how to die." Palissy did indeed die shortly after, a martyr, though not at the stake. He died in the Bastille, after enduring about a year's imprisonment—there peacefully terminating a life distinguished for heroic labor, extraordinary endurance, inflexible rectitude, and the exhibition of many rare and noble virtues. The career of Josiah Wedgwood, the English potter, was less chequered and more prosperous than that of Palissy, and his lot was cast in happier times. Down to the middle of last century England was behind most other nations of the first order in Europe in respect of skilled industry. Although there were many potters in Staffordshire, their productions were of the rudest kind, for the most part only plain brown ware, with the patterns scratched in while the clay was wet.

Josiah Wedgwood was one of those industrious men who from time to time spring from the ranks of the common people, and by their energetic character not only practically educate the working population in habits of industry, but by the example of diligence and perseverance which they set before them, largely influence the public activity in all directions, and contribute in a great degree to form the national character. He was, like Arkwright, the youngest of a family of thirteen children. His grandfather and grand-uncle were both potters, as was also his father, who died when he was a mere boy, leaving him a patrimony of twenty pounds. He had learned to read and write at the village school; but on the death of his father he was taken from it and set to work as a thrower in a small pottery carried on by his elder brother. There he began life, his working life, to use his own words, "at the lowest round of the ladder," when only eleven years old. He was shortly after seized by an attack of virulent smallpox, from the effects of which he suffered during the rest of his life, for it was followed by a disease in the right knee, which recurred at frequent intervals, and was only got rid of by the amputation of the limb many years later.

When he had completed his apprenticeship with his brother, Josiah joined partnership with another workman, and carried on a small business in making knife-hafts, boxes, and sundry articles for domestic use; but he made comparatively little progress until he began business on his own account at Burslem. There he diligently pursued his calling, introducing new articles to the trade, and gradually extending his business. What he chiefly aimed at was to manufacture cream-colored ware of a better quality than was then produced in Staffordshire as regarded shape, color, glaze, and durability. To understand the subject thoroughly, he devoted his leisure to the study of chemistry; and he made numerous experiments on fluxes, glazes, and various sorts of clay. Being a close inquirer and accurate observer, he noticed that a certain earth containing silica, which was black before calcination, became white after exposure to the heat of a furnace. This fact, observed and pondered on, led to the idea of mixing silica with the red powder of the potteries, and to the discovery that the mixture becomes white when calcined. He had but to cover this material with a vitrification of transparent glaze, to obtain one of the most important products of fictile art—that which, under the name of English earthenware, was to attain the greatest commercial value and become of the most extensive utility.

Wedgwood was for some time much troubled by his furnaces, though nothing like to the same extent that Palissy was; and he overcame his difficulties in the same way—by repeated experiments and unfaltering perseverance. His first attempts at making porcelain for table use were a succession of disastrous failures—the labors of months being often destroyed in a day. It was only after a long series of trials, in the course of which he lost time, money, and labor, that he arrived at the proper sort of glaze to be used; but he would not be denied, and at last he conquered success through patience. The improvement of pottery became his passion, and was never lost sight of for a moment. Even when he had mastered his difficulties, and become a prosperous man—manufacturing white stone ware and cream-colored ware in large quantities for home and foreign use—he went forward perfecting his manufactures, until, his example extending in all directions, the action of the entire district was stimulated, and a great branch of British industry was eventually established on firm foundations. He aimed throughout at the highest excellence, declaring his determination "to give over manufacturing any article, whatsoever it might be, rather than to degrade it."

Wedgwood called to his aid the crucible of the chemist, the knowledge of the antiquary, and the skill of the artist. He found out Flaxman when a youth, and while he liberally nurtured his genius, drew from him a large number of beautiful designs for his pottery and porcelain; converting them by his manufacture into objects of taste and excellence, and thus making them instrumental in the diffusion of art among the people. By careful experiment and study he was even enabled to rediscover the art of painting on porcelain or earthenware vases and similar articles—an art practiced by the ancient Etruscans, but which had been lost since the time of Pliny.

The result of Wedgewood's labors was, that the manufacture of pottery, which he found in the very lowest condition, became one of the staples of England; and, instead of importing what we needed for home use from abroad, England became a large exporter to other countries, supplying them with earthenware even in the face of enormous prohibitory duties on articles of British produce.

Wedgwood gave evidence as to his manufacture before Parliament in 1785, only some thirty years after he had begun his operations; from which it appeared that, instead of providing only casual employment to a small number of inefficient and badly remunerated workmen, about 20,000 persons then derived their bread directly from the manufacture of earthenware, without taking into account the increased numbers to which it gave employment in coal mines, and in the carrying trade by land and sea, and the stimulus which it gave to employment in many ways in various parts of the country.

Yet, important as had been the advances made in his time, Mr. Wedgwood was of the opinion that the manufacture was but in its infancy, and that the improvements which he had effected were but of small moment compared with those to which the art was capable of attaining, through the continued industry and growing intelligence of the manufacturers, and the natural facilities and political advantages enjoyed by Great Britain; an opinion which has been fully borne out by the progress which has since been effected in this important branch of industry.

In 1852 not fewer than 84,000,000 pieces of pottery were exported from England to other countries, besides what were made for home use. But it is not merely the quantity and value of the produce that is entitled to consideration, but the improvement of the condition of the population by whom this great branch of industry is conducted.

When Wedgwood began his labors the Staffordshire district was only in a half-civilized state. The people were poor, uncultivated, and few in number. When Wedgwood's manufacture was firmly established there was found ample employment, at good wages, for three times the number of population; while their moral advancement had kept pace with their material improvement.

Men such as these are fairly entitled to take rank as the Industrial Heroes of the civilized world. Their patient self-reliance amidst trials and difficulties, their courage and perseverance in the pursuit of worthy objects, are not less heroic than the bravery and devotion of the soldier and the sailor.

One of the first grand results of Watt's invention—which placed an almost unlimited power at the command of the producing classes—was the establishment of the cotton manufacture. The person most closely identified with the foundation of this great branch of industry was unquestionably Sir Richard Arkwright, whose practical energy and sagacity were perhaps even more remarkable than his mechanical inventiveness.

Arkwright, like most of our great mechanicians, sprang from the ranks. He was born in Preston in 1732. His parents were very poor, and he was the youngest of thirteen children. He was never at school. The only education he received he gave to himself, and to the last he was only able to write with difficulty. When a boy he was apprenticed to a barber, and after learning the business, he set up for himself in Bolton, where he occupied an underground cellar, over which he put up the sign, "Come to the subterraneous barber—he shaves for a penny." The other barbers found their customers leaving them, and reduced their prices to his standard, when Arkwright, determined to push his trade, announced his determination to give a clean shave for a half-penny. After a few years he quitted his cellar, and became an itinerant dealer in hair. At that time wigs were worn, and wig-making formed an important branch of the barbering business. Arkwright went about buying hair for the wigs. He was accustomed to attend the hiring-fairs throughout Lancashire resorted to by young women, for the purpose of securing their long tresses; and it is said that in negotiations of this sort he was very successful. He also dealt in a chemical hair-dye, which he used adroitly, and thereby secured a considerable trade. But he does not seem, notwithstanding his pushing character, to have done more than earn a bare living.

The fashion of wig-wearing having undergone a change, distress fell upon the wig-makers, and Arkwright, being of a mechanical turn, was consequently induced to turn machine inventor or "conjurer," as the pursuit was then popularly termed. Many attempts were made about that time to invent a spinning-machine, and our barber determined to launch his little bark on the sea of invention with the rest. Like other self-taught men of the same bias, he had already been devoting his spare time to the invention of a perpetual-motion machine, and from that the transition to a spinning machine was easy. He followed his experiments so assiduously that he neglected his business, lost the little money he had saved, and was reduced to great poverty. His wife, for he had by this time married, was impatient at what she conceived to be a wanton waste of time and money, and in a moment of sudden wrath she seized upon and destroyed his models, hoping thus to remove the cause of the family privations. Arkwright was a stubborn and enthusiastic man, and he was provoked beyond measure by this conduct of his wife, from whom he immediately separated.

In traveling about the country, Arkwright had become acquainted with a person named Kay, a clock-maker at Warrington, who assisted him in constructing some of the parts of his perpetual-motion machinery. It is supposed that he was informed by Kay of the principle of spinning by rollers, but it is also said that the idea was first suggested to him by accidentally observing a red-hot piece of iron become elongated by passing between iron rollers. However this may be, the idea at once took firm possession of his mind, and he proceeded to devise the process by which it was to be accomplished. Arkwright now abandoned his business of hair-collecting, and devoted himself to the perfecting of his machine, a model of which, constructed by Kay under his directions, he set up in the parlor of the Free Grammar school at Preston. Being a burgess of the town, he voted at the contested election at which General Burgoyne was returned; but such was his poverty, and such the tattered state of his dress, that a number of persons subscribed a sum sufficient to have him put in a state fit to appear in the poll-room. The exhibition of his machine in a town where so many work-people lived by the exercise of manual labor proved a dangerous experiment; ominous growlings were heard outside the school-room from time to time, and Arkwright—remembering the fate of Kay, who was mobbed and compelled to fly from Lancashire because of his invention of the fly-shuttle, and of poor Hargreaves, whose spinning-jenny had been pulled to pieces only a short time before by a Blackburn mob—wisely determined on packing up his model and removing to a less dangerous locality. He went accordingly to Nottingham, where he applied to some of the local bankers for pecuniary assistance, and the Messrs. Wright consented to advance him a sum of money on condition of sharing in the profits of the invention. The machine, however, not being perfected so soon as they had anticipated, the bankers recommended Arkwright to apply to Messrs. Strutt and Need, the former of whom was the ingenious inventor and patentee of the stocking-frame. Mr. Strutt at once appreciated the Merits of the invention, and a partnership was entered into with Arkwright, whose road to fortune was now clear. The patent was secured in the name of "Richard Arkwright, of Nottingham, clockmaker," and it is a circumstance worthy of note, that it was taken out in 1769, the same year in which Watt secured the patent for his steam engine. A cotton-mill was first erected at Nottingham, driven by horses, and another was shortly after built, on a much larger scale, turned by a water-wheel, from which circumstance the spinning machine came to be called the water-frame.

Arkwright's labors, however, were, comparatively speaking, only begun. He had still to perfect all the working details of his machine. It was in his hands the subject of constant modification and improvement, until eventually it was rendered practicable and profitable in an eminent degree. But success was only secured by long and patient labor; for some years, indeed, the speculation was disheartening and unprofitable, swallowing up a very large amount of capital without any result. When success began to appear more certain, then the Lancashire manufacturers fell upon Arkwright's patent to pull it in pieces, as the Cornish miners fell upon Boulton and Watt to rob them of the profits of their steam engine. Arkwright was even denounced as the enemy of the working people, and a mill which he built near Chorley was destroyed by a mob in the presence of a strong force of police and military. The Lancashire men refused to buy his materials, though they were confessedly the best in the market. Then they refused to pay patent-right for the use of his machine, and combined to crush him in the courts of law. To the disgust of right-minded people, Arkwright's patent was upset. After the trial, when passing the hotel at which his opponents were staying, one of them said, loud enough to be heard by him, "Well, we've done the old shaver at last"; to which he coolly replied, "Never mind, I've a razor left that will shave you all." He established new mills in Lancashire, Derbyshire, and at New Lanark, in Scotland. The mills of Cromford also came into his hands at the expiration of his partnership with Strutt, and the amount and the excellence of his products were such, that in a short time he obtained so complete a control of the trade that the prices were fixed by him, and he governed the main operations of the other cotton-spinners.

Arkwright was a man of great force of character, indomitable courage, much worldly shrewdness, with a business faculty almost amounting to genius. At one period his time was engrossed by severe and continuous labor, occasioned by the organizing and conducting of his numerous manufactories, sometimes from four in the morning till nine at night. At fifty years of age he set to work to learn English grammar, and improve himself in writing and orthography. After overcoming every obstacle, he had the satisfaction of reaping the reward of his enterprise. Eighteen years after he had constructed his first machine, he rose to such estimation in Derbyshire that he was appointed High Sheriff of the county, and shortly after George III conferred upon him the honor of knighthood. He died in 1792. Arkwright was the founder of the modern factory system, a branch of industry which has unquestionably proved a source of immense wealth to individuals and to the nation.

Among other distinguished founders of industry, the Rev. William Lee, inventor of the Stocking-frame, and John Heathcoat, inventor of the Bobbin-net Machine, are worthy of notice, as men of great mechanical skill and perseverance, through whose labors a vast amount of remunerative employment has been provided. William Lee was born about the year 1563. He was a poor scholar, and had to struggle with poverty from his earliest years.

At the time when Lee invented the Stocking-frame he was officiating as curate of Calverton, near Nottingham, and it is alleged, that being married and poor, his wife was under the necessity of contributing to their joint support by knitting; and that Lee, while watching the motion of his wife's fingers, conceived the idea of imitating their movements by a machine. For three years he devoted himself to the prosecution of the invention, sacrificing every thing to his new idea. As the prospect of success opened before him, he abandoned his curacy, and devoted himself to the art of stocking making by machinery.

Whatever may have been the actual facts as to the origin of the invention of the Stocking-loom, there can be no doubt as to the extraordinary mechanical genius displayed by its inventor. That a clergyman living in a remote village, whose life had for the most part been spent with books, should contrive a machine of such delicate and complicated movements, and at once advance the art of knitting from the tedious process of linking threads in a chain of loops by three needles in the fingers of a woman, to the beautiful and rapid process of weaving by the stocking frame, was indeed an astonishing achievement, which may be pronounced almost unequalled in the history of mechanical invention. Lee's merit was all the greater, as the handicraft arts were then in their infancy, and little attention had as yet been given to the contrivance of machinery for the purposes of manufacture. He was under -the necessity of extemporising the parts of his machine as he best could, and adopting various expedients to overcome difficulties as they arose. His tools were imperfect, and his materials were imperfect; and he had no skilled workmen to assist him. The first frame he made was a twelve gauge, without lead sinkers, and it was almost wholly of wood; the needles being also stuck in bits of wood. One of Lee's principal difficulties consisted in the formation of the stitch, for want of needle eyes; but this he eventually overcame by forming eyes to the needles with a three-square file. At length, one difficulty after another was successfully overcome, and after three years' labor the machine was sufficiently complete to be fit for use. The quondam curate, full of enthusiasm for his art, now began stocking-weaving in the village of Calverton, and he continued to work there for several years, instructing his brother James and several of his relations in the practice of the art.

Having brought his frame to a considerable degree of perfection, and being desirous of securing the patronage of Queen Elizabeth, whose partiality for knitted silk stockings was well known, Lee proceeded to London to exhibit the Loom before her Majesty. He first showed it to several members of the court, and was, through their instrumentality, at length admitted to an interview with the Queen, and worked the machine in her presence. Elizabeth, however, did not give him the encouragement that he had expected; she is said to have opposed the invention on the ground that it was calculated to deprive a large number of poor people of their employment of hand-knitting. Lee was no more successful in finding other patrons; and, considering himself and his invention treated with contempt, he embraced the offer made to him by Sully, the sagacious minister of Henry IV, to proceed to Rouen and instruct the operatives of that town in the construction and use of the stocking-frame. Lee accordingly transferred himself and his machines to France, in 1605, taking with him his brother and seven workmen. He met with a cordial reception at Rouen, and was proceeding with the manufacture of stockings on a large scale, when unhappily, misfortune again overtook him. Henry IV, his protector, on whom he relied for the rewards, honors, and promised grant of privileges, which had induced Lee to settle in France, was murdered by the fanatic Ravaillac, and the encouragement and protection which had heretofore been extended to him were at once withdrawn. To press his claims at court, Lee proceeded to Paris; but, being a Protestant as well as a foreigner, his representations were treated with neglect; and, worn out with vexation and grief, this distinguished inventor shortly after died at Paris, in a state of extreme poverty and distress.

Lee's brother, with seven of the workmen, succeeded in escaping from France with their frames, leaving two behind. On James Lee's return to Nottinghamshire, he was joined by one Ashton, a miller of Thornton, who had been instructed in the art of framework knitting by the inventor himself before he left England. These two, with the workmen and their frames, began the stocking manufacture at Thornton, and carried it on with considerable success. The place was favorably situated for the purpose, as the sheep pastured in the neighboring district of Sherwood yielded a kind of wool of the longest staple. The number of looms employed in different parts of England gradually increased; and the machine manufacture of stockings eventually became an important branch of the national industry.

John Heathcoat was the son of a cottage farmer at Long Whalton, Leicestershire, where he was born in 1778. He was taught to read and write at the village school, but was shortly removed from it to be put apprentice to a framesmith in a neighboring village. The boy soon learnt to handle tools with dexterity, and he acquired a minute knowledge of the parts of which the stocking-frame was composed, as well as of the more intricate warp-machine. At his leisure he studied how to introduce improvements in them, and his friend, Mr. Bazley, M. P., states that as early as the age of sixteen he conceived the idea of inventing a machine by which lace might be made similar to Buckingham or French lace, then all made by hand. The first practical improvement he succeeded in introducing was in the warp-frame, when, by means of an ingenious apparatus, he succeeded in producing "mitts" of a lacey appearance; and it was this success which determined him to pursue the study of mechanical lace-making.

When a little over twenty-one years of age Heathcoat married, and went to Nottingham in search of work. He there found employment as a smith and "setter-up" of hosiery and warp-frames. He also continued to pursue the subject on which his mind had before been occupied. It was a long and laborious task, requiring the exercise of great perseverance and no little ingenuity. His master, Elliott, described him at that time as plodding, patient, self-denying, and taciturn, undaunted by failures and mistakes, full of resources and expedients, and entertaining the most perfect confidence that his application of mechanical principles would eventually be crowned with success. During this time his wife was kept in almost as great anxiety as himself. She well knew of his struggles and difficulties, and she began to feel the pressure of poverty on her household; for, while he was laboring at his invention, he was frequently under the necessity of laying aside the work that brought in the weekly wages.

Many years after, when all difficulties had been successfully overcome, the conversation which took place between husband and wife one eventful Saturday evening was vividly remembered. "Well, John," said the anxious wife, looking in her husband's face, "will it work?" "No, Anne," was the sad answer, "I have had to take it all in pieces again." Though he could still speak hopefully and cheerfully, his poor wife could restrain her feelings no longer, but sat down and cried bitterly. She had, however, only a few more weeks to wait; for success, long labored for and richly deserved, came at last; and a proud and happy man was John Heathcoat when he brought home the first narrow strip of bobbin net made by his machine, and placed it in the hands of his wife.

It is difficult to describe in words an invention so complicated as the bobbin-net machine. It was indeed a mechanical pillow for making lace; imitating in an ingenious manner the motions of the lace-maker's fingers in intersecting or tying the meshes of the lace upon her pillow. Long after, he said: "The single difficulty of getting the diagonal threads to twist in the allotted space was so great, that if it had now to be done, I should probably not attempt its accomplishment." At the age of twenty-four he was enabled to secure his invention by a patent.

As in the case of nearly all inventions which have proved productive, Heathcoat's rights as a patentee were disputed, and his claims as an inventor called in question. On the supposed invalidity of the patent, the lace-makers boldly adopted the bobbin-net machine, and set the inventor at defiance. But other patents were taken out for alleged improvements and adaptations; and it was only when these new patentees fell out and went to law with each other that Heathcoat's rights became established. One lace manufacturer having brought an action against another for an alleged infringement of his patent, the jury brought in a verdict for the defendant, in which the judge concurred, on the ground that *both* the machines in question were infringements of Heathcoat's patent.

After the trial was over, Mr. Heathcoat, on inquiry, found about six hundred machines at work after his patent, and he proceeded to levy royalty upon the owners of them, which amounted to a large sum. But the profits realized by the manufacturers of lace were very great, and the use of the machines rapidly extended, while the price of the article was reduced from five pounds the square yard to about five pence in the course of twenty-five years. During the same period the average annual returns of the lace trade have been at least four millions sterling, and it gives remunerative employment to about 150,000 workpeople.

In 1809 we find him established as a lace manufacturer at Loughborough, in Leicestershire. There he carried on a prosperous business, giving employment to a large number of operatives, at wages varying from $25 to $50 a week.

Not only did he carry on the manufacture of lace, but the various branches of business connected with it, yarn doubling, silk spinning, net making and finishing. He also established an iron-foundry and works for the manufacture of agricultural implements, which proved of great convenience to the district, It was a favorite idea of his that steam power was capable of being applied to perform all the heavy drudgery of life, and he labored for a long time at the invention of a steam plough. In 1832 he so far completed his invention as to be enabled to take out a patent for it, and Heathcoat's steam plough, though it has since been superseded by Fowler's, was considered the best machine of the kind that had up to that time been invented.

Mr. Heathcoat was a man of great natural gifts. He possessed a sound understanding, quick perception, and a genius for business of the highest order. With these he combined uprightness, honesty and integrity—qualities which are the true glory of human character. Himself a diligent self-educator, he gave ready encouragement to deserving youths in his employment, stimulating their talents and fostering their energies. During his own busy life, he contrived to save time to master French and Italian, of which he acquired an accurate and grammatical knowledge. His mind was largely stored with the results of a careful study of the best literature, and there was few subjects on which he had not formed for himself shrewd and accurate views. The two thousand workpeople in his employment regarded him almost as a father, and he carefully provided for their comfort and improvement. Prosperity did not spoil him, as it does so many, nor close his heart against the claims of the poor and struggling, who were always sure of his sympathy and help. To provide for the education of the children of his work-people, he built schools for them at the cost of about $30,000. He was also a man of singularly cheerful and buoyant disposition, a favorite with men of all classes, and most admired and beloved by those who knew him best.

In 1831 the electors of Tiverton, of which town Mr. Heathcoat had proved himself so genuine a benefactor, returned him to represent them in Parliament, and he continued their member for nearly thirty years. During a great part of that time he had Lord Palmerston for his colleague, and the noble lord, on more than one public occasion, expressed the high regard which he entertained for his venerable friend. On retiring from the representation in 1859, thirteen hundred of his workmen presented him with a silver inkstand and gold pen, in token of their esteem. He enjoyed his leisure for only two more years, dying in January, 1861, at the age of seventy-seven, and leaving behind him a character for probity, virtue, manliness and mechanical genius, of which his descendants may well be proud.

Chapter 9

Application and Perseverance

"Our greatest glory is not in never falling, but in rising every time we fall."
—*Confucius.*

"Learn as if you were to live forever; live as if you were to die tomorrow."
—*Ansalus De Insulis.*

THE GREATEST RESULTS in life are usually attained by simple means, and the exercise of ordinary qualities. The common life of every day, with its cares, necessities and duties, affords ample opportunity for acquiring experience of the best kind, and its most beaten paths provide the true worker with abundant scope for effort and room for self-improvement. The road of human welfare lies along the old highway of steadfast well-doing; and they who are the most persistent, and work in the truest spirit, will usually be the most successful.

Fortune has often been blamed for her blindness; but fortune is not so blind as men are. Those who look into practical life will find that fortune is usually on the side of the industrious, as the winds and waves are on the side of the best navigators. In the pursuit of even the highest branches of human inquiry, the commoner qualities are found the most useful—such as common sense, attention, application and perseverance.

Genius may not be necessary, though even genius of the highest sort does not disdain the use of these ordinary qualities. The very greatest men have been among the least believers in the power of genius, and as worldly wise and persevering as successful men of the commoner sort. Some have even defined genius to be only common sense intensified. A distinguished teacher and president of a college spoke of it as the power of making efforts. John Foster held it to be the power of lighting one's own fire, Buffon said of genius, "it is patience."

Newton's was unquestionably a mind of the very-highest order, and yet, when asked by what means he had worked out his extraordinary discoveries, he modestly answered, "by always thinking unto them." At another time he thus expressed his method of study: "I keep the subject continually before me, and wait till the first dawnings open slowly by little and little into a full and clear light." It was in Newton's case as in every other, only by diligent application and perseverance that his great reputation was achieved. Even his recreation consisted in change of study, laying down one subject to take up another. To Dr. Bentley he said: "If I have done the public any service, it is due to nothing but industry and patient thought."

When the late President Garfield began the study of finance, he discovered that many of the best books upon that subject were written in the French language. He immediately set himself at work to learn it, and amid his diversified duties, soon found time to so far conquer this language as to be able to both read and speak it well.

Dalton, the chemist, repudiated the notion of his being "a genius," attributing everything which he had accomplished to simple industry and accumulation. John Hunter said of himself, "My mind is like a beehive; but full as it is of buzz and apparent confusion, it is yet full of order and regularity, and food collected with incessant industry from the choicest stores of nature." We have, indeed, but to glance at the biographies of great men to find that the most distinguished inventors, artists, thinkers and workers of all kinds, owe their success, in a great measure, to their patient industry and application. They were men who turned all things to gold—even time itself. Disraeli, the elder, held that the secret of success consisted in being master of your subject, such mastery being attainable only through continuous application and study. Hence it happens that the men who have most moved the world, have not been so much men of genius, strictly so called, as men of intense mediocre abilities, and untiring perseverance; not so often the gifted, of naturally bright and shining qualities, as those who have applied themselves diligently to their work, in whatsoever line that might lie.

Hence, a great point to be aimed at is to get the working quality well trained. When that is done, the race will be found comparatively easy. We must repeat and again repeat, facility will come with labor. Not even the simplest art can be accomplished without it, and what difficulties it is found capable of achieving! It was by early discipline and repetition that the late Sir Robert Peel cultivated those remarkable, though still mediocre powers, which rendered him so illustrious an ornament of the British Senate. When a boy at Drayton Manor, his father was accustomed to set him up at table to practice speaking extempore, and he early accustomed him to repeat as much of the Sunday's sermon as he could remember. Little progress was

Application and Perseverance

made at first, but by steady perseverance the habit of attention became powerful, and the sermon was at length repeated almost verbatim. When afterwards replying in succession to the arguments of his parliamentary opponents—an art in which he was perhaps unrivalled—it was little surmised that the extraordinary power of accurate remembrance which he displayed on such occasions, had been originally trained under the discipline of his father in the parish church of Drayton.

Progress, however, of the best kind, is comparatively slow. Great results can not be achieved at once; and we must be satisfied to advance in life as we walk, step by step. De Maistre says that "To know *how to wait* is the great secret of success." We must sow before we can reap, and often have to wait long, content meanwhile to look patiently forward in hope; the fruit best worth waiting for often ripening the slowest. But "Time and patience," says the Eastern proverb, "change the mulberry leaf to satin."

To wait patiently, however, men must work cheerfully. Cheerfulness is an excellent working quality, imparting great elasticity to the character. As a bishop has said, "Temper is nine-tenths of Christianity"; so are cheerfulness and diligence nine-tenths of practical wisdom. They are the life and soul of success, as well as of happiness; perhaps the very highest pleasure in life consisting in clear, brisk, conscious working; energy, confidence, and every other good quality mainly depending upon it. Sydney Smith, when laboring as a parish priest at Foston-le-Clay, in Yorkshire—though he did not feel himself to be in his proper clement—went cheerfully to work in the firm determination to do his best. "I am resolved," he said, "to like it, and reconcile myself to it, which is more manly than to feign myself above it, and to send up complaints by the post, of being thrown away, and being desolate, and such like trash." So Dr. Hook, when leaving Leeds for a new sphere of labor, said, "Wherever I may be, I shall, by God's blessing, do with my might what my hand findeth to do; and, if I do not find work, I shall make it."

It was a maxim of Dr. Young, the philosopher, that "Any man can do what any other man has done"; and it is unquestionable that he himself never recoiled from any trials to which he determined to subject himself. It is related of him that the first time he mounted a horse he was in company with the grandson of Mr. Barclay, of Ury, the well-known sportsman, when the horseman who preceded them leaped a high fence. Young wished to imitate him, but fell off his horse in the attempt. Without saying a word he remounted, made a second effort, and was again unsuccessful, but this time was not thrown further off than on to the horse's neck, to which he clung. At the third trial he succeeded, and cleared the fence. The story of Timour the Tartar learning a lesson of perseverance under adversity from the spider is well known. Not less interesting is the anecdote of Audubon, the American ornithologist, as related by himself: "An accident," he says, "which happened to two hundred of my original drawings, nearly put a stop to my researches in ornithology. I shall relate it, merely to show how far enthusiasm—for by no other name can I call my perseverance—may enable the preserver of nature to surmount the most disheartening difficulties. I left the village of Henderson, in Kentucky, situated on the banks of the Ohio, where I resided for several years, to proceed to Philadelphia on business. I looked to my drawings before my departure, placed them carefully in a wooden box, and gave them in charge of a relative, with injunctions to see that no injury should happen to them. My absence was of several months, and when I returned, after having enjoyed the pleasures of home for a few days, I inquired after my box, and what I was pleased to call my treasure. The box was produced and opened; but, reader, feel for me—a pair of Norway rats had taken possession of the whole, and reared a young family among the gnawed bits of paper, which, but a month previous, represented nearly a thousand inhabitants of air! The burning heat which instantly rushed through my brain was too great to be endured without affecting my whole nervous system. I slept for several nights, and the days passed like days of oblivion—until the animal powers being recalled into action, through the strength of my constitution, I took up my gun, my note-book and my pencils, and went forth to the woods as gaily as if nothing had happened. I felt pleased that I might now make better drawings than before; and, ere a period not exceeding three years had elapsed, my portfolio was again filled."

The accidental destruction of Sir Isaac Newton's papers, by his little dog "Diamond" upsetting a lighted taper upon his desk, by which the elaborate calculations of many years were in a moment destroyed, is a well-known anecdote, and need not be repeated: it is said that the loss caused the philosopher such profound grief that it seriously injured his health, and impaired his understanding. An accident of a somewhat similar kind happened to the manuscript of Mr. Carlyle's first volume of his "French Revolution." He had lent the manuscript to a literary neighbor to peruse. By some mischance it had been left lying on the parlor floor, and become forgotten. Weeks ran on, and the historian sent for his work, the printers being loud for "copy." Inquiries were made, and it was found that the maid-of-all-work, finding what she conceived to be a bundle of waste paper on the floor, had used it to light the kitchen and parlor fires! Such was the answer returned to Mr. Carlyle, and his feelings may be imagined. There was, however, no help for him but to set resolutely to work to re-write the book, and he turned to and did it. He had no draft, and was compelled to rake up from his memory, facts, ideas, and expressions which had been long since dismissed. The composition of the book in the first instance had been a work of pleasure; the writing of it a second time was one of pain and anguish almost beyond belief. That he persevered and finished the volume under such circumstances, affords an instance of determination of purpose which has seldom been surpassed.

The lives of eminent inventors are eminently illustrative of the same quality of perseverance. George Stephenson, when addressing young men, was accustomed to sum up his best advice to them in the words, "Do as I have done—persevere." He had worked at the improvement of his locomotive for some fifteen years before achieving his decisive victory at Rainhill; and Watt was engaged for some thirty years upon the condensing-engine before he brought it to perfection. But there are equally striking illustrations of perseverance to be found in every other branch of science, art, and industry. Perhaps one of the most interesting is that connected with the disentombment of the Nineveh marbles, and the discovery of the long lost cuneiform or arrow-headed character in which the inscriptions on them are written—a kind of writing which had been lost to the world since the period of the Macedonian conquest of Persia.

An intelligent cadet of the East India Company, stationed at Kermanshah, in Persia, had observed the curious cuneiform inscriptions on the old monuments in the neighborhood—so old that all historical traces of them had been lost—and amongst the inscriptions which he copied was that on the celebrated rock of Behistun—a perpendicular rock rising abruptly some 1700 feet from the plain, the lower part bearing inscriptions for the space of about 300 feet in three languages—Persian, Scythian, and Assyrian. Comparison of the known with the unknown, of the language which survived with the language that had been lost, enabled this cadet to acquire some knowledge of the cuneiform character, and even to form an alphabet. Mr. Rawlinson sent his tracings home for examination. No professors in colleges as yet knew anything of the cuneiform character; but there was a clerk of the East India House—a modest unknown man by the name of Norris—who had made this little-understood subject his study, to whom the tracings were submitted; and so accurate was his knowledge, that, though he had never seen the Behistun rock, he pronounced that the cadet had not copied the puzzling inscription with proper exactness. Rawlinson, who was still in the neighborhood of the rock, compared his copy with the original, and found that Norris was right; and, by further comparison and careful study the knowledge of the cuneiform writing was thus greatly advanced.

But to make the learning of these two self-taught men of avail, a third laborer was necessary, in order to supply them with material for the exercise of their skill. Such a laborer presented himself in the person of Austen

Layard, originally an articled clerk in the office of a London solicitor. One would scarcely have expected to find in these three men, a cadet, an India-House clerk, and a lawyer's clerk, the discoverers of a forgotten language, and of the buried history of Babylon; yet it was so. Layard was a youth of only twenty-two, traveling in the East, when he was possessed with a desire to penetrate the regions beyond the Euphrates. Accompanied by a single companion, trusting to his arms for protection, and what was better, to his cheerfulness, politeness, and chivalrous bearing, he passed safely amidst tribes at deadly war with each other; and, after the lapse of many years, with comparatively slender means at his command, but aided by application and perseverance, resolute will and purpose, and almost sublime patience—borne up throughout by his passionate enthusiasm for discovery and research—he succeeded in laying bare and digging up an amount of historical treasures, the like of which has probably never before been collected by the industry of any one man. Not less than two miles of bas-reliefs were thus brought to light by Mr. Layard. The selection of these valuable antiquities, now placed in the British Museum, was found so curiously corroborative of the scriptural records of events which occurred some three thousand years ago, that they burst upon the world almost like a new revelation. And the story of the disentombment of these remarkable works, as told by Mr. Layard himself, in his "Monuments of Nineveh," will always be regarded as one of the most charming and unaffected records which we possess of individual enterprise, industry, and energy.

The career of the Comte de Buffon presents another remarkable illustration of the power of patient industry, as well as of his own saying, that "Genius is patience." Notwithstanding the great results achieved by him in natural history, Buffon, when a youth, was regarded as of mediocre talents. His mind was slow in forming itself, and slow in reproducing what it had acquired. He was also constitutionally indolent; and, being born to good estate, it might be supposed that he would indulge his liking for ease and luxury. Instead of which, he early formed the resolution of denying himself pleasure, and devoting himself to study and self-culture. Regarding time as a treasure that was limited, and finding that he was losing many hours by lying abed in the mornings, he determined to break himself of the habit. He struggled hard against it for some time, but failed in being able to rise at the hour he had fixed. He then called his servant, Joseph, to his help, and promised him the reward of a crown every time he succeeded in getting him up before six. At first, when called, Buffon declined to rise—pleaded that he was ill, or pretended anger at being disturbed; and on the Count at length getting up, Joseph found that he had earned nothing but reproaches for having permitted his master to lay abed contrary to his express orders. At length the valet determined to earn his crown; and again and again he forced Buffon to rise, notwithstanding his entreaties, expostulations, and threats of immediate discharge from his service. One morning Buffon was unusually obstinate, and Joseph found it necessary to resort to the extreme measure of dashing a basin of ice-cold water under the bed-clothes, the effect of which was instantaneous. By the persistent use of such means, Buffon at length conquered his habit; and he was accustomed to say, that he owed to Joseph three or four volumes of his Natural History.

For forty years of his life, Buffon worked every morning at his desk from nine till two, and again in the evening from five till nine. His diligence was so continuous and so regular that it became habitual. His biographer has said of him, "Work was his necessity; his studies were the charm of his life; and towards the last years of his glorious career he frequently said that he still hoped to be able to consecrate to them a few more years." He was a most conscientious worker, always studying to give the reader his best thoughts, expressed in the very best manner. He was never wearied with touching and retouching his compositions, so that his style may be pronounced almost perfect. He wrote the "Époques de la Nature" not fewer than eleven times before he was satisfied with it; although he had thought over the work about fifty years. He was a thorough man of business, most orderly in every thing; and he was accustomed to say that genius without order lost three-fourths of its power. His great success as a writer was the result mainly of his painstaking labor and diligent application. "Buffon," observed Madame Necker, "strongly persuaded that genius is the result of a profound attention directed to a particular subject, said that he was thoroughly wearied out when composing his first writings, but compelled himself to return to them and go over them carefully again, even when he thought he had already brought them to a certain degree of perfection; and that at length he found pleasure instead of weariness in this long and elaborate correction." It ought also to be added that Buffon wrote and published all his great works while afflicted by one of the most painful diseases to which the human frame is subject.

True wisdom and humility are such that the more a man really knows, the less conceited he is. The student at Trinity College who went up to his professor to take leave of him because he had "finished his education," was wisely rebuked by the professor's reply, "Indeed! I am only beginning mine." The superficial person, who has obtained a smattering of many things but knows nothing well, may pride himself upon his gifts; but the sage humbly confesses that "all he knows is, that he knows nothing," or, like Newton, that he has been only engaged in picking shells by the sea-shore while the great ocean of truth lies all unexplored before him

Loudon, the landscape gardener, was a man of extraordinary working power. The son of a farmer near Edinburgh, he was early inured to work. His skill in drawing plans and making sketches of scenery induced his father to train him for a landscape gardener. During his apprenticeship he sat up two whole nights every week to study; yet he worked harder during the day than any laborer. In the course of his night studies he learnt French, and before he was eighteen he translated a life of Abelard for an Encyclopedia. He was so eager to make progress in life, That when only twenty, while working as a gardener in England, he wrote down in his notebook, "I am now twenty years of age, and perhaps a third part of my life has passed away, and yet what have I done to benefit my fellow-men?" an unusual reflection for a youth of only twenty. From French he proceeded to learn German, and rapidly mastered that language. Having taken a large farm, for the purpose of introducing Scotch improvements in the art of agriculture, he shortly succeeded in realizing a considerable income. The continent being thrown open at the end of the war, he traveled abroad for the purpose of inquiring into the system of gardening and agriculture in other countries. He twice repeated his journeys, and the results were published in his Encyclopaedias, which are among the most remarkable works of their kind—distinguished for the immense mass of useful matter which they contain, collected by an amount of industry and labor which has rarely been equalled.

The career of Samuel Drew is not less remarkable than any of those which we have cited. His father was a hard-working laborer of Cornwall. Though poor, he contrived to send his two sons to a penny-a-week school. Jabez, the elder, took delight in learning, and made great progress in his lessons; but Samuel, the younger, was a dunce, notoriously given to mischief and playing truant. When he was eight years old he was put to manual labor, earning three halfpence a day. At ten he was apprenticed to a shoemaker, and while in this employment he endured much hardship—living, as he used to say, "like a toad under a harrow." He often thought of running away and becoming a pirate, or something of the sort, and he seems to have grown in recklessness as he grew in years. In robbing orchards, he was usually a leader; and, as he grew older, he delighted to take part in any poaching or smuggling adventure. When about seventeen, before his apprenticeship was out, he ran away, intending to enter on board a man-of-war; but, sleeping in a hay-field at night cooled him a little, and he returned to his trade.

Drew next removed to the neighborhood of Plymouth to work at the shoemaking business. While there, he had nearly lost his life in a smuggling exploit which he had joined, partly induced by the love of adventure, and partly by the love of gain, for his regular wages were not more than eight shillings a week. One night, notice was given throughout Crafthole, that a smuggler was off the coast, ready to land her cargo; on which the male population of the place—nearly all smugglers—made for the shore. One party remained on the rocks to make signals and dispose of the goods as they were landed; and another manned the boats, Drew being of the latter party. The night was intensely dark, and very little of the cargo had been landed, when the wind rose, with a heavy sea. The men in the boats, however, determined to persevere, and several trips were made between the smuggler, now standing farther out to sea, and the shore. One of the men in the boat in which Drew was, had his hat blown off by the wind, and in attempting to recover it, the boat was upset. Three of the men were immediately drowned; the others clung to the boat for a time, but finding it drifting out to sea, they took to swimming. They were two miles from land, and the night was intensely dark. After being about three hours in the water, Drew reached a rock near the shore, with one or two others, where he remained benumbed with cold till morning, when he and his companions were discovered and taken off, more dead than alive. This was a very unpromising beginning of a life; and yet this same Drew, scapegrace, orchard-robber, shoemaker and smuggler, outlived the recklessness of his youth, and became distinguished as a minister of the Gospel and a writer of good books. Happily, before it was too late, the energy which characterized him was turned into a more healthy direction, and rendered him as eminent in usefulness as he had been before in wickedness. His father again took him back and found employment for him as a journeyman shoemaker. Perhaps his recent escape from death had tended to make the young man serious, as we shortly find him, attracted by the forcible preaching of Dr. Adam Clarke. His brother having died about the same time, the impression of seriousness was deepened; and thenceforward he was an altered man. He began anew the work of education, for he had almost forgotten how to read and write; and even after several years' practice, a friend compared his writing to the traces of a spider dipped in ink set to crawl upon paper. Speaking of himself, about that time, Drew afterwards said, "The more I read, the more I felt my own ignorance; and the more I felt my ignorance, the more invincible became my energy to surmount it. Every leisure moment was now employed in reading one thing or another. Having to support myself by manual labor, my time for reading was but little, and to overcome this disadvantage, my usual method was to place a book before me while at meat, and at every repast I read five or six pages." The perusal of Locke's "Essay on the Understanding" gave the first metaphysical turn to his mind. "It awakened me from my stupor," said he, "and induced me to form a resolution to abandon the groveling views which I had been accustomed to entertain."

Drew began business on his own account, with a capital of a few shillings; but his character for steadiness was such that a neighboring miller offered him a loan, which was accepted, and, success attending his industry, the debt was repaid at the end of a year. He started with a determination to "owe no man any thing," and he held to it in the midst of many privations. Often he went to bed supperless, to avoid rising in debt. His ambition was to achieve independence by industry and economy, and in this he gradually succeeded. In the midst of incessant labor, he sedulously strove to improve his mind, studying astronomy, history, and metaphysics. He was induced to pursue the latter study chiefly because it required fewer books to consult than either of the others. "It appeared to be a thorny path," he said, "but I determined, nevertheless, to enter, and accordingly began to read it."

Added to his labors in shoemaking and metaphysics, Drew became a local preacher and a class-leader. He took an eager interest in politics, and his shop became a favorite resort with the village politicians. And when they did not come to him, he went to them to talk over public affairs. This so encroached upon his time that he found it necessary sometimes to work until midnight to make up for the hours lost during the day. His political fervor became the talk of the village. While busy one night hammering away at a shoe-sole, a little boy, seeing a light in the shop, put his mouth to the keyhole of the door, and called out in a shrill pipe, "Shoemaker! shoemaker! work by night and run about by day!" A friend, to whom Drew afterwards told the story, asked, "And did not you run after the boy and strap him?" "No, no," was the reply; "had a pistol been fired off at my ear, I could not have been more dismayed or confounded. I dropped my work, and said to myself 'True, true! but you shall never have that to say of me again.' To me that cry was as the voice of God, and it has been a word in season throughout my life. I learnt from it not to leave till tomorrow the work of today, or to idle when I ought to be working."

From that moment Drew dropped politics, and stuck to his work, reading and studying in his spare hours; but he never allowed the latter pursuit to interfere with his business, though it frequently broke in upon his rest. He married, and thought of emigrating to America; but he remained working on. His literary taste first took the direction of poetical composition; and from some of the fragments which have been preserved, it appears that his speculations as to the immateriality and immortality of the soul had their origin in these poetical musings. His study was the kitchen, where his wife's bellows served him for a desk; and he wrote amidst the cries and cradlings of his children. Paine's "Age of Reason" having appeared about this time and excited much interest, he composed a pamphlet in refutation of its arguments, which was published. He used afterwards to say that it was the

"Age of Reason" that made him an author. Various pamphlets from his pen shortly appeared in rapid succession, and a few years later, while still working at shoemaking, he wrote and published his admirable "Essay on the Immateriality and Immortality of the Human Soul," which he sold for twenty pounds, a great sum in his estimation at the time. The book went through many editions, and is still prized.

Drew was in no wise puffed up by his success, as many young authors are, but, long after he had become celebrated as a writer, used to be seen sweeping the street before his door, or helping his apprentices to carry in the winter's coals. Nor could he, for some time, bring himself to regard literature as a profession to live by. His first care was to secure an honest livelihood by his business, and to put into the "lottery of literary success," as he termed it, only the surplus of his time. At length, however, he devoted himself wholly to literature, more particularly in connection with the Wesleyan body; editing one of their magazines, and superintending the publication of several of their denominational works. He also wrote in the "Eclectic Review," and compiled and published a valuable history of his native county, Cornwall, with numerous other works. Towards the close of his career he said of himself: "Raised from one of the lowest stations in society, I have endeavored through life to bring my family into a state of Respectability, by honest industry, frugality, and a high regard for my moral character. Divine providence has smiled on my exertions, and crowned my wishes with success."

Chapter 10

Helps and Opportunities—Scientific Pursuits

"Opportunity has hair in front, behind she is bald; if you seize her by the forelock you may hold her, but, if suffered to escape, not Jupiter himself can catch her again." —From the Latin.

ACCIDENT DOES VERY LITTLE towards the production of any great result in life. Though sometimes what is called "a happy hit" may be made by a bold venture, the common highway of steady industry and application is the only safe road to travel. It is said of the landscape painter Wilson, that when he had nearly finished a picture in a tame, correct manner, he would step back from it, his pencil fixed at the end of a long stick, and after gazing earnestly on the work, he would suddenly walk up and by a few bold touches give a brilliant finish to the painting. But it will not do for everyone who would produce an effect, to throw his brush at the canvas in the hope of producing a picture. The capability of putting in these last vital touches is acquired only by the labor of a life; and the probability is, that the artist who has not carefully trained himself beforehand, in attempting to produce a brilliant effect at a dash, will only produce a blotch.

Sedulous attention and painstaking industry always mark the true worker. The greatest men are not those who "despise the day of small things," but those who improve them the most carefully. Michael Angelo was one day explaining to a visitor to his studio what he had been doing at a statue since his previous visit. "I have retouched this part—polished that—softened this feature—brought out that muscle—given some expression to this lip, and more energy to that limb." "But these are trifles," remarked the visitor. "It may be so," replied the sculptor, "but recollect that trifles make perfection, and perfection is no trifle." So it was said of Nicolas Poussin, the painter, that the rule of his conduct was, that "whatever was worth doing at all was worth doing well"; and when asked, late in life, by a friend, by what means he had gained so high a reputation among the painters of Italy, Poussin emphatically answered, "Because I have neglected nothing."

Although there are discoveries which are said to have been made by accident, if carefully inquired into, it will be found that there has really been very little that was accidental about them. For the most part these so-called accidents have only been opportunities, carefully improved by genius. The fall of the apple at Newton's feet has often been quoted in proof of the accidental character of some discoveries. But Newton's whole mind had already been devoted for years to the laborious and patient investigation of the subject of gravitation; and the circumstances of the apple falling before his eyes was suddenly apprehended only as genius could apprehend it, and served to flash upon him the brilliant discovery then opening to his sight. In like manner, the brilliantly-colored soap-bubbles blown from a common tobacco-pipe—though "trifles light as air" in most eyes—suggested to Dr. Young his beautiful theory of "interferences," and led to his discovery relating to the diffraction of light. Although great men are popularly supposed only to deal with great things, men such as Newton and Young were ready to detect the significance of the most familiar and simple facts; their greatness consisting mainly in their wise interpretation of them.

The difference between men consists, in a great measure, in the intelligence of their observation. The Russian proverb says of the non-observant man, "He goes through the forest and sees no firewood." "The wise man's eyes are in his head," says Solomon, "but the fool walketh in darkness." "Sir," said Johnson, on one occasion, to a fine gentleman just returned from Italy, "some men will learn more in the Hampstead stage than others in the tour of Europe." It is the mind that sees as well as the eye. Where unthinking gazers observe nothing, men of intelligent vision penetrate into the very fibre of the phenomena presented to them, attentively noting differences, making comparisons, and recognizing their underlying idea. Many before Galileo had seen a suspended weight swing before their eyes with a measured beat; but he was the first to detect the value of the fact. One of the vergers in the cathedral at Pisa, after replenishing with oil a lamp which hung from the roof, left it swing to and fro; and Galileo, then a youth of only eighteen, noting it attentively, conceived the idea of applying it to the measurement of time. Fifty years of study and labor, however, elapsed, before he completed the invention of his Pendulum—the importance of which, in the measurement of time and in astronomical calculations, can scarcely be overrated. In like manner, Galileo, having casually heard that a Dutch spectacle-maker had presented to Count Maurice an instrument by means of which distant objects appeared nearer to the beholder, addressed himself to the cause of such a phenomenon, which led to the invention of the telescope, and proved the beginning of the modern science of astronomy. Discoveries such as these could never have been made by a negligent observer, or by a mere passive listener.

While Captain Brown was occupied in studying the construction of bridges, with a view of contriving one of a cheap description to be thrown across the Tweed, near which he lived, he was walking in his garden one dewy autumn morning, when he saw a tiny spider's net suspended across his path. The idea immediately occurred to him that a bridge of iron ropes or chains might be constructed in like manner, and the result was the invention of his Suspension Bridge. Sir James Watt when consulted about the mode of carrying water by pipes under the Clyde, along the unequal bed of the river, turned his attention one day to the shell of a lobster presented at table; and from that model he invented an iron tube, which, when laid down, was found effectually to answer the purpose. Sir Isambert Brunel took his first lessons in forming the Thames Tunnel It is the intelligent eye of the careful observer which gives these apparently trivial phenomena their value. So trifling a matter as the sight of seaweed floating past his ship enabled Columbus to quell the mutiny which arose amongst his sailors at not discovering land, and to assure them that the eagerly sought New World was not far off. There is nothing so small that it should remain forgotten; and no fact, however trivial, but may prove useful in some way or other if carefully interpreted. Who could have imagined that the famous "chalk cliffs of Albion" had been built up by tiny insects—detected only by the help of the microscope—of the same order of creatures that have gemmed the sea with islands of coral! And who that contemplates such extraordinary results, arising from infinitely minute operations will venture to question the power of little things?

It is the close observation of little things which is the secret of success in business, in art, in science, and in every pursuit of life. Human knowledge is but an accumulation of small facts, made by successive generations of men, the little bits of knowledge and experience carefully treasured up by them growing at length into a mighty pyramid. Though many of these facts and observations seemed in the first instance to have but slight significance, they are all found to have their eventual uses, and to fit into their proper places. Even many speculations seemingly remote, turn out to be the basis of results the most obviously practical. In the case of the conic sections discovered by Apollonius Pergazus, twenty centuries elapsed before they were made the basis of astronomy—a science which enables the modern navigator to steer his way through unknown seas and traces for him in the heavens an unerring path to his appointed haven. And had not mathematicians toiled for so long, and, to uninstructed observers, apparently so fruitlessly, over the abstract relations of lines and surfaces, it is probable that but few of our mechanical inventions would have seen the light.

The secret of Garfield's great success in life, of his culture, of his learning, and of his growth in statesmanship was disclosed in a brief speech to the students of Hiram College, delivered many years ago. He said: "I was thinking, young ladies and gentlemen, as I sat here this morning, that life is almost wholly made up of margins. The bulk itself of almost anything is not what tells. That exists anyway. That is expected. That is not what gives the profit or makes the distinguishing difference. The grocer cares little for the great bulk of the price of his tea. It is the few cents between the cost and selling price, which he calls the margin, that particularly interests him. Is this to be great or small? is the thing of importance. Millions of dollars change hands in our great marts of trade just on the question of margins. This same thing is all-important in the subject of thought. One mind is not greater than another, perhaps, in the great bulk of its contents; but its margin is greater, that's all. I may know just as much as you do about the general details of a subject, but you can go just a little further than I can. You have a greater margin than I. You can tell me of some single thought just beyond where I have gone. Your margin has got me. I must succumb to your superiority."

A good way to carry out the same idea, and better illustrate it, is by globes. Did you ever see two globes whose only difference was, that one had half an inch larger diameter than the other? The larger one, although there is so little difference, will entirely enclose the other, and have a quarter of an inch in every direction to spare besides. Let those globes be minds, with a living principle of some kind at their centres, which throws out its little tentacle-like arms in every direction as if to explore for knowledge. The one goes a certain distance and stops. It can reach no farther. It has come to a standstill. It has reached its maximum of knowledge in that direction. The other sends its arms out, and can reach just a quarter of an inch farther. So far as the first mind is able to tell, the other has gone infinitely farther than it can reach. It goes out to its farthest limit and must stop; the other tells him things he did not know before. Many minds you may consider wonderful in their capacity. They may be able to go only a quarter of an inch beyond you. What an incentive this should be for any young man to work, to make his margin as great as, if not greater than, the margin of his fellows!

I recall a good illustration of this when I was in college. A certain young man was leading the class in Latin. I thought I was studying hard. I couldn't see how he got the start of us all so. To us he seemed to have an infinite knowledge. He knew more than we did. Finally, one day I asked him when he learned his Latin lesson. "At night," he replied. I learned mine at the same time. His window was not far from mine, and I could see him from my own. I had finished my lesson the next night as well as usual, and, feeling sleepy, was about to go to bed. I happened to saunter to my window, and there I saw my classmate still bending diligently over his book. "There's where he gets the margin on me," I thought. "But he shall not have it for once," I resolved. "I will study just a little longer than he does tonight." So I took down my books again, and, opening to the lesson, went to work with renewed vigor. I watched for the light to go out in my classmate's room. In fifteen minutes it was all dark. "There is his margin," I thought. It was fifteen minutes more time. It was hunting out fifteen minutes more of rules and root-derivatives. How often, when a lesson is well prepared, just five minutes spent in perfecting it will make one the best in the class. The margin in such a case as that is very small, but it is all-important. The world is made up of little things.

When Franklin made his discovery of the identity of lightning and electricity, it was sneered at, and people asked, "Of what use is it?" To which his reply was, "What is the use of a child? It may become a man!" When Galvani discovered that a frog's leg twitched when placed in contact with different metals, it could scarcely have been imagined that so apparently insignificant a fact could have led to important results. Yet therein lay the germ of the Electric Telegraph, which binds the intelligence of continents together, and, probably before many years have elapsed will "put a girdle round the globe." So, too, little bits of stone and fossil, dug out of the earth, intelligently interpreted, has issued in the science of geology and the practical operations of mining, in which large capitals are invested and vast numbers of persons profitably employed.

The gigantic machinery employed in pumping our mines, working our mills and manufactures, and driving our steamships and locomotives, in like manner depends for its supply of power upon so slight an agency as little drops of water expanded by heat—that familiar agency called steam, which we see issuing from that common tea-kettle spout, but which, when pent up within an ingeniously contrived mechanism, displays a force equal to that of millions of horses, and contains a power to rebuke the waves and set even the hurricane at defiance. The same power at work within the bowels of the earth has been the cause of those volcanoes and earthquakes which have played so mighty a part in the history of the globe.

It is said that the Marquis of Worcester's attention was first accidently directed to the subject of steam power by the tight cover of a vessel containing hot water having been blown off before his eyes, when confined a prisoner in the Tower. He published the result of his observations in his "Century of Inventions," which formed a sort of text-book for inquiries into the powers of steam for a time, until Savary, Newcomen, and others, applying it to practical purposes, brought the steam-engine to the state in which Watt found it when called upon to repair a model of Newcomen's engine, which belonged to the University of Glasgow. This accidental circumstance was an opportunity for Watt, which he was not slow to improve; and it was the labor of his life to bring the steam-engine to perfection.

This art of seizing opportunities and turning even accidents to accounts, bending them to some purpose, is a great secret of success. Dr. Johnson has defined genius to be "a mind of large general powers accidentally determined in some particular direction." Men who are resolved to find a way for themselves, will always find opportunities enough; and if they do not lie ready to their hand, they will make them. It is not those who have enjoyed the advantages of colleges, museums, and public galleries, that have accomplished the most for science and art; nor have the greatest mechanics and inventors been trained in mechanics' institutes. Necessity, oftener than facility, has been the mother of invention; and the most prolific school of all has been the school of difficulty. Some of the very best workmen have had the most indifferent tools to work with. But it is not tools that make the workman, but the trained skill and perseverance of the man himself. Indeed it is proverbial that the bad workman never yet had a good tool. Some one asked Opie by what wonderful process he mixed his colors. "I mix them with *my* brains, sir," was his reply. It is the same with every workman who would excel. Ferguson made marvellous things—such as his wooden clock, that accurately measured the hours—by means of a common penknife, a tool in everybody's hand; but then everybody is not a Ferguson. A pan of water and two thermometers were the tools by which Dr. Black discovered latent heat; and a prism, a lens, and a sheet of pasteboard enabled Newton to unfold the composition of light and the origin of colors. An eminent foreign *savant* once called upon Dr. Wollaston, and requested to be shown over his laboratories in which science had been enriched by so many important discoveries, when the doctor took him into a little study, and, pointing to an old tea-tray on the table, containing a few watch-glasses, test-papers, a small balance, and a blow-pipe, said, "There is all the laboratory that I have!"

Stothard learned the art of combining colors by closely studying butterflies' wings. He would often say that no one knew what he owed to these tiny insects. A burnt stick and a barn-door served Wilkie in lieu of pencil and canvas. Bewick first practiced drawing on the cottage walls of his native village, which he covered with his sketches in chalk; and Benjamin West made his first brushes out of the cat's tail. Ferguson laid himself down in the fields at night in a blanket, and made a map of the heavenly bodies by means of a thread with small beads on it stretched between his eye and the stars. Franklin first robbed the thunder-cloud of its lightning by means of a kite made with two cross sticks and a silk handkerchief. Watt made his first model of the condensing steam-engine out of an old anatomist's syringe, used to inject the arteries previous to dissection. Gifford worked his first problems in mathematics, when a cobbler's apprentice, upon small scraps of leather, which he beat smooth for the purpose; whilst Rittenhouse, the astronomer, first calculated eclipses on his plough-handle.

The most ordinary occasions will furnish a man with opportunities or suggestions for improvement, if he be but prompt to take advantage of them. Professor Lee was attracted to the study of Hebrew by finding a Bible in that tongue in a synagogue, while working as a common carpenter at the repairs of the benches. He became possessed with a desire to read the book in the original, and, buying a cheap second-hand copy of a Hebrew grammar, he sat to work and learned the language for himself. As Edmund Stone said to the Duke of Argyle, in answer to his grace's inquiry how he, a poor gardener's boy, had contrived to be able to read Newton's Principia in Latin, "One needs only to know the twenty-four letters of the alphabet in order to learn everything else that one wishes." Application and perseverance, and the diligent improvement of opportunities will do the rest.

Sir Walter Scott found opportunities for self-improvement in every pursuit, and turned even accidents to account. Thus it was in the discharge of his functions as a writer's apprentice that he first visited the Highlands, and formed those friendships among the surviving heroes of 1745 which served to lay the foundation of a large class of his works. Later in life, when employed as quartermaster of the Edinburgh Light Cavalry, he was accidently disabled by the kick of a horse, and confined for some time to his house; but Scott was a sworn enemy to idleness, and he forthwith set his mind to work. In three days he had composed the first canto of "The Lay of the Last Minstrel," which he shortly after finished—his first great original work.

The attention of Dr. Priestly, the discoverer of so many gases, was accidentally drawn to the subject of chemistry through his living in the neighborhood of a brewery. When visiting the place one day, he noted the peculiar appearances attending the extinction of lighted chips in the gas floating over the fermented liquor. He was forty years old at the time, and knew nothing of chemistry. He consulted books to ascertain the cause, but they told him little, for as yet nothing was known on the subject. Then he began to experiment, with some rude apparatus of his own contrivance. The curious results of his first experiments led to others, which in his hands shortly became the science of pneumatic chemistry. About the same time Scheele was obscurely working in the same direction in a remote Swedish village; and he discovered several new gases, with no more effective apparatus at his command than a few apothecaries' vials and pigs' bladders. Sir Humphrey Davy, when an apothecary's apprentice, performed his first experiments with instruments of the rudest description. He extemporized the greater part of them himself; out of the motley materials which chance threw in his way—the pots and pans of the kitchen, and the vials and vessels of his master's surgery. It happened that a French ship was wrecked off the Land's End, and the surgeon escaped, bearing with him his case of instruments, amongst which was an old-fashioned glyster apparatus; this article he presented to Davy, with whom he had become acquainted. The apothecary's apprentice received it with great exultation, and forthwith employed it as a part of a pneumatic apparatus which he contrived, afterwards using it to perform the duties of an air-pump in one of his experiments on the nature and sources of heat.

In like manner Professor Faraday, Sir Humphrey Davy's scientific successor, made his first experiments in electricity by means of an old bottle, while he was still a working bookbinder. And it is a curious fact, that Faraday was first attracted to the study of chemistry by hearing one of Sir Humphrey Davy's lectures on the subject at the Royal Institution. A gentleman, who was a member, calling one day at the shop where Faraday was employed in binding books found him poring over the article "Electricity" in an Encyclopaedia placed in his hands to bind. The gentleman, having made inquiries, found that the young bookbinder was curious about such subjects, and gave him an order of admission to the Royal Institution, where he attended a course of four lectures delivered by Sir Humphrey. He took notes of them, which he showed to the lecturer, who acknowledged their scientific accuracy, and was surprised when informed of the humble position of the reporter. Faraday then expressed his desire to devote himself to the prosecution of chemical studies, from which Sir Humphrey at first endeavored to dissuade him; but the young man persisting, he was at length taken into the Royal Institution as an assistant; and eventually the mantle of the brilliant apothecary's boy fell upon the worthy shoulders of the equally brilliant bookbinder's apprentice.

The words which Davy entered in his note-book when about twenty years of age, working in Dr. Beddoes laboratory at Bristol, were eminently characteristic of him: "I have neither riches, nor power, nor birth to recommend me; yet, if I live, I trust I shall not be of less service to mankind and my friends, than if I had been born with all these advantages." Davy possessed the capability of devoting the whole power of his mind to the practical and experimental investigation of a subject in all its bearings; and such a mind will rarely fail, by dint of mere industry and patient thinking, in-producing results of the highest order. Coleridge said of Davy, "There is an energy and elasticity in his mind which enables him to seize on and analyze all questions, pushing them to their legitimate consequences Every subject in Davy's mind has the principle of vitality. Living thoughts spring up like turf under his feet." Davy, on his part, said of Coleridge, whose abilities he greatly admired, "With the most exalted genius, enlarged views, sensitive heart, and enlightened mind, he will be the victim of a want of order, precision, and regularity."

The great Cuvier was a singularly accurate, careful, and industrious observer. When a boy he was attracted to the subject of natural history by the sight of a volume of Buffon which accidentally fell in his way. He at once proceeded to copy the drawings, and to color them after the description given in the text. While still at school, one of the teachers made him a present of "Linnaeus's System of nature"; and for more than ten years this constituted his library of natural history. At eighteen he was offered the situation of tutor in a family residing in Normandy. Living close to the sea-shore, he was brought face to face with the wonders of marine life. Strolling along the sands one day he observed a stranded cuttle-fish. He was attracted by the curious object, took it home to dissect, and thus began the study of the molluscan, in the pursuit of which he achieved so distinguished a reputation. He had no books to refer to, excepting only the great book of Nature which lay open before him. The study of the novel and interesting objects which it daily presented to his eyes made a much deeper impression on his mind than any written or engraved descriptions could possibly have done. Three years thus passed, during which he compared the living species of marine animals with the fossil remains found in the neighborhood, dissected the specimens of marine life that came under his notice, and, by careful observation, prepared the way for a complete reform in the classification of the animal kingdom. It is not accident, then, that helps a man in the world so much as purpose and persistent industry. To the feeble, the sluggish and purposeless, the happiest acct-dents will avail nothing—they pass them by, seeing no meaning in them. But it is astonishing how much can be accomplished if we are prompt to seize and improve the opportunities for action and effort which are constantly presenting themselves. Watt taught himself chemistry and mechanics while working at his trade of a mathematical-instrument maker, at the same time that he was learning German from a Swiss dyer. Stephenson taught himself arithmetic and mensuration while working as an engine-man, during the night shifts; and when he could snatch a few moments in the intervals allowed for meals during the day, he worked his sums with a bit of chalk upon the sides of the colliery wagons. Dalton's industry was the habit of his life. He began from his boyhood, for he taught a little village school when he was only about twelve years old—keeping the school in winter, and working upon his father's farm in summer He would sometimes urge himself and companions to study by the stimulus of a bet, and on one occasion by his satisfactory solution of a problem, he won as much as enabled him to buy a winter's store of candles. He continued his meteorological observations until a day or two before he died—having made and recorded upwards of 200,000 in the course of his life.

With perseverance, the very odds and ends of time may be worked up into results of the greatest value. An hour in every day withdrawn from frivolous pursuits would, if profitably employed, enable a person of ordinary capacity to go far towards mastering a science. It would make an ignorant man a well-informed one in less than ten years. Time should not be allowed to pass without yielding fruits, in the form of something learned worthy of being known, some good principle cultivated, or some good habit strengthened. Dr Mason Good translated Lucretius while riding in his carriage in the streets of London, going the round of his patients. Dr. Darwin composed nearly all his works in the same way while driving about in his sulky from house to house in the country—writing down his thoughts on little scraps of paper, which he carried about with him for the purpose. Hale wrote his "Contemplations" while traveling on circuit. Dr. Burney learned French and Italian while traveling on horseback from one musical pupil to another in the course of his profession. Kirke White learned Greek while walking to and from a lawyer's office; and we personally know a man of eminent position who learned Latin and French while going messages as an errand-boy in the streets of Manchester.

Daguesseau, one of the great chancellors of France, by carefully working up his odd bits of time, wrote a bulky and able volume in the successive intervals of waiting for dinner, and Madame de Geniis composed several of her charming volumes while waiting for the princess to whom she gave her daily lessons. Elihu Burritt attributed his first success in self-improvement, not to genius, which he disclaimed, but simply to the careful employment of those invaluable fragments of time called "odd moments." While working and earning his living as a blacksmith, he mastered some eighteen ancient and modern languages, and twenty two European dialects.

What a solemn and striking admonition to youth is that inscribed on the dial at All Souls, Oxford—"The hours perish, and are laid to our charge." Time is the only little fragment of Eternity that belongs to man; and, like life, it can never be recalled. "In the dissipation of worldly treasure," says Jackson of Exeter, "the frugality of the future may balance the extravagance of the past; but who can say, I will take from minutes tomorrow to compensate for those I have lost today?" Melanchthon noted down the time lost by him, that he might thereby reanimate his industry, and not lose an hour. An Italian scholar put over his door an inscription intimating that whosoever remained there should join in his labors. "We are afraid," said some visitors to Baxter, "that we break in upon your time." "To be sure you do," replied the disturbed and blunt divine. Time was the estate out of which these great workers, and all other workers, formed that rich treasury of thoughts and deeds which they have left to their successors.

The mere drudgery undergone by some men in carrying on their undertakings has been something extraordinary, but the drudgery they regarded as the price of success. Addison amassed as much as three folios of manuscript materials before he began his "Spectator." Newton wrote his "Chronology" fifteen times over before he was satisfied with it; and Gibbon wrote out his "Memoir" nine times. Hale studied for many years at the rate of sixteen hours a day, and when wearied with the study of the law, he would recreate himself with philosophy and the study of the mathematics. Hume wrote thirteen hours a day while preparing his "History of England." Montesquieu, speaking of one part of his writings, said to a friend, "You will read it in a few hours; but I assure you it has cost me so much labor that it has whitened my hair."

The practice of writing down thoughts and facts for the purpose of holding them fast and preventing their escape into the dim region of forgetfulness, has been much resorted to by thoughtful and studious men. Lord Bacon left behind him many manuscripts entitled "Sudden thoughts set down for use." Erskine made great extracts from Burke; and Eldon copied Coke upon Littleton twice over with his own hand, so that the book became, as it were, part of his own mind. The late Dr. Pye Smith, when apprenticed to his father as a bookbinder, was accustomed to make copious memoranda of all the books he read, with extracts and criticisms. This indomitable industry in collecting materials distinguished him through life, his biographer describing him as "always at work, always in advance, always accumulating." These note-books afterwards proved like Richter's "quarries," the great storehouse from which he drew his illustrations.

The same practice characterized the eminent John Hunter, who adopted it for the purpose of supplying the defects of memory; and he was accustomed thus to illustrate the advantages which one derives from putting one's thoughts in writing: "It resembles," he said, "a tradesman taking stock, without which he never knows either what he possesses or in what he is deficient." John Hunter—whose observation was so keen that Abernethy was accustomed to speak of him as "the Argus-eyed"—furnished an illustrious example of the power of patient industry. He received little or no education till he was about twenty years of age, and it was with difficulty that he acquired the arts of reading and writing. He worked for some years as a carpenter at Glasgow, after which he joined his brother William, who had settled in London as a lecturer and anatomical demonstrator. John entered his dissecting room as an assistant, but soon shot ahead of his brother, partly by virtue of his great natural ability, but mainly by reason of his patient application and indefatigable industry. He was one of the first in this country to devote himself assiduously to the study of comparative anatomy, and the objects he dissected and collected took the eminent Professor Owen no less than ten years to arrange, The collection contains some twenty thousand specimens, and is the most precious treasure of the kind that has ever been accumulated by the industry of one man. Hunter used to spend every morning from sunrise until eight o'clock in his museum; and throughout the day, he carried on his extensive private practice, performed his laborious duties as surgeon to St. George's Hospital and deputy surgeon-general to the army; delivered lectures to students, and superintended a school of practical anatomy at his own house; finding leisure, amidst all, for elaborate experiments on the animal economy, and the composition of various works of great scientific importance. To find time for this gigantic amount of work he allowed himself only four hours of sleep at night, and an hour after dinner. When once asked what method he had adopted to insure success in his undertakings, he replied, "My rule is, deliberately to consider, before I commence, whether the thing be practicable. If it be not practicable, I do not attempt it. If it be practicable, I can accomplish it if I give sufficient pains to it; and having begun, I never stop till the thing is done. To this rule I owe all my success."

Hunter occupied a great deal of his time in collecting definite facts respecting matters which, before his day, were regarded as exceedingly trivial. Thus it was supposed by many of his cotemporaries that he was only wasting his time and thought in studying so carefully as he did the growth of a deer's horn. But Hunter was impressed with the conviction that no accurate knowledge of scientific facts is without its value. By the study referred to he learned how arteries accommodate themselves to circumstances, and enlarge as occasion requires; and the knowledge thus acquired emboldened him, in a case of aneurism in a branch artery, to tie the main trunk where no surgeons before him had dared to tie it, and the life of his patient was saved. Like many original men, he worked for a long time, as it were, underground, digging and laying foundations

Harvey was as zealous a laborer as any we have named. He spent not less than eight long years of investigation and research before he published his views of the circulation of the blood. He repeated and verified his experiments again and again, probably anticipating the opposition he would have to encounter from the profession in making known his discovery. The tract in which he at length announced his views was a most modest one, but simple, perspicuous, and conclusive. It was nevertheless received with ridicule, as the utterance of a cracked-brained impostor. For some time he did not make a single convert, and gained nothing but contumely and abuse. He had called in question the revered authority of the ancients; and it was even averred that his views were calculated to subvert the authority of the Scriptures and undermine the very foundation of morality and religion. His little practice fell away, and he was left almost without a friend. This lasted for some years, until the great truth, held fast by Harvey amidst all his adversity, and which had dropped into many thoughtful minds, gradually ripened by further observation, and after a period of about twenty-five years it became generally recognized as an established scientific truth.

The difficulties encountered by Dr. Jenner in promulgating and establishing his discovery of vaccination as a preventive of small-pox, were even greater than those of Harvey, Many, before him, had witnessed the cowpox, and had heard of the report current among the milk maids in Gloucestershire, that whoever had taken that disease was secure against small-pox. It was a trifling, vulgar rumor, supposed to have no significance whatever, and no one had thought it worthy of investigation, until it was accidentally brought under the notice of Jenner. He was a youth, pursuing his studies at Sodbury, when his attention was arrested by the casual observation made by a country girl, who came to his master's shop for advice. The small-pox was mentioned, when the girl said, "I can't take that disease, for I have had cowpox." The observation immediately riveted Jenner's attention, and he forthwith set about inquiring and making observations on the subject. His professional friends, to whom he mentioned his views as to the prophylactic virtues of cow-pox, laughed at him, and even threatened to expel him from their society, if he persisted in harassing them with the subject. In London he was so fortunate as to study under John Hunter, to whom he communicated his views. The advice of the great anatomist was thoroughly characteristic: "Don't think, but *fly;* be patient, be accurate." Jenner's courage was supported by the advice, which conveyed to him the true art of philosophical investigation. He went back to the country to practice his profession and make observations and experiments, which he continued to pursue for a period of twenty years. His faith in his discovery was so implicit that he vaccinated his own son on three several occasions. At length he published his views in a quarto of about seventy pages, in which he gave the details of twenty-three cases of successful vaccination of individuals, in whom it was found afterwards impossible to communicate the small-pox either by contagion or inoculation. It was in 1798 that this treatise was published; though he had been working out his ideas since the year 1775, when they had begun to assume a definite form. How was the discovery received? First with indifference, then with active hostility. Jenner proceeded to London to exhibit to the profession the process of vaccination and its results; but not a single medical man could be induced to make trial of it, and after fruitlessly waiting for nearly three months, he returned to his native village. He was even caricatured and abused for his attempt to "bestialize" his species by the introduction into their systems of diseased matter from the cow's udder. Vaccination was denounced from the pulpit as "diabolical." It was averred that vaccinated children became "ox-faced," that abscesses broke out to "indicate sprouting horns," and that the countenance was gradually "transmuted into the visage of a cow, the voice into the bellowing of bulls." Vaccination, however, was a truth, and, notwithstanding the violence of the opposition, belief in it spread slowly. In one village, where a gentleman tried to introduce the practice, the first persons who permitted themselves to be vaccinated were absolutely pelted and driven into their houses if they appeared out of doors. Two ladies of title had the courage to vaccinate their children, and the prejudices of the day were at once broken through. The medical profession gradually came round, and there were several who even sought to rob Dr. Jenner of the merit of the discovery, when its importance came to be recognized. Jenner's cause at last triumphed, and he was publicly honored and rewarded. In his prosperity he was as modest as he had been in his obscurity. He was invited to settle in London, and told that he might command a practice Of $50,000 a year. But his answer was, "No! In the morning of my days I sought the sequestered and lowly paths of life— the valley, and not the mountain—and now, in the evening of my days, it is not meet for me to hold myself up as an object for fortune and for fame." During Jenner's own lifetime the practice of vaccination became adopted all over the civilized world; and when he died, his title as a benefactor of his kind was recognized far and wide. Cuvier has said, "If vaccine were the only discovery of the epoch, it would serve to render it illustrious forever; yet it knocked twenty times in vain at the doors of the Academies."

Not less patient, resolute, and persevering was Sir Charles Bell in the prosecution of his discoveries relating to the nervous system. Previous to his time, the most confused notions prevailed as to the functions of the nerves, and this branch of study was little more advanced than it had been at the time of Democritus and Anaxagoras three thousand years before. Sir Charles Bell, in the valuable series of papers the publication of which was commenced in 1821, took an entirely original view of the subject, based upon a long series of careful, accurate, and oft repeated experiments. Elaborately tracing the development of the nervous system up from the lowest order of animated being, to man—the lord of the animal kingdom—he displayed it, to use his own words, "as plainly as if it were written in our mother-tongue." His discovery consisted in the fact, that the spinal nerves are double in their function, and arise by double roots from the spinal marrow—volition being conveyed by that part of the nerves springing from the one root, and sensation by the other. The subject occupied the mind of Sir Charles Bell for a period of forty years, when, in 1840, he laid his last paper before the Royal Society. As in the case of Harvey and Jenner, when he had lived down the ridicule and opposition with which his views were first received, and their truth came to be recognized, numerous claims for priority in making the discovery were set up at home and abroad. Like them, too, he lost practice by the publication of his papers; and he left it on record that, after every step in his discovery, he was obliged to work harder than ever to preserve his reputation as a practitioner. The great merits of Sir Charles Bell were, however, at length fully recognized; and Cuvier himself, when on his death-bed, finding his face distorted and drawn to one side, pointed out the symptom to his attendants as a proof of the correctness of Sir Charles Bell's theory.

The life of Sir William Herschel affords another remarkable illustration of the force of perseverance in another branch of science. His father was a poor German musician, who brought up his four sons to the same calling. William came over to England to seek his fortune, and he joined the band of the Durham Militia, in which he played the oboe. The regiment was lying at Doncaster, where Dr. Miller first became acquainted with Herschel, having heard him perform a solo on the violin in a surprising manner. The Doctor entered into conversation with the youth, and was so pleased with him, that he urged him to leave the militia and take up his residence at his house for a time. Herschel did so, and while at Doncaster was principally occupied as a violin-player at concerts, availing himself of the advantages of Dr. Miller's library to study at his leisure hours. A new organ having been built for the parish church at Halifax, an organist was advertised for, on which Herschel applied for the office and was selected. Leading the wandering life of an artist, he was next attracted to Bath, where he played in the Pump-room band, and also officiated as organist in the Octagon chapel. Some recent discoveries in astronomy having arrested his mind, and awakened in him a powerful spirit of curiosity, he sought and obtained from a friend the loan of a two-foot Gregorian telescope. So fascinated was the poor musician by the science, that he even thought of purchasing a telescope, but the price asked by the London optician was so alarming that he determined to make one. Those who know what a reflecting telescope is, and the skill which is required to prepare the concave metallic speculum which forms the most important part of the apparatus, will be able to form some idea of the difficulty of this undertaking. Nevertheless, Herschel succeeded, after long and painful labor, in completing a five-foot reflector, with which he had the gratification of observing the ring and satellites of Saturn. Not satisfied with his triumph, he proceeded to make other instruments in succession, of seven, ten, and even twenty feet. In constructing the seven-foot reflector, he finished no fewer than two hundred specula before he produced one that would bear any power that was applied to it—a striking instance of the persevering laboriousness of the man. While gauging the heavens with his instruments, continued patiently to earn his bread by piping to the fashionable frequenters of the Pump-room. So eager was he in his astronomical observations, that he would steal away from the room during an interval of the performance, give a little turn at his telescope, and contentedly return to his oboe. Thus working away Herschel discovered the Georgium Sidus, the orbit and rate of motion of which he carefully calculated, and sent the result to the Royal Society; when the humble oboe-player found himself at once elevated from obscurity to fame. He was shortly after appointed Astronomer Royal, and by the kindness of George III was placed in a position of honorable competency for life. He bore his honors with the same meekness and humility which had distinguished him in the days of his obscurity. So gentle and patient, and withal so distinguished and successful a follower of science under difficulties, perhaps can not be found in the entire history of biography.

Hugh Miller was a man of like observant faculties, who studied literature as well as science with zeal and success. While Hugh was but a child, his father, who was a sailor, was drowned at sea, and he was brought up by his widowed mother. He had a school training after a sort, but his best teachers were the boys with whom he played, the men amongst whom he worked, the friends and relatives with whom he lived. He read much and miscellaneously, and picked up odd sorts of knowledge from many quarters—from workmen, carpenters, fishermen, and sailors, and above all, from the old boulders strewed along the shores of the Cromarty Frith. With a big hammer which had belonged to his great-grandfather, an old buccaneer, the boy went about chipping the stones, and accumulating specimens of mica, porphyry, garnet, and such like. Sometimes he had a day in the Woods, and there, too, the boy's attention was excited by the peculiar geological curiosities which came in his way. When of a suitable age he was apprenticed to the trade of his choice—that of a working stone-mason; and he began his laboring career in a quarry looking out upon the Cromarty Frith. This quarry proved one of his best schools. The remarkable geological formation which it displayed awakened his curiosity. The bar of deep-red stone beneath, and the bar of pale-red clay above, were noted by the young quarryman, who even in such unpromising subjects found matter of observation and reflection. Where other men saw nothing, he detected analogies, differences and peculiarities, which set him thinking. He simply kept his eyes and his mind open; was sober, diligent and persevering; and this was the secret of his intellectual growth.

His curiosity was excited and kept alive by the curious organic remains, principally of old and extinct species of fishes, ferns, and ammonites, which were revealed along the coast by the washings of the waves, or were exposed by the stroke of his mason's hammer. He never lost sight of the subject, but went on accumulating observations and comparing formations, until at length many years afterwards, when no longer a working mason, he gave to the world his highly interesting work on the Old Red Sandstone, which at once established his reputation as a scientific geologist. But this work was the fruit of long years of patient observation and research. As he modestly states in his autobiography, "The only merit to which I lay claim in the case is that of patient research—a merit in which whoever wills may rival or surpass me; and this humble faculty of patience, when rightly developed, may lead to more extraordinary developments of idea than even genius itself."

Not long ago Sir Roderick Murchison discovered in the far north of Scotland a profound geologist, in the person of a baker named Robert Dick. When Sir Roderick called upon him at the bakehouse in which he baked and earned his bread, Robert Dick delineated to him, by means of flour upon the board, the geographical features and geological phenomena of his native country, pointing out the imperfections in the existing maps, which he had ascertained by traveling over the country in his leisure hours. On further inquiry, Sir Roderick ascertained that the humble individual before him was not only a capital baker and geologist, but a first-rate botanist. "I found," said the President of the Geographical Society, "to my great humiliation, that the baker knew more of botanical science, ay, ten times more, than I did; and that there were only some twenty or thirty specimens of flowers which he had not collected. Some he had obtained as presents, some he had purchased, but the greater portion he had accumulated by his industry, in his native county of Caithness; and the specimens were all arranged in the most beautiful order, with their scientific names affixed."

Chapter 11

Energy and Will

"Kites rise against, not with the wind. . . . No man ever worked his passage anywhere in a dead calm." —Jno. Neal.

THERE IS A FAMOUS SPEECH recorded of an old Norseman, thoroughly characteristic of the Teuton. "I believe neither in idols nor demons," said he, "I put my sole trust in my own strength of body and soul." The ancient crest of a pickaxe with the motto of "Either I will find a way or make one," was an exposition of the same sturdy independence which to this day distinguishes the descendants of the Northmen. Indeed nothing could be more characteristic of the Scandinavian mythology, than that it had a God with a hammer. A man's character is seen in small matters; and from even so slight a test as the mode in which a man wields a hammer, his energy may in some measure be inferred. Thus an eminent Frenchman hit off in a single phrase the characteristic quality of the inhabitants of a particular district, in which a friend of his proposed to settle and buy land. "Beware," said he, "of making a purchase there; I know the men of that department; the pupils who come from it to our veterinary school at Paris *do not strike hard upon the anvil;* they want energy; and you will not get a satisfactory return on any capital you may invest there." A fine and just appreciation of character, indicating the thoughtful observer; and strikingly illustrative of the fact that it is the energy of the individual men that gives strength to a State, and confers a value even upon the very soil which they cultivate.

The cultivation of this quality is of the greatest importance; resolute determination in the pursuit of worthy objects being the foundation of all true greatness of character. Energy enables a man to force his way through irksome drudgery and dry details, and carries him onward and upward in every station in life. It accomplishes more than genius, with not one half the disappointment and peril. It is not eminent talent that is required to insure success in any pursuit, so much as purpose—not merely the power to achieve, but the will to labor energetically and perseveringly. Hence energy of will may be defined to be the very central power of character in a man—in a word, it is the Man himself. It gives impulse to his every action, and soul to every effort. True hope is based on it—and it is hope that gives the real perfume to life. "Woe unto him that is faint-hearted," says the son of Sirach. There is, indeed, no blessing equal to the possession of a stout heart. Even if a man fail in his efforts, it will be a satisfaction to him to enjoy the consciousness of having done his best. In humble life nothing can be more cheering and beautiful than to see a man combating suffering by patience, triumphing in his integrity, and who, when his feet are bleeding and his limbs failing him, still walks upon his courage. When Luther said to Erasmus, "You desire to walk upon eggs without crushing them, and among glasses without breaking them," the timorous, hesitating Erasmus replied, "I will not be unfaithful to the cause of Christ, at least *so far as the age will permit me.*" Luther was of a very different character. "I will go to Worms though devils were combined against me as thick as the tiles upon the housetops."

Nothing that is of real worth can be achieved without courageous working. Man owes his growth chiefly to that active striving of the will, that encounter with difficulty which we call effort; and it is astonishing to find how often results apparently impracticable are thus made possible. An intense anticipation itself transforms possibility into reality; our desires being often but the precursors of the things which we are capable of performing. On the contrary, the timid and hesitating find every thing impossible, chiefly because it seems so. It is related of a young French officer, that he used to walk about his apartment exclaiming, "I *will* be Marshal of France and a great general." His ardent desire was the presentiment of his success; for the young officer did become a distinguished commander, and he died a Marshal of France.

"You are now at the age," said Lamennais once, addressing a gay youth, "at which a decision must be formed by you; a little later and you may have to groan within the tomb which you yourself have dug, without the power of rolling away the stone. That which the easiest becomes a habit in us is the will. Learn, then, to will strongly and decisively; thus fix your floating life, and leave it no longer to be carried hither and thither, like a withered leaf, by every wind that blows."

Buxton held the conviction that a young man might be very much what he pleased, provided he formed a strong resolution and held to it. Writing to one of his sons, he said to him, "You are now at that period of life, in which you must make a turn to the right or the left. You must now give proofs of principle, determination, and strength of mind; or you must sink into idleness, and acquire the habits and character of a desultory, ineffective young man; and if once you fall to that point, you will find it no easy matter to rise again. I am sure that a young man may be very much what he pleases. In my own case it was so. Much of my happiness, and all my prosperity in life, have resulted from the change I made at your age. If you seriously resolve to be energetic and industrious, depend upon it that you will for your whole life have reason to rejoice that you were wise enough to form and to act upon that determination." As will, considered without regard to direction, is simply constancy, firmness, perseverance, it will be obvious that everything depends upon right direction and motives. Directed wards the enjoyment of the senses, the strong will may be a demon, and the intellect merely its debased slave; but directed towards good, the strong will is a king, and the intellect the minister of man's highest well-being.

"Where there is a will there is a way," is an old and true saying. He who resolves upon doing a thing, by that very resolution often scales the barriers to it, and secures its achievement. To think we are able, is almost to be so—to determine upon attainment is frequently attainment itself. Thus, earnest resolution has often seemed to have about it almost a savor of omnipotence. The strength of Suwarrow's character lay in his power of willing, and, like most resolute persons, he preached it up as a system. "You can only half will," he would say to people who failed. Like Richelieu and Napoleon, he would have the word "impossible" banished from the dictionary. "I don't know," "I can't," and "impossible," were words which he detested above all others. "Learn! Do! Try!" he would exclaim. His biographer has said of him, that he furnished a remarkable illustration of what may be effected by the energetic development and exercise of faculties, the germs of which at least are in every human heart.

One of Napoleon's favorite maxims was, "The truest wisdom is a resolute determination." His life, beyond most others, vividly showed what a powerful and unscrupulous will could accomplish. He threw his whole force of body and mind direct upon his work. Imbecile rulers and the nations they governed went down before him in succession. He was told that the Alps stood in the way of his armies—"There shall be no Alps," he said, and the road across the Simplon was constructed, through a district formerly almost inaccessible. "Impossible," said he, "is a word only to be found in the dictionary of fools." He was a man who toiled terribly; sometimes employing and exhausting four secretaries at a time. He spared no one, not even himself. His influence inspired other men, and put a new life into them. "I made my generals out of mud," he said. But all was of no avail; for Napoleon's intense selfishness was his ruin, and the ruin of France, which he left a prey to anarchy. His life taught the lesson that power, however energetically wielded, without beneficence, is fatal to its possessor and its subjects; and that knowledge without goodness, is but the incarnate principle of evil.

Our own Wellington was a far greater man. Not less resolute, firm, and persistent, but more self-denying, conscientious, and truly patriotic. Napoleon's aim was "Glory"; Wellington's watchword, like Nelson's, was "Duty." The former word, it is said, does not once occur in his dispatches, the latter often, but never accompanied by any high-sounding professions. The greatest difficulties could neither embarrass nor intimidate Wellington; his energy invariably rising in proportion to the obstacles to be surmounted. The patience, the firmness, the resolution, with which he bore through the maddening vexations and gigantic difficulties of the Peninsular campaigns, is, perhaps one of the sublimest things to be found in history. Though his natural temper was irritable in the extreme, his high sense of duty enabled him to restrain it; and to those about him his patience seemed absolutely inexhaustible. His great character stands untarnished by ambition, avarice, or any low passion. Though a man of powerful individuality, he yet displayed a great variety of endowment. The equal of Napoleon in generalship, he was as prompt, vigorous, and daring as Clive; as wise a statesman as Cromwell; and as pure and high-minded as Washington. The great Wellington left behind him an enduring reputation, founded on toilsome campaigns won by skillful combination, by fortitude which nothing could exhaust, by sublime daring, and perhaps by still sublimer patience.

Energy usually displays itself in promptitude and decision. When Ledyard the traveler was asked by the African Association when he would be ready to set out for Africa, he immediately answered, "Tomorrow morning." Blucher's promptitude obtained for him the cognomen of "Marshal Forward" throughout the Prussian army. When John Jervis, afterwards Earl St. Vincent, was asked when he would be ready to join his ship, he replied "Directly." And when Sir Colin Campbell, appointed to the command of the Indian army, was asked when he could set out, his answer was, "Tomorrow"— an earnest of his subsequent success. For it is rapid decision, and a similar promptitude in action, such as taking instant advantage of an enemy's mistakes, that so often wins battles. "At Arcola," said Napoleon, "I won the battle with twenty-five horsemen. I seized a moment of lassitude, gave every man a trumpet, and gained the day with this handful. Two armies are two bodies which meet and endeavor to frighten each other; a moment of panic occurs, and *that moment* must be turned to advantage." "Every moment lost," said he at another time, "gives an opportunity for misfortune"; and he declared that he beat the Austrians because they never knew the value of time. Another great but sullied name is that of Warren Hastings—a man of dauntless will and untiring industry. His family was ancient and illustrious; but their vicissitudes of fortune and ill-requited loyalty in the cause of the Stuarts, brought them to poverty, and the family estate at Daylesford, of which they had been lords of the manor for hundreds of years, at length passed from their hands. The last Hastings of Daylesford had, however, presented the parish-living to his second son; and it was in his house, many years later, that Warren Hastings, his grandson, was born. The boy learned his letters at the village school, on the same bench with the children of the peasantry. He played in the fields which his fathers had owned; and what the loyal and brave Hastings of Daylesford *had* been was ever in the boy's thoughts. His young ambition was fired, and it is said that one summer's day, when only seven years old, as he laid him down on the bank of the stream which flowed through the domain, he formed in his mind the resolution that he would yet recover possession of the family lands. It was the romantic vision of a boy; yet he lived to realize it. The dream became a passion, rooted in his very life; and he pursued his determination through youth up to manhood, with that calm but indomitable force of will which was the most striking peculiarity of his character. The orphan boy became one of the most powerful men of his time; he retrieved the fortunes of his line; bought back the old estate, and rebuilt the family mansion.

Sir Charles Napier was another Indian leader of extraordinary courage and determination. He once said of the difficulties with which he was surrounded in one of his campaigns, "They only make my feet go deeper into the ground." His battle of Meeanee was one of the most extraordinary feats in history. With 2,000 men, of whom only 400 were Europeans, he encountered an army of 35,000 hardy and well-armed Beloochees. It was an act, apparently, of the most daring temerity, but the General had faith in himself and in his men. He charged the Belooch centre, up a high bank which formed their rampart in front, and for three mortal hours the battle raged. Each man of that small force, inspired by the chief, became for the time a hero. The Beloochees, though twenty to one, were driven back, but with their faces to the foe. It is this sort of pluck, tenacity, and determined perseverance which wins soldiers' battles, and, indeed, every battle. It is the one neck nearer that wins the race and shows the blood; it is the one march more that wins the campaign; the five minutes' more persistent courage that wins the fight. Though your force be less than another's, you equal and outmaster your opponent if you continue it longer and concentrate it more: The reply of the Spartan father, who said to his son, when complaining that his sword was too short. "Add a step to it," is applicable to everything in life.

Napier took the right method of inspiring his men with his own heroic spirit. He worked as hard as any private in the ranks. "The great art of commanding," he said, "is to take a fare share of the work. The man who leads an army can not succeed unless his whole mind is thrown into his work. The more trouble, the more labor must be given; the more danger, the more pluck must be shown, till all is overpowered." A young officer who accompanied him in his campaigns in the Cutchee Hills, once said, "When I see that old man incessantly on his horse, how can I be idle who am young and strong? I would go into a loaded cannon's mouth if he ordered me." This remark, when repeated to Napier, he said was ample reward for his toils. The anecdote of his interview with the Indian juggler strikingly illustrates his cool courage, as well as his remarkable simplicity and honesty of character. On one occasion, after the Indian battles, a famous juggler visited the camp and performed his feats before the General, his family, and staff. Among other performances this man cut in two with a stroke of his sword a lime or lemon placed in the hand of his assistant Napier thought there was some collusion between the juggler and his retainer. To divide by a sweep of the sword on a man's hand so small an object without touching the flesh he believed to be impossible, though a similar incident is related by Scott in his romance of the "Talisman." To determine the point, the General offered his own hand for the experiment, and he stretched out his right arm. The juggler looked attentively at the hand and said he would not make the trial. "I thought I would find you out!" exclaimed Napier. "But stop," added the other, "let me see your left hand." The left hand was submitted, and the man then said firmly, "If you will hold your arm steady I will perform the feat." "But why the left hand and not the right?" "Because the right is hollow to the cent-re, and there is a risk of cutting off the thumb; the left is high, and the danger will be less." Napier was startled. "I got frightened," he said; "I saw it was an actual feat of delicate swordsmanship, and if I had not abused the man as I did before my staff, and challenged him to the trial, I honestly acknowledge I would have retired from the encounter. However, I put the lime on my hand, and held out my arm steadily. The juggler balanced himself, and, with a swift stroke, cut the lime in two pieces. I felt the edge of the sword on my hand as if a cold thread had been drawn across it. So much (he added) for the brave swordsmen of India, whom our fine fellows defeated at Meeanee."

Patriotism and nobility culminate in the life of Washington, the leader and deliverer of his country. He was one of the greatest men of the eighteenth century—not so much by his genius as by his purity and trustworthiness. His English descent was a goodly heritage. He came from an Anglian stock settled in the county of Durham; from thence his ancestors emigrated to America, and settled in Virginia about the year 1657.

The character of George Washington was such that at an early age he was appointed to positions of great trust and confidence. At the age of nineteen he was appointed one of the adjutants-general of Virginia, with the rank of major—nor did he ever deceive those who put trust in him. He was ever prompt, obedient, and dutiful. At the age of twenty-three he was appointed colonel and commander-in-chief of all the forces raised in Virginia for co-operation with the English troops in the defense of the western territory against the French. He was trained not only in success, but in failure, which evoked his indomitable spirit.

No man could be more pure, no man could be more self-denying. In victory he was self-controlled; in defeat he was unshaken. Throughout he was magnanimous and pure. In General Washington it is difficult to know which to admire the most—the nobility of his character, the ardor of his patriotism, or the purity of his conduct.

Toward the close of his address to the Governors of the several States, on resigning his position of commander-in-chief, he said: "I make it my constant prayer, that God would have you and the State over which you preside in his holy protection; that he would incline the hearts of the citizens to cultivate a spirit of subordination and obedience to government; to entertain a brotherly affection and love for one another, for their fellow-citizens of the United States at large, and particularly for their brethren who have served in the field; and finally, that he would most graciously be pleased to dispose us all to do justice, to love mercy, and to demean ourselves with that charity, humility, and pacific temper of mind, which were the characteristics of the Divine Author of our blessed religion; without a humble imitation of whose example in these things, we can never hope to be a happy nation." How simple, truthful, and beautiful are the words of Washington!

It is not the size of a country, but the character of its people, that gives it sterling value. We find men constantly calling for liberty, but who do nothing to deserve it. They remain inert, lazy and selfish. There is a so-called patriotism that has no more dignity in it than the howling of wolves. True patriotism is of another sort. It is based on honesty, truthfulness, generosity, self-sacrifice, and genuine love of freedom.

Look for instance, at the little Republic of Switzerland, which has been hemmed in by tyrannical governments for hundreds of years. But the people are brave and frugal, honest and self-helping. They would have no master, but governed themselves. They elected their representatives, as at Apenzell, by show of hands in the public market-places. They proclaimed liberty of conscience, and Switzerland, like England, has always been the refuge of the persecuted for conscience' sake.

It was not without severe struggles that Switzerland conquered its independence The leaders of these brave men have often sacrificed themselves for the good of their country. Take for instance, the example of Arnold von Winkelried. In 1481 the Austrians invaded Switzerland, and a comparatively small number of men determined to resist them. Near the little town of Sempach the Austrians were observed advancing in a solid, compact body, presenting an unbroken line of spears. The Swiss met them, but their spears were shorter, and being much fewer in number, they were compelled to give way. Observing this, Arnold von Winkelried, seeing that all the efforts of the Swiss to break the ranks of their enemy had failed, exclaimed to his countrymen, "I will open a path to freedom! Protect, dear comrades, my wife and children!" He rushed forward, and, gathering in his arms as many spears as he could grasp, he buried them in his bosom. He fell, but a gap was made, and the Swiss rushed in, and achieved an exceeding great victory. Arnold von Winkelried died, but saved his country. The little mountain republic preserved its liberty. The battle took place on the 9th of July, and to this day the people of the country assemble to celebrate their deliverance from the Austrians, through the self-sacrifice of their leader.

The career of Dr. Livingstone is one of the most interesting. His ancestors were poor but honest Highlanders, and it is related of one of them, renowned in his district for wisdom and prudence, that when on his death-bed, he called his children around him and left them these words, the only legacy he had to bequeath—"In my life-time," said he, "I have searched most carefully through all the traditions I could find of our family, and I never could discover that there was a dishonest man among our forefathers; if, therefore, any of you or any of your children should take to dishonest ways, it will not be because it runs in our blood; it does not belong to you: I leave this precept with you—Be honest." At the age of ten Livingstone was sent to work in a cotton-factory near Glasgow as a "piecer." With part of his first week's wages he bought a Latin grammar, and began to learn that language, pursuing the study for years at a night-school. He would sit up conning his lessons till twelve or later, when not sent to bed by his mother, for he had to be up and at work in the factory every morning by six. In this way he plodded through Virgil and Horace, also reading extensively all books, excepting novels, that came in his way, but more especially scientific works and books of travels. He occupied his spare hours, which were but few, in the pursuit of botany, scouring the neighborhood to collect plants. He even carried on his reading amidst the roar of the factory machinery, so placing the book upon the spinning-jenny which he worked that he could catch sentence after sentence as he passed it. In this way the persevering youth acquired much useful knowledge; and as he grew older, the desire possessed him of becoming a missionary to the heathen. With this object he set himself to obtain a medical education, in order the better to be qualified for the work. He accordingly economized his earnings, and saved as much money as enabled him to support himself while attending the Medical and Greek classes, as well as the Divinity Lectures, at Glasgow, for several winters, working as a cotton-spinner during the remainder of each year. He thus supported himself, during his college career, entirely by his own earnings as a factory workman, never having received a farthing of help from any source. "Looking back now," he honestly says, "at that life of toil, I can not but feel thankful that it formed such a material part of my early education; and, were it possible, I should like to begin life over again in the same lowly style, and to pass through the same hardy training." At first he thought of going to China, but the war then waging with that country prevented his following out the idea; and having offered his services to the London Missionary Society, he was by them sent out to Africa, which he reached in 1840. He had intended to proceed to China by his own efforts; and he says the only pang he had in going to Africa at the charge of the London Missionary Society was, because "it was not quite agreeable to one accustomed to work his own way to become, in a manner, dependent upon others." Arrived in Africa, he set to work with great zeal. He could not brook the idea of merely entering upon the labors of others, but cut out a large sphere of independent work, preparing himself for it by undertaking manual labor in building and other handicraft employment, in addition to teaching, which, he says, "made me generally as much exhausted and unfit for study in the evenings as ever I had been when a cotton-spinner." Whilst laboring amongst the Bechuanas, he dug canals, built houses, cultivated fields, reared cattle, and taught the natives to work as well as worship.

John Howard was another of the many patient and persevering men who have made England what it is—content simply to do with energy the work they have been appointed to do, and to go to their rest thankfully when it is done—

"Leaving no memorial but a world made better by their lives."

His sublime life proved that even physical weakness could remove mountains in the pursuit of an end recommended by duty. The idea of ameliorating the condition of prisoners engrossed his whole thoughts and possessed him like a passion, and no toil, nor danger, nor bodily suffering could turn him from that great object of his life. Though a man of no genius and but moderate talent, his heart was pure and his will was strong. Even in his own time he achieved a remarkable degree of success; and his influence did not die with him, for it has continued powerfully to affect not only the legislation of England, but of all civilized nations, down to the present hour.

Andrew Marvell was a patriot of the old Roman build. He lived in troublous times. He was born at Hull at the beginning of the reign of Charles I. When a young man, he spent four years at Trinity College, Cambridge. He afterwards traveled through Europe. In Italy he met Milton, and continued his friend through life. On his return to England the civil war was raging. It does not appear that he took any part in the struggle, though he was always a defender and promoter of liberty. In 1660 he was elected member of Parliament for his native town, and during his membership he wrote to the mayor and his constituents by almost every post, telling them of the course of affairs in Parliament. Marvell did not sympathize with Milton's anti-monarchical tendencies. His biographer styles him "the friend of England, Liberty and Magna Charta." He had no objections to a properly restricted monarchy, and therefore favored the restoration. The people longed for it, believing that the return of Charles II would prove the restoration of peace and loyalty. They were much mistaken. Marvell was appointed to accompany Lord Carlisle on an embassy to Russia, showing that he was not reckoned an enemy to the court. During his absence much evil had been done. The restored king was constantly in want of money. He took every method, by selling places and instituting monopolies, to supply his perpetual need. In one of Marvell's letters to his constituents he said, "The court is at the highest pitch of want and luxury, and the people are full of discontent."

The king continued to raise money unscrupulously, by means of his courtiers and apostate patriots. He bought them up by bribes of thousands of pounds. But Marvell was not to be bought. His satires upon the court and its parasites were published. They were read by all classes, from the king to the tradesman. The king determined to win him over. He was threatened, he was flattered, he was thwarted, he was caressed, he was beset with spies, he was waylaid by ruffians, and courted by beauties. But no Delilah could discover the secret of his strength. His integrity was proof alike against danger and against corruption. Against threats and bribes, pride is the ally of principle. In a court which held no man to be honest, and no woman chaste, this soft sorcery was cultivated to perfection; but Marvell, revering and respecting himself; was proof against its charms.

It has been said that Lord Treasurer Danby, thinking to buy over his old school-fellow, called upon Marvell in his garret. At parting the lord treasurer slipped into his hand an order on the treasury for $5,000, and then went to his chariot. Marvell, looking at the paper, calls after the treasurer, "My lord, I request another moment." They went up again to the garret, and Jack, the servant-boy, was called. "Jack, child, what had I for dinner yesterday?" "Don't you remember, sir? you had the little shoulder of mutton that you ordered me to bring from a woman in the market." "Very right, child. What have I for dinner today?" "Don't you know, sir, that you bid me lay by the blade-bone to broil?" "'Tis so, very right, child; go away." "My lord, said Marvell, turning to the treasurer, "do you hear that? Andrew Marvell's dinner is provided; there's your piece of paper. I want it not. I knew the sort of kindness you intended. I live here to serve my constituents; the ministry may seek men for their purpose; I am not one."

Buxton was a dull, heavy boy, distinguished for his strong self-will, which first exhibited itself in violent, domineering, and headstrong obstinacy. His father died when he was a child; but fortunately he had a wise mother, who trained his will with great tare, constraining him to obey, but encouraging the habit of deciding and acting for himself in matters which might safely be left to him. His mother believed that a strong will, directed upon worthy objects, was a valuable manly quality if properly guided, and she acted accordingly. When others about her commented on the boy's self-will, she would merely say, "Never mind—he is self-willed now—you will see it will turn out well in the end." Fowell learned very little at school, and was regarded as a dunce and an idler. He got other boys to do his exercises for him, while he romped and scrambled about. He returned home at fifteen, a great, growing, awkward lad, fond only of boating, shooting, riding, and field-sports—spending his time principally with the game-keeper, a man possessed of a good heart, an intelligent observer of life and nature, though he could neither read nor write. Buxton had excellent raw material in him, but he wanted culture, training and development. At this juncture of his life, when his habits were being formed for good or evil, he was happily thrown into the society of the Gurney family, distinguished for their fine social qualities not less than for their intellectual culture and public-spirited philanthropy. This intercourse with the Gurneys, he used after wards to say gave the coloring to his life They encouraged his efforts at self-culture; and when he went to the University of Dublin and gained high honors there, the animating passion in his mind, he said, "was, to carry back to them the prizes which they prompted and enabled him to win." He married one of the daughters of the family and started in life, commencing as a clerk. His power of will, which made him so difficult to deal with as a boy, now formed the backbone of his character, and made him most industrious and energetic in whatever he undertook. He threw his whole strength and bulk right down upon his work; and the great giant—"Elephant Buxton," they called him, for he stood some six feet four in height—became one of the most vigorous and practical of men. There was invincible energy and determination in whatever he did. Admitted a partner, he became the active manager of the concern; and the vast business which he conducted felt his influence through every fibre, and prospered far beyond its previous success. Nor did he allow his mind to lie fallow, for he gave his evenings diligently to self-culture, studying and digesting Blackstone, Montesquieu, and solid commentaries on English law. His maxims in reading were, "never to begin a book without finishing it"; "never to consider a book finished until it is mastered"; and "to study everything with the whole mind." When only thirty-two Buxton entered Parliament, and at once assumed that position of influence there of which every honest, earnest, well-informed man is secure, who enters that assembly.

Buxton was no genius—not a great intellectual leader nor discoverer, but mainly an earnest, straightforward, resolute, energetic man. Indeed, his whole character is most forcibly expressed in his own words, which every young man might well stamp upon his soul: "The longer I live," said he, "the more I am certain that the great difference between men, between the feeble and the powerful, the great and the insignificant, is *energy—invincible determination—a* purpose once fixed, and then death or victory! That quality will do any thing that can be done in this world; and no talents, no circumstances, no opportunities, will make a two-legged creature a Man without it."

Chapter 12

Self—Culture—Facilities and Difficulties

"Every person has two educations, one which he receives from others, and one, more important, which he gives to himself." —Gibbon.

"Is there one whom difficulties dishearten—who bends to the storm? He will do little. Is there one who will conquer? That kind of man never fails." —John Hunter.

"THE BEST PART of man's education," said Sir Walter Scott, "is that which he gives to himself." The late Sir Benjamin Brodie delighted to remember this saying, and he used to congratulate himself on the fact that professionally he was self-taught. But this is necessarily the case with all men who have acquired distinction in letters, science, or art. The education received at school or college is but a beginning, and is valuable mainly inasmuch as it trains the mind and habituates it to continuous application and study. That which is put into us by others is always far less ours than that which we acquire by our own diligent and persevering effort. Knowledge conquered by labor becomes a possession—a property entirely our own. Our own active effort is the essential thing; and no facilities, no books, no teachers, no amount of lessons learnt by rote will enable us to dispense with it. The best teachers have been the readiest to recognize the importance of self-culture, and of stimulating the student to acquire knowledge by the active exercise of his own faculties. They have relied more upon *training* than upon *telling*, and sought to make their pupils themselves active parties to the work in which they were engaged; thus making teaching something far higher than the mere passive reception of the scraps and details of knowledge. This was the spirit in which the great Dr. Arnold worked; he strove to teach his pupils to rely upon themselves, and develop their powers by their own active efforts, himself merely guiding, directing, stimulating, and encouraging them.

"I would far rather," he said, "send a boy to Van Dieman's Land, where he must work for his bread, than send him to Oxford to live in luxury, without any desire in his mind to avail himself of his advantages." "If there be one thing on earth," he observed on another occasion, "which is truly admirable, it is to see God's wisdom blessing an inferiority of natural powers, when they have been honestly, truly, and zealously cultivated." Speaking of a pupil of this character, he said, "I would stand to that man hat in hand." Once at Laleham, when teaching a rather dull boy, Arnold spoke somewhat sharply to him, on which the pupil looked up in his face and said, "Why do you speak angrily, sir? *indeed* I am doing the best I can." Years afterwards, Arnold used to tell the story to his children, and added, "I never felt so much in my life—that look and that speech I have never forgotten."

Practical success in life depends more upon physical health than is generally imagined. Hodson, writing home to a friend in England, said, "I believe if I get on well in India, it will be owing, physically speaking, to a sound digestion." The use of early labor in self-imposed mechanical employments may be illustrated by the boyhood of Sir Isaac Newton. Though comparatively a dull scholar, he was very assiduous in the use of his saw, hammer, and hatchet—"knocking and hammering in his lodging room"—making models of windmills, carriages, and machines of all sorts; and as he grew older, he took delight in making little tables and cupboards for his friends. Smeaton, Watt, and Stephenson, were equally handy with tools when mere boys; and but for such kind of self-culture in their youth, it is doubtful whether they would have accomplished so much in their manhood. Such was also the early training of the great inventors and mechanics described in the preceding pages, whose contrivance and intelligence were practically trained by the constant use of their hands in early life. Elihu Burritt says he found hard labor *necessary* to enable him to study with effect; and more than once he gave up school-teaching and study, and, taking to his leather apron again, went back to his blacksmith's forge and anvil for his health of body and mind's sake.

The training of young men in the use of tools would, at the same time that it educated them in "common things," teach them the use of their hands and arms, familiarize them with healthy work, exercise their faculties upon things tangible and actual, give them some practical acquaintance with mechanics, impart to them the ability of being useful, and implant in them the habit of persevering physical effort. This is an advantage which the working classes, strictly so called, certainly possess over the leisure classes—that they are in early life under the necessity of applying themselves laboriously to some mechanical pursuit or other—thus acquiring manual dexterity and the use of their physical powers. The chief disadvantage attached to the calling of the laborious classes is, not that they are employed in physical work, but that they are too exclusively so employed, often to the neglect of their moral and intellectual faculties. While the youths of the leisure classes, having been taught to associate labor with servility, have shunned it, and been allowed to grow up practically ignorant, the poorer classes, confining themselves within the circle of their laborious callings, have been allowed to grow up, in a large proportion of cases, absolutely illiterate. It seems possible, however, to avoid both these evils by combining physical training or physical work with intellectual culture, and there are various signs abroad which seem to mark the gradual adoption of this healthier system of education.

While it is necessary, then, in the first place to secure this solid foundation of physical health, it must also be observed that the cultivation of the habit of mental application is quite indispensable for the education of the student. The maxim that "Labor conquers all things," holds especially true in the case of the conquest of knowledge. The road into learning is alike free to all who will give the labor and the study requisite to gather it; nor are there any difficulties so great that the student of resolute purpose may not surmount and overcome them. It was one of the characteristic expressions of Chatterton, that God had sent his creatures into the world with arms long enough to reach any thing if they chose to be at the trouble. In study, as in business, energy is the great thing. We must not only strike the iron while it is hot, but strike it till it is made hot. It is astonishing how much may be accomplished in self-culture by the energetic and the persevering, who are careful to avail themselves of opportunities, and use up the fragments of spare time which the idle permit to run to waste. Thus Ferguson learned astronomy from the heavens while wrapt in a sheepskin on the highland hills. Thus Stone learned mathematics while working as a journeyman gardener; thus Drew studied the highest philosophy in the intervals of cobbling shoes; and thus Miller taught himself geology while working as a day-laborer in a quarry.

Sir Joshua Reynolds, as we have already observed, was so earnest a believer in the force of industry, that he held that all men might achieve excellence if they would but exercise the power of assiduous and patient working. He held that drudgery lay on the road to genius, and that there was no limit to the proficiency of an artist except the limit of his own painstaking. He would not believe in what is called inspiration, but only in study and labor. "Excellence," he said, "is never granted to man but as the reward of labor." "If you have great talents, industry will improve them; if you have but moderate abilities, industry will supply their deficiency. Nothing is denied to well-directed labor; nothing is to be obtained without it." Sir Fowell Buxton was an equal believer in the power of study; and he entertained the modest idea that he could do as well as other men if he devoted to the pursuit double the time and labor that they did. He placed his great confidence in ordinary means and extraordinary application.

Thoroughness and accuracy are two principal points to be aimed at in study. Francis Horner, in laying down rules for the cultivation of his mind, placed great stress upon the habit of continuous application to one subject for the sake of mastering it thoroughly; he confined himself with this object to only a few books, and resisted with the greatest firmness "every approach to a habit of desultory reading." The value of knowledge to any man consists not in its quantity, but mainly in the good uses to which he can apply it. Hence a little knowledge of an exact and perfect character, is always found more valuable for practical purposes than any extent of superficial learning,

One of Ignatius Loyola's maxims was, "He who does well one work at a time, does more than all." By spreading our efforts over too large a surface we inevitably weaken our force, hinder our progress, and acquire a habit of fitfulness and ineffective working. Lord St. Leonards once communicated to Sir Fowell Buxton the mode in which he had conducted his studies, and thus explained the secret of his success. "I resolved," said he, "when beginning to read law, to make everything I acquired perfectly my own, and never to go to a second thing till I had entirely accomplished the first. Many of my competitors read as much in a day as I read in a week; but, at the end of twelve months, my knowledge was as fresh as the day it was acquired, while theirs had glided away from recollection." It is not the quantity of study that one gets through, or the amount of reading, that makes a wise man; but the appositeness of the study to the purpose for which it is pursued; the concentration of the mind, for the time being, on the subject under consideration; and the habitual discipline by which the whole system of mental application is regulated. The most profitable study is that which is conducted with a definite aim and object. By thoroughly mastering any given branch of knowledge we render it more available for use at any moment. Hence it is not enough merely to have books, or to know where to read for information as we want it. Practical wisdom, for the purposes of life, must be carried about with us, and be ready for use at call. It is not sufficient that we have a fund laid up at home, but not a farthing in the pocket: we must carry about with us a store of the current coin of knowledge ready for exchange on all occasions, else we are comparatively helpless when the opportunity for using it occurs.

Decision and promptitude are as requisite in self-culture as in business. The growth of these qualities may be encouraged by accustoming young people to rely upon their own resources, leaving them to enjoy as much freedom of action in early life as is practicable. Too much guidance and restraint hinder the formation of habits of self-help. They are like bladders tied under the arms of one who has not taught himself to swim. Want of confidence is perhaps a greater obstacle to improvement than is generally imagined. Dr. Johnson was accustomed to attribute his success to confidence in his own powers. True modesty is quite compatible with a due estimate of one's own merits, and does not demand the abnegation of all merit. Though there are those who deceive themselves by putting a false figure before their ciphers, the want of confidence, the want of faith in one's self, and consequently the want of promptitude in action, is a defect of character which is found to stand very much in the way of individual progress; and the reason why so little is done, is generally because so little is attempted.

It is the use we make of the powers entrusted to us, which constitutes our only just claim to respect. He who employs his one talent aright is as much to be honored as he to whom ten talents have been given. There is really no more personal merit attaching to the possession of superior intellectual powers than there is in the succession to a large estate. How are those powers used—how is that estate employed? The mind may accumulate large stores of knowledge without any useful purpose; but the knowledge must be allied to goodness and wisdom, and embodied in upright character, else it is naught. Pestalozzi even held intellectual training by itself to be pernicious; insisting that the roots of all knowledge must strike and feed in the soil of the rightly-governed will. The acquisition of knowledge may, it is true, protect a man against the meaner felonies of life; but not in any degree against its selfish vices, unless fortified by sound principles and habits. Hence do we find in daily life so many instances of men who are well-informed in intellect, but utterly deformed in character; filled with the learning of the schools, yet possessing little practical wisdom, and offering examples for warning rather than imitation. An often quoted expression at this day is that "Knowledge is power"; but so, also, are fanaticism, despotism, and ambition. Knowledge of itself, unless wisely directed, might merely make bad men more dangerous, and the society in which it was regarded as the highest good, little better than a pandemonium.

It is also to be borne in mind that the experience gathered from books, though often valuable, is but of the nature of *learning;* whereas the experience gained from actual life is of the nature of *wisdom;* and a small store of the latter is worth vastly more than any stock of the former. Lord Bolingbroke truly said that "Whatever study tends neither directly nor indirectly to make us better men and citizens, is at best but a specious and ingenious sort of idleness, and the knowledge we acquire by it only a creditable kind of ignorance—nothing more."

Useful and instructive though good reading may be, it is yet only one mode of cultivating the mind; and is much less influential than practical experience and good example in the formation of character. There were wise, valiant, and true-hearted men bred in England, long before the existence of a reading public. Magna Charta was secured by men who signed the deed with their marks. Though altogether unskilled in the art of deciphering the literary signs by which principles were denominated upon paper, yet they understood and appreciated, and boldly contended for, the things themselves. Thus the foundations of English liberty were laid by men who, though illiterate, were nevertheless of the very highest stamp of character. And it must be admitted that the chief object of culture is, not merely to fill the mind with other men's thoughts, and to be the passive recipient of their impressions of things, but to enlarge our individual intelligence, and render us more useful and efficient workers in the sphere of life to which we may be called. Many of our most energetic and useful workers have been but sparing readers. Brindley and Stephenson did not learn to read and write until they reached manhood, and yet they did great works and lived manly lives; John Hunter could barely read or write when he was twenty years old, though he could make tables and chairs with any carpenter in the trade. When told that one of his contemporaries had charged him with being ignorant of the dead languages, he said, "I would undertake to teach him that on the dead body which he never knew in any language, dead or living."

It is not then how much a man may know, that is of importance, but the end and purpose for which he knows it. The object of knowledge should be to mature wisdom and improve character, to render us better, happier, and more useful; more benevolent, more energetic, and more efficient in the pursuit of every high purpose in life. When people once fall into the habit of admiring and encouraging ability as such, without reference to moral character they are on the highway to all sorts of degradation. We must ourselves *be* and *do,* and not rest satisfied merely with reading and meditating over what other men have been and done. Our best light must be made life, and our best thought action. At least we ought to be able to say, as Richter did, "I have made as much out of myself as could be made of the stuff, and no man should require more"; for it is every man's duty to discipline and guide himself, with God's help, according to his responsibilities and the faculties with which he has been endowed.

Self-respect is the noblest garment with which a man may clothe himself—the most elevating feeling with which the mind can be inspired. One of Pythagoras's wisest maxims, in his "Golden Verses," is that with which he enjoins the pupil to "reverence himself." Borne up by this high idea, he will not defile his body by sensuality, nor his mind by servile thoughts. This sentiment, carried into daily life, will be found at the root of all the virtues—cleanliness, sobriety, chastity, morality, and religion. "The pious and just honoring of ourselves," said Milton, "may be thought the radical moisture and fountain-head from whence every laudable and worthy enterprise issues forth." To think meanly of one's self, is to sink in one's own estimation as well as in the estimation of others. And as the thoughts are, so will the acts be. Man can not aspire if he look down; if he will rise, he must look up. The very humblest may be sustained by the proper indulgence of this feeling. Poverty itself may be lifted and lighted up by self-respect; and it is truly a noble sight to see a poor man hold himself upright amidst his temptations, and refuse to demean himself by low actions.

Self-culture may not, however, end in eminence, as in the numerous instances above cited. The great majority of men, in all times, however enlightened, must necessarily be engaged in the ordinary avocations of industry; and no degree of culture which can be conferred upon the community at large will ever enable them—even were it desirable, which it is not—to get rid of the daily work of society, which must be done. But this, we think, may also be accomplished. We can elevate the condition of labor by allying it to noble thoughts, which confer a grace upon the lowliest as well as the highest rank. For no matter how poor or humble a man may be, the great thinker of this And other days may come in and sit down with him, and be his companion for the time, though his dwelling be the meanest hut. It is thus that the habit of well-directed reading may become a source of the greatest pleasure and self-improvement, and exercise a gentle coercion, with the most beneficial results, over the whole tenor of a man's character and conduct. And even though self-culture may not bring wealth, it will at all events give one the companionship of elevated thoughts. A nobleman once contemptuously asked of a sage, "What have you got by all your philosophy?" "At least I have got society in myself," was the wise man's reply.

But many are apt to feel despondent, and become discouraged in the work of self-culture, because they do not "get on" in the world so fast as they think they deserve to do. Having planted their acorn, they expect to see it grow into an oak at once. They have perhaps looked upon knowledge in the light of a marketable commodity, and are consequently mortified because it does not sell as they expected it would do. Mr. Tremenheere, in one of his "Education Reports," states that a schoolmaster in Norfolk, finding his school rapidly falling off, made inquiry into the cause, and ascertained that the reason given by the majority of the parents for withdrawing their children was, that they had expected "education was to make them better off than they were before," but that having found it had "done them no good," they had taken their children from school, and would give themselves no further trouble about education!

The same low idea of self-culture is but too prevalent in other classes, and is encouraged by the false views of life which are always more or less current in society. But to regard self-culture either as a means of getting past others in the world, or of intellectual dissipation and amusement, rather than as a power to elevate the character and expand the spiritual nature, is to place it on a very low level. To use the words of Bacon, "Knowledge is not a shop for profit or sale, but a rich store-house for the glory of the Creator and the relief of man's estate." It is doubtless most honorable for a man to labor to elevate himself, and to better his condition in society, but this is not to be done at the sacrifice of himself. To make the mind the mere drudge of the body, is putting it to a very servile use; and to go about whining and bemoaning our pitiful lot because we fail in achieving that success in life which, after all, depends rather upon habits of industry and attention to business details than upon knowledge, is the mark of a small, and often of a sour mind. Such a temper can not better be reproved than in the words of Robert Southey, who thus wrote to a friend who sought his counsel: "I would give you advice if it could be of use; but there is no curing those who choose to be diseased. A good and wise man may at times be angry with the world, at times grieved for it; but be sure no man was ever discontented with the world if he did his duty in it. If a man of education, who has health, eyes, hands, and leisure, wants an object, it is only because God Almighty has bestowed all those blessings upon a man who does not deserve them."

Amusement in moderation is wholesome, and to be commended; but amusement in excess vitiates the whole nature, and is a thing to be carefully guarded against. The maxim is often quoted of "All work and no play makes Jack a dull boy"; but all play and no work makes him something greatly worse. Nothing can be more hurtful to a youth than to have his soul surfeited with pleasure. The best qualities of his mind are impaired; common enjoyments become tasteless; his appetite for the higher kind of pleasure is vitiated; and when he comes to face the work and the duties of life, the result is usually aversion and disgust. "Fast" men waste and exhaust the powers of life, and dry up the sources of true happiness. Having forestalled their spring, they can produce no healthy growth of either character or intellect. A child without simplicity, a maiden without innocence, a boy without truthfulness, are not more piteous sights than the man who has wasted and thrown away his youth in self-indulgence. Mirabeau said of himself; "My early years have already in a great measure disinherited the succeeding ones, and dissipated a great part of my vital powers." As the wrong done to another today returns upon ourselves tomorrow, so the sins of our youth rise up in our age to scourge us. "I assure you," wrote Giusti the Italian to a friend, "I pay a heavy price for existence. It is true that our lives are not at our own disposal. Nature pretends to give them gratis at the beginning, and then sends in her account." The worst of youthful indiscretions is not that they destroy health, so much as that they sully manhood. The dissipated youth becomes a tainted man; and often he can not be pure, even if he would. If cure there be, it is only to be found in inoculating the mind with a fervent spirit of duty, and in energetic application to useful work.

Robert Nicoll wrote to a friend, after reading the "Recollections of Coleridge," "What a mighty intellect was lost in that man for want of a little energy—a little determination!" Nicoll himself was a true and brave spirit, who died young, but not before he had encountered and overcome great difficulties in life. At his outset, while carrying on a small business as a bookseller, he found himself weighed down with a debt of only twenty pounds, which he said he felt "weighing like a millstone round his neck," and that "if he had it paid he never would borrow again from mortal man." Writing to his mother at the time he said, "Fear not for me, dear mother, for I feel myself daily growing firmer and more hopeful in spirit. The more I think and reflect—and thinking, not reading, is now my occupation—I feel that, whether I be growing richer or not, I am growing a wiser man, which is far better. Pain, poverty, and all the other wild beasts in life which so frighten others, I am so bold as to think I could look in the face without shrinking, without losing respect for myself, faith in man's high destinies, or trust in God. There is a point which it costs much mental toil and struggling to gain, but which, when once gained, a man can look down from, as a traveler from a lofty mountain, on storms raging below, while he is walking in sunshine. That I have yet gained this point in life I will not say, but I feel myself daily nearer to it."

It is not ease, but effort—not facility, but difficulty, that makes men. There is, perhaps, no station in life, in which difficulties have not to be encountered and overcome before any decided measure of success can be achieved. Those difficulties are, however, our best instructors, as our mistakes are often our best experience. Charles James Fox was accustomed to say that he hoped more from a man who failed, and yet went on in spite of his failure, than from the buoyant career of the successful. "It is all very well," said he, "to tell me that a young man has distinguished himself by a brilliant first speech. He may go on, or he may be satisfied with his first triumph; but show me a young man who has *not* succeeded at first, and nevertheless has gone on, and I will back that young man to do better than most of those who have succeeded at the first trial." We learn wisdom from failure much more than from success. We often discover what *will* do by finding out what will not do; and probably he who never made a mistake never made a discovery. It was the failure in the attempt to make a sucking-pump act, when the working bucket was more than thirty-three feet above the surface of the water to be raised, that led observant men to study the law of atmospheric pressure, and opened a new field of research to the genius of Galileo, Torrecelli, and Boyle. John Hunter used to remark that the art of surgery would not advance until professional men had the courage to publish their failures as well as their successes. Watt the engineer said, of all things most wanted in mechanical engineering was a history of failures. "We want," he said, "a book of blots." When Sir Humphrey Davy was once shown a dexterously manipulated experiment, he said—"I thank God I was not made a dexterous manipulator, for the most important of my discoveries have been suggested to me by failures." Another distinguished investigator in physical science has left it on record that, whenever in the course of his researches he encountered an apparently insuperable obstacle, he generally found himself on the brink of some discovery The very greatest things—great thoughts, great discoveries, inventions—have usually been nurtured in hardship, often pondered over in sorrow and at length established with difficulty.

Beethoven said of Rossini, that he had in him the stuff to have made a good musician if he had only, when a boy, been well flogged; but that he had been spoilt by the facility with which he produced. Men who feel their strength within them need not fear to encounter adverse opinions; they have far greater reason to fear undue praise and too friendly criticism. When Mendelssohn was about to enter the orchestra at Birmingham, on the first performance of his "Elijah," he said laughingly to one of his friends and critics, "stick your claws into me! Don't tell me what you like, but what you don't like!"

It has been said, and truly, that it is the defeat that tries the general more than the victory. Washington lost more battles than he gained; but he succeeded in the end. The Romans, in their most victorious campaigns, almost invariably began with defeats. Moreau used to be compared by his companions to a drum, which nobody hears of except it be beaten. Wellington's military genius was perfected by encounter with difficulties of apparently the most overwhelming character, but which only served to move his resolution, and bring out more prominently his great qualities as a man and a general. So the skillful mariner obtains his best experience amidst storms and tempests, which train him to self-reliance, courage, and the highest discipline; and we probably owe to rough seas and wintry nights the best training of the race of British seamen, who are certainly not surpassed by any in the world.

"Sweet indeed are the uses of adversity." They reveal to us our powers, and call forth our energies. If there be real worth in the character, like sweet herbs, it will give forth its finest fragrance when pressed.

"Crosses," says the old proverb, "are the ladders that lead to heaven." "What is even poverty itself"; asks Richter, "that a man should murmur under it? It is but as the pain of piercing a maiden's ear, and you hang precious jewels in the wound." In the experience of life it is found that the wholesome discipline of adversity in strong natures usually carries with it a self-preserving influence. Many are found capable of bravely bearing up under privations, and cheerfully encountering obstructions, who are afterwards found unable to withstand the more dangerous influences of prosperity. It is only a weak man whom the wind deprives of his cloak; a man of average strength is more in danger of losing it when assailed by the beams of a too genial sun. Thus it often needs a higher discipline and a stronger character to bear up under good fortune than under adverse. Some generous natures kindle and warm with prosperity, but there are many on whom wealth has no such influence. Base hearts it only hardens, making those who were mean and servile, mean and proud. But while prosperity is apt to harden the heart to pride, adversity in a man of resolution will serve to ripen it into fortitude. To use the words of Burke, "Difficulty is a severe instructor, set over us by the supreme ordinance of a parental guardian and instructor, who knows us better than we know ourselves, as He loves us better too. He that wrestles with us strengthens our nerves, and sharpens our skill; our antagonist is thus our helper." Without the necessity of encountering difficulty, life might be easier, but men would be worth less. For trials, wisely improved, train the character, and teach self-help; thus hardship itself may often prove the wholesomest discipline for us, though we recognize it not.

The battle of life is, in most cases, fought up-hill; and to win it without a struggle were perhaps to win it without honor. If there were no difficulties there would be no success; if there were nothing to struggle for, there would be nothing to be achieved. Difficulties may intimidate the weak, but they act only as a wholesome stimulus to men of resolution and valor. All experience of life, indeed, serves to prove that the impediments thrown in the way of human advancement may, for the most part, be overcome by steady good conduct, honest zeal, activity, perseverance, and above all, by a determined resolution to surmount difficulties, and stand up manfully against misfortune.

The school of Difficulty is the best school of moral discipline, for nations as for individuals. Indeed, the history of difficulty would be but a history of all the great and good things that have yet been accomplished by men. It is hard to say how much northern nations owe to their encounter with a comparatively rude and changeable climate, and an originally sterile soil, which is one of the necessities of their condition—involving a perennial struggle with difficulties such as the natives of sunnier climes know nothing of. And thus it may be, that though our finest products are exotic, the skill and industry which have been necessary to rear them, have issued in the production of a native growth of men not surpassed on the globe.

Wherever there is difficulty, the individual man must come out for better or for worse. Encounter with it will train his strength, and discipline his skill; heartening him for future effort, as the racer, by being trained to run against the hill, at length courses with facility. The road to success may be steep to climb, and it puts to the proof the energies of him who would reach the summit. But by experience a man soon learns that obstacles are to be overcome by grappling with them; that the nettle feels as soft as silk when it is boldly grasped; and that the most effective help towards realizing the object proposed is the moral conviction that we can and will accomplish it. Thus difficulties often fall away of themselves before the determination to overcome them.

Much will be done if we do but try. Nobody knows what he can do till he has tried; and few try their best till they have been forced to do it. "*If* I could do, such and such a thing," sighs the desponding youth. But nothing will be done if he only wishes. The desire must ripen into purpose and effort; and one energetic attempt is worth a thousand aspirations. It is these thorny "ifs" which so often hedge around the field of possibility, and prevent anything being done or even attempted. "A difficulty," said Lord Lyndhurst, "is a thing to be overcome"; grapple with it at once; facility will come with practice, and strength and fortitude with repeated effort. Thus the mind and character may be trained to an almost perfect discipline, and enabled to act with a grace, spirit, and liberty, almost incomprehensible to those who have not passed through a similar experience. Carissimi, when praised for the ease and grace of his melodies, exclaimed, "Ah! you little know with what difficulty this ease has been acquired." Sir Joshua Reynolds, when once asked how long it had taken him to paint a certain picture, replied, "All my life." Henry Clay, the American orator, when giving advice to young men, thus described to them the secret of his success in the cultivation of his art: "I owe my success in life," said he, "chiefly to one circumstance—that at the age of twenty-seven I commenced, and continued for years, the process of daily reading and speaking upon the contents of some historical or scientific book. These offhand efforts were made, sometimes in a cornfield, at others in the forest, and not infrequently in some distant barn, with the horse and the ox for my auditors. It is to this early practice of the art of all arts that I am indebted for the primary and leading impulses that stimulated me onward and have shaped and moulded my whole subsequent destiny."

Curran, the Irish orator, when a youth, had a strong defect in his articulation, and at school he was known as "stuttering Jack Curran." While he was engaged in the study of the law, and still struggling to overcome his defect, he was stung into eloquence by the sarcasms of a member of a debating club, who characterized him as "Orator Mum"; for, like Cowper, when he stood up to speak on a previous occasion, Curran had not been able to utter a word. The taunt stung him and he replied in a triumphant speech. This accidental discovery in himself of the gift of eloquence encouraged him to proceed in his studies with renewed energy. He corrected his enunciation by reading aloud, emphatically and distinctly, the best passages in literature for several hours every day, studying his features before a mirror, and adopting a method of gesticulation suited to his rather awkward and ungraceful figure. He also proposed cases to himself, which he argued with as much care as if he had been addressing a jury. Curran began business with the qualification which Lord Eldon stated to be the first requisite for distinction, that is, "to be not worth a shilling." While working his way laboriously at the bar, still oppressed by the diffidence which had overcome him in his debating, club, he was on one occasion provoked by the Judge into making a very severe retort. In the case under discussion, Curran observed, "that he had never met the law as laid down by his lordship in any book in his library." "That may be, sir," said the judge, in a contemptuous tone, "but I suspect that *your* library is very small." His lordship was notoriously a furious political partisan, the author of several anonymous pamphlets characterized by unusual violence and dogmatism. Curran, roused by the allusion to his straightened circumstances, replied thus: "It is very true, my lord, that I am poor, and the circumstance has certainly curtailed my library; my books are not numerous, but they are select, and I hope they have been perused with proper dispositions. I have prepared myself for this high profession by the study of a few good works, rather than by the composition of a great many bad ones. I am not ashamed of my poverty; but I should be ashamed of my wealth, could I have stooped to acquire it by servility and corruption. If I rise not to rank, I shall at least be honest; and should I ever cease to be so, many an example shows me that an ill-gained elevation, by making me the more conspicuous, would only make me the more universally and the more notoriously contemptible."

The extremest poverty has been no obstacle in the way of men devoted to the duty of self-culture. Professor Alexander Murray, the linguist, learned to write by scribbling his letters on an old wool-card with the end of a burned feather stem. The only book which his father, who was a poor shepherd, possessed, was a penny Catechism; but that, being thought too valuable for common use, was carefully preserved in a cupboard for the Sunday catechisings. Professor Moor, when a young man, being too poor to purchase Newton's "Principia," borrowed the book, and copied the whole of it with his own hand. Many poor students, while laboring daily for their living, have only been able to snatch an atom of knowledge here and there at intervals, as birds do their food in winter-time when the fields are covered with snow. They have struggled on, and faith and hope have come to them. A well-known author and publisher, William Chambers, of Edinburgh, speaking before an assemblage of young men in that city, thus briefly described to them his humble beginnings, for their encouragement: "I stand before you," he said, "a self-educated man. My education is that which is supplied at the humble parish schools of Scotland; and it was only when I went to Edinburgh, a poor boy, that I devoted my evenings, after the labors of the day, to the cultivation of that intellect which the Almighty has given me. From seven or eight in the morning till nine or ten at night was I at my business as a bookseller's apprentice, and it was only during hours after these, stolen from sleep, that I could devote myself to study. I did not read novels; my attention was devoted to physical science, and other useful matters. I also taught myself French. I look back to those times with great pleasure, and am almost sorry I have not to go through the same experience again; for I reaped more pleasure when I had not a sixpence in my pocket, studying in a garret in Edinburgh, than I now find when sitting amidst all the elegancies and comforts of a parlor."

William Cobbett's account of how he learned English grammar is full of interest and instruction for all students laboring under difficulties. "I learned grammar," said he, "when I was a private soldier on the pay of sixpence a day. The edge of my berth, or that of my guard-bed, was my seat to study in; my knapsack was my book-case; a bit of board lying on my lap was my writing table; and the task did not demand any thing like a year of my life. I had no money to purchase candle or oil; in winter-time it was rarely that I could get any evening light but that of the fire, and only my turn even at that. And if I, under such circumstances, and without parent or friend to advise or encourage me, accomplished this undertaking, what excuse can there be for any youth, however poor, however pressed with business, or however circumstanced as to room or other convenience? To buy a pen or a sheet of paper I was compelled to forego some portion of food, though in a state of half-starvation; I had no moment of time that I could call my own; and I had to read and write amidst the talking, laughing, singing, whistling, and brawling of at least half a score of the most thoughtless of men, and that, too, in the hours of their freedom from all control. Think not lightly of the farthing that I had to give, now and then, for ink, pen, or paper! That farthing was, alas! a great sum to me! I was as tall as I am now; I had great health and great exercise. The whole of the money, not expended for us at market, was four cents a week for each man. I remember, and well I may! that on one occasion I, after all necessary expenses, had, on a Friday, made shifts to have a halfpenny in reserve, which I had destined for the purchase of a red herring in the morning; but, when I pulled off my clothes at night, so hungry then as to be hardly able to endure life, I found that I had lost my halfpenny! I buried my head under the miserable sheet and rug, and cried like a child! And again I say, if I, under circumstances like these, could encounter and overcome this task, can there be, in the whole world, a youth to find an excuse for the nonperformance?"

We have been informed of an equally striking instance of perseverance and application in learning on the part of a French political exile in London. His original occupation was that of a stonemason, at which he found employment for some time; but work becoming slack, he lost his place, and poverty stared him in the face. In his dilemma, he called upon a fellow-exile profitably engaged in teaching French, and consulted him what he ought to do to earn a living. The answer was, "Become a professor?" "A professor?" answered the mason—"I, who am only a workman, speaking but a patois! Surely you are jesting?" "On the contrary, I am quite serious," said the other, "and again I advise you—become a professor; place yourself under me, and I will undertake to teach you how to teach others." "No, no!" replied the mason, "it is impossible; I am too old to learn; I am too little of a scholar; I can not be a professor." He went away, and again he tried to obtain employment at his trade. From London he went into the provinces, and traveled several hundred miles in vain; he could not find a master. Returning to London, he went direct to his former adviser and said, "I have tried every where for work, and failed; I will now try to be a professor!" He immediately placed himself under instruction; and being a man of close application, of quick apprehension, and vigorous intelligence, he speedily mastered the elements of grammar, the rules of construction and composition, and the correct pronunciation of classical French. When his friend and instructor thought him sufficiently competent to undertake the teaching of others, an appointment, advertised as vacant, was applied for and obtained; and behold our artisan at length become professor! It so happened, that the seminary to which he was appointed was situated in a suburb of London where he had formerly worked as a stonemason; every morning the first thing which met his eyes, on looking out of his dressing-room window was a stack of cottage-chimneys which he had himself built! He feared for a time lest he should be recognized in the village as the quondam workman, and thus bring discredit on his seminary, which was of high standing. But he need have been under no such apprehension, as he proved a most efficient teacher, and his pupils were on more than one occasion publicly complimented for their knowledge of French. Meanwhile, he secured the respect and friendship of all who knew him—fellow-professors as well as pupils; and when the story of his struggles, his difficulties, and his past history became known to them, they admired him more than ever.

Sir Samuel Romilly was not less persevering as a self-cultivator. The son of a jeweler, descended from a French refugee, he received little education in his early years, but overcame all his disadvantages by unwearied application, and by efforts constantly directed towards the same end. "I determined," he said, in his autobiography, "when I was between fifteen and sixteen years of age, to apply myself seriously to learning Latin, of which I, at that time, knew little more than some of the most familiar rules of grammar. In the course of three or four years, during which I thus applied myself, I had read almost every prose writer of the age of pure Latinity. I had gone three times through the whole of Livy, Sallust, and Tacitus. I had studied the most celebrated orations of Cicero, and translated a great deal of Homer. Terence, Virgil, Horace, Ovid, and Juvenal I had read over and over again." He also studied geography, natural history, and natural philosophy, and obtained a considerable acquaintance with general knowledge. At sixteen he was articled to a clerk in Chancery; worked hard; was admitted to the bar; and his industry and perseverance insured success. He became Solicitor-General under the Fox administration in 1806, and steadily worked his way to the highest celebrity in his profession. Yet he was always haunted by a painful and almost oppressive sense of his own disqualifications, and never ceased laboring to remedy them. His autobiography is a lesson of instructive facts, worth volumes of sentiment, and well deserves a careful perusal.

Sir Walter Scott was accustomed to cite the case of his young friend John Leyden as one of the most remarkable illustrations of the power of perseverance which he had ever known. The son of a shepherd in one of the wildest valleys in Roxburghshire, he was almost entirely self-educated. Like many Scotch shepherds' sons—like Hogg, who taught himself to write by copying the letters of a printed book as he lay watching his flock on the hillside—like Cairns, who from tending sheep on the Lammermoors, raised himself by dint of application and industry to the professor's chair which he now so worthily holds—like Maurey, Ferguson, and many more, Leyden was early inspired by a thirst for knowledge. When a poor barefooted boy, he walked six or eight miles across the moors daily to learn reading at the little village schoolhouse of Kirkton; and this was all the education he received; the rest he acquired for himself. He found his way to Edinburgh to attend the college there, setting the extremest penury at defiance. He was first discovered as the frequenter of a small bookseller's shop kept by Archibald Constable, afterwards so well known as a publisher. He would pass hour after hour perched on a ladder in mid-air, with some great folio in his hand, forgetful of the scanty meal of bread and water which awaited him at his miserable lodging. Access to books and lectures comprised all within the bounds of his wishes. Thus he toiled and battled at the gates of science until his unconquerable perseverance carried everything before it. Before he had attained his nineteenth year he had astonished all the professors in Edinburough by his profound knowledge of Greek and Latin, and the general mass of information he had acquired. Having turned his views to India, he sought employment in the civil service, but failed. He was however informed that a surgeon's assistant's commission was open to him. But he was no surgeon, and knew no more of the profession than a child. He could, however, learn. Then he was told that he must be ready to pass in six months. Nothing daunted, he sat to work to acquire in six months what usually required three years. At the end of six months he took his degree with honor. Scott and a few friends helped to fit him out; and he sailed for India, after publishing his beautiful poem, "The Scenes of Infancy." In India he promised to become one of the greatest of oriental scholars, but was unhappily cut off by fever caught by exposure, and died at an early age.

The life of the late Dr. Lee, Professor of Hebrew at Cambridge, furnishes one of the most remarkable instances in modern times of the power of patient perseverance and resolute purpose in working out an honorable career in literature. He received his education at a charity school at Lognor, near Shrewsbury, but so little distinguished himself there, that his master pronounced him one of the dullest boys that ever passed through his hands. He was put apprentice to a carpenter, and worked at that trade until he arrived at manhood. To occupy his leisure hours he took to reading; and, some of his books containing Latin quotations, he became desirous of ascertaining what they meant. He bought a Latin grammar, and proceeded to learn Latin. As Stone, the Duke of Argyle's gardener, said, long before, "Does one need to know more than the twenty-four letters in order to learn everything else that one wishes?" Lee rose early and sat up late, and he succeeded in mastering the Latin before his apprenticeship was out. Whilst working one day in some place of worship, a copy of a Greek Testament fell in his way, and he was immediately filled with the desire to learn that language. He accordingly sold some of his Latin books and purchased a Greek Grammar and Lexicon. Taking pleasure in learning, he soon mastered the language. Then he sold his Greek books and bought Hebrew ones, and learned that language, unassisted by any instructor, without any hope of fame or reward, but simply following the bent of his genius. He next proceeded to learn the Chaldee, Syriac, and Samaritan dialects. His character as a tradesman being excellent, his business improved, and his means enabled him to marry, which he did when twenty-eight years old. He determined now to devote himself to the maintenance of his family, and to renounce the luxury of literature. Accordingly he sold all his books. He might have continued a working carpenter all his life had not the chest of tools upon which he depended for subsistence been destroyed by fire, and destitution stared him in the face. He was too poor to buy new tools, so he bethought him of teaching children their letters—a profession requiring the least possible capital. But though he had mastered many languages, he was so defective in the common branches of knowledge, that at first he could not teach them. Resolute of purpose however, he assiduously set to work, and taught himself arithmetic and writing to such a degree as to be able to impart the knowledge of these branches to little children. His unaffected, simple, and beautiful character gradually attracted friends, and the acquirements of the "learned carpenter" became bruited abroad. Dr. Scott, a neighboring clergyman, obtained for him the appointment of master of a charity school and introduced him to a distinguished Oriental scholar. These friends supplied him with books, and Lee successively mastered Arabic, Persic, and Hindostanee. He continued to pursue his studies while on duty as a private in the local militia of the county; gradually acquiring greater proficiency in languages. At length his kind patron, Dr. Scott, enabled Lee to enter Queen's College, Cambridge; and after a course of study, in which he distinguished himself by his mathematical acquirements, a vacancy occurring in the professorship of Arabic and Hebrew, he was worthily elected to fill the honorable office. Besides ably performing his duties as a professor, he voluntarily gave much of his time to the instruction of missionaries going forth to preach the Gospel to Eastern tribes in their own tongue. He also made translations of the Bible into several Asiatic dialects; and having mastered the New Zealand language, he arranged a grammar and vocabulary for two New Zealand chiefs who were then in England, which books are now in daily use in the New Zealand schools. Such, in brief; is the remarkable history of Dr. Samuel Lee; and it is but the counterpart of numerous similarly instructive examples of the power of perseverance in self-culture, as displayed in the lives of many of the most distinguished of our literary and scientific men.

There are many other illustrious names which might be cited to prove the truth of the common saying that "it is never to late to learn." Even at advanced years men can do much, if they will determine on making a beginning. Sir Henry Spelman did not begin the study of science until he was between fifty and sixty years of age. Franklin was fifty before he fully entered upon the study of Natural Philosophy. Dryden and Scott were not known as authors until each was in his fortieth year. Boccaccio was thirty-five when he commenced his literary career, and Alfieri was forty-six when he began the study of Greek. Dr. Arnold learned German at an advanced age, for the purpose of reading Niebuhr in the original; and in like manner James Watt, when about forty, while working at his trade of an instrument-maker in Glasgow, learned French, German, and Italian, to enable himself to peruse the valuable works on mechanical philosophy which existed in those languages. Thomas Scott was fifty-six before he began to learn Hebrew. Robert Hall was once found lying upon the floor, racked by pain, learning Italian in his old age, to enable him to judge of the parallel drawn by Macaulay between Milton and Dante. Handel was forty-eight before he published any of his great works. Indeed, hundreds of instances might be given of men who struck out an entirely new path, and successfully entered on new studies, at a comparatively advanced time of life. None but the frivolous or the indolent will say, "I am too old to learn."

And here we would repeat what we have said before, that it is not men of genius who move the world and take the lead in it, so much as men of steadfastness, purpose, and industry. Notwithstanding the many undeniable instances of the precocity of men of genius, it is nevertheless true that early advancement gives no indication of the height to which the grown man will reach. Precocity is sometimes a symptom of disease rather than of intellectual vigor. What becomes of all the "remarkably forward children?" Trace them through life, and it will frequently be found that the dull boys, who were beaten at school, have shot ahead of them. The precocious boys are rewarded, but the prizes which they gain by their greater quickness and facility do not always prove of use to them. What ought rather to be rewarded is the endeavor, the struggle, and the obedience; for it is the youth who does his best, though endowed with an inferiority of natural powers, that ought above all others to be encouraged.

An interesting chapter might be written on the subject of illustrious dunces—dull boys, but brilliant men. Newton, when at school, stood at the bottom of the lowest form but one. The boy above Newton having kicked him, the dunce showed his pluck by challenging him to a fight, and beat him. Then he set to work with a will, and determined also to vanquish his antagonist as a scholar, which he did, rising to the top of his class. Isaac Barrow, when a boy at the Charterhouse School, was notorious chiefly for his strong temper, pugnacious habits, and proverbial idleness as a scholar; and he caused such grief to his parents that his father used to say that, if it pleased God to take from him any of his children, he hoped it might be Isaac, the least promising of them all. Adam Clarke, when a boy, was proclaimed by his father to be "a grievous dunce." Dean Swift was "plucked" at Dublin University, and only obtained his recommendation to Oxford by "special favor." The well-known Dr. Chalmers and Dr. Cook were boys together at the parish school of St. Andrew's; and they were found so stupid and mischievous, that the master, irritated beyond measure, dismissed them both as incorrigible dunces. The brilliant Sheridan showed so little capacity as a boy, that he was presented to a tutor by his mother with the complimentary accompaniment that he was a hopeless dunce. Walter Scott was all but a dunce when a boy, always much readier for sport than apt at his lessons. At the Edinburg University, Professor Dalzell pronounced upon him the sentence that "Dunce he was, and dunce he would remain." Chatterton was returned on his mother's hands as "a fool, of whom nothing could be made." Burns was a dull boy, good only at athletic exercises. Goldsmith spoke of himself as a plant that flowered late. Alfieri left college no wiser than he entered it, and did not begin the studies by which he distinguished himself, until he had run half over Europe. Robert Clive was a dunce, if not a reprobate, when a youth; but always full of energy, even in badness. His family, glad to get rid of him, shipped him off to Madras; and he lived to lay the foundations of the British power in India. Napoleon and Wellington were both dull boys not distinguishing themselves in any way at school.

Ulysses Grant, the Commander-in-chief of the United States, was called "Useless Grant" by his mother—he was so dull and unhandy when a boy; and Stonewall Jackson, Lee's greatest lieutenant, was, in his youth, chiefly noted for his slowness. While a pupil at West Point Military Academy he was, however, equally remarkable for his application and perseverance. When a task was set him, he never left it until he had mastered it; nor did he ever feign to possess knowledge which he had not entirely acquired. "Again and again," wrote one who knew him, "when called upon to answer questions in the recitation of the day, he would reply, I have not yet looked at it; I have been engaged in mastering the recitation of yesterday or the day before." The result was that he graduated seventeenth in a class of seventy. There was probably in the whole class not a boy to whom Jackson at the outset was not inferior in knowledge and attainments; but at the end of the race he had only sixteen before him, and had outstripped no fewer than fifty-three. It used to be said of him by his contemporaries, that if the course had been for ten years instead of four, Jackson would have graduated at the head of his class. John Howard, the philanthropist, was another illustrious dunce, learning next to nothing during the seven years that he was at school. Watt was a dull scholar, notwithstanding the stories told about his precocity; but he was, what was better, patient and perseverant, and it was by such qualities, and by his carefully cultivated inventiveness, that he was enabled to perfect his steam-engine.

What Dr. Arnold says of boys is equally true of men—that the difference between one boy and another consists not so much in talent as in energy; Given perseverance, and energy soon becomes habitual. Provided the dunce has persistency and application, he will inevitably head the cleverer fellow without those qualities. Slow but sure wins the race. It is perseverance that explains how the position of boys at school are so often reversed in real life, and it is curious to note how some who were then so clever have since become so commonplace; while others, dull boys, of whom nothing was expected, slow in their faculties but sure in their pace, have assumed the, position of leaders of men. The tortoise in the right road will beat a racer in the wrong. It matters not, though a youth be slow, if he be but diligent. Quickness of parts may even prove a defect, is as much as the boy who learns readily will often forget as readily; and also because he finds no need of cultivating that quality of application and perseverance which the slower youth is compelled to exercise, and which proves so valuable an element in the formation of every character. Davy said, "What I am I have made myself"; and the same holds true universally.

To conclude: the best culture is not obtained from teachers when at school or college, so much as by our own diligent self-education when we have become men, Hence parents need not be in too great haste to see their children's talents forced into bloom. Let them watch and wait patiently, letting good example and quiet training do their work, and leave the rest to Providence. Let them see to it that the youth is provided, by free exercise of his bodily powers, with a full stock of physical health; set him fairly on the road of self culture; carefully train his habits of application and perseverance, and as he grows older, if the right stuff be in him, he will be enabled vigorously and effectively to cultivate himself.

Chapter 13

Workers in Art

*"If what shone afar so grand,
Turn to nothing in thy hand,
On again; the virtue lies
In the struggle, not the prize."*
—M. M. Moore.

EXCELLENCE IN ART, as in everything else, can only be achieved by dint of painstaking labor. There is nothing less accidental than the painting of a picture or the chiselling of a noble statue. Every skilled touch of the artist's brush or chisel, though guided by genius, is the product of unremitting study.

Sir Joshua Reynolds was such a believer in the force of industry, that he held that artistic excellence, "however expressed by genius, taste, or the gift of heaven, may be acquired." Writing to Barry he said, "Whoever is resolved to excel in painting, or indeed any other art, must bring all his mind to bear upon that one object from the moment that he rises till he goes to bed." And on another occasion he said, "Those who are resolved to excel must go to their work, willing or unwilling, morning, noon, and night; they will find it no play, but very hard labor."

Like Sir Joshua Reynolds, Michael Angelo was a great believer in the force of labor; and he held that there was nothing which the imagination conceived that could not be embodied in marble, if the hand were made vigorously to obey the mind. He was himself one of the most persevering of workers; and he attributed his power of studying for a greater number of hours than most of his cotemporaries to his spare habits of living. A little bread and wine was all he required for the chief part of the day when employed at his work, and very frequently he rose in the middle of the night to resume his labors. On these occasions it was his practice to fix the candle, by the light of which he chiseled, on the summit of a pasteboard cap which he wore. Sometimes he was too wearied to undress, and he slept in his clothes, ready to spring to his work as soon as refreshed by sleep. He had a favorite device of an old man in a go-cart, with an hour-glass upon it bearing the inscription, "Still I am learning."

Titian, also, was an earnest worker. His celebrated "Pietro Martire" was eight years in hand, and his "Last Supper" seven. In his letter to Charles V he said, "I send your Majesty the 'Last Supper,' after working at it almost daily for seven years." Few think of the patient labor and long training involved in the greatest works of the artist. They seem easy and quickly accomplished, yet with how great difficulty has this ease been acquired. "You charge me fifty sequins," said the Venetian nobleman to the sculptor, "for a bust that cost you only ten days' labor." "You forget," said the artist, "that I have been thirty years learning to make that bust in ten days." It was eminently characteristic of the industry of the late Sir Augustus Callcott that he made not fewer than forty separate sketches in the composition of his famous picture of "Rochester." This constant repetition is one of the main conditions of success in art, as in life itself. No matter how generous nature has been in bestowing the gift of genius, the pursuit of art is nevertheless a long and continuous labor. Many artists have been precocious, but without diligence their precocity would have come to nothing. The anecdote related of West is well known. When only seven years old, struck with the beauty of the sleeping infant of his eldest sister, whilst watching by its cradle, he ran to seek some paper, and forthwith drew its portrait in red and black ink. The little incident revealed the artist in him, and it was found impossible to draw him from his bent. West might have been a greater painter had he not been injured by too early success: his fame, though great, was not purchased by study, trials, and difficulties, and it has not been enduring.

Sir Joshua Reynolds, when a boy, forgot his lessons, and took pleasure only in drawing, for which his father was accustomed to rebuke him. The boy was destined for the profession of physic, but his strong instinct for art could not be suppressed, and he became a painter. Gainsborough, when a school-boy, went sketching in the woods, and at twelve he was a confirmed artist; he was a keen observer and a hard worker—no picturesque feature of any scene he had once looked upon escaping his;diligent pencil. William Blake, a hosier's son, employed himself in drawing designs on the backs of his father's shop-bills, and making sketches for the purpose of meeting with character. By this careful storing of his mind, he was afterwards enabled to crowd an immense amount of thought and treasured observation into his works. Hence it is that Hogarth's pictures are so truthful a memorial of the character, the manners, and even the very thoughts of the times in which he lived. True painting, he himself observed, can only be learned in one school, and that is kept by Nature. But he was not a highly cultivated man, except in his own walk. His school education had been of the slenderest kind, scarcely even perfecting him in the art of spelling; his self-culture did the rest. For a long time he was in very straightened circumstances, but nevertheless worked on with a cheerful heart. Poor though he was, he contrived to live within his small means, and he boasted, with becoming pride, that he was "a punctual paymaster." When he had conquered all his difficulties and become a famous and thriving man, he loved to dwell upon his early labors and privations, and to fight over again the battle which ended so honorably to him as a man and so gloriously as an artist. "I remember the time," said he on one occasion, "when I have gone moping into the city with scarce a shilling, but as soon as I have received ten guineas there for a plate, I have returned home, put on my sword, and sallied out with all the confidence of a man who had thousands in his pockets."

"Industry and perseverance" was the motto of the sculptor Banks, which he acted on himself, and strongly recommended to others. His well-known kindness induced many aspiring youths to call upon him and ask for his advice and assistance; and it is related that one day a boy called at his door to see him with this object, but the servant, angry at the loud knock he had given, scolded him, and was about sending him away, when Banks, overhearing her, himself went out. The little boy stood at the door with some drawings in his hand. "What do you want with me?" asked the sculptor. "I want, sir, if you please, to be admitted to draw at the Academy." Banks explained that he himself could not procure his admission, but he asked to look at the boy's drawings. Examining them, he said, "Time enough for the Academy, my little man! go home—mind your schooling—try to make a better drawing of the Apollo—and in a month come again and let me see it." The boy went home—sketched and worked with redoubled diligence—and, at the end of the month, called again on the sculptor. The drawing was better; but again Banks sent him back, with good advice, to work and study. In a week the boy was again at his door, his drawing much improved; and Banks bid him be of good cheer, for if spared he would distinguish himself. The boy was Mulready; and the sculptor's augury was amply fulfilled.

Turner was destined by his father for his own trade of a barber, which he carried on in London, until one day the sketch which the boy had made of a coat-of-arms on a silver salver having attracted the notice of a customer whom his father was shaving, the latter was urged to allow his son to follow his bias, and he was eventually permitted to follow art as a profession. Like all young artists, Turner had many difficulties to encounter, and they were all the greater that his circumstances were so straitened. But he was always willing to work, and to take pains with his work, no matter how humble it might be. He was glad to hire himself out at half-a-crown a night to wash in skies in Indian ink upon other people's drawings, getting his supper into the bargain. Thus he earned money and acquired expertness. Then lie took to illustrating guide-books, almanacs, and any sort of books that wanted cheap frontispieces. "What could I have done better?" said he afterwards; "it was first-rate practice." He did everything carefully and conscientiously, never slurring over his work because he was ill-remunerated for it. He aimed at learning as well as living; always doing his best, and never leaving a drawing without having made a step in advance upon his previous work. A man who thus labored was sure to do much; and his growth in power and grasp of thought was, to use Ruskin's words, "as steady as the increasing light of sunrise." But Turner's genius needs no panegyric; his best monument is the noble gallery of pictures bequeathed by him to the nation, which will ever be the most lasting memorial of his fame.

Very romantic and adventurous was the career of Benvenuto Cellini, the marvellous gold-worker, painter, sculptor, engraver, engineer, and author. His life, as told by himself, is one of the most extraordinary autobiographies ever written. Giovanni Cellini, his father, -was one of the Court musicians al Florence; and his highest ambition concerning his son was that he should become an expert player on the flute. But Giovanni having lost his appointment, found it necessary to send his son to learn some trade, and he was apprenticed to a goldsmith. The boy had already displayed a love of drawing and of art; and, applying himself to his business, he soon became a dexterous workman. Having got mixed up in a quarrel with some of the townspeople, he was banished for six months, during which period he worked with a goldsmith at Sienna, gaining further experience in jewelry and gold-working.

His father still insisting on his becoming a flute-player, Benvenuto continued to practice on the instrument, though he detested it. His chief pleasure was in art, which he pursued with enthusiasm. Returning to Florence, he carefully studied the best designs; and, still further to improve himself in gold-working, he went on foot to Rome, where he met with a variety of adventures. He returned to Florence with the reputation of being a most expert worker in the precious metals, and his skill was soon in great request. During his residence in Rome, Cellini met with extensive patronage, and he was taken into the Pope's service in the double capacity of goldsmith and musician. He was constantly studying and improving himself by acquaintance with the works of the best masters. He mounted jewels, finished enamels, engraved seals, and designed and executed works in gold, silver, and bronze, in such a style as to excel all other artists. Whenever he heard of a goldsmith who was famous in any particular branch, he immediately determined to surpass him. Thus it was that he rivalled the medals of one, the enamels of another, and the jewelry of a third; in fact, there was not a branch of his business that he did not feel impelled to excel in. Working in this spirit, it is not so wonderful that Cellini should have been able to accomplish so much. He was a man of ceaseless activity, and was constantly on the move. At one time we find him at Florence, at another at Rome; then he is at Mantua, at Rome, at Naples, and back to Florence again; then at Venice, and in Paris, making all his long journeys on horseback. He could not carry much luggage with him; so, wherever he went he usually began by making his own tools. He not only designed his works, but executed them himself—hammered and carved, and cast and shaped them with his own hands. Indeed, his works have the impress of genius so clearly stamped upon them, that they could never have been designed by one person and executed by another. The humblest article—a buckle for a lady's girdle, a seal, a locket, a brooch, a ring, or a button—became in his hands a beautiful work of art. Cellini was remarkable for his readiness and dexterity in handicraft. One day a surgeon entered the shop of a goldsmith, to perform an operation on his daughter's hand. On looking at the surgeon's instruments, Cellini, who was present, found them rude and clumsy, as they usually were in those days, and he asked the surgeon to proceed no further with the operation for a quarter of an hour. He then ran to his shop, and taking a piece of the finest steel, wrought out of it a beautifully finished knife, with which the operation was successfully performed. Among the statues executed by Cellini, the most important are the silver figure of Jupiter and Perseus. John Flaxman was the son of a humble seller of plaster casts. When a child he was such an invalid that it was his custom to sit behind his father's shop counter propped by pillows, amusing himself with drawing and reading. A benevolent clergyman, the Rev. Mr. Matthews, calling at the shop one day, saw the boy trying to read a book, and, on inquiring what it was, found it to be a Cornelius Nepos, which his father had picked up for a few pence at a book stall. The gentleman, after some conversation with the boy, said that was not the proper book for him to read, but that he would bring him one. The next day he called with translations of Homer and "Don Quixote," which the boy proceeded to read with great avidity. His mind was soon filled with the heroism which breathed through the pages of the former, and, with the stucco Ajaxes and Achilleses about him, ranged along the shop shelves, the ambition took possession of him that he, too, would design and embody in poetic forms those majestic heroes.

Like all youthful efforts, his first designs were crude. The proud father one day showed some of them to Roubilliac the sculptor, who turned from them with a contemptuous "pshaw!" But the boy had the right stuff in him; he had industry and patience; and he continued to labor incessantly at his books and drawings. He then tried his young powers in modelling figures in plaster of Paris, wax, and clay. Some of these early works are still preserved, not because of their merit, but because they are curious as the first healthy efforts of patient genius. It was long before the boy could walk, and he only learned to do so by hobbling along upon crutches. At length he became strong enough to walk without them.

The kind Mr. Matthews invited him to his house, where his wife explained Homer and Milton to him. They helped him also in his self-culture—giving him lessons in Greek and Latin, the study of which he prosecuted at home. By dint of patience and perseverance his drawing improved so much that he obtained a commission from a lady to execute six original drawings in black chalk of subjects in Homer. His first commission! What an event in the artist's life! The boy at once proceeded to execute the order, and he was both well praised and well paid for his work. At fifteen Flax-man entered a pupil at the Royal Academy. Notwithstanding his retiring disposition, he soon became known among the students; and great things were expected of him. Nor were their expectations disappointed; in his fifteenth year he gained the silver prize, and next year he became a candidate for the gold one. Everybody prophesied that he would carry off the medal, for there were none who surpassed him in ability and industry. Yet he lost it, and the gold medal was adjudged to a pupil who was not afterwards heard of This failure on the part of the youth was really of service to him; for defeats do not long cast down the resolute-hearted, but only serve to call forth their real powers. "Give me time," said he to his father, "and I will yet produce works that the Academy will be proud to recognize." He redoubled his efforts, spared no pains, designed and modelled incessantly, and made steady if not rapid progress. But meanwhile poverty threatened his father's household; the plaster-cast trade yielded a very bare living; and young Flaxman, with resolute self-denial, curtailed his hours of study, and devoted himself to helping his father in the humble details of his business. He laid aside his Homer to take up the plaster trowel. He was willing to work in the humblest department of the trade, so that his father's family might be supported and the wolf kept from the door. To this drudgery of his art he served a long apprenticeship; but it did him good. It familiarized him with steady work, and cultivated in him the spirit of patience. The discipline may have been hard, but it was wholesome.

Happily, young Flaxman's skill in design had reached the knowledge of Josiah Wedgwood, who sought him out for the purpose of employing him to design improved patterns of china and earthenware. It may seem a humble department of art for such a genius as Flaxman to work in; but it really was not so. An artist may be laboring truly in his vocation while designing a common teapot or water-jug. Articles in daily use amongst the people, which are before their eyes at every meal, may be made the vehicles of education to all, and minister to their highest culture. The most ambitious artist may thus confer a greater practical benefit on his countrymen than by executing an elaborate work which he may sell for thousands of pounds, to be placed in some wealthy man's gallery where it is hidden away from public sight. Before Wedgwood's time the designs which figured upon our china and stoneware were hideous both in drawing and execution, and he determined to improve both. Flax-man did his best to carry out the manufacturer's views. He supplied him from time to time with models and designs of various pieces of earthenware, the subjects of which were principally from ancient verse and history. Many of them are still in existence, and some are equal in beauty and simplicity to his after-designs for marble. The celebrated Etruscan vases, specimens of which were to be found in public museums and in the cabinets of the curious, furnished him with the best examples of form, and these he embellished with his own elegant devices. "Stuart's Athens," then recently published, furnished him with specimens of the purest-shaped Greek utensils; of these he adopted the best, and worked them into new shapes of elegance and beauty. Flaxman then saw that he was laboring in a great work—no less than the promotion of popular education; and he was proud, in after life, to allude to his early labors in this walk, by which he was enabled at the same time to cultivate his love of the beautiful, to diffuse a taste for art among the people, and to replenish his own purse, while he promoted the prosperity of his friend and benefactor. When twenty-seven years of age, he quitted his father's roof and rented a small house and studio; and what was more, he married—Ann Denman was the name of his wife—and a cheerful, bright-souled, noble woman she was. He believed that in marrying her he should be able to work with an intenser spirit; for, like him, she had a taste for poetry and art; and besides was an enthusiastic admirer of her husband's genius. Yet when Sir Joshua Reynolds—himself a bachelor—met Flaxman shortly after his marriage, he said to him, "So, Flaxman, I am told you are married; if so, sir, I tell you you are ruined for an artist." Flaxman went straight home, sat down beside his wife, took her hand in his, and said, "Ann, I am ruined for an artist." "How so, John? How has it happened? and who has done it?" "It happened," he replied, "in the church, and Ann Denman has done it." He then told her of Sir Joshua's remark—whose opinion was well known, and had often been expressed, that if students would excel they must bring the whole power of their mind to bear upon their art, from the moment they rose until they went to bed; and also, that no man could be a *great* artist unless he studied the grand works at Rome and Florence. "And I," said Flaxman, drawing up his little figure to its full height, "would be a great artist." "And a great artist you shall be," said his wife, "and visit Rome, too, if that be really necessary to make you great." "But how?" asked Flaxman. "*Work and economize*," rejoined the brave wife, "I will never have it said that Ann Denman ruined John Flaxman for an artist." And so it was determined by the pair that the journey to Rome was to be made when their means would admit. "I will go to Rome," said Flaxman, "and show the President that wedlock is for a man's good rather than his harm; and you, Ann, shall accompany me."

Patiently and happily the affectionate couple plodded on during five years in their humble little home, always with the long journey to Rome before them. It was never lost sight of for a moment, and not a penny was uselessly spent that could be saved towards the necessary expenses. They said no word to any one about their project; solicited no aid from the Academy; but trusted only to their own patient labor and love to pursue and achieve their object. During this time Flax-man exhibited very few works. He could not afford marble to experiment in original designs; but he obtained frequent commissions for monuments, by the profits of which he maintained himself. He still worked for Wedgwood, who was a prompt paymaster; and, on the whole, he was thriving, happy, and hopeful.

At length Flaxman and his wife having accumulated a sufficient store of savings, set out for Rome. Arrived there, he applied himself diligently to study; maintaining himself, like other poor artists, by making copies from the antique. English visitors sought his studio, and gave him commissions; and it was then that he composed his beautiful designs illustrative of Homer, Aeschylus, and Dante. He then prepared to return to England, his taste improved and cultivated by careful study; but before he left Italy the Academies of Florence and Carrara recognized his merit by electing him a member.

His fame had preceded him to London, where he soon found abundant employment. While at Rome he had been commissioned to execute his famous monument in memory of Lord Mansfield, and it was erected in the North transept of Westminster Abbey shortly after his return. It stands there in majestic grandeur, a monument to the genius of Flaxman himself—calm, simple, and severe. No wonder that Banks, the sculptor, then at the zenith of his fame, exclaimed, when he saw it, "This little man cuts us all out! "

When the members of the Royal Academy heard of Flaxman's return, and especially when they had an opportunity of seeing and admiring his portrait-statue of Mansfield, they were eager to have him enrolled among their number. He allowed his name to be proposed in the candidates' list of associates, and was immediately elected. Shortly after he appeared in an entirely new character. The little boy who had began his studies behind the plaster-cast seller's shop-counter was now a man of high intellect and recognized supremacy in art, instructing students, in the character of Professor of Sculpture to the Royal Academy. And no man better deserved to fill that distinguished office; for none is so able to instruct others as he who, for himself and by his own efforts, has learned to grapple with and overcome difficulties. After a long, peaceful, and happy life, Flaxman found himself growing old. The loss which he sustained by the death of his affectionate wife Ann was a severe shock to him; but he survived her several years, during which he executed his celebrated "Shield of Achilles," and his noble "Archangel Michael vanquishing Satan"—perhaps his two greatest works.

The same honest and persistent industry was throughout distinctive of the career of David Wilkie. The son of a Scotch minister, he gave early indications of an artistic turn; and though he was a negligent and inapt scholar, he was a sedulous drawer of faces and figures. A silent boy, he already displayed that quiet concentrated energy of character which distinguished him through life. He was always on the lookout for an opportunity to draw— and the walls of the manse, or the smooth sand by the river side, were alike convenient for his purpose. Any sort of tool would serve him; like Giotto, he found a pencil in a burnt stick, a prepared canvas in any smooth stone, and the subject for a picture in every ragged mendicant he met. When he visited a house he generally left his mark on the walls as an indication of his presence, sometimes to the disgust of cleanly housewives. In short, notwithstanding the aversion of his father, the minister, to the "sinful" profession of painting, Wilkie's strong propensity was not to be thwarted, and he became an artist; working his way manfully up the steep of difficulty. Though rejected on his first application as a candidate for admission to the Scottish Academy, at Edinburgh, on account of the rudeness and inaccuracy of his introductory specimens, he persevered in producing better, until he was admitted. But his progress was slow. He applied himself diligently to the drawing of the human figure, and held on with the determination to succeed, as if with a resolute confidence as to the result. He displayed none of the eccentric humor and fitful application of many youths who conceive themselves geniuses, but kept up the routine of steady application to such an extent that he himself was afterwards accustomed to attribute his success to his dogged perseverance rather than to any higher innate power. "The single element," he said, "in all the progressive movements of my pencil was persevering industry." At Edinburgh he gained a few premiums, thought of turning his attention to portrait-painting, with a view to its higher and more certain remuneration, but eventually went boldly into the line in which he earned his fame—and painted his Pitlessie Fair. What was bolder still, he determined to proceed to London, on account of its presenting so much wider a field for study and work; and the poor Scotch lad arrived in town, and painted his "Village Politicians" while living in a humble lodging on eighteen shillings a week.

Notwithstanding the success of this picture, and the commissions which followed it, Wilkie long continued poor. The prices which his works realized were not great, for he bestowed upon them so much time and labor, that his earnings continued comparatively small for many years. Every picture was carefully studied and elaborated beforehand; nothing was struck off at a heat; many occupied him for years—touching, retouching, and improving them until they finally passed out of his hands. As with Reynolds, his motto was, "Work! work! work!" and, like him, he expressed great dislike for talking artists. Talkers may sow, but the silent reap. "Let us be *doing* something," was his oblique mode of rebuking the loquacious and admonishing the idle. He once related to his friend Constable that when he studied at the Scottish Academy, Graham, the master of it, was accustomed to say to the students, in the words of Reynolds, "If you have genius, industry will improve it; if you have none, industry will supply its place." "So," said Wilkie, "I was determined to be very industrious, for I knew I had no genius." He also told Constable that when Linnell and Burnett, his fellow-students in London, were talking about art, he always contrived to get as close to them as he could to hear all they said, "for," said he, "they know a great deal, and I know very little." This was said with perfect sincerity, for Wilkie was habitually modest. One of the first things that he did with the sum of thirty pounds which he obtained from Lord Mansfield for his "Village Politicians," was to buy a present—of bonnets, shawls, and dresses—for his mother and sister at home; though but little able to afford it at the time. Wilkie's early poverty had trained him in the habits of strict economy, which were however, consistent with a noble liberality.

Many artists have had to encounter privations which have tried their courage and endurance to the utmost before they succeeded. What number may have sunk under them we can never know. Martin encountered difficulties in the course of his career such as perhaps fall to the lot of few. More than once he found himself on the verge of starvation while engaged on his first great picture. It is related of him that on one occasion he found himself reduced to his last shilling—a *bright* shilling—which he had kept because of its very brightness, but at length he found it necessary to exchange it for bread. He went to a baker's shop, bought a loaf, and was taking it away, when the baker snatched it from him, and tossed back the shilling to the starving painter. The bright shilling had failed him in his hour of need—it was a bad one! Returning to his lodgings, he rummaged his trunk for some remaining crust to satisfy his hunger. Upheld throughout by the victorious power of enthusiasm, he pursued his design with unsubdued energy. He had the courage to work on and to wait; and when, a few days after, he found an opportunity to exhibit his picture, he was from that time famous. Like many other great artists, his life proves that, despite outward circumstances, genius, aided by industry, will be its own protector, and that fame, though she comes late, will never ultimately refuse her favors to real merit.

Another striking exemplification of perseverance and industry in the cultivation of art in humble life is presented in the career of James Sharples, a working blacksmith at Blackburn. He was one of a family of thirteen children. His father was a working iron-founder. The boys received no school education, but were all sent to work as soon as they were able; and at about ten James was placed in a foundry, where he was employed for about two years as smithy-boy. After that he was sent into the engine-shop where his father worked as engine-smith. The boy's employment was to heat and carry rivets for the boiler-makers. Though his hours of labor were very long—often from six in the morning until eight at night—his father contrived to give him some little teaching after working hours; and it was thus that he partially learned his letters. An incident occurred in the course of his employment among the boiler-makers, which first awakened in him the desire to learn drawing. He had occasionally been employed by the foreman to hold the chalked line with which he made the designs of boilers upon the floor of the workshop; and on such occasions the foreman was accustomed to hold the line, and direct the boy to make the necessary dimensions. James soon became so expert at this as to be of considerable service to the foreman; and at his leisure hours at home his great delight was to practice drawing designs of boilers upon his mother's floor. On one occasion, when a female relative was expected from Manchester to pay the family a visit, and the house had been made as decent as possible for her reception, the boy, on coming in from the foundry in the evening, began his usual operations upon the floor. He had proceeded some way with his design of a large boiler in chalk, when his mother arrived with the visitor, and to her dismay, found the boy unwashed, and the floor chalked all over. The relative, however, professed to be pleased with the boy's industry, praised his design, and recommended his mother to provide "the little sweep," as she called him, with paper and pencils.

Encouraged by his elder brother, he began to practice figure and landscape drawing, making copies of lithographs, but as yet without any knowledge of the rules of perspective and the principles of light and shade. He worked on, however, and gradually acquired expertness in copying. At sixteen, he entered the Bury Mechanic's Institution in order to attend the drawing-class, taught by an amateur who followed the trade of a barber. There he had a lesson a week during three months. The teacher recommended him to obtain from the library Burnet's "Practical Treatise on Painting"; but as he could not yet read with ease, he was under the necessity of getting his mother, and sometimes his elder brother, to read passages from the book for him while he sat by and listened. Feeling hampered by his ignorance of the art of reading, and eager to master the contents of Burnet's book, he ceased attending the drawing-class at the Institute after the first quarter, and devoted himself to learning reading and writing at home. In this he soon succeeded; and when he again entered the Institute and took out "Burnet" a second time, he was not only able to read it, but to make written extracts for future use. So ardently did he study the volume, that he used to rise at four o'clock in the morning to read it and copy out passages; after which he went to the foundry at six, worked until six and sometimes eight in the evening; and returned home to enter with fresh zest upon the study of Burnet, which he continued often until a late hour. Parts of his nights were also occupied in drawing and making copies of drawings. On one of these he spent an entire night. He went to bed, indeed, but his mind was so engrossed with the subject that he could not sleep, and rose again to resume his pencil. He next proceeded to try his hand at painting in oil, for which purpose he procured some canvas from a draper, stretched it on a frame, coated it over with white lead, and began painting on it with colors bought from a house-painter. But his work proved a total failure; for the canvas was rough and knotty, and the paint would not dry. In his extremity he applied to his old teacher, the barber, from whom he first learnt that prepared canvas was to be had, and that there were colors and varnishes made for the special purpose of oil-painting. As soon, therefore, as his means would allow, he bought a small stock of the necessary articles and began afresh— his amateur master showing him how to paint; and the pupil succeeded so well that he excelled the master's copy. His first picture was a copy from an engraving called "Sheep-shearing" and was afterwards sold by him for half-a-crown. Aided by a shilling Guide to Oil-Painting, he went on working at his leisure hours, and gradually acquired a better knowledge of his materials. He made his own easel and palette, palette-knife, and paint-chest; he bought his paint, brushes, and canvas, as he could raise the money by working over-time. This was the slender fund which his parents consented to allow him for the purpose; the burden of supporting a very large family precluding them from doing more. Often he would walk to Manchester and back in the evenings to buy two or three shillings' worth of paint and canvas, returning almost at midnight, after his eighteen miles' walk, sometimes wet through and completely exhausted, but borne up throughout by his inexhaustible hope and invincible determination. The further progress of the self-taught artist is best narrated in his own words.

"The next pictures I painted," he says, "were a Landscape by Moonlight, a Fruit-piece, and one or two others; after which I conceived the idea of painting 'The Forge.' I had for some time thought about it, but had not attempted to embody the conception in a drawing. I now, however, made a sketch of the subject upon paper, and then proceeded to paint it on canvas. The picture simply represents the interior of a large workshop such as I have been accustomed to work in, although not of any particular shop. It is, therefore, to this extent, an original conception. Having made an outline of the subject, I found that, before I could proceed with it successfully, a knowledge of anatomy was indispensable to enable me accurately to delineate the muscles of the figure. My brother Peter came to my assistance at this juncture, and kindly purchased for me Flaxman's 'Anatomical Studies'—a work altogether beyond my means at the time, for it cost twenty-four shillings. This book I looked upon as a great treasure, and I studied it laboriously, rising at three o'clock in the morning to draw after it, and occasionally getting my brother Peter to stand for me as a model at that untimely hour. Although I gradually improved myself by this practice, it was some time before I felt sufficient confidence to go on with my picture. I also felt hampered by my want of knowledge of perspective, which I endeavored to remedy by carefully studying Taylor's 'Principles'; and shortly after I resumed my painting. While engaged in the study of perspective at home, I used to apply for and obtain leave to work at the heavier kinds of smith-work at the foundry, and for this reason—the time required for heating the heaviest iron work is so much longer than that required for heating the lighter, that it enabled me to secure a number of spare minutes in the course of each day, which I carefully employed in making diagrams in perspective upon the sheet-iron casings in front of the hearth at which I worked."

Thus assiduously working and studying, James Sharpies steadily advanced in his knowledge of the principles of art, and acquired greater facility in its practice. Some eighteen months after the expiration of his apprenticeship he painted a portrait of his father, which attracted considerable notice in the town; as also did the picture of "The Forge," which he finished soon after. His success in portrait-painting obtained for him a commission from the foreman of the shop to paint a family group, and Sharples executed it so well that the foreman not only paid him the agreed price of eighteen pounds, but thirty shillings to boot. While engaged on this group he ceased to work at the foundry, and he had thoughts of giving up his trade altogether and devoting himself exclusively to painting. But not obtaining sufficient employment at portraits to occupy his time, or give him the prospect of a steady income, he had the good sense to resume his leather apron, and go on working at his honest trade of a blacksmith; employing his leisure hours in engraving his picture of "The Forge," since published.

The execution of this work occupied Sharples' leisure evening hours during a period of five years; and it was only when he took the plate to the printer that he for the first time saw an engraved slate produced by any other man. To this unvarnished picture of industry and genius we add one other trait, and it is a domestic one. "I have been married seven years," says he, "and during that time my greatest pleasure, after I have finished my daily labor at the foundry, has been to resume my pencil or graver, frequently until a late hour of the evening, my wife meanwhile sitting by my side and reading to me from some interesting book"—a simple but beautiful testimony to the thorough common sense as well as the genuine right-heartedness of this most interesting and deserving workman.

Haydn, speaking of his art, said, "It consists in taking up a subject and pursuing it." "Work," said Mozart, "is my chief pleasure." Beethoven's favorite maxim was, "The barriers are not erected which can say to aspiring talents and industry, 'Thus far and no farther.'" When Moscheles submitted his score of "Fidelio" for the pianoforte to Beethoven, the latter found written at the bottom of the last page, "Finis, with God's help." Beethoven immediately wrote underneath, "O man! help thyself!" This was the motto of his artistic life. John Sebastian Bach said of himself, "I was industrious; whoever is equally sedulous will be equally successful." Of Meyerbeer, Bayle thus wrote: "He is a man of some talent, but no genius; he lives solitary, working fifteen hours a day at music." Years passed, and Meyerbeer's hard work fully brought out his genius, as displayed in his "Hugenots," and other works, confessedly amongst the greatest operas which have been produced in modern times.

Chapter 14

Men of Business

"Seest thou a man diligent in his business? He shall stand before kings."
—*Proverbs of Solomon.*

"That man is but of the lower part of the world that is not brought up to business and affairs." —*Owen Feltham.*

HAZLITT, in one of his clever essays, represents the man of business as a mean sort of person put in a go-cart, yoked to a trade or profession; alleging that all he has to do is, not to go out of the beaten track, but merely to let his affairs take their own course. "The great requisite," he says, "for the prosperous management of ordinary business is the want of imagination, or of any ideas but those of custom and interest on the narrowest scale." But nothing could be more one-sided, and in effect untrue, than such a definition. Of course there are narrow-minded men of business, as there are narrow-minded scientific men, literary men, and legislators; but there are also business men of large and comprehensive minds, capable of action on the very largest scale. As Burke said in his speech on the India Bill, he knew statesmen who were peddlers, and merchants who acted in the spirit of statesmen.

If we take into account the qualities necessary for the successful conduct of any important undertaking—that it requires special aptitude, prompitude of action on emergencies, capacity for organizing the labors often of large numbers of men, great tact and knowledge of human nature, constant self-culture, and growing experience in the practical affairs of life—it must, we think, be obvious that the school of business is by no means so narrow as some writers would have us believe. Mr. Helps has gone much nearer the truth when he said that consummate men of business are as rare almost as great poets—rarer, perhaps, than veritable saints and martyrs. Indeed, of no other pursuit can it so emphatically be said, as of this, that "Business makes men."

It has, however, been a favorite fallacy with dunces in all times, that men of genius are unfitted for business, as well as that business occupations unfit men for the pursuits of genius. The unhappy youth who committed suicide a few years since because he had been "born to be a man and condemned to be a grocer," proved by the act that his soul was not equal even to the dignity of a grocer; for it is not the calling that degrades a man, but the man that degrades the calling. All work that brings honest gain is honorable, whether it be of hand or mind. The fingers may be soiled, yet the heart remain pure; for it is not material so much as moral dirt that defiles—greed far more than crime, and vice than verdigris.

The greatest have not disdained to labor honestly and usefully for a living, though at the same time aiming after higher things. Thales, the first of the seven sages, Solon, the second founder of Athens, and Hyperates, the mathematician, were all traders. Plato, called the Divine by reason of the excellence of his wisdom, defrayed his traveling expenses in Egypt by the profits derived from the oil which he sold during his journey. Spinoza maintained himself by polishing glasses while he pursued his philosophical investigations. Linnaeus, the great botanist, prosecuted his studies while hammering leather and making shoes. Shakespeare was a successful manager of a theatre—perhaps priding himself more upon his practical qualities in that capacity than on his writing of plays and poetry. Pope was of opinion that Shakespeare's principal object in cultivating literature was to secure an honest independence. Indeed he seems to have been altogether indifferent to literary reputation. It is not known that he superintended the publication of a single play, or even sanctioned the printing of one; and the chronology of his writings is still a mystery. It is certain, however, that he prospered in his business, and realized sufficient to enable him to retire upon a competency to his native town.

We have abundant illustrations, in our own day, of the fact that the highest intellectual power is not incompatible with the active and efficient performance of routine duties. Grote, the great historian of Greece, was a London banker. And it is not long since John Stuart Mill, one of our greatest living thinkers, retired from the Examiner's department of the East India Company, carrying with him the admiration and esteem of his fellow-officers, not on account of his high views of philosophy, but because of the high standard of efficiency which he had established in his office, and the thoroughly satisfactory manner in which he had conducted the business of his department.

The path of success in business is usually the path of common sense. Patient labor and application are as necessary here as in the acquisition of knowledge or the pursuit of science. The old Greeks said, "To become an able man in any profession, three things are necessary—nature, study, and practice." In business, practice, wisely and diligently improved, is the great secret of success. Some may make what are called "lucky hits," but like money earned by gambling, such "hits" may only serve to lure one to ruin.

Every youth should be made to feel that his happiness and well-doing in life must necessarily rely mainly on himself and the exercise of his own energies, rather than upon the help and patronage of others. The late Lord Melbourne embodied a piece of useful advice in a letter which he wrote to Lord John Russell, in reply to an application for a provision for one of Moore the poet's sons: "My dear John," he said, "I return you Moore's letter. I shall be ready to do what you like about it when we have the means. I think whatever is done should be done for Moore himself. This is more distinct, direct, and intelligible. Making a small provision for young men is hardly justifiable; and it is of all things the most prejudicial to themselves. They think what they have much larger than it really is; and they make no exertion. The young should never hear any language but this: 'You have your own way to make, and it depends upon your own exertions whether you starve or not.' Believe me, etc., *Melbourne*."

Practical industry, wisely and vigorously applied, always produces its due effects. It carries a man onward, brings out his individual character, and stimulates the actions of others. All may not rise equally, yet each, on the whole, very much according to his deserts. "Though all cannot live on the piazza," as the Tuscan proverb has it, "everyone may feel the sun."

On the whole, it is not good that human nature should have the road of life made too easy. Better to be under the necessity of working hard and faring meanly, than to have every thing done ready to our hand and a pillow of down to repose upon. Indeed, to start in life with comparatively small means seems so necessary as a stimulus to work, that it may almost be set down as one of the conditions essential to success in life. Hence, an eminent judge, when asked what contributed most to success at the bar, replied, "Some succeed by great talent, some by high connections, some by miracle, but the majority by commencing without a shilling."

We have heard of an architect of considerable accomplishments—a man who had improved himself by long study, and travel in the classical lands of the East—who came home to commence the practice of his profession. He determined to begin anywhere, provided he could be employed; and he accordingly undertook a business connected with dilapidations—one of the lowest and least remunerative departments of the architect's calling. But he had the good sense not to be above his trade, and he had the resolution to work his way upward, so that he only got a fair start. One hot day in July a friend found him sitting astride of a house-roof occupied with his dilapidation business. Drawing his hand across his perspiring countenance, he exclaimed, "Here's a pretty business for a man who has been all over Greece!" However, he did his work, such as it was, thoroughly and well; he persevered until he advanced by degrees to more remunerative branches of employment, and eventually he rose to the highest walks of his profession.

The necessity of labor may, indeed, be regarded as the main root and spring of all that we call progress in individuals, and civilization in nations; and it is doubtful that any heavier curse could be imposed on man than the gratification of all his wishes without effort on his part, leaving nothing for his hopes, desires, or struggles. The feeling that life is destitute of any motive or necessity for action, must be of all others the most distressing and insupportable to a rational being. The Marquis de Spinola asking Sir Horace Vere what his brother died of, Sir Horace replied, "He died, sir, of having nothing to do." "Alas!" said Spinola, "that is enough to kill any general of us all."

Those who fail in life are, however, very apt to assume a tone of injured innocence, and conclude too hastily that everybody excepting themselves has had a hand in their personal misfortune. There is a Russian proverb which says that misfortune is next door to stupidity; and it will often be found that men who are constantly lamenting their luck, are in some way or other reaping the consequences of their own neglect, mismanagement, improvidence, or want of application. Dr. Johnson, who came up to London with a single guinea in his pocket, and who once accurately described himself in his signature to a letter addressed to a noble lord, as *Impransus*, or Dinnerless, has honestly said, "All the complaints which are made of the world are unjust; I never knew a man of merit neglected; it was generally by his own fault that he failed of success."

Washington Irving held like views. "As for the talk," he said, "about modest merit being neglected, it is too often a cant, by which indolent and irresolute men seek to lay their want of success at the door of the public. Modest merit is, however, too apt to be inactive, or negligent, or uninstructed merit. Well-matured and well disciplined talent is always sure of a market, provided it exerts itself; but it must not cower at home and expect to be sought for. There is a good deal of cant, too, about the success of forward and impudent men, while men of retiring worth are passed over with neglect. But it usually happens that those forward men have that valuable quality of promptness and activity without which worth is a mere inoperative property. A barking dog is often more useful than a sleeping lion."

Attention, application, accuracy, method, punctuality, and dispatch, are the principal qualities required for the efficient conduct of business of any sort. These, at first sight, may appear to be small matters; and yet they are of essential importance to human happiness, well-being, and usefulness. They are little things, it is true; but human life is made up of comparative trifles. It is the repetition of little acts which constitutes not only the sum of human character, but which determines the character of nations. And where men or nations have broken down, it will almost invariably be found that neglect of little things was the rock on which they split. Every human being has duties to be performed, and, therefore, has need of cultivating the capacity for doing them; whether the sphere of action be the management of a household, the conduct of a trade or profession, or the government of a nation.

The examples we have already given of great workers in various branches of industry, art, and science, render it unnecessary further to enforce the importance of persevering application in any department of life. It is the result of every-day experience, that steady attention to matters of detail lies at the root of human progress; and that diligence, above all, is the mother of good luck. Accuracy is also of much importance, and an invariable mark of good training in a man—accuracy in observation, accuracy in speech, accuracy in the transaction of affairs. What is done in business must be well done; for it is better to accomplish perfectly a small amount of work, than to half-do ten times as much. A wise man used to say, "Stay a little, that we may make an end the sooner."

Too little attention, however, is paid to this highly important quality of accuracy. As a man eminent in practical sciences lately observed to us, "It is astonishing how few people I have met with the course of my experience who can define a fact accurately." Yet in business affairs, it is the manner in which even small matters are transacted, that often decides men for or against you. With virtue, capacity, and good conduct in other respects, the person who is habitually inaccurate can not be trusted; his work has to be gone over again; and he thus causes an infinity of annoyance, vexation, and trouble. It was one of the characteristic qualities of Charles James Fox, that he was thoroughly pains-taking in all that he did. When appointed Secretary of State, being piqued at some observation as to his bad writing, he actually took a writing-master, and wrote copies like a school-boy until he had sufficiently improved himself.

Method is essential, and enables a larger amount of work to be got through with satisfaction. "Method," said the Rev. Richard Cecil, "is like packing things in a box; a good packer will get in half as much again as a bad one." Cecil's dispatch of business was extraordinary, his maxim being, "the shortest way to do many things is to do only one thing at once"; and he never left a thing undone with a view of recurring to it at a period of more leisure. When business pressed he rather chose to encroach on his hours of meals and rest than omit any part of his work. DeWitt's maxim was like Cecil's: "One thing at a time." "If," said he, "I have any necessary dispatches to make, I think of nothing else till they are finished; if any domestic affairs require my attention, I give myself wholly up to them till they are set in order."

A French minister, who was alike remarkable for his dispatch of business and his constant attendance at places of amusement, being asked how he contrived to combine both objects, replied, "Simply by never postponing till tomorrow what should be done today." Men are apt to rely upon agents, who are not always to be relied upon. Important affairs must be attended to in person. "If you want your business done," says the proverb, "go and do it; if you don't want it done, send some one else." An indolent country gentleman had a freehold estate producing about five hundred a year. Becoming involved in debt, be sold half the estate, and let the remainder to an industrious farmer for twenty years. About the end of the term the farmer called to pay his rent, and asked the owner whether he would sell the farm. "Will *you* buy it?" asked the owner, surprised. "Yes, if we can agree about the price." "That is exceedingly strange," observed the gentleman; "pray tell me how it happens that, while I could not live upon twice as much land, for which I paid no rent, you are regularly paying me two hundred a year for your farm, and are able, in a few years, to purchase it." "The reason is plain," was the reply; "you sat still and said *Go,* I got up and said *Come;* you lay in bed and enjoyed your estate, I rose in the morning and minded my business."

Promptitude in action may be stimulated by a due consideration of the value of time. An Italian philosopher was accustomed to call time his estate—an estate which produces nothing of value without cultivation, but, duly improved, never fails to recompense the labors of the diligent worker. Allowed to lie waste, the product will be only noxious weeds and vicious growths of all kinds. One of the minor uses of steady employment is, that it keeps one out of mischief, for truly an idle brain is the devil's workshop, and a lazy man the devil's bolster. To be occupied is to be possessed as by a tenant, whereas to be idle is to be empty; and when the doors of the imagination are opened, temptation finds a ready access, and evil thoughts come trooping in. It is observed at sea, that men are never so much disposed to grumble and mutiny as when least employed. Hence, an old captain, when there was nothing else to do, would issue the order to "scour the anchor!" Men of business are accustomed to quote the maxim that Time is money; but it is more; the proper improvement of it is self-culture, self-improvement, and growth of character. An hour wasted daily on trifles or in indolence would, if devoted to self-improvement, make an ignorant man wise in a few years, and, employed in good works, would make his life fruitful, and death a harvest of worthy deeds. Fifteen minutes a day devoted to self-improvement, will be felt at the end of the year. Good thoughts and carefully gathered experience take up no room, and may be carried about as our companions everywhere, without cost or encumbrance. An economical use of time is the true mode of securing leisure; it enables us to get through business and carry it forward, instead of being driven by it. On the other hand, the miscalculation of time involves us in perpetual hurry, confusion and difficulties; and life becomes a mere shuffle of expedients, usually followed by disaster. Nelson once said, "I owe all my success in life to having been always a quarter of an hour before my time." Some take no thought of the value of money until they have come to an end of it, and many do the same with their time. The hours are allowed to flow by unemployed, and then, when life is fast waning, they bethink themselves of the duty of making a wiser use of it. But the habit of listlessness and idleness may already have become confirmed, and they are unable to break the bonds with which they have permitted themselves to become bound. Lost wealth may be replaced by industry, lost knowledge by study, lost health by temperance or medicine, but lost time is gone forever. A proper consideration of the value of time will also inspire habits of punctuality. Nothing begets confidence in a man sooner than the practice of this virtue, and nothing shakes confidence sooner than the want of it. He who holds to his appointment and does not keep you waiting for him, shows that he has regard for your time as well as for his own. Thus punctuality is one of the modes by which we testify our personal respect for those whom we are called upon to meet in the business of life. It is also conscientiousness, in a measure; for an appointment is a contract, express or implied, and he who does not keep it breaks faith, as well as dishonestly uses other people's time, and thus inevitably loses character. We naturally come to the conclusion that the person who is careless about time is careless about business, and that he is not the one to be trusted with the transaction of matters of importance. When Washington's secretary excused himself for the lateness of his attendance and laid the blame upon his watch, his master quietly said, "Then you must get another watch, or I another secretary."

 The truth of the good old maxim, that "Honesty is the best policy," is upheld by the daily experience of life, uprightness and integrity being found as successful in business as in every thing else. Integrity of word and deed ought to be the very corner-stone of all business transactions. To the tradesman, the merchant, and manufacturer, it should be what honor is to the soldier, and charity is to the Christian. In the humblest calling there will always be found scope for the exercise of this uprightness of character. Hugh Miller speaks of the mason with whom he served his apprenticeship, as one who *"put his conscience info every stone that lie laid."* So the true mechanic will pride himself upon the thoroughness and solidity of his work, and the high-minded contractor upon the honesty of performance of his contract in every particular. The upright manufacturer will find not only honor and reputation, but substantial success, in the genuineness of the article which he produces, and the merchant in the honesty of what he sells, and that it really is what it seems to be. Baron Dupin, speaking of the general probity of Englishmen, which he held to be a principle cause of their success, observed, "We may succeed for a time by fraud, by surprise, by violence; but we can succeed permanently only by means directly opposite. It is not alone the courage, the intelligence, the activity of the merchant and manufacturer which maintains the superiority of their productions and the character of their country; it is far more their wisdom, their economy, and, above all, their probity. If ever in the British Islands the useful citizen should lose these virtues, we may be sure that, for England, as for every other country, the vessels of a degenerate commerce, repulsed from every shore, would speedily disappear from those seas whose surface they now cover with the treasures of the universe, bartered for the treasures of the industry of the three kingdoms."

It must be admitted, that trade tries character perhaps more severely than any other pursuit in life. It puts to the severest tests honesty, self-denial, justice, and truthfulness; and men of business who pass through such trials unstained are perhaps worthy of as great honor as soldiers who prove their courage amidst the fire and perils of battle. And, to the credit of the multitudes of men engaged in the various departments of trade, we think it must be admitted that on the whole they pass through their trials nobly. If we reflect but for a moment on the vast amount of wealth daily entrusted even to the subordinate persons, who themselves probably earn but a bare competency—the loose cash which is constantly passing through the hands of shopmen, agents, brokers, and clerks in banking-houses—and note how comparatively few are the breaches of trust which occur amidst all this temptation, it will probably be admitted that this steady daily honesty of conduct is more honorable to human nature, if it do not even tempt us to be proud of it. The same trust and confidence reposed by men of business in each other, as implied by the system of credit, which is mainly based upon the principle of honor, would be surprising if it were not so much a matter of ordinary practice in business transactions. Dr. Chalmers has well said that the implicit trust with which merchants are accustomed to confide in distant agents, separated from them perhaps by half the globe—often consigning vast wealth to persons recommended only by their character, whom perhaps they have never seen—is probably the finest act of homage which men can render to one another.

The fortunes of the house of Rothschild were based upon the honesty of their founder—Meyer Anslem. He was born at Frankfort-on-the-Maine in 1743. His parents were Jews. What a frightful history might be written of the persecutions, tortures and martyrdoms of the Jews in the Middle Ages, and even down to our own times. At Frankfort, as well as at other towns and cities in Germany, the Jews were compelled to resort to their quarters at a certain hour in the evening, under penalty of death. The Juden-gasse at Frankfort was shut in by gates, which were locked at night. Napoleon blew them down with cannon, one of the best things he ever did; yet the persecutions of the Jews continued.

Young Anslem lost his parents at eleven, and had to fight his way through life alone. After a slight modicum of education, the boy had the good fortune to find a place as clerk to a small banker and money changer at Hanover. He returned to Frankfort in 1772, and established himself as a broker and moneylender. Over his shop he hung the sign of the Red Shield—in German, Rothschild. He collected ancient and rare coins, and among the amateurs who frequented his shop was the Landgrave William, afterward Elector of Hesse.

When Napoleon overran Europe, William of Hesse was driven from his states, and left all the money he could gather together in the hands of Anselm, his agent. It amounted to $1,250,000. How to take care of this money and make it grow in his hands was Anselm's greatest object. Money in those days was very dear; it returned twelve or even twenty percent on good security. The war went on. Russia was invaded by Napoleon. His army was all but lost in the snow. The battle of Leipzig was fought, and Napoleon and his army were hurled across the Rhine. The Land-grave of Hesse then returned to his states. A few days after, the eldest son of Meyer Anselm presented himself at court and handed over to the Landgrave the three millions of florins which his father had taken care of. The Landgrave was almost beside himself with joy. He looked upon the restored money as a windfall. In his exultation he knighted the young Rothschild at once. "Such honesty," his Highness exclaimed, "had never been known in the world." At the Congress of Vienna, where he went shortly after, he could talk of nothing else than the honesty of the Rothschilds. Anselm had a large family. They followed his example, and thus the Rothschilds became the largest moneylenders in the world.

Chapter 15

Money—Its Use and Abuse

"Not for to hide it in a hedge,
Nor for a train attendant,
But for the glorious privilege
Of being independent."
—Burns.

"Neither a borrower nor a lender be:
For loan oft loses both itself and friend;
And borrowing dulls the edge of husbandry."
—Shakespeare.

"Whoever has a sixpence is sovereign over all men to the extent of that sixpence, commands cooks to feed him, philosophers to teach him, kings to guard over him—to the extent of that sixpence." —Carlyle.

How a man uses money—makes it, saves it, and spends it—is perhaps one of the best tests of practical wisdom. Although money ought by no means to be regarded as the chief end of man's life, neither is it a trifling matter, to be held in philosophic contempt, representing, as it does, to so large an extent, the means of physical comfort and social well-being. Indeed, some of the finest qualities of human nature are intimately related to the right use of money—such as generosity, honesty, justice, and self-sacrifice, as well as the practical virtues of economy and providence. On the other hand, there are their counterparts of avarice, fraud, injustice, and selfishness, as displayed by the inordinate lovers of gain; and the vices of thriftlessness, extravagance, and improvidence, on the part of those who misuse and abuse the means entrusted to them. "So that," as is wisely observed by Henry Taylor, in his thoughtful 'Notes from Life,' "a right measure and manner in getting, saving, spending, giving, taking, lending, borrowing, and bequeathing, would almost argue a perfect man."

Comfort in worldly circumstances is a condition which every man is justified in striving to attain by all worthy means. It secures that physical satisfaction which is necessary for the culture of the better part of his nature, and enables him to provide for those of his own household, without which, says the apostle, a man is "worse than an infidel." Nor ought the duty to be any the less pleasing to us that the respect which our fellowmen entertain for us in no slight degree depends upon the manner in which we exercise the opportunities which present themselves for our honorable advancement in life. The very effort required to be made to succeed in life with this object is of itself an education, stimulating a man's sense of self-respect, bringing out his practical qualities, and disciplining him in the exercise of patience, perseverance, and such like virtues. The provident and careful man must necessarily be a thoughtful man, for he lives not merely for the present, but with provident forecast makes arrangements for the future. He must also be a temperate man, and exercise the virtue of self-denial, than which nothing is so much calculated to give strength to the character. John Sterling says truly, that "the worst education which teaches self-denial, is better than the best which teaches everything else, and not that."

Hence the lesson of self-denial—the sacrificing of a present gratification for a future good—is one of the last that is learned. Those classes which work the hardest might naturally be expected to value the most the money which they earn. Yet the readiness with which so many are accustomed to eat up and drink up their earnings as they go, renders them to a great extent helpless and dependent upon the frugal. There are large numbers of persons among us who, though enjoying sufficient means of comfort and independence, are often found to be barely a day's march ahead of actual want when a time of pressure occurs; and hence a great cause of social helplessness and suffering. On one occasion a deputation waited on Lord John Russell, respecting the taxation levied on the working classes of the country, when the noble lord took the opportunity of remarking, "You may rely upon it that the Government of this country durst not tax the working classes to anything like the extent to which they tax themselves in their expenditure upon intoxicating drinks alone!" "Providence, frugality, and good management," said Samuel Drew, the philosophical shoemaker, "are excellent artists for mending bad times: they occupy but little room in any dwelling, but would furnish a more effectual remedy for the evils of life than any Reform Bill that ever passed the Houses of Parliament." Socrates said, "Let him that would move the world move first himself."

Any class of men that lives from hand to mouth will ever be an inferior class. They will necessarily remain impotent and helpless, hanging on to the skirts of -society, the sport of times and seasons. Having no respect for themselves, they will fail in securing the respect of others. In commercial crisis, such men must inevitably go to the wall. Wanting that husbanded power with a store of savings, no matter how small, invariably gives them, they will be at every man's mercy, and, if possessed of right feelings, they can not but regard with fear and trembling the future possible fate of their wives and children. "The world," said Mr. Cobden, "has always been divided into two classes—those who have saved, and those who have spent—the thrifty and the extravagant. The building of all the houses, the mills, the bridges, and the ships, and the accomplishment of all other great works which have rendered man civilized and happy, has been done by the savers, the thrifty; and those who have wasted their resources have always been their slaves. It has been the law of nature and of Providence that this should be so; and I were an impostor if I promised any class that they would advance themselves if they were improvident, thoughtless, and idle."

Equally sound was the advice given by Mr. Bright to an assembly of working men, when, after expressing his belief that, "so far as honesty was concerned, it was to be found in pretty equal amount among all classes," he used the following words: "There is only one way that is safe for any man, or any number of men, by which they can maintain their present position if it be a good one, or raise themselves above it if it be a bad one—that is, by the practice of the virtues of industry, frugality, temperance, and honesty." There is no royal road by which men can raise themselves from a position which they feel to be uncomfortable and unsatisfactory, as regards their mental or physical condition, except by the practice of those virtues by which they find numbers amongst them are continually advancing and bettering themselves. There is no reason why the condition of the average workman should not be a useful, honorable, respectable, and happy one. The whole body of the working classes might be as frugal, virtuous, well-informed, and well-conditioned as many individuals of the same class have already made themselves. What some men are, all without difficulty, might be. Employ the same means, and the same results will follow. The healthy spirit of self-help created amongst working people would more than any other measure serve to raise them as a class, and this, not by pulling down others, but by leveling them up to a higher and still advancing standard of religion, intelligence, and virtue. "All moral philosophy," says Montaigne, "is as applicable to a common and private life as to the most splendid. Every man carries the entire form of the human condition with him."

When a man casts his glance forward, he will find that the three chief temporal contingencies for which he has to provide are want of employment, sickness, and death. The two first he may escape, but the last is inevitable. It is, however, the duty of the prudent man so to live, and so to arrange, that the pressure of suffering, in the event of either contingency occurring, shall be mitigated to as great an extent as possible, not only to himself, but also to those who are dependent upon him for their comfort and subsistence. Viewed in this light, the honest earning and the frugal use of money are of the greatest importance. Rightly earned, it is the representative of patient industry and untiring effort, of temptation resisted and hope rewarded; and rightly used, it affords indications of prudence, forethought, and self-denial—the true basis of manly character. Though money represents a crowd of objects without any real worth or utility, it also represents many things of great value; not only food, clothing, and household satisfaction, but personal self-respect and independence. Thus a store of savings is to the working man as a barricade against want; it secures him a footing, and enables him to wait, it may be in cheerfulness and hope, until better days come round. The very endeavor to gain a firmer position in the world has a certain dignity in it, and tends to make a man stronger and better. At all events, it gives him greater freedom of action, and enables him to husband his strength for future effort. But the man who is always hovering on the verge of want is in a state not far removed from that of slavery. He is in no sense his own master, but is in constant peril of falling under the bondage of others, and accepting the terms which they dictate to him. He can not help being in a measure servile, for he dares not look the world boldly in the face; and in adverse times he must look either to alms or the poor's rates. If work fails him altogether, he has not the means of moving to another field of employment

To secure independence, the practice of simple economy is all that is necessary. Economy requires neither superior courage nor eminent virtue; it is satisfied with ordinary energy, and the capacity of average minds. Economy, at bottom, is but the spirit of order applied in the administration of domestic affairs; it means management, regularity, prudence, and the avoidance of waste. Francis Horner's father gave him this advice on entering life: "Whilst I wish you to be comfortable in every respect, I can not too strongly inculcate economy. It is a necessary virtue to all; and however the shallow part of mankind may despise it, it certainly leads to independence, which is a grand object to every man of a high spirit."

It was a maxim of Lord Bacon, that when it was necessary to economize, it was better to look after petty savings than to descend to petty gettings. The loose cash which many persons throw away uselessly, and worse, would often form a basis of fortune and independence for life. These wasters are their own worst enemies, though generally found amongst the ranks of those who rail at the injustice of "the world." But if a man will not be his own friend, how can he expect that others will? Orderly men of moderate means have always something left in their pockets to help others; whereas your prodigal and careless fellows who spend all never find an opportunity for helping any body. It is poor economy, however, to be a scrub. Narrow-mindedness in living and in dealing is generally short-sighted, and leads to failure. The penny soul, it is said never came to twopence. Generosity and liberality, like honesty, prove the best policy after all.

The proverb says that "an empty bag can not stand upright"; neither can a man who is in debt. It is also difficult for a man who is in debt to be truthful; hence it is said that lying rides on debt's back. The debtor has to frame excuses to his creditor for postponing payment of the money he owes him, and probably also to contrive falsehoods. It is easy enough for a man who will exercise a healthy resolution, to avoid incurring the first obligation; but the facility with which that has been incurred often becomes a temptation to a second; and very soon the unfortunate borrower becomes so entangled that no late exertion of industry can set him free. The first step in debt is like the first step in falsehoods; almost involving the necessity of proceeding in the same course, debt following debt, as lie follows lie. Haydon, the painter, dated his decline from the day on which he first borrowed money. He realized the truth of the proverb, "Who goes a-borrowing, goes a-sorrowing." The significant entry in his diary is, "Here began debt and obligation, out of which I have never been and never shall be extricated as long as I live." His autobiography shows but too painfully how embarrassment in money matters produces poignant distress of mind, utter incapacity for work, and constantly recurring humiliations. The written advice which he gave to a youth when entering the navy was as follows: "Never purchase any enjoyment if it can not be procured without borrowing of others. Never borrow money; it is degrading. I do not say never lend, but never lend if by lending you render yourself unable to pay what you owe; but under any circumstances never borrow." Fichte, the poor student, refused to accept even presents from his still poorer parents.

Dr. Johnson held that early debt is ruin. His words on the subject are weighty, and worthy of being held in remembrance. "Do not," said he, "accustom yourself to consider debt only as an inconvenience; you will find it a calamity. Poverty takes away so many means of doing good, and produces so much inability to resist evil, both natural and moral, that it is by all virtuous means to be avoided. . . . Let it be your first care, then, not to be in any man's debt. Resolve not to be poor; whatever you have, spend less. Poverty is a great enemy to human happiness; it certainly destroys liberty, and it makes some virtues impracticable and others extremely difficult. Frugality is not only the basis of quiet, but of beneficence. No man can help others that wants help himself; we must have enough before we have to spare."

It is the bounden duty of every man to look his affairs in the face, and to keep an account of his incomings and outgoings in money matters. The exercise of a little simple arithmetic in this way will be found of great value. Prudence requires that we shall pitch our scale of living a degree below our means. But this can only be done by carrying out faithfully a plan of living by which both ends may be made to meet. John Locke strongly advised this course: "Nothing," said he, "is likelier to keep a man within compass-than having constantly before his eyes the state of his affairs in a regular course of account." The Duke of Wellington kept an accurate detailed account of all the money received and expended by him. Washington was very particular in matters of business detail; and it is a remarkable fact, that he did not disdain to scrutinize the smallest outgoings of his household—determined as he was to live honestly within his means—even when holding the high office of President of the American Union.

Admiral Jervis has told the story of his early struggles, and, amongst other things, of his determination to keep out of debt. "My father had a very large family," said he, "with limited means. He gave me twenty pounds at starting, and that was all he ever gave me. After I had been a considerable time at the station I drew for twenty more, but the bill came back protested. I was mortified at this rebuke, and made a promise, which I have ever kept, that I would never draw another bill without a certainty of its being paid. I immediately changed my mode of living, quitted my mess, lived alone, and took up the ship's allowance, which I found quite sufficient; washed and mended my own clothes; made a pair of trousers out of the ticking of my bed; and having by these means saved as much money as would redeem my honor, I took up my bill, and from that time to this I have taken care to keep within my means." Jervis for six years endured pinching privation, but preserved his integrity, studied his profession with success, and gradually and steadily rose by merit and bravery to the highest rank. Middle-class people are too apt to live up to their incomes, if not beyond them, affecting a degree of "style" which is most unhealthy in its effects upon society at large. There is an ambition to bring up boys as gentlemen, or rather "genteel" men, though the result frequently is only to make them gents. They acquire a taste for dress, style, luxuries, and amusements, which can never form any solid foundation for manly or gentlemanly character; and the result is that we have a vast number of gingerbread young gentry thrown upon the world, who remind one of the abandoned hulls sometimes picked up at sea, with only a monkey on board. There is a dreadful ambition abroad for being "genteel." We keep up appearances, too often at the expense of honesty; and, though we may not be rich, yet we must seem to be so. We must be "respectable," though only in the meanest sense—in mere vulgar outward show. We have not the courage to go patiently onward in the condition in life in which it has pleased God to call us; but must needs live in some fashionable state to which we ridiculously please to call ourselves, and to gratify the vanity of that unsubstantial genteel world of which we form a part. There is a constant struggle and pressure for front seats in the social amphitheatre; in the midst of which all noble self-denying resolve is trodden down, and many fine natures are inevitably crushed to death. What waste, what misery, what bankruptcy, come from all this ambition to dazzle others with the glare of apparent worldly success, we need not describe. The mischievous results show themselves in a thousand ways—in the rank frauds committed by men who dare to be dishonest, but do not dare to seem poor. There are rogues innumerable, who are ready to sell their bodies and souls for money and for drink. Who has not heard of the elections which have been made void through bribery and corruption? This is not the way to enjoy liberty or to keep it. The men who sell themselves are slaves; their buyers are dishonest and unprincipled. Freedom has its humbugs. "I'm standing on the soil of liberty," said an orator. "You ain't," replied a boot-maker in the audience. "You are standing on a pair of boots you never paid me for."

The ignorant and careless are at the mercy of the unprincipled; and the ignorant are as yet greatly in the majority. When a French quack was taken before the Correctional Tribunal at Paris for obstructing the Pont Neuf, the magistrate said to him, "Sirrah! how is it you draw such crowds about you, and extract so much money from them in selling your infallible rubbish?" "My lord," replied the quack, "how many people do you think cross the Pont Neuf in the hour?" "I don't know," said the judge. "Then I can tell you—about ten-thousand; and how many of these do you think are wise?" "Oh, perhaps a hundred!" "It is too many," said the quack; "but I leave the hundred persons to you, and take the nine thousand and nine hundred for my customers!"

Aristides was called "The Just" from his unbending integrity. His sense of justice was spotless, and his self-denial unimpeachable. He fought at Marathon, at Salamis, and commanded at the battle of Plaitea. Though he had borne the highest offices in the state, he died poor. Nothing could buy him; nothing could induce him to swerve from his duty. It is said that the Athenians became more virtuous from contemplating his bright example.

In the representation of one of the tragedies of Aeschylus, a sentence was uttered in favor of moral goodness, on which the eyes of the audience turned involuntarily from the actor to Aristides.

Phocion, the Athenian general, a man of great bravery and foresight, was surnamed "The Good." Alexander the Great, when overrunning Greece, endeavored to win him from his loyalty. He offered him riches, and the choice of four cities in Asia. The answer of Phocion bespoke the spotless character of the man. "If Alexander really esteems me," he said, "let him leave me my honesty."

Yet Demosthenes, the eloquent, could be bought. When Harpalus, one of Alexander's chiefs, Came to Athens, the orators had an eye upon his gold. Demosthenes was one of them. What is eloquence without honesty? On his visit to Harpalus, the chief perceived that Demosthenes was much pleased with one of the king's beautifully engraved cups. He desired him to take it in his hand that he might feel its weight. "How much might it bring?" asked Demosthenes. "It will bring you twenty talents," replied Harpalus. That night the cup was sent to Demosthenes, with twenty talents in it. The present was not refused. The circumstance led to the disgrace of the orator, and he soon after poisoned himself. Cicero, on the other hand, refused all presents from friends, as well as from the enemies of his country. Some time after his assassination, Caesar found one of his grandsons with a book of Cicero's in his hands. The boy endeavored to hide it, but Caesar took it from him. After having run over it, he returned it to the boy, saying, "My dear child, this was an eloquent man, and a lover of his country." Goldsmith also was a man who would not be bought. He had known the depths of poverty. He had wandered over Europe, paying his way with his flute. He had slept in barns and under the open sky. He tried acting, ushering, doctoring. He starved amid them all. Then he tried authorship, and became a gentleman. But he never quite escaped from the clutches of poverty. He described himself as "in a garret writing for bread, and expecting to be dunned for a milk score." One day Johnson received a message from Goldsmith, stating that he was in great distress. The Doctor went to see him, and found that his landlady had arrested him for his rent. The only thing he had to dispose of was a packet of manuscript. Johnson took it up, and found it to be the "Vicar of Wakefield." Having ascertained its merit, Johnson took it to a bookseller and sold it for sixty pounds. Poor though he was then, and poor though he was at the end of his life—for he died in debt—Goldsmith couldn't be bought. He refused to do dirty political work. About $250,000 annually was then expended by Sir Robert Walpole in secret service money. Daily scribblers were suborned to write up the acts of the administration, and to write down those of their opponents. In the time of Lord North, "Junius" was in opposition. It was resolved to hire Goldsmith to baffle his terrible sarcasm. Dr. Scott, chaplain to Lord Sandwich, was deputed to negotiate with him. "I found him," says Dr. Scott, "in a miserable suite of chambers in the Temple. I told him my authority. I told him how I was empowered to pay for his exertions; and, would you believe it? he was so absurd as to say, I can earn as much as will supply my wants without writing for any party; the assistance you offer is therefore unnecessary to me; and so I left him in his garret."

Nothing is more creditable to American statesmanship than the fact that most of our Presidents at death have left their families in very moderate circumstances. Garfield and Lincoln, whose positions would have enabled them, by accepting gifts and bribes to have accumulated immense wealth, died poor and in debt, although they were rich in the affection of a grateful people. The same is true of our most honored statesmen. That bribery and corruption exists in our politics and often controls legislation cannot be denied. But it should also be said, to the great credit of a vigilant popular censorship, that corrupt and venal statesmen, when they become known as such, are promptly relegated to private life.

The young man, as he passes through life, advances through a long line of tempters ranged on either side of him; and the inevitable effect of yielding is degradation in a greater or a less degree. Contact with them tends insensibly to draw away from him some portion of the divine electric element with which his nature is charged; and his only mode of resisting them is to utter and act out his "No" manfully and resolutely. He must decide at once, not waiting to deliberate and balance reasons: for the youth, like "the woman who deliberates, is lost." Temptation will come to try the young man's strength; and, once yielded to, the power to resist grows weaker and weaker. Yield once, and a portion of virtue is gone. Resist manfully, and the first decision will give strength for life; repeated, it will become a habit. It is in the outworks of the habits formed in early life that the real strength of the defense must lie; for it has been wisely ordained that the machinery of moral existence should be carried on principally through the medium of the habits, so as to save the wear and tear of the great principles within. It is good habits, which insinuate themselves into the thousand inconsiderable acts of life, that really constitute by far the greater part of man's moral conduct.

Hugh Miller has told how, by an act of youthful decision, he saved himself from one of the strong temptations so peculiar to a life of toil. When employed as a mason, it was usual for his fellow-workmen to have an occasional treat of drink, and one day two glasses of whisky fell to his share, which he swallowed. When he reached home he found, on opening his favorite book—"Bacon's Essays"—that the letters danced before his eyes, and that he could no longer master the sense. "The condition," he says, "into which I had brought myself was, I felt, one of degradation. I had sunk, by my own act, for the time, to a lower level of intelligence than that on which it was my privilege to be placed; and, though the state could have been no very favorable one for forming a resolution, I in that hour determined that I should never again sacrifice my capacity of intellectual enjoyment to a drinking usage; and, with God's help, I was enabled to hold by the determination." It is such decisions as this that often form the turning points in a man's life, and furnish the foundation of his future character. And this rock, on which Hugh Miller might have been wrecked, if he had not at the right moment put forth his moral strength to strike away from it, is one that youth and manhood alike need to be constantly on their guard against. It is about one of the worst and most deadly, as well as extravagant temptations which lie in the way of youth. Sir Walter Scott used to say that "of all vices, drinking is the most incompatible with greatness." Not only so, but it is incompatible with economy, decency, health and honest living. Dr. Johnson said, referring to his own habits, "Sir, I can abstain; but I can't be moderate."

Many popular books have been written for the purpose of communicating to the public the grand secret of making money. But there is no secret whatever about it, as the proverbs of every nation abundantly testify. "Take care of the pennies and the pounds will take care of themselves." "Diligence is the mother of good luck." "No pains, no gains." "No sweat, no sweet." "Work and thou shalt have." "The world is his who has patience and industry." "Better go to bed supperless than rise in debt." Such are specimens of the proverbial philosophy, embodying the hoarded experience of many generations, as to the best means of thriving in the world. They were current in people's mouths long before books were invented; and, like other popular proverbs, they were the first popular morals. Moreover, they have stood the test of time, and the experience of every day still bears witness to their accuracy, force, and soundness. The proverbs of Solomon are full of wisdom as to the force of industry, and the use and abuse of money:—"He that is slothful in work is brother to him that is a great waster." "Go to the ant, thou sluggard; consider her ways, and be wise." Poverty, says the preacher, shall come upon the idler, as one that traveleth, and want as an armed man; "but of the industrious and upright, the hand of the diligent maketh rich." "The drunkard and the glutton shall come to poverty; and drowsiness shall clothe a man with rags." "Seest thou a man diligent in his business, he shall stand before kings." But, above all, "It is better to get wisdom than gold; for wisdom is better than rubies, and all the things that may be desired are not to be compared to it."

Simple industry and thrift will go far towards making any person of ordinary working faculty comparatively independent in his means. Even a working man may be so, provided he will carefully husband his resources, and watch the little outlets of useless expenditure. A penny is a very small matter, yet the comfort of thousands of families depends upon the proper spending and saving of pennies. If a man allows the little pennies, the results of his hard work, to slip out of his fingers—some to the beer shop, some this way and some that—he will find that his life is little raised above one of mere animal drudgery. On the other hand, if he takes care of the pennies—putting some weekly into a saving's bank, and confiding the rest to his wife to be carefully laid out, with a view to the comfortable maintenance and education of his family—he will soon find that this attention to small matters will abundantly repay him, in increasing means, growing comfort at home, and a mind comparatively free from fears as to the future. And if a working man have high ambition and possess richness in spirit—a kind of wealth which far transcends all mere worldly possessions—he may not only help himself, but be a profitable helper of others in his path through life. That this is no impossible thing even for a common laborer in a workshop, may be illustrated by the remarkable career of Thomas Wright of Manchester, who not only attempted but succeeded in the reclamation of many criminals while working for weekly wages in a foundry.

Accident first directed Thomas Wright's attention to the difficulty encountered by liberated convicts in returning to habits of honest industry. His mind was shortly possessed by the subject, and to remedy the evil became the purpose of his life. Though he worked from six in the morning till six at night, still there were leisure minutes that he could call his own—more especially his Sundays—and these he employed in the service of convicted criminals; a class then far more neglected than they are now. But a few minutes a day, well employed, can effect a great deal; and it will scarcely be credited, that in ten years this working man, by steadfastly holding to his purpose, succeeded in rescuing not fewer than three hundred felons from continuance in a life of villainy! He came to be regarded as the moral physician of the Manchester Old Bailey; and where the chaplain and all others failed, Thomas Wright often succeeded. Children he thus restored reformed to their parents; sons and daughters, otherwise lost, to their homes; and many a returned convict did he contrive to settle down to honest and industrious pursuits. The task was by no means easy. It required money, time, energy, prudence, and above all, character, and the confidence which character invariably inspires. The most remarkable circumstance was that Wright relieved many of these poor outcasts out of the comparatively small wages earned by him at foundry work. He did all this on an income which did not average, during his working career, $500 per annum; and yet, while he was able to bestow substantial aid on criminals, to whom he owed no more than the service of kindness which every human being owes to another, he also maintained his family in comfort, and was, by frugality and carefulness, enabled to lay by a store of savings against his approaching old age. Every week he apportioned his income with deliberate care; so much for the indispensable necessaries of food and clothing, so much for the landlord, so much for the schoolmaster, so much for the poor and needy; and the lines of distribution were resolutely observed. By such means did this humble workman pursue his great work, with the results we have so briefly described. Indeed, his career affords one of the most remarkable and striking illustrations of the force of purpose in a man, of the might of small means carefully and sedulously applied, and, above all, of the power which an energetic and upright character invariably exercises upon the lives and conduct of others.

There is no discredit, but honor, in every right walk of industry, whether it be in tilling the ground, making tools, weaving fabrics, or selling the products behind a counter. A youth may handle a yard-stick, or measure a piece of ribbon; and there will be no discredit in doing so, unless he allows his mind to have no higher range than the stick and ribbon; to be as short as the one and as narrow as the other. "Let not those blush who *have*," said Fuller, "but those who *have not* a lawful calling." And Bishop Hall said, "Sweet is the destiny of all trades, whether of the brow or of the mind." One of our Presidents, when asked what was his coat-of-arms, remembering that he had been a hewer of wood in his youth, replied, "a pair of shirt-sleeves."

Nothing is more common than energy in moneymaking, quite independent of any higher object than its accumulation. A man who devotes himself to this pursuit, body and soul, can scarcely fail to become rich. Very little brains will do: spend less than you earn; add guinea to guinea; scrape and save; and the pile of gold will gradually rise. John Foster has cited a striking illustration of what determination will do in money-making. A young man who ran through his patrimony, spending it in profligacy, was at length reduced to utter want and despair. He rushed out of his house intending to put an end to his life, and stopped on arriving at an eminence overlooking what were once his estates. He sat down ruminated for a time, and rose with the determination that he would recover them. He returned to the streets, saw a load of coal which had been shot out of a cart on to the pavement before a house, offered to carry it in, and was employed. He thus earned a few pence, requested some meat and drink as a gratuity, which was given him, and the pennies were laid by. Pursuing this menial labor, he earned and saved more pennies; accumulated sufficient to enable him to purchase some cattle, the value of which he understood, and these he sold to advantage. He proceeded by degrees to undertake larger transactions, until at length he became rich. The result was that he more than recovered his possessions, and died an inveterate miser. When he was buried mere earth went to earth. With a nobler spirit, the same determination might have enabled such a man to be a benefactor to others as well as to himself. But the life and its end in this case were alike sordid. To provide for others and for our own comfort and independence in old age, is honorable and greatly to be commended; but to hoard for mere wealth's sake is the characteristic of the narrow-souled and the miserly. It is against the growth of this habit of inordinate saving that the wise man needs most carefully to guard himself; else, what in youth was simple economy, may in old age grow into avarice, and what was a duty in the one case, may become a vice in the other. It is one of the defects of business too exclusively followed, that it insensibly tends to a mechanism of character. The business man gets into a rut, and often does not look beyond it. If he lives for himself only, he becomes apt to regard other human beings only in so far as they minister to his ends. Take a leaf from such a man's ledger and you have his life.

"Respectability," in its best sense, is good. The respectable man is one worthy of regard, literally worth turning to look at. But the respectability that consists in merely keeping up appearances is not worth looking at in any sense. Far better and more respectable is the good poor man than the bad rich one—better the humble silent man than the agreeable, well-appointed rogue who keeps his gig. A well-balanced and well-stored mind, a life full of useful purpose, whatever the position occupied in it may be, is of far greater importance than average worldly respectability. The highest object of life we take to be to form a manly character, and to work out the best development possible, of body and spirit—of mind, conscience, heart, and soul. This is the end: all else ought to be regarded but as the means. Accordingly, that is not the most successful life in which a man gets the most pleasure, the most money, the most power or place, honor or fame; but that in which a man gets the most manhood, and performs the greatest amount of useful work and of human duty. Money is power after its sort, it is true; but intelligence, public spirit, and moral virtue, are powers, too, and far nobler ones. When Sir Humphrey Davy, after great labor, invented his safety lamp, for the purpose of mitigating the dangers to colliers working in inflammable gas, he would not take out a patent for it, but made it over to the public. A friend said to him, "You might as well have secured this invention by a patent, and received your five or ten thousand a year for it." "No, my good friend," said Davy, "I never thought of such a thing; my sole object was to serve the cause of humanity. I have enough for all my views and purposes. More wealth might distract my attention from my favorite pursuits. More wealth could not increase either my fame or my happiness. It might undoubtedly enable me to put four horses to my carriage; but what would it avail me to have it said that Sir Humphrey drives his carriage and four?"

The making of a fortune may no doubt enable some people to "enter society," as it is called; but, to be esteemed there, they must possess qualities of mind, manners, or heart, else they are merely rich people, nothing more. There are men in "society" now, as rich as Croesus, who have no consideration extended towards them, and elicit no respect. For why? They are but as money-bags: their only power is in their till. The men of mark in society—the guides and rulers of opinion—the really successful and useful men—are not necessarily rich men; but men of sterling character, of disciplined experience, and of moral excellence. Even the poor man, like Thomas Wright, though he possess but little of this world's goods, may, in the enjoyment of a cultivated nature, of opportunities used and not abused, of a life spent to the best of his means and ability, look down, without the slightest feeling of envy, upon the person of mere worldly success, the man of money-bags and acres.

Chapter 16

Habits of Thrift

"We are taxed twice as heavily by our pride as by the state." —Poor Richard.

Economy is of itself a great revenue." —Cicero.

THRIFT OR PRIVATE ECONOMY began with civilization. It began when men found it necessary to provide for tomorrow as well as for today. It began long before money was invented.

While it is the object of private economy to create and promote the well-being of individuals, it is the object of political economy to create and increase the wealth of nations. Private and public wealth have the same origin. Wealth is obtained by labor; it is preserved by savings and accumulations; and it is increased by diligence and perseverance. It is the savings of individuals which compose the wealth and the well-being of every nation. On the other hand, it is the wastefulness of individuals which occasions the impoverishment of states. So that every thrifty person may be regarded as a public benefactor, and every thriftless person as a public enemy.

Prodigality is much more natural to man than thrift. The savage is the greatest of spendthrifts, for he has no forethought, no tomorrow. The prehistoric man saved nothing. He lived in caves, or in hollows of the ground, covered with branches. He subsisted on shell-fish which he picked up on the sea-shore, or upon fruits which he gathered in the woods. He killed animals with stones. He lay in wait for them, or ran them down on foot. Then he learned to use stones as tools; making stone arrow-heads and spear-points, thereby utilizing his labor, and killing birds and animals more quickly. The original savage knew nothing of agriculture. It was only in comparatively recent times that men gathered seeds for food, and saved a portion of them for next year's crop. When minerals were discovered, and fire was applied to them, and the minerals became smelted into metal, man made an immense stride. He could then fabricate hard tools, chisel stone, build houses, and proceed by unwearying industry to devise the manifold means and agencies of civilization. The dweller by the ocean burned a hollow in a felled tree, launched it, went to sea in it, and fished for food. The hollow tree became a boat, held together with iron nails. The boat became a galley, a ship, a paddle-boat, a screw-steamer, and the world was opened up for colonization and civilization. Man would have continued a savage, but for the results of the useful labors of those who preceded him. The soil was reclaimed by them, and made to grow food for human uses. They invented tools and fabrics, and we reap the useful results. They discovered art and science, and we succeed to the useful effects of their labors.

The history of industry is uniform in the character of its illustrations. Industry enables the poorest man to achieve honor, if not distinction. The greatest names in the history of art, literature and science, are those of laboring men. By the working-man we do not mean merely the man that labors with his muscles and sinews. A horse can do this. But *lie* is pre-eminently the working-man who works with his brain also, and whose whole physical system is under the influence of his higher faculties. The man who paints a picture, who writes a book, who makes a law, who creates a poem, is a working-man of the highest order; not so necessary to the physical sustainment of the community as the plowman or the shepherd, but not less important as providing for society its highest intellectual nourishment.

Having said so much of the importance and the necessity of industry, let us see what uses are made of the advantages derivable from it. It is clear that man would have continued a savage but for the accumulations of savings made by our forefathers—the savings of skill, of art, of invention, and of intellectual culture. It is the savings of the world that have made the civilization of the world. Savings arc the result of labor; and it is only when laborers begin to save that the results of civilization accumulate. We have said that thrift began with civilization; we might almost have said that thrift produced civilization. Thrift produces capital, and capital is the conserved result of labor. The capitalist is merely a man who does not spend all that is earned by work. But a large proportion of men do not provide for the future. They do not remember the past. They think only of the present, They preserve nothing. They spend all that they earn. They do not provide for themselves; nor for their families. They may make high wages, but eat and drink the whole of what they earn. Such people are constantly poor, and hanging on the verge of destitution. The men who economize by means of labor become the owners of capital which sets other labor in motion. Capital accumulates in their hands, and they employ other laborers to work

Habits of Thrift

for them. Thus trade and commerce begin. The thrifty build houses, warehouses, and mills. They fit manufactories with tools and machines. They build ships, and send them to various parts of the world. They put their capital together, and build railroads, harbors, and docks. They open up mines of coal, iron, and copper; and erect pumping-engines to keep them clear of water. They employ laborers to work the mines, and thus give rise to an immense amount of employment. All this is the result of thrift. It is the result of economizing money, and employing it for beneficial purposes. The thriftless man has no share in the progress of the world. He spends all that he gets, and can give no help to anybody. No matter how much money he makes, his position is not in any respect raised. He husbands none of his resources. He is always calling for help. He is, in fact, the born slave of the thrifty. Competence and comfort lie within the reach of most people, were they to take the adequate means to secure and enjoy them. Men who are paid good wages might also become capitalists, and take their fair share in the improvement and well-being of the world. But it is only by the exercise of labor, energy, honesty, and thrift, that they can advance their own position or that of their class.

Society at present suffers far more from waste of money than from want of money. It is easier to make money than to know how to spend it. It is not what a man gets that constitutes his wealth, but his manner of spending and economizing. And when a man obtains by his labor more than enough for his personal and family wants, and can lay by a little store of savings besides, he unquestionably possesses the elements of social well-being. The savings may amount to little, but they may be sufficient to make him independent. There is no reason why the highly paid workman of today may not save a store of capital. It is merely a matter of self-denial and private economy. Indeed, the principal industrial leaders of today consist, for the most part, of men who have sprung directly from the ranks. Thrift of time is equal to thrift of money. Franklin said, "Time is gold." If one wishes to earn money, it may be done by the proper use of time. But time may also be spent in doing many good and noble actions. It may be spent in learning, in study, in art, in science, in literature. Time can be economized by system. System is an arrangement to secure certain ends, so that no time may be lost in accomplishing them. Every business man must be systematic and orderly; so must every housewife. There must be a place for every thing, and every thing in its place. There must also be a time for every thing, and every thing must be done in time. Thrift does not require superior courage, superior intellect, nor any superhuman virtue. It merely requires common sense, and the power of resisting selfish enjoyments. In fact, thrift is merely common sense in every-day working action. It needs no fervent resolution, but only a little patient self-denial. *Begin* is its device! The more the habit of thrift is practiced, the easier it becomes, and the sooner it compensates the self-denier for the sacrifices which it has imposed.

The question may be asked: Is it possible for a man working for small wages to save anything, and lay it by in a savings-bank, when he requires every penny for the maintenance of his family? But the fact remains, that it is done by many industrious and sober men; that they do deny themselves, and put their spare earnings into savings-banks, and the other receptacles provided for poor men's savings. And if some can do this, all may do it under similar circumstances, without depriving themselves of any genuine pleasure or any real enjoyment.

How intensely selfish is it for any one in the receipt of good pay to spend everything upon himself; or, if he has a family, to spend his whole earnings from week to week, and lay nothing by. When we hear that a man who has been in the receipt of a good salary, has died and left nothing behind him—that he has left his wife and family destitute—left them to chance—to live or perish anywhere—we can not but regard it as the most selfish thriftlessness. And yet comparatively little is thought of such cases. Perhaps the hat goes round. Subscriptions may produce something—perhaps nothing; and the ruined remnants of the unhappy family sink into poverty and destitution. Money represents a multitude of objects without value, or without real utility; but it also represents something much more precious, and that is independence. In this light it is of great moral importance. No class ever accomplished anything that lived from hand to mouth. People who spend all that they earn are ever hanging on the brink of destitution. They must necessarily be weak and impotent—the slaves of time and circumstance. They keep themselves poor. They lose self-respect as well as the respect of others. It is impossible that they can be free and independent. To be thriftless is enough to deprive one of all manly spirit and virtue.

But a man with something saved, no matter now little, is in a different position. The little capital he has stored up is always a source of power. He is no longer the sport of time and fate. He can boldly look the world in the face. He is, in a manner, his own master. He can dictate his own terms. He can neither be bought nor sold. He can look forward with cheerfulness to an old age of comfort and happiness.

What a serious responsibility does the man incur who marries! Not many seriously think of this responsibility. Perhaps this is wisely ordered, for much serious thinking might end in the avoidance of married life and its responsibilities. But, once married, a man ought forthwith to determine that, so far as his own efforts are concerned, want shall never enter his household; and that his children shall not, in the event of his being removed from the scene of fife and labor, be left a burden upon society. When economy is looked upon as a thing that *must* be practiced, it will never be felt as a burden; and those who have not before observed it, will be astonished to find what a few pence or shillings laid aside weekly will do toward securing moral elevation, mental culture, and personal independence. There is a dignity in every attempt to economize. Its very practice is improving. It indicates self-denial, and imparts strength to the character. It produces a well-regulated mind. It fosters temperance. It is based on forethought. It makes prudence the dominating characteristic. It gives virtue the mastery over self-indulgence. Above all, it secures comfort, drives away, care, and dispels many vexations and anxieties which might otherwise prey upon us.

The number of well paid workmen in this country has become very large, who might easily save and economize, to the improvement of their moral wellbeing, of their respectability and independence, and of their status in society as men and citizens. They are improvident and thriftless to an extent which proves not less hurtful to their personal happiness and domestic comfort than it is injurious to the society of which they form so important a part. In "prosperous times" they spend their gains recklessly; and when adverse times come they are at once plunged in misery. Money is not used, but abused; and, when people should be providing against old age, or for the wants of a growing family, they are, in too many cases, feeding folly, dissipation and vice. Let no one say that this is an exaggerated picture. It is enough to look round in any neighborhood, and see how much is spent and how little is saved; what a large proportion of savings goes to the beer-shop, and how little to the savings-bank.

"Prosperous times" are very often the least prosperous of all times. There are demands for higher wages; and the higher wages, when obtained, are spent as soon as earned. Intemperate habits are formed, and, once formed, the habit of intemperance continues. Increased wages, instead of being saved, are, for the most part, spent in drink. Thus, when a population are thoughtless and improvident, no kind of material prosperity will benefit them. Unless they exercise forethought and economy they will alternately be in a state of "hunger and burst." When trade falls off; as it does after exceptional prosperity, they will not be comforted by the thought of what they *might* have saved, had it ever occurred to them that the "prosperous times" might not have proved permanent. "Where are all the workmen?" said a master to his foremen, on going the rounds among his builders: "this work must be pushed on, and covered in while the fine weather lasts." "Why, sir," said the foreman, "this is Monday, and they have not spent all their money yet."

The difference in thriftiness between the English working people and the inhabitants of Guernsey is thus referred to by Mr. Denison: "The difference between poverty and pauperism is brought home to us very strongly by what I see here. In England we have people faring sumptuously while they are getting good wages; and coming on the parish as paupers the moment those wages are suspended. Here, people are never dependent on any support but their own; but they live, of their own free will, in a style of frugality which a landlord would be hooted at for suggesting to his cottagers. We pity Hodge, reduced to bacon and greens, and to meat only once a week. The principal meal of a Guernsey farmer consists of cabbage and pease stewed with a little dripping. This is the daily dinner of men who *own* perhaps three or four cows, a pig or two, and poultry. But the produce and flesh of these creatures they sell in the market, investing their gains in extension of land or stock, or in rent-charges on land, certificates of which are readily bought and sold in the market."

No one can reproach the American workman with want of industry. He works harder and more skillfully than the workman of any other country; and he might be more comfortable and independent in his circumstances, were he as prudent as he is laborious. But improvidence is unhappily the defect of the class. Even the best-paid American workmen, though earning more money than the average of professional men, are still for the most part poor because of their thoughtlessness. In prosperous times they are not accustomed to make provision for adverse times; and when a period of social pressure occurs, they are rarely found more than a few weeks ahead of positive want.

Franklin, with his shrewd common sense, observed: "The taxes are indeed very heavy; and if those laid on by the Government were the only ones we had to pay, we might more easily discharge them; but we have many others, and much more grievous to some of us. We are taxed quite as much by our idleness, three times as much by our pride, and four times as much by our folly; and from these taxes the commissioners can not ease or deliver us by allowing an abatement."

It is difficult to account for the waste and extravagance of working-people. It must be the hereditary remnant of the original savage. It must be a survival. The savage feasts and drinks until everything is gone; and then he hunts or goes to war. Or it may be the survival of slavery in the State. Slavery was one of the first of human institutions. The strong man made the weak man work for him. The warlike race subdued the less warlike race, and made them their slaves. Thus slavery existed from the earliest times. In Greece and Rome the fighting was done by freemen, the labor by helots and bondsmen. But slavery also existed in the family. The wife was the slave of her husband, as much as the slave whom he bought in the public market. Matters have now become entirely different. The workman, no matter what his trade, is comparatively free. The worst slavery from which he suffers is his passion for drink. In this respect he still resembles the Esquimaux and the North American Indians. Would he be really free? Then he must exercise the powers of a free, responsible man. He must exercise self-control and self-restraint, and sacrifice present personal gratifications for prospective enjoyments of a much higher kind. It is only by self-respect and self-control that the position of the workman can be really elevated.

Thrift is the spirit of order applied to domestic management and organization. Its object is to manage frugally the resources of the family, to prevent waste, and avoid useless expenditure. Thrift is under the influence of reason and forethought, and never works by chance or by fits. It endeavors to make the most and the best of every thing. It does not save money for saving's sake. It makes cheerful sacrifices for the present benefits of others; or it submits to voluntary privation for some future good.

Mrs. Inchbald, author of the "Simple Story," was, by dint of thrift, able to set apart the half of her small income for the benefit of her infirm sister. There were thus about two pounds a week for the maintenance of each. "Many times," she says, "during the winter, when I was crying with cold, have I said to myself, 'Thank God, my dear sister need not leave her chamber; she will find her fire ready for her each morning, for she is now far less able than I am to endure privation.'" Mrs. Inchbald's family were, for the most part, very poor; and she felt it right to support the during their numerous afflictions. There is one thing that may be said of benevolence; that it has never ruined any one, though selfishness and dissipation have ruined thousands. The words, "Waste not, want not," carved in stone over Sir Walter Scott's kitchen fireplace at Abbotsford, expresses in a few words the secret of order in the midst of abundance. Order is most useful in the management of every thing—of a household, of a business, of a manufactory, of an army. Its maxim is, "A place for every thing, and every thing in its place." Order is wealth; for, whoever properly regulates the use of his income, almost doubles his resources. Disorderly persons are rarely rich, and orderly persons are rarely poor. Order is the best manager of time; for unless work is properly arranged, time is lost; and, once lost, is gone forever.

Thrift is the spirit of order in human life. It is the prime agent in private economy. It preserves the happiness of many a household. And as it is usually woman who regulates the order of the household, it is mainly upon her that the well-being of society depends. It is therefore all the more necessary that she should early be educated in orderly habits.

Upon an income not exceeding two hundred a year the Tenth Earl of Buchan brought up a numerous family of children, one of whom afterwards rose to be Lord Chancellor of England. It is not the amount of income, so much as the good use of it, that marks the true man; and, viewed in this light, good sense, good taste, and sound mental culture are among the best of all economists. The late Dr. Aiton said that his father brought a still larger family up on only half the income of the Earl of Buchan. The following dedication, prefixed to his work on "Clerical Economics," is worthy of being remembered: "This work is respectfully dedicated to a father, now in the eighty-third year of his age, who, on an income which never exceeded a hundred pounds yearly, educated, out of a family of twelve children, four sons to liberal-professions, and who has often sent his last shilling to each of them in their turn, when they were at college."

Many men, in order to advance themselves in the world, and to raise themselves in society, have "scorned delights and lived laborious days." They have lived humbly and frugally, in order to accomplish greater things. They have supported themselves by their hand-labor, until they could support themselves by their head-labor. When Lord Elcho addressed the East Lothian colliers, he named several men who had raised themselves from the coal-pit; and, first of all, he referred to Mr. Macdonald, member for Stafford. "The beginning of my acquaintance with Mr. Macdonald," he said, "was when I was told a miner wanted to see me in the lobby of the House of Commons. I went out and saw Mr. Macdonald, who gave me a petition from his district, which he asked me to present. I entered into conversation with him, and was much struck by his intelligence. He told me that he had begun life as a boy in the pit at Lanarkshire, and that the money he saved as a youth in the summer he spent at Glasgow University in the winter; and that is where he got whatever book-learning or power of writing he possesses. I say that is an instance that does honor to the miners of Scotland. Another instance was that of Dr. Hogg, who began as a pitman in this country; worked in the morning, attended school in the afternoon; then went to the university for four years, and to the Theological Hall for five years; and afterward, in consequence of his health failing he went abroad, and is now engaged as a missionary in Upper Egypt. Or take the case of Mr. Elliott, member for North Durham, who has represented the miners all the better for having had practical knowledge of their work. He began as a miner in the pit, and he worked his way up till he has in his employment many thousand men. He has risen to his great wealth and station from the humblest position, as every man who now hears me is capable of doing, to a greater or less degree, if he will only be thrifty and industrious."

George Stephenson worked his way from the pithead to the highest position as an engineer. George began his life with industry, and when he had saved a little money he spent it in getting a little learning. What a happy man he was when his wages were increased to twelve shillings a week! He declared upon that occasion that he was "a made man for life!" He was not only enabled to maintain himself upon his earnings, but to help his poor parents, and to pay for his own education. When his skill had increased, and his wages had advanced to a pound a week, he immediately began, like a thoughtful, intelligent workman, to lay by his surplus money; and when he had saved his first guinea he proudly declared to one of his colleagues that he was now a rich man! And he was right, for the man who, after satisfying his wants, has something to spare, is no longer a poor man. It is certain that from that day Stephenson never looked back; his advance as a self-improving man was as steady as the light of sunrise. A person of large experience has indeed stated that he never knew, among working-people, a single instance of a man having out of his small earnings laid by a pound who had in the end became a pauper.

When Stephenson proposed to erect his first locomotive, he had not sufficient means to defray its cost. But in the course of his life as a workman he had established a character. He was trusted. He was faithful. He was a man who could be depended on. Accordingly, when the Earl of Ravensworth was informed of Stephenson's desire to erect a locomotive he at once furnished him with the means for enabling him to carry his wishes into effect. Watt, also, when inventing the condensing steam-engine, maintained himself by making and selling mathematical instruments. He made flutes, organs, compasses—anything that would maintain him, until he had completed his invention. At the same time he was perfecting his own education—learning French German, mathematics, and the principles of natural philosophy. This lasted for many years; and by the time Watt developed his steam-engine and discovered Mathew Boulton, he had by his own efforts, become an accomplished and scientific man.

These great workers did not feel ashamed of laboring with their hands for a living; but they also felt within themselves the power of doing head-work as well as hand-work. And while thus laboring with their hands, they went on with their inventions, the perfecting of which has proved of so much advantage to the world. Hugh Miller furnished, in his own life, an excellent instance of that practical common sense in the business of life which he so strongly recommended to others. When he began to write poetry, and felt within him the growing powers of a literary man, he diligently continued his labor as a stone-cutter. A man who feels he has some good work in him, which study and labor might yet bring out, is fully justified in denying himself, and in applying his energies to the culture of his intellect. And it is astonishing how much carefulness, thrift, the reading of books, and diligent application, will help such men onward. Franklin long maintained himself by his trade of printing. He was a hard-working man—thrifty, frugal, and a great saver of time. He worked for character as much as for wages, and when it was found that he could be relied on, he prospered. At length he was publicly recognized as a great statesman, and as one of the most scientific men of his time. Samuel Richardson, while writing his novels, stuck to his trade of a book-seller. He sold his books in the front shop, while he wrote them in the back. He would not give himself up to authorship, because he loved his independence. "You know," he said to his friend Defreval, "how my business engages me. You know by what snatches of time I write in order that I may preserve that independence which is the comfort of my life. I never sought out of myself for patrons. My own industry and God's providence have been my whole reliance. The great are not great to me unless they are good. And it is a glorious privilege that a middling man enjoys, who has preserved his independence, and can occasionally tell the world what he thinks of that world, in hopes to contribute, by his mite, to mend it."

Lough, the English sculptor, is another instance of self-denial and hard-work. When a boy, he was fond of drawing. At school he made drawings of horses, dogs, cows, and men, for pins; that was his first pay, and he used to go home with his jacket-sleeve stuck full of them. He and his brother next made figures in clay. Pope's Homer lay on his father's window. The boys were so delighted with it that they made thousands of models—one taking the Greeks and the other the Trojans. An odd volume of Gibbon gave an account of the Coliseum. After the family were in bed the brothers made a model of the Coliseum, and filled it with fighting gladiators. As the boys grew up they were sent to their usual outdoor work, following the plow, and doing the usual agricultural labor; but still adhering to their modelling at leisure hours. At Christmas-time Lough was very much in demand. Everybody wanted him to make models in pastry for Christmas pies—the neighboring farmers especially. "It was capital practice," he afterward said.

At length Lough went from Newcastle to London, to push his way in the world of art. He obtained a passage in a collier, the skipper of which he knew. When he reached London, he slept on board the collier as long as it remained in the Thames. He was so great a favorite with the men, that they all urged him to go back. He had no friends, no patronage, no money! What could he do with everything against him? But, having already gone so far, he determined to proceed. He would not go back—at least, not yet. The men all wept when he took farewell of them. He was alone in London, alone under the shadow of St. Paul's.

His next step was to take a lodging in an obscure first floor in Burleigh street, over a green-grocer's shop; and there he began to model his grand statue of "Milo." He had to take the roof off to let Milo's head out. There Hayden found him, and was delighted with his genius. "I went," he says "to young Lough, the sculptor, who has just burst out, and has produced great effect. His 'Milo' is really the most extraordinary thing, considering all the circumstances, in modern sculpture. It is another proof of the efficacy of inherent genius." That Lough must have been poor enough at this time, is evident from the fact that, during the execution of his 'Milo,' he did not eat meat for three months; and when Peter Coxe found him out, he was tearing up his shirt to make wet rags for his figure, to keep the clay moist. He had a bushel and a half of coal during the whole winter; and he used to lie down by the side of his clay model of the immortal figure, damp as it was, and shiver for hours till he fell asleep.

Chapter 17

Methods of Economy

"The only true secret of assisting the poor is to make them agents in bettering their own condition." —Archbishop Sumner.

THE METHODS of practising economy are very simple. Spend less than you earn. That is the first rule. A portion should always be set apart for the future. The person who spends more than he earns is a fool. The civil law regards the spendthrift as akin to the lunatic, and frequently takes from him the management of his own affairs.

The next rule is, to pay ready money, and never, on any account, to run in debt. The person who runs in debt is apt to get cheated; and if he runs in debt to any extent, he will himself be apt to get dishonest. "Who pays what he owes, enriches himself."

The next is, never to anticipate uncertain profits by expending them before they are secured. The profits may never come, and in that case you will have taken upon yourself a load of debt which you may never get rid of. It will sit upon your shoulders like the old man in Sinbad.

Another method of economy is, to keep a regular account of all that you earn and of all that you expend. An orderly man will know before hand what he requires, and will be provided with the necessary means for obtaining it. Thus his domestic budget will be balanced, and his expenditure kept within his income. John Wesley regularly adopted this course. Although he possessed a small income, he always kept his eyes upon the state of his affairs. A year before his death, he wrote, with a trembling hand, in his Journal of Expenses: "For more than eighty-six years I have kept my accounts exactly. I do not care to continue to do so any longer, having the conviction that I economize all that I obtain, and give all that I can—that is to say, all that I have."

It is the duty of all persons to economize their means—of the young as well as of the old. The Duke of Sully mentions, in his "Memoirs," that nothing contributed more to his fortune than the prudent economy which he practiced, even in his youth, of always preserving some ready money in hand for the purpose of meeting circumstances of emergency. Is a man married? Then the duty of economy is still more binding. His wife and children plead to him most eloquently. Are they, in the event of his early death, to be left to buffet with the world unaided? The hand of charity is cold, the gifts of charity are valueless compared with the gains of industry and the honest savings of frugal labor, which carry with them comforts, without inflicting any wound upon the feelings of the helpless and bereaved. Let every man, therefore, who can, endeavor to economize and to save; not to hoard, but to nurse his little savings, for the sake of promoting the welfare and happiness of himself while here, and of others when he has departed.

There is a dignity in the very effort to save with a worthy purpose, even though the attempt should not be crowned with eventual success. It produces a well-regulated mind; it gives prudence a triumph over extravagance; it gives virtue the mastery over vice; it puts the passions under control; it drives away care; it secures comfort. Saved money, however little, will serve to dry up many a tear—will ward off many sorrows and heartburnings, which otherwise might prey upon us. Possessed of a little store of capital, a man walks with a lighter step, his heart beats more cheerily. When interruption of work or adversity happens, he can meet it; he can recline on his capital, which will either break his fall or prevent it altogether. By prudential economy, we can realize the dignity of man; life will be a blessing, and old age an honor. We can ultimately, under a kind Providence, surrender life, conscious that we have been no burden upon society, but rather, perhaps, an acquisition and ornament to it; conscious, also, that, as we have been independent, our children after us, by following our example and availing themselves of the means we have left behind us, will walk in like manner through the world in happiness and independence.

Every man's first duty is, to improve, to educate, and elevate himself, helping forward his brethren at the same time by all reasonable methods. Each has within himself the capability of free will and free action to a large extent; and the fact is proved by the multitude of men who have successfully battled with and overcome the adverse circumstances of life in which they have been placed; and who have risen from the lowest depths of poverty and social debasement, as if to prove what energetic man, resolute of purpose, can do for his own elevation, progress, and advancement in the world. Is it not a fact that the greatness of humanity, the glory of communities, the power of nations, are the result of trials and difficulties encountered and overcome?

Let a man resolve and determine that he will advance, and the first step of advancement is already made. The first step is half the battle. In the very fact of advancing himself, he is in the most effectual possible way advancing others. He is giving them the most eloquent of all lessons—that of example; which teaches far more emphatically than words can teach. He is doing what others are by imitation incited to do. Beginning with himself, he is in the most emphatic manner teaching the duty of self-reform and of self-improvement; and if the majority of men acted as he did, how much wiser, how much happier, how much more prosperous, as a whole, would society become! For, society being made up of units, will be happy and prosperous, or the reverse, exactly in the same degree as the respective individuals who compose it.

Complaints about the inequality of conditions are as old as the world. In the "Economy" of Xenophon, Socrates asks, "How is it that some men live in abundance, and have something to spare, while others can scarcely obtain the necessaries of life, and at the same time run into debt?" "The reason is," replied Isomachus, "because the former occupy themselves with their business, while the latter neglect it."

The difference between men consists, for the most part, in intelligence, conduct, and energy. The best character never works by chance, but is under the influence of virtue, prudence and forethought.

There are, of course many failures in the world. The man who looks to others for help, instead of relying on himself, will fail. The man who is undergoing the process of perpetual waste will fail. The miser, the extravagant, the thriftless, will necessarily fail. Indeed, most people fail because they do not deserve to succeed. They set about their work in the wrong way, and no amount of experience seems to improve them. There is not so much in luck as some people profess to believe. Luck is only another word for good management in practical affairs. Richelieu used to say that he would not continue to employ an unlucky man—in other words, a man wanting in practical qualities, and unable to profit by experience; for failures in the past are very often the auguries of failures in the future.

Some of the best and ablest of men are wanting in tact. They will neither make allowance for circumstances, nor adapt themselves to circumstances; they will insist on trying to drive the wedge the broad end foremost. They raise walls only to run their own heads against. They make such great preparations, and use such great precautions, that they defeat their own object—like the Dutchman mentioned by Washington Irving, who having to leap a ditch, went so far back to have a good run at it, that when he came up he was completely winded, and had to sit down on the wrong side to recover his breath.

No idle or thriftless man ever became great. It is among those who never lost a moment that we find the men who have moved and advanced the world—by their learning, their science, or their inventions. Labor of some sort is one of the conditions of existence. The thought has come down to us from pagan times that "labor is the price which the gods have set upon all that is excellent." The thought is also worthy of Christian times.

Most men have it in their power, by prudent arrangements, to defend themselves against adversity, and to throw up a barrier against destitution. They can do this by their own individual efforts, or by acting on the principle of co-operation, which is capable of an almost indefinite extension. People of the most humble condition, by combining their means and associating together, are enabled in many ways to defend themselves against the pressure of poverty, to promote their physical well-being, and even to advance the progress of the nation

A solitary individual may be able to do very little to advance and improve society; but when he combines with his fellows for the purpose, he can do a very great deal. Civilization itself is but the effect of combining. Mr. Mill has said that "almost all the advantages which man possesses over the inferior animals arise from his power of acting in combination with his fellows, and of accomplishing, by the united efforts of numbers, what could not be accomplished by the detached efforts of individuals." The secret of social development is to be found in co-operation; and the great question of improved economical and social life can only receive a satisfactory solution through its means. To effect good on a large scale men must combine their efforts; and the best social system is that in which the organization for the common good is rendered the most complete in all respects.

The middle classes have accomplished more by the principle of co-operation than the classes who have so much greater need of it. All the joint-stock companies are the result of association. The railways, the telegraphs, the banks, the mines, the manufactories, have for the most part, been established and are carried on by means of the savings of the middle classes.

The working-classes have only begun to employ the same principle. Yet how much might they accomplish by this means! They might co-operate in saving as well as in producing. They might, by putting their saved earnings together, become, by combination, their own masters. Within a few years past many millions sterling have been expended in strikes for wages. Five hundred million dollars a year are thrown away upon drink and other unnecessary articles. Here is an enormous capital. Men who expend or waste such an amount can easily become capitalists. It requires only will, energy, and self-denial. So much money spent on buildings, plant, and steam-engines would enable them to manufacture for themselves, instead of for the benefit of individual capitalists. The steam-engine is impartial in its services. It is no respecter of persons; it will work for the benefit of the laborer as well as for the benefit of the millionaire. It will work best for those who make the best use of it, and who have the greatest knowledge of its powers.

The greater number of workmen possess little capital save their labor; and, as we have already seen, many of them uselessly and wastefully spend most of their earnings, instead of saving them and becoming capitalists. By combining in large numbers for the purposes of economical working, they might easily become capitalists, and operate upon a large scale. As society is now constituted, every man is not only justified, but bound in duty as a citizen, to accumulate his earnings by all fair and honorable methods, with the view of securing a position of ultimate competence and independence. We do not say that men should save and hoard their gains for the mere sake of saving and hoarding; that would be parsimony and avarice. But we do say that all men ought to aim at accumulating a sufficiency—enough to maintain them in comfort during the helpless years that are to come; to maintain them in time of sickness and of sorrow, and in old age, which, if it does come, ought to find them with a little store of capital in hand, sufficient to secure them from dependence upon the charity of others.

Workmen are for the most part disposed to associate; but the association is not always of a healthy kind. It sometimes takes the form of unions against masters; and displays itself in the strikes that are so common, and usually so unfortunate. Workmen also strike against men of their own class, for the purpose of excluding them from their special calling. One of the principal objects of trades-unions is to keep up wages at the expense of the lower-paid and unassociated working people. They endeavor to prevent poorer men learning their trade, and thus keep the supply of labor below the demand. This system may last for a time, but it becomes ruinous in the end.

It is not the want of money that prevents skilled workmen from becoming capitalists, and opening the door for the employment of laboring men who are poorer and less skilled than themselves. The working people threw away two and a half millions of dollars during the Preston strike, after which they went back to work at the old terms. The London building trades threw away over one and a half million dollars during their strike; and even had they obtained the terms for which they struck, it would have taken six years to make up for their loss. The colliers in the Forest of Dean went back to work at the old terms after eleven weeks' play, at the loss of $250,000. The iron-workers of Northumberland and Durham, after spending a third of a year in idleness, and losing one million dollars in wages, went back to work at a reduction of ten percent. The colliers and iron-workers of South Wales, during the recent strike, were idle for four months, and, according to Lord Aberdare, lost, in wages alone, not less than fifteen million dollars.

Here, then, is abundance of money within the power of working men—money which they might utilize, but do not. Think only of a solitary million, out of the fifteen million dollars which they threw away during the coal strike, being devoted to the starting of collieries, or iron-mills, or manufactories, to be worked by cooperative production for the benefit of the operatives themselves. "With frugal habits," says Mr. Greg, "the well-conditioned workman might in ten years easily have five hundred pounds in the bank; and, combining his savings with twenty other men similarly disposed, they might have fifty thousand dollars for the purpose of starting any manufacture in which they are adepts. The annual expenditure of the working-classes alone, on drink and tobacco, is not less than $300,000,000. Every year, therefore, the working-classes have it in their power to become capitalists *(simply by saving wasteful and pernicious expenditure)* to an extent which would enable them to start at least five hundred cotton-mills, or coal-mines, or iron-works, *on their own account*, or to purchase at least 500,000 acres, and so set up 50,000 families each with a nice little estate of their own of ten acres, on fee simple. No one can dispute the facts. No one can deny the inference."

That this is not an impracticable scheme is capable of being easily proved. The practice of co-operation has long been adopted by working people throughout England. A large proportion of the fishery industry has been conducted on that principle for hundreds of years. Fishermen join in building, rigging, and manning a boat; the proceeds of the fish they catch at sea is divided among them—so much to the boat, so much to the fishermen. The company of oyster-dredgers of Whitstable "has existed time out of mind," though it was only in 1793 that they were incorporated by act of Parliament. The tin-miners of Cornwall have also acted on the same principle. They have mined, washed, and sold the tin, dividing the proceeds among themselves in certain proportions—most probably from the time that the Phoenicians carried away the produce to their ports in the Mediterranean.

In our own time co-operation has been practiced to a considerable extent. In 1795, the Hull Anti-Mill Industrial Society was founded. The reasons for its association are explained in the petition addressed to the mayor and aldermen of Hull by the first members of the society. The petition begins thus: "We, the poor inhabitants of the said town, have lately experienced much trouble and sorrow in ourselves and families, on the occasion of the exorbitant price of flour; and though the price is much reduced at present, yet we judge it needful to take every precaution to preserve ourselves from the invasions of covetous and merciless men in the future." They accordingly entered into a subscription to build a mill, in order to supply themselves with flour. The corporation granted their petition, and supported them by liberal donations. The mill was built, and exists to this day. It now consists of more than four thousand members, each holding a share of twenty-five shillings. The members belong principally to the laboring-classes. The millers endeavored by action at law to put down the society, but the attempt was successfully resisted. The society manufactures flour, and sells it to the members at market price, dividing the profits annually among the share-holders, according to the quantity consumed in each member's family. The society has proved eminently remunerative.

Many years passed before the example of the "poor inhabitants" of Hull was followed. It was only in 1847 that the co-operators of Leeds purchased a flour mill, and in 1850 that those of Rochdale did the same; since which time they have manufactured flour for the benefit of their members. The corn-millers of Leeds attempted to undersell the Leeds Industrial Society. They soon failed, and the price of flour was permanently reduced. The Leeds mill does business amounting to more than half a million dollars yearly; its capital amounts to $110,000; and it paid more than eight thousand pounds of profits and bonuses to its three thousand six hundred members in 1866, besides supplying them with flour of the best quality. The Rochdale District Co-operative Corn-mill Society has also been eminently successful. It supplies flour to consumers residing within a radius of about fifteen miles around Rochdale. It also supplies flour to sixty-two co-operative societies, numbering over twelve thousand members. Its business in 1866 amounted to $1,120,000, and its profits to over $90,000.

The Rochdale Corn-mill grew out of the Rochdale Equitable Pioneers' Society, which formed an epoch in the history of industrial co-operative institutions. The Equitable Pioneers' Society was established in the year 1844, at a time when trade was in a very bad condition, and working-people generally were heartless and hopeless as to their future state. Some twenty-eight or thirty men, mostly flannel-weavers, met and formed themselves into a society for the purpose of economizing their hard-won earnings. It is pretty well known that working-men generally pay at least ten percent more for the articles they consume than they need to do under a sounder system. Professor Fawcett estimates their loss at nearer twenty percent than ten percent. At all events, these working-men wished to save this amount of profit, which before went into the pockets of the distributors of the necessaries—in other words, into the pockets of the shop-keepers. The weekly subscription was twopence each; and when about fifty-two calls of twopence each had been made, they found that they were able to buy a sack of oatmeal, which they distributed at cost price among the members of the society. The number of members grew, and the subscription so increased that the society was enabled to buy tea, sugar, and other articles, and distribute them among the members at cost price. They superseded the shop-keepers, and became their own tradesmen. They insisted from the first on payments in cash. No credit was given. The society grew. It established a store for the sale of food, firing, clothes and other necessaries. In a few years the members set on foot the Co-operative Corn-mill. They increased the capital by the issue of one pound shares and began to make and sell clothes and shoes. They also sold drapery. But the principal trade consisted in the purchase and sale of provisions—butchers' meat, groceries, flour, and such like. Notwithstanding the great distress during the period of the cotton famine, the society continued to prosper. From the first, it set apart a portion of its funds for educational purposes, and established a newsroom and a library, which now contains over six thousand volumes. The society continued to increase until it possessed eleven branches for the sale of goods and stores in or near Rochdale, besides the original office in Toad Lane. At the end of 1866, it had six thousand two hundred and forty-six members, and a capital of $499,540. Its income for goods sold and cash received during the year was $1,245,610, and the gross profit $159,655.

But this was not all. Two and a half percent were appropriated from the net profits to support the newsrooms and library; and there are now eleven news and reading rooms at different places in or near the town where the society carries on its business; the sum devoted to this object amounting to over seven hundred pounds per annum. The members play at chess and draughts, and use the stereoscopic views, microscopes, and telescopes placed in the libraries. No special arrangements have been made to promote temperance; but the news-room and library exercise a powerful and beneficial influence in promoting sobriety. It has been said that the society has done more to remove drunkenness from Rochdale than all that the advocates of temperance have been able to effect.

The example of the Rochdale Pioneers has exercised a powerful influence on working-men throughout the northern counties of England. There is scarcely a town or village but has a co-operative institution of one kind or another. These societies have promoted habits of saving, of thrift, and of temperance. They have given the people an interest in money matters and enabled them to lay out their earnings to the best advantage. They have also given the working-people some knowledge of business; for the whole of their concerns are managed by committees selected at the general meetings of the members.

One of the most flourishing co-operative societies is that established at Over Darwen. The society has erected a row of handsome buildings in the centre of the town. The shops for the sale of provisions, groceries, clothing, and other necessaries occupy the lower story. Over the shops are the library, reading-rooms, and class-rooms, which are open to the members and their families. The third story consists of a large public hall, which is used for lectures, concerts, and dances. There are six branches of the society established in different parts of the town. A large amount of business is done, and the profits are very considerable. These are divided among the members, in proportion to the purchases made by them. The profits are for the most part re-in-vested in joint-stock paper-mills, cotton-mills, and collieries, in the neighborhood of Darwen. One of the most praiseworthy features of the society is the provision made for the free education of the members and their families. Two and a half percent of the profits are appropriated for the purpose. While inspecting the institution a few months ago, we were informed that the science classes were so efficiently conducted that one of the pupils had just obtained a Government scholarship of fifty pounds a year, for three years, including free instruction at a School of Mines, with a free use of the laboratories during that period. There are also two other co-operative institutions in the same place; and we were informed that the working-people of Darwen are, for the most part, hard-working, sober, and thrifty.

The sole secret of its success consists in "ready money." It gives no credit. Everything is done for cash, the profit of the trade being divided among the members. Every business man knows that cash payment is the soundest method of conducting business; the Rochdale Pioneers having discovered the secret, have spread it among their class. In their "advice to members of this and other societies," they say: "Look well after money matters. Buy your goods as much as possible in the first markets; or, if you have the produce of your industry to sell, contrive, if possible, to sell it in the last. Never depart from the principle of buying and selling for ready money. Beware of long reckonings." In short, the co-operative societies became tradesmen on a large scale; and, besides the pureness of the food sold, their profit consisted in the discount for cash payments, which was divided among the members.

Land and building societies constitute another form of co-operation. By their means portions of land are bought, and dwelling houses are built. By means of a building society, a person who desires to possess a house enters the society as a member, and, instead of paying his rent to the landlord, pays his subscriptions and interest to a committee of his friends; and in course of time, when his subscriptions are paid up, the house is purchased, and conveyed to him by the society. The building society is thus a savings bank, where money accumulates for a certain purpose. But even those who do not purchase a house receive a dividend and bonus on their shares, which sometimes amount to a considerable sum.

The accumulation of property has the effect which it always has upon thrifty men; it makes them steady, sober, and diligent. It weans them from revolutionary notions, and makes them conservative. When workmen, by their industry and frugality, have secured their own independence, they will cease to regard the sight of others' well-being as a wrong inflicted on themselves; and it will no longer be possible to make political capital out of their imaginary woes.

It is said that there is a skeleton in every household. The skeleton is locked up—put away in a cupboard—and rarely seen. Only the people inside the house know of its existence. But the skeleton, nevertheless, cannot long be concealed. It comes to light in some way or another. The most common skeleton is poverty. Poverty, says Douglas Jerrold, is the great secret, kept at any pains by one-half the world from the other half. When there is nothing laid by—nothing saved to relieve sickness when it comes—nothing to alleviate the wants of old age—then is the skeleton hidden away in many a cupboard.

In a country such as this, where business is often brought to a standstill by overtrading and overspeculation, many masters, clerks, and workpeople are thrown out of employment. They must wait until better times come round. But in the meantime how are they to live? If they have accumulated no savings, and have nothing laid by, they are comparatively destitute.

It often happens that workmen lose their employment in "bad times." Mercantile concerns become bankrupt, clerks are paid off, and servants are dismissed when their masters can no longer employ them. If the disemployed people have been in the habit of regularly consuming all their salaries and wages, without laying anything by, their case is the most pitiable that can be imagined. But if they have saved something, at home or in the savings-bank, they will be enabled to break their fall. They will obtain some breathing time before they again fall into employment. Suppose they have as much as fifty dollars saved. It may seem a very little sum, yet in distress it amounts to much. It may even prove a man's passport to future independence.

We do not value money for its own sake, and we should be the last to encourage a miserly desire to hoard among any class; but we cannot help recognizing in money the means of life, the means of comfort, the means of maintaining an honest independence. We would, therefore, recommend every young man and every young woman to begin life by learning to save; to lay up for the future a certain portion of every week's earnings, be it little or much; to avoid consuming every week or every year the earnings of that week or year; and we counsel them to do this, as they would avoid the horrors of dependence, destitution, or beggary. We would have men and women of every class able to help themselves—relying upon their own resources—upon their own savings; for it is a true saying that "a penny in the purse is better than a friend at court." The first penny saved is a step in the world. The fact of its being saved and laid by indicates self-denial, forethought, prudence, wisdom. It may be the germ of future happiness. It may be the beginning of independence.

It is not the highly paid class of working men and women who invest money in the savings-banks, but those who earn comparatively moderate incomes. Thus the most numerous class of depositors in the Manchester and Salford Savings-bank is that of domestic servants. After them rank clerks, shop-men, porters and miners. Only about a third part of the deposits belongs to the operatives, artisans and mechanics. It is the same in manufacturing districts generally. A few years since, it was found that of the numerous female depositors at Dundee only one was a factory worker; the rest were for the most part servants.

There is another fact that is remarkable. The habit of saving does not so much prevail in those counties where wages are the highest as in those counties where wages are the lowest. Previous to the era of post-office savings-banks, the inhabitants of Wilts and Dorset—where wages are about the lowest in England—deposited more money in the savings-banks, per head of the population, than they did in Lancashire and Yorkshire, where wages are about the highest in England. Taking Yorkshire itself, and dividing it into manufacturing and agricultural, the manufacturing inhabitants of the West Riding of York invested about twenty-five shillings per head of the population in the savings-banks, while the agricultural population of the East Riding invested about three times that amount.

A magistrate at Bilston, not connected with the employment of workmen, has mentioned the following case: "I prevailed," he says, "upon a workman to begin a deposit in the savings-bank. He came most unwillingly. His deposits were small, although I knew his gains to be great. I encouraged him by expressing satisfaction at the course he was taking. His deposits became greater, and at the end of five years he drew out the fund he had accumulated, bought a piece of land, and has built a house upon it. I think if I had not spoken to him, the whole amount would have been spent in feasting, or clubs, or contributions to the trades unions. That man's eyes are now open; his social position is raised; he sees and feels as we do, and will influence others to follow his example."

From what we have said, it will be obvious that there can be no doubt as to the ability of a large proportion of the better-paid classes of workingmen to lay by a store of savings. When they set their minds upon any subject, they have no difficulty in finding the requisite money. A single town in Lancashire contributed $150,000 to support their fellow-workmen when on a strike in an adjoining town. At a time when there are no strikes, why should they not save as much money on their own account for their own permanent comfort? Many workmen already save with this object, and what they do, all might do. We know of one large mechanical establishment, situated in an agricultural district, where the temptations to useless expenditure are few, in which nearly all the men are habitual economists, and have saved sums varying from $1,000 to $2,500 each.

Many factory operatives, with their families, might easily lay by from five to ten shillings a week, which in a few years would amount to considerable sums. At Darwen, only a short time ago, an operative drew his savings out of the bank to purchase a row of cottages, now become his property. Many others, in the same place, and in the neighboring towns, are engaged in building cottages for themselves, some by means of their contributions to building societies, and others by means of their savings accumulated in the bank.

A respectably dressed workingman, when making a payment one day at the Bradford Savings-bank, which brought his account up to nearly eighty pounds, informed the manager how it was that he had been induced to become a depositor. He had been a drinker, but one day accidentally finding his wife's savings-bank deposit-book, from which he learned that she had laid by about $100, he said to himself, "Well, now, if this can be done while I am spending, what might we do if both were saving?" The man gave up his drinking, and became one of the most respectable persons of his class. "I owe it all," he said, "to my wife and the savings-bank."

The Denny bank reaches a class of persons of very small means, whose ability to save is much Tess than that of the highly paid workmen, and who, if the money were left in their pockets, would in most cases spend it in the nearest public house. When a penny bank was established at Putney, and the deposits were added up at the end of the first year, a brewer, who was on the committee, made the remark, "Well, that represents thirty thousand pints of beer *not drunk.*" But the principal supporters of the penny banks are boys, and this is their most hopeful feature; for it is out of boys that men are made. At Huddersfield many of the lads go in bands from the mills to the penny banks; emulation as well as example urging them on. They save for various purposes—one to buy a chest of tools; another, a watch; a third, a grammar or a dictionary.

Thus these institutions give help and strength in many ways, and, besides enabling young people to keep out of debt and honestly to pay their way, furnish them with the means of performing kindly and generous acts in times of family trial and emergency. It is an admirable feature of the ragged schools that almost everyone of them has a penny bank connected with it, for the purpose of training the scholars in good habits, which they most need; and it is a remarkable fact that in one year not less than $44,000 was deposited, in 25,637 sums, by the scholars connected with the Ragged-school Union. And when this can be done by the poor boys of the ragged schools, what might not be accomplished by the highly paid operatives and mechanics of England?

But another capital feature in the working of penny banks, as regards the cultivation of prudent habits among the people, is the circumstance that the example of boys and girls depositing their spare weekly pennies has often the effect of drawing their parents after them. A boy goes on for weeks paying his pence, and taking home his pass-book. The book shows that he has a "ledger folio" at the bank, expressly devoted to him; that his pennies are all duly entered, together with the respective dates of their deposits; that these savings are not lying idle, but bear interest at two and a half percent per annum, and that he can have them restored to him at any time, if under twenty shillings, without notice; and if above twenty shillings, then after a week's notice has been given.

The book is a little history in itself, and can not fail to be interesting to the boy's brothers and sisters, as well as to his parents. They call him "good boy," and they see he is a well-conducted boy. The father, if he is a sensible man, naturally bethinks him that if his boy can do so creditable a thing, worthy of praise, so might he himself, Accordingly, on the next Saturday night, when the boy goes to deposit his threepence at the penny bank, the father often sends his shilling. Thus a good beginning is often made, and a habit initiated, which, if persevered in, very shortly exercises a most salutary influence on the entire domestic condition of the family. The observant mother is quick to observe the effects of this new practice upon the happiness of the home; and in course of time, as the younger children grow up and earn money, she encourages them to follow the elder boy's example. She herself takes them by the hand, leads them to the penny bank, and accustoms them to invest their savings there. Women have even more influence in such matters than men; and where they exercise it, the beneficial effects are much more lasting.

One evening, a strong, muscular mechanic appeared at the Bradford Savings-bank in his working dress, bringing with him three children, one of them in his arms. He placed on the counter their deposit-books, which his wife had previously been accustomed to present, together with ten shillings, to be equally apportioned among the three. Pressing to his bosom the child in his arms, the man said, "Poor things! they have lost their mother since they were here last; but I must do the best I can for them." And he continued the good lesson to his children which his wife had begun, bringing them with him each time to see their little deposits made.

There is an old English proverb which says, "He that would thrive must first ask his wife"; but the wife must not only let her husband thrive, but help him, otherwise she is not the "helpmeet" which is as needful for the domestic comfort and satisfaction of the working man, as of every other man who undertakes the responsibility of a family. Women form the moral atmosphere in which we grow when children; and they have a great deal to do with the life when we become men. It is true that the men may hold the reins; but it is generally the women who tell them which way to drive. What Rousseau said is very near the truth: "Men will always be what women make them."

Neglect of small things is the rock on which the great majority of the human race have split. Human life consists of a succession of small events, each of which is comparatively unimportant, and yet the happiness and success of every man depend upon the manner in which these small events are dealt with. Character is built up on little things—little things well and honorably transacted. The success of a man in business depends on his attention to little things. The comfort of a household is the result of small things well arranged and duly provided for. Good government can only be accomplished in the same way—by well-regulated provision for the doing of little things.

Accumulations of knowledge and experience of the most valuable kind are the result of little bits of knowledge and experience carefully treasured up. Those who learn nothing, or accumulate nothing in life, are set down as failures, because they have neglected little things. They may themselves consider that the world has gone against them; but, in fact, they have been their own enemies. There has long been a popular belief in "good luck"; but, like many other popular notions, it is gradually giving way. The conviction is extending that diligence is the mother of good luck; in other words, that a man's success in life will be proportionate to his efforts, to his industry, to his attention to small things. Your negligent, shiftless, loose fellows never meet with luck; because the results of industry are denied to those who will not use the proper efforts to secure them.

It is not luck, but labor, that makes men. "Luck is ever waiting for something to turn up; Labor, with keen eye and strong will, always turns up something. Luck lies in bed, and wishes the postman would bring him news of a legacy; Labor turns out at six, and with busy pen or ringing hammer lays the foundation of a competence. Luck whines; Labor whistles. Luck relies on chance; Labor, on character. Luck slips downward to self-indulgence; Labor strides upward, and aspires to independence."

There are many little things in the household, attention to which is indispensable to health and happiness. Cleanliness consists in attention to a number of apparent trifles—the scrubbing of a floor, the dusting of a chair, the cleansing of a tea-cup; but the general result of the whole is an atmosphere of moral and physical wellbeing—a condition favorable to the highest growth of human character. The kind of air which circulates in a house may seem a small matter, for we can not see the air, and few people know any thing about it; yet if we do not provide a regular supply of pure air within our houses, we shall inevitably suffer for our neglect. A few specks of dirt may seem unimportant, and a closed door or window would appear to make little difference; but it may make the difference of a life destroyed by fever; and therefore the little dirt and the little bad air are really very serious matters. The whole of the household regulations are, taken by themselves, trifles, but trifles tending to important results.

A man may work hard, and earn high wages; but if he allow the pennies, which are the result of hard work, to slip out of his fingers—some going to the beer-shop, some this way, and some that—he will find that his life of hard work is little raised above a life of animal drudgery. On the other hand, if he take care of the pennies, putting some weekly into a benefit society or an insurance fund, others into a savings-bank, and confide the rest to his wife to be carefully laid out, with a view to the comfortable maintenance and culture of his family, he will soon find that his attention to small matters will abundantly repay him, in increasing means, in comfort at home, and in a mind comparatively free from fears as to the future.

If a man does not know how to save his pennies or his pounds, his nose will always be kept to the grindstone. Want may come upon him any day, "like an armed man." Careful saving acts like magic; once begun, it grows into a habit. It gives a man a feeling of satisfaction, of strength, of security. The pennies he has put aside in his savings-box, or in the savings-bank, give him an assurance of comfort in sickness, or of rest in old age. The man who saves has something to weather-fend him against want; while the man who saves not has nothing between him and bitter, biting poverty.

A man may be disposed to save money, and lay it by for sickness or for other purposes; but he can not do this unless his wife lets him, or helps him. A prudent, frugal, thrifty woman is a crown of glory to her husband. She helps him in all his good resolutions; she may, by quiet and gentle encouragement, bring out his better qualities; and by her example she may implant in him noble principles, which are the seeds of the highest practical virtues. A man's daily life is the best test of his moral and social state.

Take two men, for instance, both working at the same trade and earning the same money; yet how different they may be as respects their actual condition! The one looks a free man; the other a slave. The one lives in a snug cottage; the other in a mud hovel. The one has always a decent coat to his back; the other is in rags. The children of the one are clean, well-dressed, and at school; the children of the other are dirty, filthy, and often in the gutter. The one possesses the ordinary comforts of life, as well as many of its pleasures and conveniences—perhaps a well-chosen library; the other has few of the comforts of life, certainly no pleasures, enjoyments, nor books. And yet these two men earn the same wages. What is the cause of the difference between them?

It is this: The one man is intelligent and prudent; the other is the reverse. The one denies himself for the benefit of his wife, his family, and his home; the other denies himself nothing, but lives under the tyranny of evil habits. The one is a sober man, and takes pleasure in making his home attractive and his family comfortable; the other cares nothing for his home and family, but spends the greater part of his earnings in the gin-shop or the public-house. The one man looks up; the other looks down. The standard of enjoyment of the one is high, and of the other low. The one man likes books, which instruct and elevate his mind; the other likes drink, which tends to lower and brutalize him. The one saves his money; the other wastes it.

Chapter 18

Courage

"If thou canst plan a noble deed,
And never flag till it succeed,
Though in the strife thy heart should bleed,
Whatever obstacles control,
Thine hour will come—go on, true soul!
Thou'lt win the prize, thou'lt reach the goal."
—C. Mackay.

"The heroic example of other days is in great part the source of the courage of each generation; and men walk up composedly to the most perilous enterprises, beckoned onward by the shades of the braves that were." —Helps.

THE WORLD OWES MUCH to its men and women of courage. We do not mean physical courage, in which man is at least equalled by the bull-dog; nor is the bull-dog considered the wisest of his species.

The courage that displays itself in silent effort and endeavor—that dares to endure all and suffer all for truth and duty—is more truly heroic than the achievements of physical valor, which are rewarded by honors and titles, or by laurels sometimes steeped in blood.

It is moral courage that characterizes the highest order of manhood and womanhood—the courage to seek and to speak the truth; the courage to be just; the courage to be honest; the courage to resist temptation; the courage to do one's duty. If men and women do not possess this virtue, they have no security whatever for the preservation of any other.

Every step of progress in the history of our race has been made in the face of opposition and difficulty, and been achieved and secured by men of intrepidity and valor—by leaders in the van of thought—by great discoverers, great patriots and great workers in all walks of life. There is scarcely a great truth or doctrine but has had to fight its way to public recognition in the face of detraction, calumny, and persecution. "Everywhere," says Heine, "that a great soul gives utterance to its thoughts, there also is a Golgotha."

Socrates was condemned to drink the hemlock at Athens in his seventy-second year, because his lofty teaching ran counter to the prejudices and party spirit of his age. He was charged by his accusers with corrupting the youth of Athens by inciting them to despise the tutelary deities of the state. He had the moral courage to brave not only the tyranny of the judges who condemned him, but of the mob who could not understand him. He died discoursing of the doctrine of the immortality of the soul; his last words to his judges being, "it is now time that we depart—I to die, you to live; but which has the better destiny is unknown to all except to God."

How many great men and thinkers have been persecuted in the name of religion! Bruno was burnt alive at Rome, because of his exposure of the fashionable but false philosophy of his time. When the judges of the Inquisition condemned him to die, Bruno said proudly, "You are more afraid to pronounce my sentence than I am to receive it."

There was scarcely a great discovery in astronomy, in natural history, or in physical science, which was not once denounced as leading to infidelity. The followers of Copernicus were branded as unbelievers. After Lippersley had invented the telescope, Galileo took up the idea, and constructed a telescope of his own, with which he ascended the tower of St. Mark, at Venice, to view the heavenly bodies. He directed it to the planets and fixed stars, which he observed with "incredible delight." He discovered the satellites and rings of Jupiter, the phases of Venus, and the spots on the sun. He faithfully recorded the revelations that came down to him direct from the skies. But all this was at variance with the received ideas of the time. The Inquisition undertook to regulate the astronomical science. Galileo was called to Rome and summoned before the Inquisitors to answer for the heretical doctrines he had published. He was compelled to renounce his opinions, he declared that he abandoned the doctrine of the earth's motion round the sun. The Inquisitors inserted in the prohibited index the works of Galileo, Kepler, and Copernicus. Galileo plucked up heart again, and published a new work, in the form of a dialogue, defending his doctrines. He was summoned before the Inquisition, and compelled, on bended knees, to renounce and abjure his glorious discovery. Galileo wanted the courage of his opinions. But he was an old man of seventy when he denied his faith. Galileo would not have been persecuted could he have been answered. Yet the truth lived, and men were set on the right track of observation for all ages to come. Pascal said of his condemnation: "It is in vain that you have procured against Galileo a decree from Rome condemning his opinions of the earth's motion.

Assuredly that will never prove it to be at rest; and if we have unerring observations proving that it turns round, not all mankind together can keep it from turning, nor themselves from turning with it."

The life of Kepler was as sad as that of Galileo. Originally a poor boy, he was admitted to the school at the monastery of Maulbroom, and eventually became a learned man. He accepted the astronomical chair at Gratz and devoted himself to the study of the planets. He was afterward appointed imperial mathematician to the emperor; though his salary was insufficient to maintain himself and his family. He was excommunicated by the church because of some opinions he had expressed respecting transubstantiation. "Judge" he said to Hoffman, "how far I can assist you, in a place where the priest and school inspector have combined to brand me with the public stigma of heresy, because in every question I take that side which seems to me consonant with the will of God."

Kepler was then offered the professorship of mathematics at Bologna, but having the recantation and condemnation of Galileo before him he declined the chair. "I might," he said, "notably increase my fortune, but, living a German among Germans, I am accustomed to a freedom of speech and manners which, if persevered in at Bologna, would draw upon me, if not danger, at least notoriety, and might expose me to suspicion and party malice."

In 1619 Kepler discovered the celebrated law which will be ever memorable in the history of science, "that the squares of the periodic times of the planets are to one another as the cubes of their distances." He recognized with transport the absolute truth of a principle which, for seventeen years, had been the object of his incessant labors. "The die is cast," he said; "the book is written, to be read either now or by posterity—I care not which. It may well wait a century for a reader, as God has waited six thousand years for an observer."

The next book Kepler published, "The Epitome of the Copernican Astronomy," was condemned at Rome and placed in the prohibited Index. In the meantime, his mind was distracted by a far greater trouble. His mother, seventy-nine years old, was thrown into prison, condemned to torture, and was about to be burned as a witch. Kepler immediately flew to her relief, and arrived at his Swabian home in time to save her from further punishment. But more troubles followed. The States of Styria ordered all the copies of his "Kalendar" for 1624 to be publicly burned. His library was sealed up by order of the Jesuits, and he was compelled to leave Lintz by the popular insurrection which then prevailed. He went to Sagan in Silesia, and shortly after died there of disease of the brain, the result of too much study.

When Columbus stated his views to King Ferdinand the clergy declared that the theory of an antipodes was hostile to the faith. The earth, they said, was an immense flat disc; and if there was a new earth beyond the ocean, then all men could not be descended from Adam. Columbus was dismissed as a fool.

Roger Bacon, the Franciscan monk, was persecuted on account of his studies in natural philosophy, and he was charged with dealing in magic, because of his investigations in chemistry. His writings were condemned, and he was thrown into prison, where he lay for ten years, during the lives of four successive popes. It is even averred that he died in prison. Ockham, the early English speculative philosopher, was excommunicated, and died in exile at Munich, where he was protected by the friendship of the Emperor of Germany.

The Inquisition branded Vesalius as a heretic for revealing man to man, as it had before branded Bruno and Galileo for revealing the heavens to man. Vesalius had the boldness to study the structure of the human body by actual dissection, a practice until then almost entirely forbidden. He laid the foundations of a science, but he paid for it with his life. Condemned by the Inquisition, his penalty was commuted, by the intercession of the Spanish king, into a pilgrimage to the Holy Land; and when on his way back, while still in the prime of life, he died miserably at Zante, of fever and want—a martyr to his love of science.

When the "Novum Organon" appeared, a hue and cry was raised against it, because of its alleged tendency to produce "dangerous revolutions," to "subvert governments," and to "overturn the authority of religion"; and one Dr. Henry Stubbe wrote a book against the new philosophy, denouncing the whole tribe of experimentalists as a "Bacon-faced generation." Even the establishment of the Royal Society was op-nosed, on the ground that "experimental philosophy is subversive of the Christian faith." Even the pure and simple-minded Newton, of whom Bishop Burnet said that he had the *whitest soil* he ever knew—who was a very infant in the purity of his mind—even Newton was accused of "dethroning the Deity" by his sublime discovery of the law of gravitation; and a similar charge was made against Franklin for explaining the nature of the thunderbolt.

Spinoza was excommunicated by the Jews, to whom he belonged, because of his views of philosophy, which were supposed to be adverse to religion; and his life was afterwards attempted by an assassin for the same reason. Spinoza remained courageous and self-reliant to the last, dying in obscurity and poverty.

The philosophy of Descartes was denounced as leading to irreligion; the doctrines of Locke were said to produce materialism, and in our own day, Dr.

Buck-land, Mr. Sedgewick, and other leading geologists, have been accused of overturning revelation with regard to the constitution and history of the earth. Indeed, there has scarcely been a discovery in astronomy, in natural history, or in physical science, that has not been attacked by the bigoted and narrow-minded as leading to infidelity.

Other great discoverers, though they may not have been charged with irreligion, have had not less obloquy of a professional and public nature to encounter. When Dr. Harvey published his theory of the circulation of the blood, his practice fell off, and the medical profession stigmatised him as a fool. "The few good things I have been able to do," said John Hunter, "have been accomplished with the greatest difficulty, and encountered the greatest opposition." Sir Charles Bell, while employed in his important investigations as to the nervous system, which issued in one of the greatest of physiological discoveries, wrote to a friend: "If I were not so poor, and had not so many vexations to encounter, how happy would I be!" But he himself observed that his practice sensibly fell off after the publication of each successive stage of his discovery.

Thus nearly every enlargement of the domain of knowledge, which has made us better acquainted with the heavens, with the earth, and with ourselves, has been established by the energy, the devotion, the self-sacrifice, and the courage of the great spirits of past times, who, however much they have been opposed or reviled by their contemporaries, now rank among those whom the enlightened of the human race most delight to honor.

Nor is the unjust intolerance displayed towards men of science in the past without its lesson for the present. It teaches us to be forbearant towards those who differ from us, provided they observe patiently, think honestly, and utter their convictions freely and truthfully. It was a remark of Plato, that "the world is God's epistle to mankind"; and to read and study that epistle, so as to elicit its true meaning, can have no other effect on a well-ordered mind than to lead to a deeper impression of His power, a clearer perception of His wisdom, and a more grateful sense of His goodness.

While such has been the courage of the martyrs of science, not less glorious has been the courage of the martyrs of faith. The passive endurance of the man or woman who, for conscience sake, is found ready to suffer and to endure in solitude, without so much as the encouragement of even a single sympathizing voice, is an exhibition of courage of a far higher kind than that displayed in the roar of battle, where even the weakest feels encouraged and inspired by the enthusiasm of sympathy and the power of numbers. Time would fail to tell of the deathless names of those who through faith in principles, and in the face of difficulty, danger and suffering, "have wrought righteousness and waxed valiant" in the moral warfare of the world, and been content to lay down their lives rather than prove false to their conscientious convictions of the truth.

Men of this stamp, inspired by a high sense of duty, have in past times exhibited character in its most heroic aspects, and continue to present to us some of the noblest spectacles to be seen in history. Even women, full of tenderness and gentleness, not less than men, have in this cause been found capable of exhibiting the most unflinching courage, Such, for instance, as that of Anne Askew, who, when racked until her bones were dislocated, uttered no cry, moved no muscle, but looked her tormentors calmly in the face, and refused either to confess or to recant; or such as that of Latimer and Ridley, who, instead of bewailing their hard fate and beating their breasts, went as cheerfully to their death as a bridegroom to the altar—the one bidding the other to "be of good comfort," for that "we shall this day light such a candle in England, by God's grace, as shall never be put out"; or such, again, as that of Mary Dyer, the Quakeress, hanged by the Puritans of New England for preaching to the people, who ascended the scaffold with a willing step, and, after calmly addressing those who stood about, resigned herself into the hands of her persecutors, and died in peace and joy.

Not less courageous was the behavior of the good Sir Thomas More, who marched willingly to the scaffold, and died cheerfully there, rather than prove false to his conscience. When More had made his final decision to stand upon his principles, he felt as if he had won a victory, and said to his son-in-law Roper. "Son Roper, I thank our Lord, the field is won!" The Duke of Norfolk told him of his danger, saying: "By the mass, Master More, it is perilous striving with princes; the anger of a prince brings death!" "Is that all, my lord?" said More; "then the difference between you and me is this—that I shall die today, and you tomorrow."

Martin Luther was not called upon to lay down his life for his faith; but, from the day that he declared himself against the pope he daily ran the risk of losing it. At the beginning of his great struggle he stood almost entirely alone. The odds against him were tremendous. "On one side," said he himself, "are learning, genius, numbers, grandeur, rank, power, sanctity, miracles; on the other Wycliffe, Lorenzo Valla, Augustine, and Luther—a poor creature, a man of yesterday, standing well-nigh alone with a few friends." Summoned by the emperor to appear at Worms, to answer the charge made against him for heresy, he determined to answer in person. Those about him told him he would lose his life if he went, and they urged him to fly. "No," said he, "I will repair thither, though I should find there twice as many devils as there are tiles upon the house-tops!" Warned against the bitter enmity of a certain Duke George, he said, "I will go there, though for nine whole days running it rained Duke Georges!"

Luther was as good as his word, and he set forth upon his perilous journey. When he came in sight of the old bell-towers of Worms, he stood up in his chariot and sang, *"Einfeste Burg isi unser Gal"*—the "Marseillaise" of the Reformation—the words and music of which he is said to have improvised only two days before. Shortly before the meeting of the Diet, an old soldier, George Freundesburg, put his hand upon Luther's shoulder, and said to him: "Good monk, good monk, take heed what thou doest; thou art going into a harder fight than any of us have ever yet been in." But Luther's only answer to the veteran was, that he had "determined to stand upon the Bible and his conscience."

Luther's courageous defense before the Diet is on record, and forms one of the most glorious pages in history. When finally urged by the emperor to retract, he said, firmly: "Sire, unless I am convinced of my error by the testimony of scripture, or by manifest evidence, I can not and will not retract, for we must never act contrary to our conscience. Such is my profession of faith, and you must expect none other from me. Here stand I: I can not do otherwise; God help me!" He had to do his duty—to obey the orders of a power higher than that of kings; and he did it at all hazards.

Afterwards, when hard pressed by his enemies at Augsburg, Luther said that, "if he had five hundred heads, he would lose them all rather than recant his article concerning faith." Like all courageous men, his strength only seemed to grow in proportion to the difficulties he had to encounter and overcome. "There is no man in Germany," said Hutten, "who more utterly despises death than does Luther." And to his moral courage, perhaps more than to that of any other single man, do we owe the liberation of modern thought, and the vindication of the great rights of the human understanding.

But it is a mistake to suppose that the days requiring self-sacrifice and suffering for conscience or the truth's sake are past. "Modern freedom," says Thoreau, "is only the exchange of the slavery of feudality for the slavery of opinion." The tyranny of a multitude is worse than the tyranny of an individual. How many, even in our own progressive age, have suffered persecution for bravely advocating principles and doctrines which they believed to be true? The decisions reached by counsels and conferences are but an expression of the average or popular opinion. Men of earnest thought are generally far in advance of the average sentiment. What wonder is it then that the most profound, the best, the most earnest men of every age have been men who were abused by their associates, or through charges of heresy expelled from the churches?

William Penn was of opinion that there was no greater mistake than to suppose that a country or a people were strengthened by all the people holding one opinion, whether upon religious doctrine or religious practice; and that a variety of opinions, of professions, and of practice, was a strength to a people and to a government, if all were alike tolerated. Individuality must be upheld; for without individuality there can be no liberty. Individuality is everywhere to be spared and respected, as the root of every thing good. "Even despotism does not produce its worst effects," says John Stuart Mill, "so long as individuality exists under it; and whatever crushes individuality *is* despotism, by whatever name it may be called, and whether it professes to be enforcing the will of God or the injunctions of men."

But the greater part of the courage that is needed in the world is not of a heroic kind. Courage may be displayed in every-day life as well as in historic fields of action. There needs, for example, the common courage to be honest—the courage to resist temptation—the courage to speak the truth—the courage to be what we really are, and not to pretend to be what we are not—the courage to live honestly within our own means, and not dishonestly upon the means of others. A great deal of the unhappiness, and much of the vice, of the world is owing to weakness and indecision of purpose—in other words, to lack of courage. Men may know what is right, and yet fail to exercise the courage to do it; they may understand the duty they have to do, but will not summon up the requisite resolution to perform it. The weak and undisciplined man is at the mercy of every temptation; he can not say "No," but falls before it. And if his companionship be bad, he will be all the easier led away by bad example into wrong-doing.

Nothing can be more certain than that the character can only be sustained and strengthened by its own energetic action. The will, which is the central force of character must be trained to habits of decision—otherwise it will neither be able to resist evil nor to follow good. Decision gives the power of standing firmly, when to yield, however slightly, might be only the first step in a down-hill course to ruin.

Calling upon others for help in forming a decision is worse than useless. A man must so train his habits as to rely upon his own powers, and depend upon his own courage in moments of emergency. Plutarch tells of a King of Macedon who, in the midst of an action, withdrew into the adjoining town to sacrifice to Hercules; while his opponent Emilius, at the same time that he implored the Divine aid, sought for victory sword in hand, and won the battle. And so it ever is in the actions of daily life.

There needs also the exercise of no small degree of moral courage to resist the corrupting influences of what is called "Society." Although "Mrs. Grundy" may be a very vulgar and commonplace personage, her influence is nevertheless prodigious. Most men, but especially women, are the moral slaves of the class or caste to which they belong. There is a sort of unconscious conspiracy existing among them against each other's individuality.

Each circle and section, each rank and class, has its respective customs and observances, to which conformity is required at the risk of being tabooed. Some are immured within a Bastille of fashion, others of custom, others of opinion; and few there are who have the courage to think outside their sect, to act outside their party, and to step out into the free air of individual thought and action. We dress, and eat, and follow fashion, though it may be at the risk of debt, ruin and misery; living not so much according to our means as according to the superstitious observances of our class. Though we may speak contemptuously of the Indians who flatten their heads, and of the Chinese who cramp their toes, we have only to look at the deformities of fashion among ourselves, to see that the reign of "Mrs. Grundy" is universal.

It is the strong and courageous men who lead and guide and rule the world. The weak and timid leave no trace behind them; while the life of a single upright and energetic man is like a track of light. His example is remembered and appealed to, and his thoughts, his spirit, and his courage continue to be the inspiration of succeeding generations.

Men often conquer difficulties because they feel they can. Their confidence in themselves inspires the confidence of others. When Caesar was at sea, and a storm began to rage, the captain of the ship which carried him became unmanned by fear. "What art thou afraid of?" cried the great captain; "thy vessel carries Caesar!" The courage of the brave man is contagious, and carries others along with it. His stronger nature awes weaker natures into silence, or inspires them with his own will and purpose.

The persistent man will not be baffled or repulsed by opposition. Diogenes, desirous of becoming the disciple of Antisthenes, went and offered himself to the cynic. He was refused. Diogenes still persisting, the cynic raised his knotty staff and threatened to strike him if he did not depart. "Strike!" said Diogenes; "you will not find a stick hard enough to conquer my perseverance." Antisthenes, overcome, had not another word to say, but forthwith accepted him as his pupil.

Inspired by energy of purpose, men of comparatively mediocre powers have often been enabled to accomplish extraordinary results. The men who have most powerfully influenced the world have not been so much men of genius as men of strong convictions and enduring capacity for work, impelled by irresistible energy and invincible determination; such men, for example, as were Mohammed, Luther, Knox, Calvin, Loyola and Wesley.

Courage, combined with energy and perseverance, will overcome difficulties apparently insurmountable. It gives force and impulse to effort, and does not permit it to retreat. Tyndall said of Faraday, that "in his warm moments he formed a resolution, and in his cool ones he made that resolution good." Perseverance, working in the right direction, grows with time, and when steadily practiced, even by the most humble, will rarely fail of its reward. Trusting in the help of others is of comparatively little use. When one of Michael Angelo's principal patrons died, he said: "I begin to understand that the promises of the world are for the most part vain phantoms, and that to confide in one's self, and become something of worth and value, is the best and safest course."

It is the courageous man who can best afford to be generons; or, rather, it is his nature to be so. When Fairfax, at the battle of Naseby, seized the colors from an ensign whom he had struck down in the fight, he handed them to a common soldier to take care of. The soldier, unable to resist the temptation, boasted to his comrades that he himself seized the colors, and the boast was repeated to Fairfax. "Let him retain the honor," said the commander; "I have enough beside."

So when Douglas, at the battle of Bannockburn, saw Randolph, his rival, outnumbered and apparently overpowered by the enemy, he prepared to hasten to his assistance; but seeing that Randolph was already driving them back, he cried out, "hold and halt! We are come too late to aid them; let us not lessen the victory they have won by affecting to claim a share in it."

It is related of Charles V that, after the siege and capture of Whittenberg by the Imperialist army, the monarch went to see the tomb of Luther. While reading the inscription on it, one of the servile courtiers who accompanied him proposed to open the grave and give the ashes of the "heretic" to the winds. The monarch's cheek flushed with honest indignation. "I war not with the dead," said he; "let this place be respected." The portrait which the great Aristotle drew of the Magnanimous Man, in other words, the True Gentleman, more than two thousand years ago, is as faithful now as it was then. "The magnanimous man," he said, "will behave with moderation under both good fortune and bad. He will know how to be exalted and how to be abased. He will neither be delighted with success nor grieved by failure. He will neither shun danger nor seek it, for there are few things which he cares for. He is reticent, and somewhat slow of speech, but speaks his mind openly and boldly when occasion calls for it. He overlooks injuries. He is not given to talk about himself or about others; for he does not care that he himself should be praised, or that other people should be blamed. He does not cry out about trifles, and craves help from none."

On the other hand, mean men admire meanly. They have neither modesty, generosity, nor magnanimity. They are ready to take advantage of the weakness or defenselessness of others, especially where they have themselves succeeded, by unscrupulous methods, in climbing to positions of authority. Snobs in high places are always much less tolerable than snobs of low degree, because they have more frequent opportunities of making their want of manliness felt. They assume greater airs, and are pretentious in all that they do; and the higher their elevation, the more conspicuous is the incongruity of their position. "The higher the monkey climbs," says the proverb, "the more he shows his tail."

Much depends on the way in which a thing is done. An act which might be taken as a kindness if done in a generous spirit, when done in a grudging spirit may be felt as stingy, if not harsh and even cruel. When Ben Johnson lay sick and in poverty, the king sent him a paltry message, accompanied by a gratuity. The sturdy, plain-spoken poet's reply was: "I suppose he sends me this because I live in an alley; tell him his soul lives in an alley."

From what we have said, it will be obvious that to be of an enduring and courageous spirit is of great importance in the formation of character. It is a source not only of usefulness in life, but of happiness. On the other hand, to be of a timid and, still more, of a cowardly nature, is one of the greatest misfortunes. A wise man was accustomed to say that one of the principal objects he aimed at in the education of his sons and daughters was to train them in the habit of fearing nothing so much as fear. And the habit of avoiding fear is, doubtless, capable of being trained like any other habit, such as the habit of attention, of diligence, of study, or of cheerfulness.

Much of the fear that exists is the offspring of imagination, which creates the images of evils which *may* happen, but perhaps rarely do; and thus many persons who are capable of summoning up courage enough to grapple with and overcome real dangers, are paralyzed or thrown into consternation by those which are imaginary. Hence, unless the imagination be held under strict discipline, we are prone to meet evils more than halfway—to suffer them by forestallment, and to assume the burdens which we ourselves create. Education in courage is not usually included among the branches of female training, and yet it is really of much greater importance than either music, French, or the use of the globes. Contrary to the view of Sir Richard Steele, that women should be characterized by a "tender fear," and "an inferiority which makes her lovely," we would have women educated in resolution and courage, as a means of rendering them more helpful, more self-reliant, and vastly more useful and happy.

There is, indeed, nothing attractive in timidity, nothing lovable in fear. All weakness, whether of mind or body, is equivalent to deformity, and the reverse of interesting. Courage is graceful and dignified; while fear, in any form, is mean and repulsive. Yet the utmost tenderness and gentleness are consistent with courage. Ary Scheffer, the artist, once wrote to his daughter: "Dear daughter, strive to be of good courage, to be gentle-hearted; these are the true qualities for woman. 'Troubles' every body must expect. There is but one way of looking at fate—whatever that be, whether blessings or afflictions—to behave with dignity under both. We must not lose heart, or it will be the worse both for ourselves and for those whom we love. To struggle, and again and again to renew the conflict—*this* is life's inheritance."

In sickness and sorrow none are braver and less complaining sufferers than women. Their courage, where their hearts are concerned, is indeed proverbial. Experience has proved that women can be as enduring as men under the heaviest trials and calamities; but too little pains are taken to teach them to endure petty terrors and frivolous vexations with fortitude. Such little miseries, if petted and indulged, quickly run into sickly sensibility, and become the bane of their life, keeping themselves and those about them in a state of chronic discomfort.

The best corrective of this condition of mind is wholesome moral and mental discipline. Mental strength is as necessary for the development of woman's character as of man's. It gives her capacity to deal with the affairs of life, and presence of mind, which enable her to act with vigor and effect in moments of emergency. Character in a woman, as in a man, will always be found the best safeguard of virtue, the best nurse of religion, the best corrective of Time. Personal beauty soon passes; but beauty of mind and character increases in attractiveness the older it grows.

Women have not only distinguished themselves for their passive courage, but, impelled by affection, or the sense of duty, they have become heroic. When the band of conspirators who sought the life of James II, of Scotland, burst into his lodgings at Perth, the king called to the ladies, who were in the chamber outside his room, to keep the door as well as they could, and give him time to escape. The conspirators had previously destroyed the locks of the doors, so that the keys could not be turned; and When they reached the ladies' apartment, it was found that the bar also had been removed. But, on hearing them approach, the brave Catherine Douglas, with the hereditary courage of her family, boldly thrust her arm across the door instead of the bar, and held it there until, her arm being broken, the conspirators burst into the room with drawn swords and daggers, overthrowing the ladies, who, though unarmed, still endeavored to resist them.

The defense of Lathom House by Charlotte de Tremouille, the worthy descendant of William of Nassau and Admiral Coligny, was another striking instance of heroic bravery on the part of a noble woman. When summoned by the Parliamentary forces to surrender, she declared that she had been entrusted by her husband with the defence of the house, and that she could not give it up without her dear lord's order, but trusted in God for protection and deliverance. In her arrangements for the defense, she is described as having "left nothing with her eye to be excused afterwards by fortune or negligence, and added to her former patience a most resolved fortitude." The brave lady held her house and home against the enemy for a whole year—during three months of which the place was strictly besieged and bombarded—until at length the siege was raised, after a most gallant defense, by the advance of the Royalist army.

Nor can we forget the courage of Lady Franklin, who persevered to the last, when the hopes of all others had died out, in prosecuting the search after the Franklin Expedition. On the occasion of the Royal Geographical Society determining to award the "Founder's Medal" to Lady Franklin, Sir Roderick Murchison observed that, in the course of a long friendship with her, he had abundant opportunity of observing and testing the sterling qualities of a woman who had proved herself worthy of the admiration of mankind. "Nothing daunted by failure after failure, through twelve long years of hope deferred, she had persevered, with a singleness of purpose and a sincere devotion which were truly unparalleled. And now that her last expedition, under the gallant M'Clintock, had realized the two great facts—that her husband had traversed wide seas unknown to former navigators, and died in discovering a northwest passage—then, surely, the adjudication of the medal would be hailed by the nation as one of the many recompenses to which the widow of the illustrious Franklin was so eminently entitled."

But that devotion to duty which marks the heroic character has more often been exhibited by women in deeds of charity and mercy. The greater part of these are never known, for they are done in private, out of the public sight, and for the mere love of doing good. Where fame has come to them, because of the success which has attended their labors in a more general sphere, it has come unsought and unexpected, and is often felt as a burden. Who has not heard of Mrs. Fry and Miss Carpenter as prison-visitors and reformers; of Mrs. Chisholm and Miss Rye as promoters of emigration; and of Miss Nightingale and Miss Garrett as apostles of hospital nursing? That these women should have emerged from the sphere of private and domestic life to become leaders in philanthropy, indicates no small degree of moral courage on their part; for to women, above all others, quiet and ease and retirement are most natural and welcome. Very few women step beyond the boundaries of home in search of a larger field of usefulness. But when they have desired one, they have had no difficulty in finding it. The ways in which men and women can help their neighbors are innumerable. It needs but the willing heart and ready hand. Most of the philanthropic workers we have named, however, have scarcely been influenced by choice. The duty lay in their way—it seemed to be the nearest to them—and they set about doing it without desire for fame, or any other reward but the approval of their own conscience.

Among prison-visitors the name of Sarah Martin is much less known than that of Mrs. Fry, although she preceded her in the work. How she was led to undertake it, furnishes at the same time an illustration of womanly true-heartedness and earnest womanly courage.

Sarah Martin was the daughter of poor parents, and was left an orphan at an early age. She was brought up by her grandmother, and earned her living by going out to families as assistant dress-maker, at a shilling a day. In 1819 a woman was tried and sentenced to imprisonment in Yarmouth Jail, for cruelly beating and ill-using her child, and her crime became the talk of the town. The young dress-maker was much impressed by the report of the trial, and the desire entered her mind of visiting the woman in jail and trying to reclaim her. She had often before, on passing the walls of the borough jail, felt impelled to seek admission, with the object of visiting the inmates, reading the Scriptures to them, and endeavoring to lead them back to the society whose laws they had violated.

At length she could not resist the impulse to visit the imprisoned mother. She entered the jail-porch, lifted the knocker, and asked the jailer for admission. For some reason or other she was refused, but she returned, repeated her request, and this time she was admitted. The culprit mother shortly stood before her. When Sarah Martin told the motive of her visit, the criminal burst into tears, and thanked her. Those tears and thanks shaped the whole course of Sarah Martin's after-life, and the poor seamstress, while maintaining herself by her needle, continued to spend her leisure hours in visiting the prisoners and endeavoring to alleviate their condition. She constituted herself their chaplain and school-mistress, for at that time they had neither; she read to them and taught them to read and write. She gave up an entire day in the week for this purpose, besides Sundays, as well as other intervals of spare time. She taught the women to knit, to sew, and to cut out—the sale of the articles enabling her to buy other materials, and to continue the industrial education thus begun. She also taught the men to make straw hats, men's and boys' caps, gray cotton shirts, and even patchwork, anything to keep them out of idleness, and from preying on their own thoughts. Out of the earnings of the prisoners in this way she formed a fund, which she applied to furnishing them with work on their discharge; thus enabling them again to begin the world honestly, and at the same time affording her, as she herself says, "the advantage of observing their conduct."

By attending too exclusively to this prison-work, however, Sarah Martin's dress-making business fell off; and the question arose with her whether, in order to recover her business, she was to suspend her prison-work. But her decision had already been made. "I had counted the cost," she said, "and my mind was made up. If, while imparting truth to others, I became exposed to temporal want, the privations so momentary to an individual would not admit of comparison with following the Lord, in thus administering to others." She now devoted six or seven hours every day to the prisoners, converting what would otherwise have been a scene of dissolute idleness into a hive of orderly industry. Newly-admitted prisoners were sometimes refractory, but her persistent gentleness eventually won their respect and co-operation. Men old in years and crime, pert London pickpockets, depraved boys and dissolute sailors, profligate women, smugglers and the promiscuous horde of criminals which usually fill the jail of a sea-port and county town, all submitted to the benign influence of this good woman; and under her eyes they might be seen, for the first time in their lives, striving to hold a pen, or to master the characters in a penny primer. She entered into their confidence—watched, wept, prayed, and felt for all by turns. She strengthened their good resolutions, cheered the hopeless and despairing, and endeavored to put all, and hold all, in the right road of amendment.

For more than twenty years this good and true-hearted woman pursued her noble course, with little encouragement and not much help; almost her only means of subsistence consisting in an annual income of ten or twelve pounds left by her grandmother, eked out by her little earnings at dressmaking. During the last two years of her ministration, the borough magistrates, knowing that her self-imposed labors saved them the expense of a schoolmaster and chaplain, made a proposal to her of an annual salary of £12 a year; but they did it in so indelicate a manner as to greatly wound her sensitive feelings. She shrank from becoming the salaried official of the corporation, and bartering for money those services which had throughout been labors of love. But the Jail Committee coarsely informed her "that, if they permitted her to visit the prison, she must submit to their terms, or be excluded." For two years, therefore, she received the salary of £12 a year—the acknowledgement of the Yarmouth corporation for her services as jail chaplain and schoolmistress! She was now, however, becoming old and infirm, and the unhealthy atmosphere of the jail did much toward finally disabling her. While she lay on her death-bed, she resumed the exercise of a talent she had occasionally practiced before in her moments of leisure—the composition of sacred poetry. As works of art, they may not excite admiration; yet never were verses written truer in spirit, or fuller of Christian love. But her own life was a nobler poem than any she ever wrote—full of true courage, perseverance, charity, and wisdom. It was indeed a commentary upon her own words:

"The high desire that others may be blest Savors of Heaven."

Chapter 19

Self-Control

"Honor and profit do not always lie in the same sack." —George Herbert.

"The government of one's self is the only true freedom for the individual."
—Frederick Perthes.

SELF-CONTROL IS ONLY COURAGE under another form. It may almost be regarded as the primary essence of character. It is in virtue of this quality that Shakespeare defines man as a being "looking before and after." It forms the chief distinction between man and the mere animal; and, indeed, there can be no true manhood without it.

Self-control is at the root of all the virtues. Let a man give the reins to his impulses and passions, and from that moment he yields up his moral freedom. He is carried along the current of life, and becomes the slave of his strongest desires for the time being.

To be morally free—to be more than an animal—man must be able to resist instinctive impulse, and this can only be done by the exercise of self-control. Thus it is this power which constitutes the real distinction between a physical and a moral life, and that form the primary basis of individual character.

The best support of character will always be found in habit, which, according as the will is directed rightly or wrongly, as the case may be, will prove either a benignant ruler or a cruel despot. We may be its willing subject on the one hand, or its servile slave on the other. It may help us on the road to good, or it may hurry us on the road to ruin.

Habit is formed by careful training. And it is astonishing how much can be accomplished by systematic discipline and drill. See how, for instance, out of the most unpromising materials—such as roughs picked up in the streets, or raw unkempt country lads taken from the plough—steady discipline and drill will bring out the unsuspected qualities of courage, endurance, and self-sacrifice; and how, in the field of battle, or even On the more trying occasions of perils by sea, such men, carefully disciplined, will exhibit the unmistakable characteristics of true bravery and heroism!

Nor is moral discipline and drill less influential in the formation of character. Without it, there will be no proper system and order in the regulation of the life. Upon it depends the cultivation of our sense of self-respect, the education of the habit of obedience, the development of the idea of duty. The most self-reliant, self-governing man is always under discipline; and the more perfect the discipline, the higher will be his moral condition. He has to drill his desires, and keep them in subjection to the higher powers of his nature. They must obey the word of command of the internal monitor, the conscience—otherwise they will be but the mere slaves of their inclinations, the sport of feeling and impulse. "In the supremacy of self-control," says Herbert Spencer, "consists one of the perfections of the ideal man. Not to be impulsive—not to be spurred hither and thither by each desire that in turn comes uppermost—but to be self-restrained, self-balanced, governed by the joint decision of the feelings in counsel assembled, before whom every action shall have been fully debated and calmly determined—that it is which education, moral education at least, strives to produce."

The first seminary of moral discipline, and the best, as we have already shown, is the home; next comes the school, and after that the world, the great school of practical life. Each is preparatory to the other, and what the man or woman becomes, depends for the most part upon what has gone before. If they have enjoyed the advantage of neither the home nor the school, but have been allowed to grow up untrained, untaught, and undisciplined, then woe to themselves—woe to the society of which they form a part.

The best-regulated home is always that in which the discipline is the most perfect, and yet where it is the least felt. Moral discipline acts with the force of a law of nature. Those subject to it yield themselves to it unconsciously; and though it shapes and forms the whole character, until the life becomes crystalized in habit, the influence thus exercised is for the most part unseen and almost unfelt.

Although the moral character depends in a great degree on temperament and on physical health, as well as on domestic and early training and the example of companions, it is also in the power of each individual to regulate, to restrain and to discipline it by watchful and persevering self-control. A competent teacher has said of the propensities and habits, that they are as teachable as Latin and Greek, while they are much more essential to happiness.

Dr. Johnson, though himself constitutionally prone to melancholy, and afflicted by it as few have been from his earliest years, said that "a man's being in a good or bad humor very much depends upon his will." We may train ourselves in a habit of patience and contentment on the one hand, or of grumbling and discontent on the other. We may accustom ourselves to exaggerate small evils, and to underestimate great blessings. We men even become the victim of petty miseries by giving way to them. Thus, we may educate ourselves in a happy disposition, as well as in a morbid one. Indeed, the habit of viewing things cheerfully, and of thinking about life hopefully, may be made to grow up in us like any other habit. It was not an exaggerated estimate of Dr. Johnson to say, that the habit of looking at the best side of any event is worth far more than a thousand pounds a year.

If a man have not self-control, he will lack patience, be wanting in tact, and have neither the power of governing himself nor of managing others. When the quality most needed in a prime minister was the subject of conversation in the presence of Mr. Pitt, one of the speakers said it was "eloquence"; another said it was "knowledge"; and a third said it was "toil." "No," said Pitt, it is "patience!" And patience means self-control, a quality in which he himself was superb. His friend George Rose has said of him that he never once saw Pitt out of temper. Yet, although patience is usually regarded as a "slow" virtue, Pitt combined with it the most extraordinary readiness, vigor, and rapidity of thought as well as action.

A strong temper is not necessarily a bad temper. But the stronger the temper, the greater is the need of self-discipline and self-control. Dr. Johnson says men grow better as they grow older, and improve with experience; but this depends upon the width and depth and generousness of their nature. It is not men's faults that ruin them so much as the manner in which they conduct themselves after the faults have been committed. The wise will profit by the suffering they cause, and eschew them for the future, but there are those on whom experience exerts no ripening influence, and who only grow narrower and bitterer, and more vicious with time. What is called strong temper in a young man, often indicates a large amount of unripe energy, which will expend itself in useful work if the road be fairly opened to it. It is said of Stephen Girard that when he heard of a clerk with a strong temper, he would readily take him into his employment, and set him to work in a room by himself, Girard being of opinion that such persons were the best workers, and that their energy would expend itself in work if removed from the temptation to quarrel.

Strong temper may only mean a strong and excitable will. Uncontrolled, it displays itself in fitful outbreaks of passion; but controlled and held in subjection—like steam pent-up within the organized mechanism of a steam engine, the use of which is regulated and controlled by slide-valves, governors and levers—it may become a source of energetic power and usefulness. Hence some of the greatest characters in history have been men of strong temper, but of equally strong determination to hold their motive power under strict regulation and control.

Cromwell also is described as having been of a wayward and violent temper in his youth—cross, untractable and masterless, with a vast quantity of youthful energy, which exploded in a variety of youthful mischiefs. He even obtained the reputation of a roysterer in his native town, and seemed to be rapidly going to the bad, when religion, in one of its most rigid forms, laid hold upon his strong nature, and subjected it to the iron discipline of Calvinism. An entirely new direction was thus given to his energy of temperament, which forced an outlet for itself into public life, and eventually became the dominating influence in England for a period of nearly twenty years.

The heroic princes of the house of Nassau were all distinguished for the same qualities of self-control, self denial, and determination of purpose. William the Silent was so called, not because he was a taciturn man, for he was an eloquent and powerful speaker where eloquence was necessary, but because he was a man who could hold his tongue when it was wisdom not to speak, and because he carefully kept his own counsel when to have revealed it might have been dangerous to the liberties of his country. He was so gentle and conciliatory in his manner that his enemies even described him as timid and pusillanimous. Yet, when the time for action came, his courage was heroic, his determination unconquerable. "The rock in the ocean," says Mr. Motley, the historian of the Netherlands, "tranquil amid raging billows, was the favorite emblem by which his friends expressed their sense of his firmness."

Mr. Motley compares William the Silent to Washington, whom he in many respects resembled. The American, like the Dutch patriot, stands out in history as the very impersonation of dignity, bravery, purity, and personal excellence. His command over his feelings, even in moments of great difficulty and danger, was such as to convey the impression, to those who did not know him intimately, that he was a man of inborn calmness and almost impassiveness of disposition. Yet Washington was by nature ardent and impetuous; his mildness, gentleness, politeness and consideration for others, were the result of rigid self-control and unwearied self-discipline, which he diligently practiced even from his boyhood. His biographer says of him that "his temperament was ardent, his passions strong, and, amidst the multiplied scenes of temptation and excitement through which he passed, it was his constant effort, and ultimate triumph, to check the one and subdue the other." And again: "His passions were strong, and sometimes they broke out with vehemence, but he had the power of checking them in an instant. Perhaps self-control was the most remarkable trait of his character. It was in part the effect of discipline, yet he seems by nature to have possessed this power in a degree which has been denied to other men." The Duke of Wellington's natural temper, like that of Napoleon, was irritable in the extreme, and it was only by watchful self-control that he was enabled to restrain it. He studied calmness and coolness in the midst of danger, like an Indian chief. At Waterloo and elsewhere he gave his orders in the most critical moments without the slightest excitement, and in a tone of voice almost more than usually subdued.

Wordsworth, the poet, was in his childhood "of a stiff, moody and violent temper," and "perverse and obstinate in defying chastisement." When experience of life had disciplined his temper, he learnt to exercise greater self-control; but, at the same time, the qualities which distinguished him as a child were afterwards useful in enabling him to defy the criticism of his enemies. Nothing was more marked than Wordsworth's self-respect and self-determination, as well as his self-consciousness of power, at all periods of his history.

Henry Martyn, the missionary, was another instance of a man in whom strength of temper was only so much pent-up, unripe energy. As a boy he was impatient, petulant, and perverse; but by constant wrestling against his tendency to wrongheadedness, he gradually gained the requisite strength so as to entirely overcome it, and to acquire what he so greatly coveted— the gift of patience.

A man may be feeble in organization, but, blessed with a happy temperament, his soul may be great, active, noble, and sovereign. Professor Tyndall has given us a fine picture of the character of Faraday, and of his self-denying labors in the cause of science, exhibiting him as a man of strong, original, and even fiery nature, and yet of extreme tenderness and sensibility. "Underneath his sweetness and gentleness," he says, "was the heat of a volcano. He was a man of excitable and fiery nature; but through high self-discipline, he had converted the fire into a central glow and motive-power of life, instead of permitting it to waste itself in useless passion." There was one fine feature in Faraday's character which is worthy of notice—one closely akin to self control: it was his self-denial. By devoting himself to analytical chemistry, he might have speedily realized a large fortune; but he nobly resisted the temptation, and preferred to follow the path of pure science. "Taking the duration of his life into account," says Mr. Tyndall, "this son of a blacksmith and apprentice to a book-binder had to decide between a fortune of $750,000 on the one side, and his undowered science on the other. He chose the latter, and died a poor man. But his was the glory of holding aloft among the nations the scientific name of England for a period of forty years."

Take a like instance of the self-denial of a Frenchman. The historian Anquetil was one of the small number of literary men in France who refused to bow to the Napoleonic yoke. He sank into great poverty, living on bread and milk, and limiting his expenditure to only three sous a day. "I have still two sous a day left," said he, "for the conqueror of Marengo and Austerlitz." "But if you fall sick," said a friend to him, "you will need the help of a pension. Why not do as others do? Pay court to the emperor—you have need of him to live." "I do not need him to die," was the historian's reply. But Anquetil did not die of poverty; he lived to the age of ninety-four, saying to a friend on the eve of his death, "Come, see a man who dies still full of life!"

Sir James Outram exhibited the same characteristic of noble self-denial, though in an altogether different sphere of life. Like the great King Arthur, he was emphatically a man who "forbore his own advantage." He was characterized throughout his whole career by his noble unselfishness. Though he might personally disapprove of the policy he was occasionally ordered to carry out, he never once faltered in the path of duty. Thus, he did not approve of the policy of invading Scinde; yet his services throughout the campaign were acknowledged by General Sir C. Napier to have been of the most brilliant character. But when the war was over, and the rich spoils of Scinde lay at the conqueror's feet, Outram said: "I disapprove of the policy of this war—I will accept no share of the prize-money!"

Not less marked was his generous self-denial when dispatched with a strong force to aid Havelock in fighting his way to Lucknow. As superior officer, he was entitled to take upon himself the chief command; but, recognizing what Havelock had already done, with rare disinterestedness he left to his junior officer the glory of completing the campaign, offering to serve under him as a volunteer. "With such reputation," said Lord Clyde, "as Major-general Outram has won for himself, he can afford to share glory and honor with others. But that does not lessen the value of the sacrifice he has made with such disinterested generosity."

If a man would get through life honorably and peaceably, he must necessarily learn to practice self-denial in small things as well as great. Men have to bear as well as forbear. The temper has to be held in subjection to the judgment; and the little demons of ill-humor, petulance, and sarcasm, kept resolutely at a distance. If once they find an entrance to the mind, they are very apt to return, and to establish for themselves a permanent occupation there.

It is necessary to one's personal happiness, to exercise control over one's words as well as acts: for there are words that strike even harder than blows;

and men may "speak daggers," though they use none. The stinging repartee that rises to the lips, and which, if uttered, might cover an adversary with confusion, how difficult it sometimes is to resist saying it! "Heaven keep us," says Miss Bremer, in her "Home," "from the destroying power of words! There are words which sever hearts more than sharp swords do; there are words the point of which sting the heart through the course of a whole life."

Thus character exhibits itself in self-control of speech as much as in anything else. The wise and forbearant man will restrain his desire to say a smart or severe thing at the expense of another's feelings; while the fool blurts out what he thinks, and will sacrifice his friend rather than his joke. Even statesmen might be named, who have failed through their inability to resist the temptation of saying clever and spiteful things at their adversary's expense. "The turn of a sentence," says Bentham, "has decided the fate of many a friendship, and, for aught that we know, the fate of many a kingdom." So, when one is tempted to write a clever but harsh thing, though it may be difficult to restrain it, it is always better to leave it in the inkstand. "A goose's quill," says the Spanish proverb, "often hurts more than a lion's claw."

Carlyle says, when speaking of Oliver Cromwell, "He that can not withal keep his mind to himself, can not practice any considerable thing whatsoever." It was said of William the Silent, by one of his greatest enemies, that an arrogant or indiscreet word was never known to fall from his lips. Like him, Washington was discretion itself in the use of speech, never taking advantage of an opponent, or seeking a short-lived triumph in a debate. And it is said that, in the long run, the world comes round to and supports the wise man who knows when and how to be silent.

We have heard men of great experience say that they have often regretted having spoken, but never once regretted holding their tongue, "Be silent," says Pythagoras, "or say something better than silence." "Speak fitly," says George Herbert, "or be silent wisely." St. Francis de Sales, whom Leigh Hunt styled "the Gentleman Saint," has said: "It is better to remain silent than to speak the truth ill-humoredly, and so spoil an excellent dish by covering it with bad sauce." Another Frenchman, Lacordaire, characteristically puts speech first, and silence next. "After speech," he says, "silence is the greatest power in the world." Yet a word spoken in season, how powerful it may be! As the old Welch proverb has it, "A golden tongue is in the mouth of the blessed."

There are, of course, times and occasions when the expression of indignation is not only justifiable but necessary. We are bound to be indignant at falsehood, selfishness, and cruelty. A man of true feeling fires up naturally at baseness or meanness of any sort, even in cases where he may be under no obligation to speak out. "I would have nothing to do," said Perthes, "with the man who can not be moved to indignation. There are more good people than bad in the world, and the bad get the upper hand merely because they are bolder. We can not help being pleased with a man who uses his powers with decision; and we often take his side for no other reason than because he does so use them. No doubt, I have often repented speaking; but not less often have I repented keeping silence."

The best corrective of intolerance in disposition, is increase of wisdom and enlarged experience of life. Cultivated good sense will usually save men from the entanglements in which moral impatience is apt to involve them; good sense consisting chiefly in that temper of mind which enables its possessor to deal with the practical affairs of life with justice, judgment, discretion, and charity. Hence men of culture and experience are invariably found the most forbearant and tolerant, as ignorant and narrow-minded persons are found the most unforgiving, and intolerant. Men of large and generous natures, in proportion to their practical wisdom, are disposed to make allowance for the defects and disadvantages of others—allowance for the controlling power of circumstances in the formation of character, and the limited power of resistance of weak and fallible natures to temptation and error. "I see no fault committed," said Goethe, "which I also might not have committed."

Life will always be, to a great extent, what we ourselves make it. The cheerful man makes a cheerful world, the gloomy man a gloomy one. We usually find but our own temperament reflected in the dispositions of those about us. If we are ourselves querulous, we will find them so; if we are unforgiving and uncharitable to them, they will be the same to us. A person returning from an evening party not long ago, complained to a policeman on his beat that an ill-looking fellow was following him; it turned out to be only his own shadow! And such usually is human life to each of us; it is, for the most part, but the reflection of ourselves.

Many persons give themselves a great deal of fidget concerning what other people think of them and their peculiarities. Some are too much disposed to take the ill-natured side, and, judging by themselves, infer the worst. But it is very often the case that the uncharitableness of others, where it really exists, is but the reflection of our own want of charity and want of temper. It still oftener happens, that the worry we subject ourselves to has its source in our own imagination. And even though those about us may think of us uncharitably, we shall not mend matters by exasperating ourselves against them. We may thereby only expose ourselves unnecessarily to their ill-nature or caprice. "The ill that comes out of our mouth," says George Herbert, "oft-times falls into our bosom."

The great and good philosopher Faraday communicated the following piece of admirable advice, full of practical wisdom, the result of a rich experience of life, in a letter to his friend, Professor Tyndall: "Let me, as an old man, who ought by this time to have profited by experience, say that when I was younger I found I often misrepresented the intentions of people, and that they did not mean what at the time I supposed they meant; and further, that, as a general rule, it was better to be a little dull of apprehension where phrases seemed to imply pique, and quick in perception when, on the contrary, they seemed to imply kindly feeling. The real truth never fails ultimately to appear; and opposing parties; if wrong, are sooner convinced when plied to forbearingly, than when overwhelmed. All I mean to say is that it is better to be blind to the results of partisanship, and quick to see good-will. One has more happiness in one's self in endeavoring to follow the things that make for peace. You can hardly imagine how often I have been heated in private when opposed, as I have thought, unjustly and superciliously, and yet I have striven, and succeeded, I hope, in keeping down replies of the like kind, and I know I have never lost by it."

While the painter Barry was at Rome, he involved himself, as was his wont, in furious quarrels with the artists about picture-painting and picture-dealing, upon which his friend and countryman, Edmund Burke—always the generous friend of struggling merit—wrote to him kindly and sensibly: "Believe me, dear Barry, that the arms with which the ill dispositions of the world are to be combated, and the qualities by which it is to be reconciled to us, and we reconciled to it, are moderation, gentleness, a little indulgence to others, and a great deal of distrust of ourselves, which are not qualities of a mean spirit, as some may possibly think them, but virtues of a great and noble kind, and such as dignify our nature as much as they contribute to our repose and fortune, for nothing can be so unworthy of a well-composed soul as to pass away life in bickerings and litigations—in snarling and scuffling with everyone about us. We must be at peace with our species, if not for their sakes, at least very much for our own."

Were it possible to conceive the existence of a tyrant who should compel his people to give up to him one-third or more of their earnings, and require them at the same time to consume a commodity that should brutalize and degrade them, destroy the peace and comfort of their families, and sow in themselves the seeds of disease and premature death—what indignation meetings, what monster processions there would be! What eloquent speeches and apostrophes to the spirit of liberty!—what appeals against a despotism so monstrous and so unnatural! And yet such a tyrant really exists among us—the tyrant of unrestrained appetite, whom no force of arms, or voices, or votes can resist, while men are willing to be his slaves.

The power of this tyrant can only be overcome by moral means—by self-discipline, self-respect and self-control. There is no other way of withstanding the despotism of appetite in any of its forms. No reform of institutions, no extended power of voting, no improved form of government, no amount of scholastic instruction, can possibly elevate the character of a people who voluntarily abandon themselves to sensual indulgence. The pursuit of ignoble pleasure is the degradation of true happiness; it saps the morals, destroys the energies, and degrades the manliness and robustness of individuals as of nations.

The courage of self-control exhibits itself in many ways, but in none more clearly than in honest living. Men without the virtue of self-denial are not only subject to their own selfish desires, but they are usually in bondage to others who are like-minded with themselves. What others do, they do. They must live according to the artificial standard of their class, spending like their neighbors, regardless of the consequences, at the same time that all are, perhaps, aspiring after a style of living higher than their means. Each carries the others along with him, and they have not the moral courage to stop. They cannot resist the temptation of living high, though it may be at the expense of others; and they gradually become reckless of debt, until it enthralls them. In all this there is great moral cowardice, and want of manly independence of character.

The honorable man is frugal of his means, and pays his way honestly. He does not seek to pass himself off as richer than he is, or, by running into debt, open an account with ruin. As that man is not poor whose means are small but whose desires are under control, so that man is rich whose means are more than sufficient for his wants. When Socrates saw a great quantity of riches, jewels, and furniture of great value, carried in pomp through Athens, he said, "Now do I see how many things I do *not* desire." "I can forgive every thing but selfishness," said Perthes. "Even the narrowest circumstances admit of greatness with reference to 'mine and thine'; and none but the very poorest need fill their daily life with thoughts of money, if they have but prudence to arrange their housekeeping within the limits of their income."

A man may be indifferent to money because of higher considerations, as Faraday was, who sacrificed wealth to pursue science; but if he would have the enjoyments that money can purchase, he must honestly earn it, and not live upon the earnings of others, as those do who habitually incur debts which they have no means of paying. When Maginn, always drowned in debt, was asked what he paid for his wine, he replied that he did not know, but he believed they "put something down in a book."

This "putting down in a book" has proved the ruin of a great many weak-minded people, who cannot resist the temptation of taking things upon credit which they have not the present means of paying for; and it would probably prove of great social benefit if the law which enables creditors to recover debts contracted under certain circumstances were altogether abolished. But, in the competition for trade, every encouragement is given to the incurring of debt, the creditor relying upon the law to aid him in the last extremity. When Sydney Smith once went into a new neighborhood, it was given out in the local papers that he was a man of high connections, and he was besought on all sides for his "custom." But he speedily undeceived his new neighbors. "We are not great people at all," he said: "We are only common honest people—people that pay our debts."

Sir Walter Scott was a man who was honest to the core of his nature; and his strenuous and determined efforts to pay his debts, or rather the debts of the firm with which he had become involved, has always appeared to us one of the grandest things in biography. When his publisher and printer broke down, ruin seemed to stare him in the face. There was no want of sympathy for him in his great misfortune, and friends came forward who offered to raise money enough to enable him to arrange with his creditors. "No!" said he, proudly; "this right hand shall work it all off!" "If we lose everything else," he wrote to a friend, "we will at least keep our honor unblemished." While his health was already becoming undermined by overwork, he went on "writing like a tiger," as he himself expressed it, until no longer able to wield a pen; and though he paid the penalty of his supreme efforts with his life, he nevertheless saved his honor and his self-respect. In vain his doctors told him to give up work; he would not be dissuaded. "As for bidding me not work," he said to Dr. Abercrombie, "Molly might just as well put the kettle on the fire and say, 'Now, kettle, don't boil,'" to which he added, "If I were to be idle, I should go mad!"

By means of the profits realized by these tremendous efforts, Scott saw his debts in course of rapid diminution, and he trusted that, after a few more years' work, he would again be a free man. But it was not to be. He went on turning out such works as his "Count Robert of Paris" with greatly impaired skill, until he was prostrated by another and severer attack of palsy. He now felt that the plough was nearing the end of the furrow; his physical strength was gone; he was "not quite himself in all things," and yet his courage and perseverance never failed. "I have suffered terribly," he wrote in his Diary, "though rather in body than in mind, and I often wish I could lie down and sleep without waking. But *I will fight it out if I can !*"

Chapter 20

Duty—Truthfulness

*"I slept, and dreamt that life was beauty;
I woke, and found that life was duty."*

"Be not simply good—be good for something." —Thoreau.

*The path of duty in this world is the road to salvation
in the next. —Jewish Sage.*

DUTY IS A THING that is due, and must be paid by every man who would avoid present discredit and eventual moral insolvency. It is an obligation—a debt—which can only be discharged by voluntary effort and resolute action in the affairs of life.

Duty embraces man's whole existence. It begins in the home, where there is the duty which children owe to their parents on the one hand, and the duty which parents owe to their children on the other. There are, in like manner, the respective duties of husbands and wives, of masters and servants; while outside the home there are the duties which men and women owe to each other as friends and neighbors, as employers and employed, as governors and governed.

Duty is based upon a sense of justice—justice inspired by love, which is the most perfect form of goodness. Duty is not a sentiment, but a principle pervading the life, and it exhibits itself in conduct and in acts, which are mainly determined by man's conscience and free will.

The voice of conscience speaks in duty done, and without its regulating and controlling influence, the brightest and greatest intellect may be merely as a light that leads astray. Conscience sets a man upon his feet, while his will holds him upright. Conscience is the moral governor of the heart—the governor of right action, of right thought, of right faith, of right life—and only through its dominating influence can the noble and upright character be fully developed.

The conscience, however, may speak never so loudly, but without energetic will it may speak in vain. The will is free to choose between the right course and the wrong one, but the choice is nothing unless followed by immediate and decisive action. If the sense of duty be strong, and the course of action clear, the courageous will, upheld by the conscience, enables a man to proceed on his course bravely, and to accomplish his purposes in the face of all opposition and difficulty. And should failure be the issue, there will remain at least this satisfaction, that it has been in the cause of duty.

"Be and continue poor, young man," said Heinzelmann, "while others around you grow rich by fraud and disloyalty; be without place or power, while others beg their way upward; bear the pain of disappointed hopes, while others gain the accomplishment of theirs by flattery; forego the gracious pressure of the hand, for which others cringe and crawl. Wrap yourself in your own virtue, and seek a friend and your daily bread. If you have in your own cause grown gray with unbleached honor, bless God and die!"

When the Marquis of Pescara was entreated by the princes of Italy to desert the Spanish cause, to which he was in honor bound, his noble wife, reminded him of his duty. She wrote to him: "Remember your honor, which raises you above fortune and above kings; by that alone, and not by the splendor of titles, is glory acquired—that glory which it will be your happiness and pride to transmit unspotted to your posterity." Such was the dignified view which she took of her husband's honor; and when he fell at Pavia, though young and beautiful, and besought by many admirers, she betook herself to solitude, that she might lament over her husband's loss and celebrate his exploits.

To live really is to act energetically. Life is a battle to be fought valiantly. Inspired by high and honorable resolve, a man must stand to his post, and die there, if need be. Like the old Danish hero, his determination should be, "to dare nobly, to will strongly, and never to falter in the path of duty." The power of will, be it great or small, which God has given us, is a Divine gift, and we ought neither to let it perish for want of using, on the one hand, nor profane it by employing it for ignoble purposes, on the other. Robertson, of Brighton, has truly said, that man's real greatness consists not in seeking his own pleasure, or fame, or advancement—"not that everyone shall save his own life, not that every man shall seek his own glory—but that every man shall do his own duty."

What most stands in the way of the performance of duty, is irresolution, weakness of purpose, and indecision. On the one side are conscience and knowledge of good and evil; on the other are indolence, selfishness, love of pleasure, or passion. The weak and ill-disciplined will may remain suspended for a time between these influences; but at length the balance inclines one way or the other, according as the will is called into action or otherwise. If it be allowed to remain passive, the lower influence of selfishness or passion will prevail; and thus manhood suffers abdication, individuality is renounced, character is degraded, and the man permits himself to become the mere passive slave of his senses.

Thus, the power of exercising the will promptly, in obedience to the dictates of conscience, and thereby resisting the impulses of the lower nature, is of essential importance in moral discipline, and absolutely necessary for the development of character in its best forms. To acquire the habit of well-doing, to resist evil propensities, to fight against sensual desires, to overcome inborn selfishness, may require a long and persevering discipline; but when once the practice of duty is learned, it becomes consolidated in habit, and thenceforward is comparatively easy.

The valiant good man is he who, by the resolute exercise of his free-will, has so disciplined himself as to have acquired the habit of virtue; as the bad man is he who, by allowing his free-will to remain inactive, and giving the bridle to his desires and passions, has acquired the habit of vice, by which he becomes, at last, bound as by chains of iron. A man can only achieve strength of purpose by the action of his own free-will. If he is to stand erect, it must be by his own efforts; for he can not be kept propped up by the help of others. He is master of himself and of his actions. He can avoid falsehood, and be truthful; he can shun sensualism, and be continent; he can turn aside from doing a cruel thing, and be benevolent and forgiving. All these lie within the sphere of individual efforts, and come within the range of self-discipline. And it depends upon men themselves whether in these respects they will be free, pure, and good, on the one hand; or enslaved, impure, and miserable, on the other.

The sense of duty is a sustaining power even to a courageous man. It holds him upright, and makes him strong. It was a noble saying of Pompey, when his friends tried to dissuade him from embarking for Rome in a storm, telling him that he did so at the great peril of his life: "It is necessary for me to go," he said, "it is not necessary for me to live." What it was right that he should do, he would do, in the face of danger and in defiance of storms.

"Let men of all ranks," said Plato, "whether they are successful or unsuccessful, whether they triumph or not—let them do their duty, and rest satisfied." What a lesson for future ages lies in these words!

As might be expected of the great Washington, the chief motive power in his life was the spirit of duty. It was the regal and commanding element in his character which gave it unity, compactness and vigor. When he clearly saw his duty before him, he did it at all hazards, and with inflexible integrity. He did not do it for effect, nor did he think of glory, or of fame and its rewards; but of the right thing to be done, and the best way of doing it.

Yet Washington had a most modest opinion of himself; and when offered the chief command of the American patriot army, he hesitated to accept it until it was pressed upon him. When acknowledging in Congress the honor which had been done him in selecting him to so important a trust, on the execution of which the future of his country in a great measure depended, Washington said: "I beg it may be remembered, lest some unlucky event should happen unfavorable to my reputation, that I this day declare, with the utmost sincerity, I do not think myself equal to the command I am honored with." And in his letter to his wife, communicating to her his appointment as commander-in-chief, he said: "I have used every endeavor in my power to avoid it, not only from my unwillingness to part with you and the family, but from the consciousness of its being a trust too great for my capacity, and that I should enjoy more real happiness in one month with you at home than I have the most distant prospect of finding abroad, if my stay were to be seven times seven years. But, as it has been a kind of destiny that has thrown me upon this service, I shall hope that my undertaking it is designed for some good purpose. It was utterly out of my power to refuse the appointment, without exposing my character to such censures as would have reflected dishonor upon myself, and given pain to my friends. This, I am sure, could not and ought not to be pleasing to you, and must have lessened me considerably in my own esteem."

Washington pursued his upright course through life, first as commander-in-chief; and afterwards as president, never faltering in the path of duty. He had no regard for popularity, but held to his purpose through good and through evil report, often at the risk of his power and influence. Thus, on one occasion, when the ratification of a treaty, arranged by Mr. Jay with Great Britain, was in question, Washington was urged to reject it. But his honor, and the honor of his country, was committed, and he refused to do so. A great outcry was raised against the treaty, and for a time Washington was so unpopular that he is said to have been actually stoned by the mob. But he nevertheless held it to be his duty to ratify the treaty; and it was carried out in despite of petitions and remonstrances from all quarters. "While I feel," he said in answer to the remonstrance, "the most lively gratitude for the many in stances of approbation from my country, I can no otherwise deserve it than by obeying the dictates of my conscience."

Duty was the dominant idea in Nelson's mind. The spirit in which he served his country was expressed in the famous watch-word, "England expects every man to do his duty," signalled by him to the fleet before going;into action at Trafalgar, as well as in the last words -that passed his lips— "I have done my duty; I praise God for it!" And Nelson's companion and friend—the brave, sensible, homely-minded Collingwood—he -who, as his ship bore clown into the great sea fight, said to his flag-captain, "Just about this time our wives are going to church in England"—Collingwood too was, like his commander, an ardent devotee of duty. "Do your duty to the best of your ability," was the maxim which he urged upon many young men starting on the voyage of life. To a midshipman he once gave the following manly and sensible advice:

"You may depend upon it, that it is more in your own power than in anybody else's to promote both your comfort and advancement. A strict and unwearied attention to your duty, and a complacent and respectful behavior, not only to your superiors but to everybody, will insure you their regard, and the reward will surely come; but if it should not, I am convinced you have too much good sense to let disappointment sour you. Guard carefully against letting discontent appear in you. It will be sorrow to your friends, a triumph to your competitors, and can not be productive of any good. Conduct yourself so as to deserve the best that can come to you, and the consciousness of your own proper behavior will keep you in spirits if it should not come. Let it be your ambition to be foremost in all duty. Do not be a nice observer of turns, but ever present yourself ready for everything, and, unless your officers are very inattentive men, they will not allow others to impose more duty on you than they should."

It is a grand thing, after all, this pervading spirit of Duty in a nation; and so long as it survives, no one need despair of its future. But when it has departed, or become deadened, and been supplanted by thirst for pleasure, or selfish aggrandizement, or "glory"—then woe to that nation, for its dissolution is near at hand!

Duty is closely allied to truthfulness of character; and the dutiful man is, above all things, truthful in his words as in his actions. He says and he does the right thing in the right way, and at the right time.

There is probably no saying of Lord Chesterfield that commends itself more strongly to the approval of manly-minded men, than that it is truth that makes the success of the gentleman. Clarendon, speaking of one of the noblest and purest gentlemen of his age, says of Falkland, that he "was so severe an adorer of truth, that he could as easily have given himself, leave to steal as to dissemble."

It was one of the finest things that Mrs. Hutchinson could say of her husband, that he was a thoroughly truthful and reliable man: "He never professed the thing he intended not, nor promised what he believed out of his power, nor failed in the performance of any thing that was in his power to fulfill."

Wellington was a severe admirer of truth. An illustration may be given. When afflicted by deafness, he consulted a celebrated aurist, who, after trying all remedies in vain, determined, as a last resource, to eject into the ear a strong solution of caustic. It caused the most intense pain, but the patient bore it with his usual equanimity. The family physician accidentally calling one day, found the duke with flushed cheeks and blood-shot eyes, and when he rose he staggered about like a drunken man. The doctor asked to be permitted to look at his ear, and then he found that a furious inflammation was going on, which, if not immediately checked, must shortly reach the brain and kill him. Vigorous remedies were at once applied, and the inflammation was checked. But the hearing of that ear was completely destroyed. When the aurist heard of the danger his patient had run, through the violence of the remedy he had employed, he hastened to Apsley House to express his grief and mortification; but the duke merely said: "Do not say a word more about it—you did all for the best." The aurist said it would be his ruin when it became known that he had been the cause of so much suffering and danger to his grace. "But nobody need know any thing about it; keep your own counsel, and, depend upon it, I won't say a word to any one." "Then, your grace will allow me to attend you as usual, which will show the public that you have not withdrawn your confidence from me?" "No," replied the duke, kindly but firmly; "I can't do that, for that would be a lie." He would not act a falsehood any more than he would speak one.

Another illustration of duty and truthfulness, as exhibited in the fulfillment of a promise, may be added from the life of Blucher. When he was hastening with his army over bad roads to the help of Wellington, on the 18th of June, 1815, he encouraged his troops by words and gestures. "Forward, children—forward!" "It is impossible; it can't be clone," was the answer. Again and again he urged them. "Children, we must get on; you may say it can't be done, but it *must* be done! I have promised my brother Wellington—promised, do you hear? You wouldn't have me *break my word!*" And it was done.

Truth is the very bond of society, without which it must cease to exist, and dissolve into anarchy and chaos. A household can not be governed by lying; nor can a nation. Sir Thomas Browne once asked, "Do the devils lie?" "No," was his answer; "for then even hell could not subsist." No consideration can justify the sacrifice of truth, which ought to be sovereign in all the relations of life. Of all mean vices, perhaps lying is the meanest. It is in some cases the offspring of perversity and vice, and in many others of sheer moral cowardice. Yet many persons think so lightly of it that they will order their servants to lie for them; nor can they feel surprised if, after such ignoble instruction, they find their servants lying for themselves.

When Pitt was in his last illness, the news reached England of the great deeds of Wellington in India. "The more I hear of his exploits," said Pitt, "the more I admire the modesty with which he receives the praises he merits for them. He is the only man I ever knew that was not vain of what he had done, and yet had so much reason to be so."

So it is said of Faraday by Professor Tyndall, that "pretense of all kinds, whether in life or in philosophy, was hateful to him." Dr. Marshall Hall was a man of like spirit—courageously truthful, dutiful, and manly. One of his most intimate friends has said of him that, wherever he met with untruthfulness or sinister motive, he would expose it, saying, "I neither will, nor can, give my consent to a lie." The question, "right or wrong," once decided in his own mind, the right was followed, no matter what the sacrifice or the difficulty—neither expediency nor inclination weighing one jot in the balance.

There was no virtue that Dr. Arnold labored more sedulously to instill into young men than the virtue of truthfulness, as being the manliest of virtues, as indeed the very basis of all true manliness. He designated truthfulness as "moral transparency," and he valued it more highly than any other quality. When lying was detected, he treated it as a great moral offense; but when a pupil made an assertion, he accepted it with confidence. "If you say so, that is quite enough; *of course* I believe your word." By thus trusting and believing them, he educated the young in truthfulness; the boys at length coming to say to one another: "Its a shame to tell Arnold a lie—he always believes one."

One of the most striking instances that could be given of the character of the dutiful, truthful, laborious man, is presented in the life of the late George Wilson, professor of Technology in the University of Edinburgh. Though we bring this illustration under the head of Duty, it might equally have stood under that of Courage, Cheerfulness, or Industry; for it is alike illustrative of these several qualities.

Wilson's life was, indeed, a marvel of cheerful laboriousness, exhibiting the power of the soul to triumph over the body, and almost to set it at defiance. It might be taken as an illustration of the saying of the whaling captain to Dr. Kane, as to the power of moral force over physical: "Bless you, sir, the soul will any day lift the body out of its boots!"

A fragile but bright and lively boy, he had scarcely entered manhood ere his constitution began to exhibit signs of disease. As early, indeed, as his seventeenth year, he began to complain of melancholy and sleeplessness, supposed to be the effect of bile. "I don't think I shall live long," he then said to a friend; "my mind will—must work itself out, and the body will soon follow it." A strange confession for a boy to make! But he gave his physical health no fair chance. His life was all brain-work, study, and competition. When he took exercise it was in sudden bursts, which did him more harm than good. Long walks in the Highlands jaded and exhausted him, and he returned to his brain-work unrested and unrefreshed.

It was during one of his forced walks of some twenty-four miles in the neighborhood of Stirling that he injured one of his feet, and he returned home seriously ill. The result was an abscess, disease of the ankle-joint, and long agony, which ended in the amputation of the right foot. But he never relaxed in his labors. He was now writing, lecturing and teaching chemistry. Rheumatism and acute inflammation of the eye next attacked him, and were treated by cupping and blistering. Unable himself to write, he went on preparing his lectures, which he dictated to his sister. Pain haunted him day and night, and sleep was only forced by morphia. While in this state of general prostration, symptoms of pulmonary disease began to show themselves. Yet he continued to give the weekly lectures to which he stood committed to the Edinburgh school of Arts. Not one was shirked, though their delivery before a large audience was a most exhausting duty. "Well, there's another nail put into my coffin," was the remark made on throwing off his over-coat on returning home; and a sleepless night almost invariably followed.

At twenty-seven, Wilson was lecturing ten, eleven, or more hours weekly, usually with setons or open blister-wounds upon him—his "bosom friends," he used to call them. He felt the shadow of death upon him, and he worked as if his days were numbered. "Don't be surprised," he wrote to a friend, "if any morning at breakfast you hear that I am gone." But while he said so, he did not in the least degree indulge in the feeling of sickly sentimentality. He worked on as cheerfully and hopefully as if in the very fullness of his strength. "To none," said he, "is life so sweet as to those who have lost all fear to die."

Sometimes he was compelled to desist from his labors by sheer debility, occasioned by loss of blood from the lungs; but after a few weeks' rest and change of air, he would return to his work, saying: "The water is rising in the well again!" Though disease had fastened on his lungs, and was spreading there, and though suffering from a distressing cough, he went on lecturing as usual. To add to his troubles, when one day endeavoring to recover himself from a stumble occasioned by his lameness, he overstrained his arm, and broke the bone near the shoulder. But he recovered from his successive accidents and illnesses in the most extraordinary way. The reed bent, but did not break; the storm passed, and it stood erect as before.

There was no worry or fever nor fret about him; but instead, cheerfulness, patience, and unfailing perseverance. His mind, amidst all his sufferings, remained perfectly calm and serene. He went about his daily work with an apparently charmed life, as if he had the strength of many men in him. Yet all the while he knew he was dying, his chief anxiety being to conceal his state from those about him at home, to whom the knowledge of his actual condition would have been inexpressibly distressing. "I am cheerful among strangers," he said, "and try to live day by day as a dying man."

He went on teaching as before—lecturing to the Architectural Institute and to the School of Arts. One day, after a lecture before the latter institute, he lay down to rest, and was shortly awakened by the rupture of a blood-vessel, which occasioned him the loss of a considerable quantity of blood. He appeared at the family meals as usual, and next day he lectured twice, punctually fulfilling his engagements; but the exertion of speaking was followed by a second attack of hemorrhage. He now became seriously ill, and it was doubted whether he would survive the night. But he did survive; and during his convalescence he was appointed to an important public office—that of Director of the Scottish Industrial Museum, which involved a great amount of labor, as well as lecturing, in his capacity of professor of technology, which he held in connection with the office.

From this time forward, his "dear museum," as he called it, absorbed all his surplus energies. While busily occupied in collecting models and specimens for the museum, he filled up his odds-and-ends of time in lecturing to Ragged Schools, Ragged Kirks, and Medical Missionary Societies. He gave himself no rest, either of mind or body; and to "die working" was-the fate he envied. His mind would not give in, but his poor body was forced to yield, and a severe attack of hemorrhage—bleeding from both lungs and stomach—compelled him to relax his labors. "For a month, or some forty days," he wrote—"a dreadful Lent—the wind has blown geographically from 'Araby the blest,' but thermometrically from Iceland the accursed. I have been made a prisoner of war, hit by an icicle in the lungs, and have shivered and burned alternately for a large portion of the last month, and spit blood till I grew pale with coughing. Now I am better, and tomorrow I give my concluding lecture, thankful that I have contrived, notwithstanding all my troubles, to carry on without missing a lecture to the last day of the Faculty of Arts, to which I belong."

How long was it to last? He himself began to wonder, for he had long felt his life as if ebbing away. At length he became languid, weary, and unfit for work; even the writing of a letter cost him a painful effort, and he felt "as if to lie down and sleep were the only things worth doing," Yet shortly after, to help a Sunday-school, he wrote his "Five Gateways of Knowledge," as a lecture, and afterwards expanded it into a book. He also recovered strength sufficient to enable him to proceed with his lectures to the institutions to which he belonged, besides on various occasions undertaking to do other people's work. "I am looked upon as good as mad," he wrote to his brother, "because, on a hasty notice, I took a defaulting lecturer's place at the Philosophical Institution, and discoursed on the polarization of light. . . . But I like work; it is a family weakness."

Then followed sleepless nights, days of pain, and more spitting of blood. "My only painless moments," he says, "were when lecturing." In this state of prostration and disease, the indefatigable man undertook to write the "Life of Edward Forbes"; and he did it, like every thing he undertook, with admirable ability. He proceeded with his lectures as usual. To an association of teachers he delivered a discourse on the educational value of industrial science. After he had spoken to his audience for an hour, he left them to say whether he should go on or not, and they cheered him on to another half-hour's address. "It is curious," he wrote, "the feeling of having an audience, like clay in your hands, to mould for a season as you please. It is a terribly responsible power. . . . I do not mean for a moment to imply that I am indifferent to the good opinion of others—far otherwise; but to gain this is much less a concern with me than to deserve it. It was not so once. I had no wish for unmerited praise, but I was too ready to settle that I did merit it. Now, the word *duty* seems to me the biggest word in the world, and is uppermost in all my serious doings."

This was written only about four months before his death. A little later he wrote: "I spin my thread of life from week to week, rather than from year to year." Constant attacks of bleeding from the lungs sapped his little remaining strength, but did not altogether disable him from lecturing. He was amused by one of his friends proposing to put him under trustees for the purpose of looking after his health. But he would not be restrained from working, so long as a vestige of strength remained.

One day, in the autumn of 1859, he returned from his customary lecture in the University of Edinburgh with a severe pain in his side. He was scarcely able to crawl up stairs. Medical aid was sent for, and he was pronounced to be suffering from pleurisy and inflammation of the lungs. His enfeebled frame was unable to resist so severe a disease, and he sank peacefully to the rest he so longed for, after a few days' illness:

> "Wrong not the dead with tears
> A glorious bright tomorrow
> Endeth a weary life of pain and sorrow."

Chapter 21

Temper

"Heaven is a temper, not a place." —Dr. Chalmers.

"Temper is nine-tenths of Christianity." —Bishop Wilson.

"Even Power itself hath not one-half the might of gentleness." —Hunt.

IT HAS BEEN SAID that men succeed in life quite as much by their temper as by their talents. However this may be, it is certain that their happiness in life depends mainly upon their equanimity of disposition, their patience and forbearance, and their kindness and thoughtfulness for those about them. It is really true what Plato says, that in seeking the good of others we find our own.

There are some natures so happily constituted that they can find good in every thing. There is no calamity so great but they can educe comfort or consolation from it—no sky so black but they can discover a gleam of sunshine issuing through it from some quarter or another; and if the sun be not visible to their eyes, they at least comfort themselves with the thought that it is there, though veiled from them for some good and wise purpose.

Such happy natures are to be envied. They have a beam in the eye—a beam of pleasure, gladness, religious cheerfulness, philosophy, call it what you will. Sunshine is about their hearts, and their mind gilds with its own hues all that it looks upon. When they have burdens to bear, they bear them cheerfully—not repining, nor fretting, nor wasting their energies in useless lamentations, but struggling onward manfully, gathering up such flowers as lie along their path.

Let it not for a moment be supposed that men such as those we speak of are weak and unreflective. The largest and most comprehensive natures are generally also the most cheerful, the most loving, the most hopeful, the most trustful. It is the wise man, of large vision, who is the quickest to discern the moral sunshine gleaming through the darkest cloud. In present evil, he sees prospective good; in pain, he recognizes the effort of nature to restore health; in trials, he finds correction and discipline; and in sorrow and suffering, he gathers courage, knowledge, and the best practical wisdom.

When Jeremy Taylor had lost all—when his house had been plundered, and his family driven out of doors, and all his worldly estate had been sequestrated—he could still write thus: "I am fallen into the hands of publicans and sequestrators, and they have taken all from me; what now? Let me look about me. They have left me the sun and moon, a loving wife, and many friends to pity me, and some to relieve me; and I can still discourse, and, unless I list, they have not taken away my merry countenance and my cheerful spirit, and a good conscience; they have still left me the providence of God, and all the promises of the Gospel, and my religion, and my hopes of heaven, and my charity to them, too; and still I sleep and digest, I eat and drink, I read and meditate. . . . And he that hath so many causes of joy, and so great, is very much in love with sorrow and peevishness who loves all these pleasures, and chooses to sit down upon his little handful of thorns."

Although cheerfulness of disposition is very much a matter of inborn temperament, it is also capable of being trained and cultivated like any other habit. We may make the best of life, or we may make the worst of it; and it depends very much upon ourselves whether we extract joy or misery from it. There are always two sides of life on which we can look, according as we choose—the bright side or the gloomy. We can bring the power of the will to bear in making the choice, and thus cultivate the habit of being happy or the reverse. We can encourage the disposition of looking at the brightest side of things, instead of the darkest. And while we sec the cloud, let us not shut our eyes to the silver lining.

The beam in the eye sheds brightness, beauty, and joy upon life in all its phases. It shines upon coldness, and warms it; upon suffering, and comforts it; upon ignorance, and enlightens it; upon sorrow and cheers it. The beam in the eye gives lustre to intellect, and brightens beauty itself. Without it the sunshine of life is not felt, flowers bloom in vain, the marvels of heaven and earth are not seen or acknowledged, and creation is but a dreary, lifeless, soulless blank.

While cheerfulness of disposition is a great source of enjoyment in life, it is also a great safeguard of character. A devotional writer of the present day, in answer to the question; How are we to overcome temptations? says: "Cheerfulness is the first thing, cheerfulness is the second, and cheerfulness is the third." It furnishes the best soil for the growth of goodness and virtue.

It gives brightness of heart and elasticity of spirit. It is the companion of charity, the nurse of patience, the mother of wisdom. It is also the best of moral and mental tonics. "The best cordial of all," said Dr. Marshall Hall to one of his patients, "is cheerfulness." And Solomon has said that "a merry heart doeth good like a medicine."

When Luther was once applied to for a remedy against melancholy, his advice was: "Gayety and courage—innocent gayety, and rational, honorable courage—are the best medicine for young men, and for old men too; for all men against sad thoughts." Next to music, if not before it, Luther loved children and flowers. The great gnarled man had a heart as tender as a woman's.

Cheerfulness is also an excellent wearing quality. It has been called the bright weather of the heart. It gives harmony of soul, and is a perpetual song without words. It is tantamount to repose. It enables nature to recruit its strength; whereas worry and discontent debilitate it, involving constant wear-and-tear.

How is it that we see such men as Lord Palmerston growing old in harness, working on vigorously to the end? Mainly through equanimity of temper and habitual cheerfulness. They have educated themselves in the habit of endurance, of not being easily provoked, of bearing and forbearing, of hearing harsh and even unjust things said of them without indulging in undue resentment, and avoiding worrying, petty, and self-tormenting cares. An intimate friend of Lord Palmerston, who observed him closely for twenty years, has said that he never saw him angry, with perhaps one exception; and that was when the Ministry, responsible for the calamity in Afghanistan, of which he was one, were unjustly accused by their opponents of falsehood, perjury, and willful mutilation of public documents.

So far as can be learned from biography, men of the greatest genius have been for the most part cheerful, contented men—not eager for reputation, money, or power—but relishing life, and keenly susceptible of enjoyment, as we find reflected in their works. Such seem to have been Homer, Horace, Virgil, Montaigne, Shakespeare, Cervantes. Healthy, serene cheerfulness is apparent in their great creations. Among the same class of cheerful-minded men may also be mentioned Luther, Moore, Bacon, Leonardo da Vinci, Raphael, and Michael Angelo. Perhaps they were happy because constantly occupied, and in the pleasantest of all work—that of creating out of the fulness and richness of their great minds.

Milton, too, though a man of many trials and sufferings, must have been a man of great cheerfulness and elasticity of nature. Though overtaken by blindness, deserted by friends, and fallen upon evil days—"darkness before, and danger's voice behind"—yet did he not abate heart or hope, but "still bore up, and steered right onward." Henry Fielding was a man borne down through life by debt, and difficulty and bodily sufferings; and yet Lady Mary Wortley Montague has said of him that, by virtue of his cheerful disposition, she was persuaded he "had known more happy moments than any other person on earth."

Johnson was of opinion that a man grew better as he grew older, and that his nature mellowed with age. This is certainly a much more cheerful view of human nature than that of Lord Chesterfield, who saw life through the eyes of a cynic, and held that "the heart never grows better by age, it only grows harder." But both sayings may be true, according to the point from which life is viewed and the temper by which a man is governed; for while the good, profiting by experience, and disciplining themselves by self-control, will grow better, the ill-conditioned, uninfluenced by experience, will only grow worse.

Sir Walter Scott was a man full of the milk of human kindness. Every body loved him. He was never five minutes in a room ere the little pets of the family, whether dumb or lisping, had found out his kindness for all their generation. Scott related to Captain Hall an incident of his boyhood which showed the tenderness of his nature. One day, a dog coming towards him, he took up a big stone, threw it, and hit the dog. The poor creature had strength enough left to crawl up to him and lick his feet, although he saw its leg was broken. The incident, he said, had given him the bitterest remorse in his after-life; but he added, "an early circumstance of that kind, properly reflected on, is calculated to have the best effect on one's character throughout life." "Give me an honest laugher," Scott would say; and he himself laughed the heart's laugh. He had a kind word for everybody, and his kindness acted all round him like a contagion, dispelling the reserve and awe which his great name was calculated to inspire. "He'll come here," said the keeper of the ruins of Melrose Abbey to Washington Irving—"he'll come here sometimes, wi' great folks in his company, and the first I'll know of it is hearing his voice calling out, 'Johnny! Johnny Bower!' and when I go out I am sure to be greeted wi' a joke or a pleasant word. He'll stand and crack and laugh wi' me just like an auld wife; and to think that of a man that has *such an awfu' knowledge o' history!*"

Dr. Arnold was a man of the same hearty cordiality of manner—full of human sympathy. There was not a particle of affectation or pretense of condescension about him. "I never knew such a humble man as the doctor," said the parish clerk at Laleham; "he comes and shakes us by the hand as if he was one of us." "He used to come into my house," said an old woman near Fox How, "and talk to me as if I were a lady."

Sidney Smith was another illustration of the power of cheerfulness. He was ever ready to look on the bright side of things; the darkest cloud had to him its silver lining. Whether working as country curate or as parish rector, he was always kind, laborious, patient and exemplary, exhibiting in every sphere of life the spirit of a Christian, the kindness of a pastor, and the honor of a gentleman. In his leisure he employed his pen on the side of justice, freedom, education, toleration, emancipation; and his writings, though full of common sense and bright humor, are never vulgar; nor did he ever pander to popularity or prejudice. His good spirits, thanks to his natural vivacity and stamina of constitution, never forsook him; and in his old age, when borne down by disease, he wrote to a friend; "I have gout, asthma, and seven other maladies, but am other wise very well." In one of the last letters he wrote to Lady Carlisle, he wrote: "If you hear of sixteen or eighteen pounds of flesh wanting an owner, they belong to me. I look as if a curate had been taken out of me."

One of the sorest trials of a man's temper and patience was that which befell Abauzit, the natural philosopher, while residing at Geneva—resembling in many respects a similar calamity which occurred to Newton, and which he bore with equal resignation. Among other things, Abauzit devoted much study to the barometer and its variations, with the object of deducing the general laws which regulated atmospheric pressure. During twenty-seven years he made numerous observations daily, recording them on sheets prepared for the purpose. One day, when a new servant was installed in the house, she immediately proceeded to display her zeal by "putting things to rights." Abauzit's study, among other rooms, was made tidy and set in order. When he entered it, he asked of the servant, "What have you done with the paper that was round the barometer?" "Oh, sir," was the reply, "it was so dirty that I burned it, and put in its place this paper, which you will see is quite new." Abauzit crossed his arms, and after some moments of internal struggle, he said, in a tone of calmness and resignation: "You have destroyed the results of twenty-seven years labor; in future touch nothing whatever in this room."

The study of natural history, more than that of any other branch of science, seems to be accompanied by unusual cheerfulness and equanimity of temper on the part of its votaries; the result of which is, that the life of naturalists is, on the whole, more prolonged than that of any other class of men of science. A member of the Linn Tan Society has informed us that, of fourteen members who died in 1870, two were over ninety, five were over eighty, and two were over seventy. The average of all the members who died in that year was seventy-five.

All large, healthy natures are cheerful as well as hopeful. Their example is also contagious and diffusive, brightening and cheering all who come within reach of their influence. It was said of Sir John Malcolm, when he appeared in a saddened camp in India, that "it was like a gleam of sunlight, . . . no man left him without a smile on his face. He was boy Malcolm still. It was impossible to resist the fascination of his genial presence."

The true basis of cheerfulness is love, hope, and patience. Love evokes love, and begets loving-kindness. Love cherishes hopeful and generous thoughts of others. It is charitable, gentle, and truthful. It is a discerner of good. It turns to the brightest side of things, and its face is ever directed towards happiness. It sees "the glory in the grass, the sunshine on the flower." It encourages happy thoughts, and lives in an atmosphere of cheerfulness. It costs nothing, and yet is invaluable; for it blesses its possessor, and grows up in abundant happiness in the bosoms of others. Even its sorrows are linked with pleasures, and its very tears are sweet. Bentham lays it down as a principle, that a man becomes rich in his own stock of pleasures in proportion to the amount he distributes to others. His kindness will evoke kindness, and his happiness be increased by his own benevolence. "Kind words," he says, "cost no more than unkind ones. Kind words produce kind actions, not only on the part of him to whom they are addressed, but on the part of him by whom they are employed; and this not incidentally only, but habitually, in virtue of the principal of association." "It may, indeed, happen that the effort of beneficence may not benefit those for whom it was intended; but when wisely directed it *must* benefit the person from whom it emanates."

The poet Rogers used to tell a story of a little girl, a great favorite with everyone who knew her. Some one said to her, "Why does every body love you so much?" She answered, "I think it is because I love every body so much." This little story is capable of a very wide application; for our happiness as human beings, generally speaking, will be found to be very much in proportion to the number of things we love, and the number of things that love us. And the greatest worldly success, however honestly achieved, will contribute comparatively little to happiness unless it be accompanied by a lively benevolence towards every human being. Kindness does not consist in gifts, but in gentleness and generosity of spirit. Men may give their money which comes from the purse, and withhold their kindness which comes from the heart. The kindness that displays itself in giving money does not amount to much, and often does quite as much harm as good; but the kindness of true sympathy, of thoughtful help, is never without beneficent results.

It is the kindly-dispositioned men who are the active men of the world, while the selfish and the skeptical, who have no love but for themselves, are its idlers. Buffon used to say that he would give nothing for a young man who did not begin life with an enthusiasm of some sort. It showed that at least he had faith in something good, lofty, and generous, even if unattainable. Egotism and selfishness are always miserable companions in life, and they are especially unnatural in youth. The egotist is next door to a fanatic. Constantly occupied with self, he has no thought to spare for others. He refers to himself in all things, thinks of himself, and studies himself, until his own little self becomes his own little god.

Worst of all are the grumblers and growlers at fortune—who find that "whatever is is wrong," and will do nothing to set matters right—who declare all to be barren, "from Dan even to Beersheba." These grumblers are invariably found the least efficient helpers in the school of life. As the worst workmen are usually the readiest to "strike," so the least industrious members of society are the readiest to complain. The worst wheel of all is the one that creaks. There is such a thing as the cherishing of discontent until the feeling becomes morbid. The jaundiced see everything about them yellow. The ill-conditioned think all things awry, and the whole world out of joint. All is vanity and vexation of spirit. The little girl in *Punch*, who found her doll stuffed with bran, and forthwith declared everything to be hollow, and wanted to "go into a nunnery," had her counterpart in real life. Many full-grown people are quite as morbidly unreasonable.

We have to be on our guard against small troubles, which, by encouraging, we are apt to magnify into great ones. Indeed, the chief source of worry in the world is not real but imaginary evil—small vexations and trivial afflictions. In the presence of a great sorrow, all petty troubles disappear; but we are too ready to take some cherished misery to our bosom, and to pet it there. Let the necessitarians argue as they may, freedom of will and action is the possession of every man and woman. It is sometimes our glory, and very often it is our shame; all depends upon the manner in which it is used. We can choose to look at the bright side of things or at the dark. We can follow good and eschew evil thoughts. We can be wrong-headed and wrong-hearted, or the reverse, as we ourselves determine. The world will be to each one of us very much what we make it. The cheerful are its real possessors, for the world belongs to those who enjoy it.

It must, however, be admitted that there are cases beyond the reach of the moralist. Once, when a miserable-looking dyspeptic called upon a leading physician, and laid his case before him, "Oh," said the doctor, "you only want a good hearty laugh; go and see Grimaldi!" "Alas!" said the miserable patient, "I am Grimaldi!" So, when Smollett, oppressed by disease, traveled over Europe in the hope of finding health, he saw everything through his own jaundiced eyes. "I'll tell it," said Smollett, "to the world." "You had better tell it," said Sterne, "to your physician."

Meeting evils by anticipation is not the way to overcome them. If we perpetually carry our burdens about with us, they will soon bear us down under their load. When evil comes, we must deal with it bravely and hopefully.

What Perthes wrote to a young man, who seemed to him inclined to take trifles as well as sorrows too much to heart, was doubtless good advice: "Go forward with hope and confidence. This is the advice given thee by an old man, who has had a full share of the burden and heat of life's day. We must ever stand upright, happen what may, and for this end we must cheerfully resign ourselves to the varied influences of this many-colored life. You may call this levity, and you are partly right—for flowers and colors are but trifles light as air—but such levity is a constituent portion of our human nature, without which it would sink under the weight of time. While on earth we must still play with earth, and with that which blooms and fades upon its breast. The consciousness of this mortal life being but the way to a higher goal by no means precludes our playing with it cheerfully; and, indeed, we must do so, otherwise our energy in action will entirely fail." Cheerfulness also accompanies patience, which is one of the main conditions of happiness and success in life. "He that will be served," says George Herbert, "must be patient." It was said of the cheerful and patient King Alfred, that "good fortune accompanied him like a gift of God." Marlborough's expectant calmness was great, and a principal secret of his success as a general. "Patience will overcome all things," he wrote in 1702. In the midst of a great emergency, while baffled and opposed by his allies, he said: "Having done all that is possible, we should submit with patience."

Last and chiefest of blessings is hope, the most common of possessions; for, as Thales, the philosopher, said, "Even those who have nothing else have hope." Hope is the great helper of the poor. It has even been styled "the poor man's bread." It is also the sustainer and inspirer of great deeds. It is recorded of Alexander the Great that, when he succeeded to the throne of Macedon, he gave away among his friends the greater part of the estates which his father had left him; and when Perdiccas asked him what he reserved for himself, Alexander answered, "the greatest possession of all—hope!"

Chapter 22

Manner—Art

"A beautiful behavior is better than a beautiful form; it gives a higher pleasure than statues and pictures; it is the finest of the fine arts." —Emerson.

"Manners are often too much neglected; they are most important to men, no less than to women. Life is too short to get over a bad manner; besides, manners are the shadows of virtues." —Rev. Sidney Smith.

MANNER IS ONE of the principal external graces of character. It is the ornament of action, and often makes the commonest offices beautiful by the way in which it performs them. It is a happy way of doing things, adorning even the smallest details of life, and contributing to render it, as a whole, agreeable and pleasant.

Manner has a good deal to do with the estimation in which men are held by the world; and it has often more influence in the government of others than qualities of much greater depth and substance. A manner at once gracious and cordial is among the greatest aids to success, and many there are who fail for want of it. Locke thought it of greater importance that an educator of youth should be well-bred and well-tempered, than that he should be either a thorough classicist or man of science.

While rudeness and gruffness bar doors and shut hearts, kindness and propriety of behavior, in which good manners consist, act as an "open sesame" everywhere. Doors unbar before them, and they are a passport to the hearts of every body, young and old. There is a common saying that "Manners make the man"; but this is not so true as that "Man makes the manners." A man may be gruff, and even rude, and yet be good at heart and of sterling character; yet he would doubtless be a much more agreeable, and probably a much more useful man, were he to exhibit that suavity of disposition and courtesy of manner which always gives a finish to the true gentleman.

A man's manner, to a certain extent, indicates his character. It is the external exponent of his inner nature. It indicates his taste, his feelings, and his temper, as well as the society to which he has been accustomed. There is a conventional manner, which is of comparatively little importance; but the natural manner, the outcome of natural gifts, improved by careful self-culture, signifies a great deal.

Grace of manner is inspired by sentiment, which is a source of no slight enjoyment to a cultivated mind. Viewed in this light, sentiment is of almost as much importance as talents and acquirements, while it is even more influential in giving the direction to a man's tastes and character. Sympathy is the golden key that unlocks the hearts of others. It not only teaches politeness and courtesy, but gives insight and unfolds wisdom, and may almost be regarded as the crowning grace of humanity.

Artificial rules of politeness are of very little use. What passes by the name of "Etiquette" is often of the essence of unpoliteness and untruthfulness. It consists in a great measure of posture-making, and is easily seen through. Even at best, etiquette is but a substitute for good manners, though it is often but their mere counterfeit.

Good manners consist, for the most part, in courteousness and kindness. Politeness has been described as the art of showing, by external signs, the internal regard we have for others. But one may be perfectly polite to another without necessarily paying a special regard for him. Good manners are neither more nor less than beautiful behavior. It has been well said that "a beautiful form is better than a beautiful face, and a beautiful behavior is better than a beautiful form; it give a higher pleasure than statues or pictures—it is the finest of the fine arts."

The truest politeness comes of sincerity It must be the outcome of the heart, or it will make no lasting impression; for no amount of polish can dispense with truthfulness. The natural character must be allowed to appear, freed of its angularities and asperities. Though politeness, in its best form, should resemble water—"best when clearest, most simple, and without taste"—yet genius in a man will always cover many defects of manner, and much will be excused to the strong and the original. Without genuineness and individuality, human life would lose much of its interest and variety, as well as its manliness and robustness of character.

True politeness especially exhibits itself in regard for the personality of others. A man will respect the individuality of another if he wishes to be respected himself. He will have due regards for his views and opinions, even though they differ from his own. The well-mannered man pays a compliment to another, and sometimes even secures his respect by patiently listening to him. He is simply tolerant and forbearant, and refrains from judging harshly; and harsh judgment of others will almost invariably provoke harsh judgments of ourselves.

The impolite, impulsive man will, however, sometimes rather lose his friend than his joke. He may surely be pronounced a very foolish person who secures another's hatred at the price of a moment's gratification. It was a saying of Burnel, the engineer—himself one of the kindest-natured of men—that "spite and ill-nature are among the most expensive luxuries in life." Dr. Johnson once said: "Sir, a man has no more right to *say* an uncivil thing than to *do* one—no more right to say a rude thing to another than to knock him down."

Want of respect for the feelings of others usually originates in selfishness, and issues in hardness and repulsiveness of manner. It may not proceed from malignity so much as from want of sympathy and want of delicacy—a want of that perception of, and attention to, those little and apparently trifling things by which pleasure is given or pain occasioned to others. Indeed, it may be said that in self-sacrifice in the ordinary intercourse of life, mainly consists the difference between being well and ill bred. Without some degree of self-restraint in society a man may be found almost insufferable. No one has pleasure in holding intercourse with such a person, and he is a constant source of annoyance to those about him. For want of self-restraint many men are engaged all their lives in fighting with difficulties of their own making, and rendering success impossible by their own cross-grained rudeness, while others, much less gifted, make their way and achieve success by simple patience, equanimity and self-control.

It has been said that men succeed in life quite as much by their temper as by their talents. However this may be, it is certain that their happiness depends mainly on their temperament, especially upon their disposition to be cheerful; upon their complaisance, kindliness of manner, and willingness to oblige others—details of conduct which are like the small-change in the intercourse of life, and are always in request.

Men may show their disregard of others in various impolite ways, as, for instance, by neglect of propriety in dress, by the absence of cleanliness, or by indulging in repulsive habits. The slovenly, dirty person, by rendering himself physically disagreeable, sets the tastes and feelings of others at defiance, and is rude and uncivil, only under another form.

The perfection of manner is ease—that it attracts no man's notice as such, but is natural and unaffected. Artifice is incompatible with courteous frankness of manner. Rochefoucauld has said that "nothing so much prevents our being natural as the desire of appearing so." Thus we come round again to sincerity and truthfulness, which find their outward expression in graciousness, urbanity, kindliness and consideration for the feelings of others. The frank and cordial man sets those about him at their ease. He warms and elevates them by his presence, and wins all hearts. Thus manner, in its highest form, like character, becomes a genuine motive power.

"The love and admiration," says Canon Kingsley, "which that truly brave and loving man, Sir Sidney Smith won from everyone, rich and poor, with whom he came in contact, seems to have arisen from the one fact that, without, perhaps, having any such conscious intention, he treated rich and poor, his own servants and the noblemen his guests, alike courteously, considerately, cheerfully, affectionately—so leaving a blessing, and reaping a blessing wherever he went."

Men who toil with their hands, equally with those who do not, may respect themselves and respect one another; and it is by their demeanor to each other—in other words, by their manners—that self-respect as well as mutual respect are indicated. There is scarcely a moment in their lives the enjoyment of which might not be enhanced by kindliness of this sort—in the workshop, in the street, or at home. The civil workman will exercise increased power among his class, and gradually induce them to imitate him by his persistent steadiness, civility and kindness. One may be polite and gentle with very little money in his purse. Politeness goes far, yet costs nothing. It is the cheapest of all commodities. It is the humblest of the fine arts, yet it is so useful and pleasure-giving that it might almost be ranked among the humanities.

The French and Germans, of even the humblest classes, are gracious in manner, complaisant, cordial, and well-bred. The foreign workman lifts his cap and respectfully salutes his fellow-workman in passing. There is no sacrifice of manliness in this, but grace and dignity. Even the lowest poverty of the foreign work-people is not misery, simply because it is cheerful.

Good taste is a true economist. It may be practiced on small means, and sweeten the lot of labor as well as of ease. It is all the more enjoyed, indeed, when associated with industry and the performance of duty. Even the lot of poverty is elevated by taste. It exhibits itself in the economies of the household. It gives brightness and grace to the humblest dwelling. It produces refinement, it engenders good-will, and creates an atmosphere of cheerfulness. Thus good taste, associated with kindliness, sympathy, and intelligence, may elevate and adorn even the lowliest lot.

The first and best school of manners, as of character, is always the Home, where woman is the teacher. The manners of society at large are but the reflex of the manners of our collective homes, neither better nor worse. Yet, with all the disadvantages of ungenial homes, men may practice self-culture of manner as of intellect, and learn by good examples to cultivate a graceful and agreeable behavior towards others. Most men are like so many gems in the rough, which need polishing by contact with other and better natures, to bring out their full beauty and lustre. Some have but one side polished, sufficient only to show the delicate graining of the interior; but to bring out the full qualities of the gem needs the discipline of experience, and contact with the best examples of character in the intercourse of daily life.

A good deal of the success of manner consists in tact; and it is because women, on the whole, have greater tact than men, that they prove the most influential teachers. They have more self-restraint than men, and are naturally more gracious and polite. They possess an intuitive quickness and readiness of action, have a keener insight into character, and exhibit greater discrimination and address. In matters of social detail aptness and dexterity come to them like nature; and hence well-mannered men usually receive their best culture by mixing in the society of gentle and adroit women.

Tact is an intuitive art of manner, which carries one through a difficulty better than either talent or knowledge. "Talent," says a public writer, "is power; tact is skill. Talent is weight; tact is momentum. Talent knows what to do; tact knows how to do it. Talent makes a man respectable; tact makes him respected. Talent is wealth; tact is ready-money." "At a gathering in Australia not long since, four persons met, three of them were shepherds on a sheep-farm; one of these had taken a degree at Oxford, another at Cambridge, the third at a German University. The fourth was their employer, a squatter, rich in flocks and herds, but scarcely able to read or write, much less to keep accounts."

The difference between a man of quick tact and of no tact whatever was exemplified in an interview which once took place between Lord Palmerston and Mr. Behnes, the sculptor. At the last sitting which Lord Palmerston gave him, Behnes opened the conversation with—"Any news, my lord, from France? How do we stand with Louis Napoleon?" The Foreign Secretary raised his eyebrows for an instant, and quickly replied, "Really Mr. Behnes, I don't know; I have not seen the newspapers!" Poor Behnes, with many excellent qualities and much real talent, was one of the many men who entirely missed their way in life through want of tact.

Such is the power of manner, combined with tact, that Wilkes, one of the ugliest of men, used to say that, in winning the graces of a lady, there was not more than three days' difference between him and the handsomest man in England. But this reference to Wilkes reminds us that too much importance must not be attached to manner, for it does not afford any genuine test of character. The well-mannered man may, like Wilkes, be merely acting a part, and that for an immoral purpose. Manner, like other fine arts, gives pleasure, and is exceedingly agreeable to look upon; but it may be assumed as a disguise, as men "assume a virtue though they have it not." It is but the exterior sign of good conduct, but may be no more than skin-deep. The most highly-polished person may be thoroughly depraved in heart; and his superfine manners may, after all, only consist in pleasing gestures and in fine phrases. On the other hand, it must be acknowledged that some of the richest and most generous natures have been wanting in the graces of courtesy and politeness. As a rough rind sometimes covers the sweetest fruit, so a rough exterior often conceals a kindly and hearty nature. The blunt man may seem even rude in manner, and yet at heart be honest, kind, and gentle.

John Knox and Martin Luther were by no means distinguished for their urbanity. They had work to do which needed strong and determined rather than well-mannered men. Indeed, they were both thought to be unnecessarily harsh and violent in their manner. "And who art thou," said Mary Queen of Scots to Knox, "that presumest to school the nobles and sovereign of this realm?" "Madam," replied Knox, "a subject born within the same." It is said that his boldness, or roughness, more than once made Queen Mary weep. When Regent Morton heard of this, he said, "Well, 'tis better that women should weep than bearded men." As Knox was retiring from the Queen's presence on one occasion he overheard one of the royal attendants say to another, "He is not afraid!" Turning round upon them, he said: "And why should the pleasing face of a gentleman frighten me? I have looked on the faces of angry men, and yet have not been afraid beyond measure." When the Reformer, worn out by excess of labor and anxiety, was at length laid to his rest, the regent, looking down into the open grave, exclaimed, in words which made a strong impression from their aptness and truth— "There lies he who never feared the face of man!"

Luther also was thought by some to be a mere compound of violence and ruggedness. But, as in the case of Knox, the times in which he lived were rude and violent, and the work he had to do could scarcely have been accomplished with gentleness and suavity. To rouse Europe from its lethargy, he had to speak and to write with force, and even vehemence. Yet Luther's vehemence was only in words. His apparently rude exterior covered a warm heart. In private life he was gentle, loving, and affectionate. He was simple and homely, even to commonness. Fond of all common pleasures and enjoyments, he was any thing but an austere man or a bigot; for he was hearty, genial, and even "jolly." Luther was the common people's hero in his lifetime, and he remains so in Germany to this day.

Samuel Johnson was rude and often gruff in manner. But he had been brought up in a rough school. Poverty in early life had made him acquainted with strange companions. He had wandered in the streets with Savage for nights together, unable between them to raise money enough to pay for a bed. When his indomitable courage and industry at length secured for him a footing in society, he still bore upon him the scars of his early sorrows and struggles. He was by nature strong and robust, and his experience made him unaccommodating and self-asserting. When he was once asked why he was not invited to dine out as Garrick was, he answered, "Because great lords and ladies did not like to have their mouths stopped"; and Johnson was a notorious mouth-stopper, though what he said was always worth listening to.

Johnson's companion spoke of him as "Ursa Major"; but, as Goldsmith generously said of him, "No man alive has a more tender heart; he has nothing of the bear about him but his skin." The kindliness of Johnson's nature was shown on one occasion by the manner in which he assisted a supposed lady in crossing Fleet Street. He gave her his arm and led her across, not observing that she was in liquor at the time. But the spirit of the act was not the less kind on that account. On the other hand, the conduct of the bookseller on whom Johnson once called to solicit employment, and who, regarding his athletic but uncouth person, told him he had better "go buy a porter's knot and carry trunks," in howsoever bland tones the advice might have been communicated, was simply brutal.

While captiousness of manner, and the habit of disputing and contradicting every thing said, is chilling and repulsive, the opposite habit of assenting to, and sympathizing with, every statement made, or emotion expressed, is almost equally disagreeable. It is unmanly, and is felt to be dishonest. "It may seem difficult," says Richard Sharp, "to steer always between bluntness and plain dealing, between giving merited praise and lavishing indiscriminate flattery; but it is very easy—good humor, kind-heartedness and perfect simplicity, being all that are requisite to do what is right in the right way."

At the same time many are impolite, not because they mean to be so, but because they are awkward, and perhaps know no better. Thus, when Gibbon had published the second and third volumes of his "Decline and Fall," the Duke of Cumberland met him one day, and accosted him with, "How do you do, Mr. Gibbon? I see you are always *at it* in the old *way—scribble, scribble, scribble!*" The duke probably intended to pay the author a compliment but did not know how better to do it than in this blunt and apparently rude way.

Again, many persons are thought to be stiff, reserved, and proud, when they are only shy. Shyness is characteristic of most people of Teutonic race. From all that can be learned of Shakespeare, it is to be inferred that he was an exceedingly shy man. The manner in which his plays were sent into the world—for it is not known that he edited or authorized the publication of a single one of them—and the dates at which they respectively appeared, are mere matters of conjecture. His appearance in his own plays in second and even third-rate parts, his indifference to reputation, and even his apparent aversion to be held in repute by his contemporaries, his disappearance from London (the seat and centre of histrionic art) so soon as he had realized a moderate competency, and his retirement about the age of forty, for the remainder of his days, to a life of obscurity in a small town in the midland counties, all seem to unite in proving the shrinking nature of the man, and his unconquerable shyness.

But a still more recent and striking instance is that of the late Archbishop Whately, who, in the early part of his life, was painfully oppressed by the sense of shyness. When at Oxford, his white, rough coat and white hat obtained for him the sobriquet of "The White Bear"; and his manners, according to his own account of himself; corresponded with the appellation. He was directed, by way of remedy, to copy the example of the best-mannered men he met in society; but the attempt to do this only increased his shyness, and he failed. He found that he was all the while thinking of himself, rather than of others; whereas thinking of others, rather than of one's self, is the true essence of politeness. Finding that he was making no progress, Whately was driven to utter despair; and then he said to himself; "Why should I endure this torture all my life to no purpose? I would bear it still if there was any success to be hoped for; but since there is not, I will die quietly, without taking any more doses. I have tried my very utmost, and find that I must be as awkward as a bear all my life, in spite of it. I will endeavor to think as little about it as a bear, and make up my mind to endure what can't be cured." From this time forth he struggled to shake off all consciousness as to manner, and to disregard censure as much as possible. In adopting this course, he says: "I succeeded beyond my expectations; for I not only got rid of the personal suffering of shyness, but also of most of those faults of manner which consciousness produces; and acquired at once an easy and natural manner—careless, indeed, in the extreme, from its originating in a stern defiance of opinion, which I had convinced myself must be ever against me; but unconscious, and therefore giving expression to that good-will towards men which I really feel; and these, I believe, are the main points."

Washington, who was an Englishman in his lineage, was also one in his shyness. He is described incidentally by Mr. Josiah Quincy as "a little stiff in his person, not a little formal in his manner, and not particularly at ease in the presence of strangers. He had the air of a country gentleman not accustomed to mix much in society, perfectly polite, but not easy in address and conversation, and not graceful in his movements."

True politeness is best evinced by self-forgetfulness or self-denial in the interest of others. Mr. Garfield, our martyred president, was a gentleman of royal type. His friend, Col. Rockwell, says of him: "In the midst of his suffering he never forgets others. For instance, today he said to me, 'Rockwell, there is a poor soldier's widow who came to me before this thing occurred, and I promised her she should be provided for. I want you to see that the matter is attended to at once.' He is the most docile patient I ever saw."

Although we are not accustomed to think of modern Americans as shy, the most distinguished American author of our time was probably the shyest of men. Nathaniel Hawthorne was shy to the extent of morbidity. We have observed him, when a stranger entered the room where he was, turn his back for the purpose of avoiding recognition. And yet, when the crust of his shyness was broken, no man could be more cordial and genial than Hawthorne. We observe a remark in one of Hawthorne's lately published "Note-books," that on one occasion he met Mr. Helps in society, and found him "cold." And doubtless Mr. Helps thought the same of him. It was only the case of two shy men meeting, each thinking the other stiff and reserved, and parting before their mutual film of shyness had been removed by a little friendly intercourse.

We have thus far spoken of shyness as a defect. But there is another way of looking at it; for even shyness has its bright side, and contains an element of good. Shy men and shy races are ungraceful and undemonstrative, because, as regards society at large, they are comparatively unsociable. They do not possess those elegances of manner acquired by tree intercourse, which distinguish the social races, because their tendency is to shun society rather than to seek it. They are shy in the presence of strangers, and shy even in their own families. They hide their affections under a robe of reserve, and when they do give way to their feelings, it is only in some very hidden inner chamber. And yet the feelings *are* there, and not the less healthy and genuine that they are not made the subject of exhibition to others.

It was not a little characteristic of the ancient Germans that the more social and demonstrative peoples by whom they were surrounded should have characterized them as the dumb men. And the same designation might equally apply to the modern English, as compared, for example, with their nimbler, more communicative and vocal, and in all respects, more social neighbors, the modern French and Irish. But there is one characteristic which marks the English people, as it did the races from which they have mainly sprung, and that is their intense love of home. Give the Englishman a home, and he is comparatively indifferent to society. For the sake of a holding which he can call his own, he will cross the sea, plant himself on the prairie or amidst the primeval forest, and make for himself a home. The solitude of the wilderness has no fears for him; the society of his wife and family is sufficient, and he cares for no other. Hence it is that the people of Germanic origin, from whom the English and Americans have alike sprung, make the best of colonizers, and are now rapidly extending themselves as emigrants and settlers in all parts of the habitable globe.

To remedy this admitted defect of grace and want of artistic taste in the English people, a school has sprung up among us for the more general diffusion of fine art. The Beautiful has now its teachers and preachers, and by some it is almost regarded in the light of a religion. "The Beautiful is the Good"—"The Beautiful is the True"—"The Beautiful is the priest of the Benevolent," are among their texts. It is believed that by the study of art, the tastes of the people may be improved; that by contemplating objects of beauty their nature will become purified; and that by being thereby withdrawn from sensual enjoyments, their character will be refined and elevated.

But though such culture is calculated to be elevating and purifying in a certain degree, we must not expect too much from it. Grace is a sweetener and embellisher of life, and as such is worthy of cultivation. Music, painting, dancing, and the fine arts, are all sources of pleasure; and though they may not be sensual, yet they are sensuous, and often nothing more. The cultivation of a taste for beauty of form or color, of sound or attitude, has no necessary effect upon the cultivation of the mind or the development of the character. The contemplation of fine works of art will doubtless improve the taste and excite admiration; but a single noble action done in the sight of men will more influence the mind, and stimulate the character to imitation, than the sight of miles of statuary or acres of pictures. For it is mind, soul, and heart—not taste or art-that make men great.

Art has usually flourished most during the decadence of nations, when it has been hired by wealth as the minister of luxury. Exquisite art and degrading corruption were contemporary in Greece as well as in Rome. Phidias and Iktinos had scarcely completed the Parthenon when the glory of Athens had departed; Phidias died in prison; and the Spartans set up in the city the memorials of their own triumph and of Athenian defeat. It was the same in ancient Rome, where art was at its greatest height when the people were in their most degraded condition. Nero was an artist as well as Domitian, two of the greatest monsters of the Empire. If the "Beautiful" had been the "Good," Commodus must have been one of the best of men. But according to history he was one of the worst.

Again, the greatest period of modern Roman art was that in which Pope Leo X flourished, of whose reign it has been said that "profligacy and licentiousness prevailed among the people and clergy, as they had done almost uncontrolled ever since the pontificate of Alexander VI." In like manner, the period at which art reached its highest point in the Low Countries was that which immediately succeeded the destruction of civil and religious liberty, and the prostration of the national character under the despotism of Spain. If art could elevate a nation, and the contemplation of The Beautiful were calculated to make men good—then Paris ought to contain a population of the wisest and best of human beings. Rome also is a great city of art, and yet there the virtues or valor of the ancient Romans has characteristically degenerated into *virtu,* or a taste for knickknacks; while, according to recent accounts, the city itself is inexpressibly foul.

Art would even sometimes appear to have a connection with dirt; and it is said of Mr. Ruskin that, when searching for works of art in Venice, his attendant in his explorations would sniff an ill-odor, and when it was strong, would say, "Now we are coming to something very old and fine,"—meaning in art. A little common education in cleanliness, where it is wanting, would probably be much more improving, as well as wholesome, than any amount of education in fine art. Ruffles are all very well, but it is folly to cultivate them to the neglect of the shirt.

While, therefore, grace of manner, politeness of behavior, elegance of demeanor, and all the arts that contribute to make life pleasant and beautiful, are worthy of cultivation, it must not be at the expense of the more solid and enduring qualities of honesty, sincerity, and truthfulness. The fountain of beauty must be in the heart more than in the eye, and if it do not tend to produce beautiful life and noble practice, it will prove of comparatively little avail. Politeness of manner is not worth much unless it is accompanied by polite actions. Grace may be but skin-deep—very pleasant and attractive, and yet very heartless. Art may be a source of innocent enjoyment, and an important aid to higher culture; but unless it leads to higher culture, it may be merely sensuous. And when art is merely sensuous, it is enfeebling and demoralizing rather than strengthening or elevating. Honest courage is of greater worth than any amount of grace; purity is better than elegance; and cleanliness of body, mind, and heart, than any amount of fine art.

While the cultivation of the graces is not to be neglected, it should never be forgotten that there is something far higher and nobler to be aimed at—greater than pleasure, greater than art, greater than wealth, greater than power, greater than intellect, greater than genius; and that is purity and excellence of character. Without a solid, sterling basis of individual goodness, all the grace, elegance, and art in the world would fail to save or elevate a people.

Chapter 23

Companionship of Books

*"Books, we know,
Are a substantial world, both pure and good,
Round which, with tendrils strong as flesh and blood,
Our pastime and our happiness can grow."
—Wordsworth.*

"Not only in the common speech of men, but in all art too—which is should be the concentrated and conserved essence of what men can speak and show—Biography is almost the one thing needful." —Carlyle.

A MAN MAY USUALLY BE KNOWN by the books he reads, as well as by the company he keeps; for there is a companionship of books as well as of men; and one should always live in the best company, whether it be or books or of men.

A good book may be among the best of friends. It is the same today as it always was, and it will never change. It is the most patient and cheerful of companions. It does not turn its back upon us in times of adversity or distress. It always receives us with the same kindness; amusing and instructing us in youth, and comforting and consoling us in age.

Men often discover their affinity to each other by the mutual love they have for a book—just as two persons sometimes discover a friend by the admiration which both entertain for a third. There is an old proverb, "Love me, love my dog." But there is more wisdom in this: "Love me, love my book." The book is a truer and higher bond of union. Men can think, feel and sympathize with each other through their favorite author. "Books," said Hazlitt, "wind into the heart; the poet's verse slides into the current of our blood. We read them when young, we remember them when old. We read there of what has happened to others; we feel that it has happened to ourselves.

They are to be had everywhere cheap and good. We breathe but the air of books. We owe everything to their authors, on this side barbarism."

A good book is often the best urn of a life, enshrining the best thoughts of which that life was capable; for the world of a man's life is, for the most part, but the world of his thoughts. Thus the best books are treasuries of good words and golden thoughts, which, remembered and cherished, become our abiding companions and comforters. "They are never alone," said Sir Philip Sidney, "that are accompanied by noble thoughts." The good and true thought may in time of temptation be as an angel of mercy purifying and guarding the soul. It also enshrines the germs of action, for good words almost invariably inspire to good works. Thus Sir Henry Lawrence prized above all other compositions Wordsworth's "Character of the Happy Warrior," which he endeavored to embody in his own life. It was ever before him as an exemplar. He thought of it continually, and often quoted it to others. His biographer says: "He tried to conform his own life and to assimilate his own character to it; and he succeeded, as all men succeed who are truly in earnest."

Books possess an essence of immortality. They are by far the most lasting products of human effort. Temples crumble into ruin, pictures and statues decay, but books survive. Time is of no account with great thoughts, which are as fresh today as when they first passed through their author's minds, ages ago. What was then said and thought still speaks to us as vividly as ever from the printed page. The only effect of time has been to sift and winnow out the bad products, for nothing in literature can long survive but what is really good.

Books introduce us into the best society; they bring us into the presence of the greatest minds that have ever lived. We hear what they said and did; we see them as if they were really alive; we are participators in their thoughts; we sympathize with them, enjoy with them, grieve with them; their experience becomes ours, and we feel as if we were in a measure actors with them in the scenes which they describe.

Great is the human interest felt in biography. What are all the novels that find such multitudes of readers, but so many fictitious biographies? What are the dramas that people crowd to see, but so much acted biography? Strange that the highest genius should be employed on the fictitious biography, and so much commonplace ability on the real! Yet the authentic picture of any-human being's life and experience ought to possess an interest greatly beyond that which is fictitious, inasmuch as it has the charm of reality. Every person may learn something from the recorded life of another; and even comparatively trivial deeds and sayings may be invested with interest, as being the outcome of the lives of such beings as we ourselves are. The records of the lives of good men are especially useful. They influence our hearts, inspire us with hope, and set before us great examples. And when men have done their duty through life in a great spirit, their influence will never wholly pass away. "The good life," says George Herbert, "is never out of season."

Goethe has said that there is no man so commonplace that a wise man may not learn something from him. Sir Walter Scott could not travel in a coach without gleaning some information or discovering some new trait of character in his companions. Dr. Johnson once observed that there was not a person in the streets but he should like to know his biography—his experience of life, his trials, his difficulties, his successes and his failures. How much more truly might this be said of the men who have made their mark in the world's history, and have created for us that great inheritance of civilization of which we are the possessors! Whatever relates to such men—to their habits, their manners, their modes of living, their personal history, their conversation, their maxims, their virtues, or their greatness—is always full of interest, of instruction, of encouragement, and of example.

The great lesson of Biography is to show what man can be and do at his best. A noble life put fairly on record acts like an inspiration to others. It exhibits what life is capable of being made. It refreshes our spirit, encourages our hopes, gives us new strength and courage and faith—faith in others as well as in ourselves. It stimulates our aspirations, rouses us to action, and incites us to become co-partners with them in their work. To live with such men in their biographies, and to be inspired by their example, is to live with the best of men and to mix in the best of company.

History itself is best studied in biography. Indeed, history is biography—collective humanity as influenced and governed by individual men. "What is all history," says Emerson, "but the work of ideas, a record of the incomparable energy which his infinite aspirations infuse into man?" In its pages it is always persons we see more than principles. Historical events are interesting to us mainly in connection with the feelings, the sufferings, and interests of those by whom they are accomplished. In history we are surrounded by men long dead, but whose speech and whose deeds survive. We almost catch the sound of their voices; and what they did constitutes the interest of history. We never feel personally interested in masses of men; but we feel and sympathize with the individual actors, whose biographies afford the finest and most real touches in all great historical dramas.

Among the great writers of the past, probably the two that have been most influential in forming the characters of great men of action and great men of thought have been Plutarch and Montaigne—the one by presenting heroic models for imitation, the other by probing questions of constant recurrence in which the human mind in all ages has taken the deepest interest. And the works of both are, for the most part, cast in a biographic form, their most striking illustrations consisting in the exhibitions of character and experience which they contain. Plutarch's "Lives," though written nearly eighteen hundred years ago, like Homer, still holds its ground as the greatest work of its kind. It was the favorite book of Montaigne; and to Englishmen it possesses the special interest of having been Shakespeare's principal authority in his great classical dramas. Montaigne pronounced Plutarch to be "the greatest master in that kind of writing"—the biographic; and he declared that he "could no sooner cast an eye upon him but he purloined either a leg or a wing."

Alfieri was first drawn with passion to literature by reading Plutarch. "I read," said he "the lives of Timoleon, Caesar, Brutus, Pelopidas, more than six times, with cries, with tears, and with such transports that I was almost furious. Every time that I met with one of the grand traits of these great men I was seized with such vehement agitation as to be unable to sit still." Plutarch was also a favorite with persons of such various minds as Schiller and Benjamin Franklin, Napoleon and Madam Roland. The latter was so fascinated by the book that she carried it to church with her, and read it surreptitiously during the service.

It has also been the nurture of heroic souls. It was one of Sir William Napier's favorite books when a boy. His mind was early imbued by it with a passionate admiration for the great heroes of antiquity; and its influence had, doubtless, much to do with the formation of his character, as well as the direction of his career in life. It is related of him, that in his last illness, when feeble and exhausted, his mind wandered back to Plutarch's heroes; and he descanted for hours to his son-in-law on the mighty deeds of Alexander, Hannibal, and Caesar. Indeed, if it were possible to poll the great body of readers in all ages whose minds have been influenced and directed by books, it is probable that—excepting the Bible—the immense majority of votes would be cast in favor of Plutarch.

While the best and most carefully-drawn of Plutarch's portraits are of life-size, many of them are little more than busts. They are well-proportioned but compact, and within such reasonable compass that the best of them may be read in half an hour. Reduced to this measure, they are, however, greatly more imposing than a lifeless Colossus or an exaggerated giant. They are not overlaid by disquisition and description, but the characters naturally unfold themselves. Montaigne, indeed, complained of Plutarch's brevity. "No doubt," he added, "but his reputation is the better for it, though in the mean time we are the worse. Plutarch would rather we should applaud his judgment than commend his knowledge, and had rather leave us with an appetite to read more than glutted with what we have already read. He knew very well that a man may say too much even on the best subjects. Such as have lean and spare bodies stuff themselves out with clothes; so they who are defective in matter endeavor to make amends with words."

Plutarch possessed the art of delineating the more delicate features of mind and minute peculiarities of conduct, as well as the foibles and defects of his heroes, all of which is necessary to faithful and accurate portraiture. "To see him," says Montaigne, "pick out a light action in a man's life, or a word, that does not seem to be of any importance, is itself a whole discourse." He even condescends to inform us of such homely particulars as that Alexander carried his head affectedly on one side; that Alcibiades was a dandy, and had a lisp, which became him, giving a grace and persuasive turn to his discourse; that Cato had red hair and gray eyes, and was a usurer and a screw, selling off his old slaves when they became unfit for hard work; that Caesar was bald and fond of gay dress; and that Cicero had involuntary twitching of his nose.

Such minute particulars may by some be thought beneath the dignity of biography, but Plutarch thought them requisite for the due finish of the complete portrait which he set himself to draw; and it is by small details of character—personal traits, features, habits, and characteristics—that we are enabled to see before us the men as they really lived. Plutarch's great merit consists in his attention to these little things, without giving them undue preponderance, or neglecting those which are of greater moment. Sometimes he hits off an individual trait by an anecdote, which throws more light upon the character described than pages of rhetorical description would do. In some cases he gives us the favorite maxim of his hero; and the maxims of men often reveal their hearts. Then, as to foibles, the greatest of men are not unusually symmetrical. Each has his defect, his twist, his craze; and it is by his faults that the great man reveals his common humanity. We may, at a distance, admire him as a demigod; but as we come nearer to him, we find that he is but a fallible man, and our brother.

Nor are the illustrations of the defects of great men without their uses; for, as Dr. Johnson observed, "If nothing but the bright side of characters were shown, we would sit down in despondency, and think it utterly impossible to imitate them in anything." Plutarch himself justifies his method of portraiture by averring that his design was not to write histories, but lives. "The most glorious exploits," he says, "do not always furnish us with the clearest discoveries of virtue or of vice in men. Sometimes a matter of much less moment, an expression or a jest, better informs us of their characters and inclinations than battles with the slaughter of tens of thousands, and the greater arrays of armies or sieges of cities. Therefore, as portrait-painters are more exact in their lines and features of the face and the expression of the eyes, in which the character is seen, without troubling themselves about the other parts of the body, so I must be allowed to give my more particular attention to the signs and indications of the souls of men; and while I endeavor by these means to portray their lives, I leave important events and great battles to be described by Others."

Things apparently trifling may stand for reach in biography as well as history, and slight circumstances may influence great results. Pascal has remarked that if Cleopatra's nose had been shorter, the whole face of the world would probably have been changed. But for the amours of Pepin the Fat, the Saracens might have overrun Europe, as it was his illegitimate son, Charles Martel, who overthrew them at Tours, and eventually drove them out of France.

That Sir Walter Scott should have sprained his foot in running round the room when a child, may seem unworthy of notice in his biography; yet, "Ivanhoe," "Old Mortality," and all the Waverly novels depended upon it. When his son intimated a desire to enter the army, Scott wrote to Southey, "I have no title to combat a choice which would have been my own, had not my lameness prevented." So that, had not Scott been lame, he might have fought all through the Peninsular War, and had his breast covered with medals; but we should probably have had none of those works of his which have made his name immortal and shed so much glory upon his country. Talleyrand also was kept out of the army, for which he had been destined, by his lameness; but directing his attention to the study of books, and eventually of men, he at length took rank among the greatest diplomatists of his time. Byron's club-foot had probably not a little to do with determining his destiny as a poet. Had not his mind been embittered and made morbid by his deformity, he might never have written a line—he might have been the noblest fop of his day. But his misshapen foot stimulated his mind, roused his ardor, threw him upon his own resources—and we know with what result. So, too, of Scarron, to whose hunchback we probably owe his cynical verse; and of Pope, whose satire was in a measure the outcome of his deformity—for he was, as Johnson described him, "protuberant behind and before." As in portraiture, so in biography—there must be light and shade. The portrait painter does not pose his sitter so as to bring out his deformities; nor does the biographer give undue prominence to the defects of the character he portrays. Not many men are so outspoken as Cromwell was when he sat to Cooper for his miniature: "Paint me as I am," said he, "warts and all." Yet, if we would have a faithful likeness of faces and characters, they must be painted as they are. "Biography," said Sir Walter Scott, "the most interesting of every species of composition, loses all its interest with me when the shades and lights of the principal characters are not accurately and faithfully detailed. I can no more sympathize with a mere eulogist than I can with a ranting hero on the stage."

While books are among the best companions of old age, they are often the best inspirers of youth. The first book that makes a deep impression on a young man's mind often constitutes an epoch in his life. It may fire the heart, stimulate the enthusiasm, and, by directing his efforts into unexpected channels, permanently influence his character. The new book, in which we form an intimacy with a new friend, whose mind is wiser and riper than our own, may thus form an important starting-point in the history of life. It may sometimes almost be regarded in the light of a new birth.

Good books are among the best of companions, and; by elevating the thoughts and aspirations, they act as preservatives against low associations. "A natural turn for reading and intellectual pursuits," says Thomas Hood, "probably preserved me from the moral shipwreck so apt to befall those who are deprived in early life of their parental pilotage. My books kept me from the ring, the dog-pit, the tavern, the saloon. The closest associate of Pope and Addison, the mind accustomed to the noble though silent discourse of Shakespeare and Milton, will hardly seek or put up with low company and slaves."

It has been truly said that the best books are those which most resemble good actions. They are purifying, elevating, and sustaining; they enlarge and liberalize the mind; they preserve it against vulgar worldliness; they tend to produce high-minded cheerfulness and equanimity of character; they fashion and shape, and humanize the mind.

Erasmus, the great scholar, was even of opinion that books were the necessaries of life, and clothes the luxuries; and he frequently postponed buying the latter until he had supplied himself with the former. His greatest favorites were the writings of Cicero, which he says he always felt himself the better for reading. "I can never," he says, "read the works of Cicero on 'Old Age,' or 'Friendship,' without fervently pressing them to my lips, without being penetrated with veneration for a mind little short of inspired by God himself." It was the accidental perusal of Cicero's "Hortensius" which first detached St. Augustine—until then a profligate and abandoned sensualist—from his immoral life, and started him upon the course of inquiry and study which led to his becoming the greatest among the Fathers of the Early Church. Sir William Jones made it a practice to read through, once a year, the writings of Cicero, "whose life, indeed," says his biographer, "was the great exemplar of his own."

When the good old Puritan Baxter came to enumerate the valuable and delightful things of which death would deprive him, his mind reverted to the pleasures he had derived from books and study. "When I die," he said, "I must depart, not only from sensual delights, but from the more manly pleasures of my studies, knowledge, and converse with many wise and godly men, must leave my library, and turn over those pleasant books no more."

Chapter 24

Companionship in Marriage

"Kindness in women, not their beauteous looks, Shall win my love."
—*Shakespeare.*

THE CHARACTER OF MEN, as of women, is powerfully influenced by their companionship in all the stages of life. We have already spoken of the influence of the mother in forming the character of her children. She makes the moral atmosphere in which they live, and by which their minds and souls are nourished, as their bodies are by the physical atmosphere they breathe. And while woman is the natural cherisher of infancy and the instructor of childhood, she is also the guide and counsellor of youth, and the confidant and companion of manhood, in her various relations of mother, sister, lover and wife. In short, the influence of woman more or less affects, for-good or for evil, the entire destinies of man. The respective social functions and duties of men and women are clearly defined by nature. God created man *and* woman, each to do their proper work, each to fill their proper sphere. Neither can occupy the position, nor perform the functions of the other. Their several vocations are perfectly distinct.

Though companions and equals, yet, as regards the measure of their powers, they are unequal. Man is stronger, more muscular, and of rougher fiber; woman is more delicate, sensitive and nervous. The one excels in power of brain, the other in qualities of heart; and though the head may rule, it is the heart that influences. Both are alike adapted for the respective functions they have to perform in life, and to attempt to impose woman's work upon man would be quite as absurd as to attempt to impose man's work upon woman.

Although man's qualities belong more to the head, and woman's more to the heart, yet it is not less necessary that man's heart should be cultivated as well as his head, and woman's head cultivated as well as her heart. A heartless man is as much out of keeping in civilized society as a stupid and unintelligent woman. The cultivation of all parts of the moral and intellectual nature is requisite to form the man or woman of healthy and well-balanced character. Without sympathy or consideration for others, man were a poor, stunted, sordid, selfish being; and without cultivated intelligence, the most beautiful woman were little better than a well-dressed doll.

It is too much the practice to cultivate the weakness of woman rather than her strength, and to render her attractive rather than self-reliant. Her sensibilities are developed at the expense of her health of body as well as mind. She lives, moves, and has her being in the sympathy of others. She dresses that she may attract, and is burdened with accomplishments that she may be chosen. Weak, trembling and dependent, she incurs the risk of becoming a living embodiment of the Italian proverb—"so good that she is good for nothing."

On the other hand, the education of young men too often errs on the side of selfishness. While the boy is encouraged to trust mainly to his own efforts in pushing his way in the world, the girl is encouraged to rely almost entirely upon others. He is educated with too exclusive reference to himself and she is educated with exclusive reference to him. He is taught to be self-reliant and self-dependent, while she is taught to be distrustful of herself, dependent, and self-sacrificing in all things. Thus the intellect of the one is cultivated at the expense of the affections, and the affections of the other at the expense of the intellect.

It is unquestionable that the highest qualities of woman are displayed in her relationship to others, through the medium of her affections. She is the nurse whom nature has given to all humankind. She takes charge of the helpless, and nourishes and cherishes those we love. She is the presiding genius of the fireside, where she create s an atmosphere of serenity and contentment suitable for the nurture and growth of character in its best forms. She is by her very constitution compassionate, gentle, patient, and self-denying. Loving, hopeful, trustful, her eye sheds brightness everywhere. It shines upon coldness and warms it, upon suffering and relieves it, upon sorrow and cheers it.

Woman has been styled the angel of the unfortunate. She is ready to help the weak, to raise the fallen, to comfort the suffering. It was characteristic of woman that she should have been the first to build and endow a hospital. It has been said that wherever a human being is suffering his sighs call a woman to his side. When Mungo Park, lonely, friendless, and famished, after being driven forth from an African village by the men, was preparing to spend the night under a tree, exposed to the rain and the wild beasts which there abounded, a poor negro woman, returning from the labors of the field, took compassion upon him, conducted him into her hut, and there gave him food, and succor, and shelter.

The best productions of the poet Goethe, as perhaps of most poets, were inspired by woman's sympathy. Of Fraulein von Klettenburg, Lewes says: "On him her influence was avowedly very great, not only while at Frankfort but subsequently. It was not so much the effect of religious discussion, as the experience it gave him of a deeply religious nature. She was neither bigot nor prude. Her faith was an inner light which shed mild radiance around her." Probably no poet owed more to the benign influence of woman than Goethe. But he was a man who traded in the loves of women—women whom he had attached to him by his powers of fascination. "When he had no woman in his heart," says his latest biographer, "he was like a dissecting surgeon without a subject." He said of Balzac, that each of his best novels seemed dug out of a suffering woman's heart. Balzac might have returned the compliment. In reference to his early fondness for natural history, Goethe says: "I remember that when a child I pulled flowers to pieces to see how the petals were inserted into the calyx, or even plucked birds to observe how the feathers were inserted in their wings." Bettina remarked to Lord Houghton that he treated women in much the same fashion. All his loves, high and low, were subjected to this kind of vivisection. His powers of fascination were extraordinary; and if for the purposes of art, he wanted a display of strong emotion, he deepened the passion without scruple or compunction.

But while the most characteristic qualities of woman are displayed through her sympathies and affections, it is also necessary for her own happiness, as a self-dependent being, to develop and strengthen her character, by due self-culture, self-reliance, and self-control. It is not desirable, even were it possible, to close the beautiful avenues of the heart. Self-reliance of the best kind does not involve any limitation in the range of human sympathy. But the happiness of woman, as of man, depends in a great measure upon her individual completeness of character. And that self-dependence which springs from the due cultivation of the intellectual powers, conjoined with a proper discipline of the heart and conscience, will enable her to be more useful in life as well as happy; to dispense blessings intelligently as well as to enjoy them; and most of all those which spring from mutual dependence and social sympathy.

To maintain a high standard of purity in society, the culture of both sexes must be in harmony, and keep equal pace. A pure womanhood must be accompanied by a pure manhood. The same moral law applies alike to both. It would be loosening the foundations of virtue to countenance the notion that, because of a difference in sex, man were at liberty to set morality at defiance, and to do that with impunity which, if done by a woman, would stain her character for life. To maintain a pure and virtuous condition of society, therefore, man as well as woman must be pure and virtuous; both alike shunning all acts infringing on the heart, character, and conscience—shunning them as poison, which, once imbibed, can never be entirely thrown out again, but mentally embitters, to a greater or less extent, the happiness of after-life.

Although nature spurns all formal rules and directions in affairs of love, it might at all events be possible to implant in young minds such views of character as should enable them to discriminate between the true and the false, and to accustom them to hold in esteem those qualities of moral purity and integrity without which life is but a scene of folly and misery. It may not be possible to teach young people to love wisely, but they may at least be guarded by parental advice against the frivolous and despicable passions which so often usurp its name. "Love," it has been said, "in the common acceptation of the term, is folly; but love, in its purity, its loftiness, its unselfishness, is not only a consequence, but a proof, of our moral excellence. The sensibility to moral beauty, the forgetfulness of self in the admiration engendered by it, all prove its claim to a high moral influence. It is the triumph of the unselfish over the selfish part of our nature."

It is by means of this divine passion that the world is kept ever fresh and young. It is the perpetual melody of humanity. It sheds an effulgence upon youth, and throws a halo round age. It glorifies the present by the light it casts backward, and it lightens the future by the beams it casts forward. The love which is the outcome of esteem and admiration has an elevation and purifying effect on the character. It tends to emancipate one from the slavery of self. It is altogether unsordid; itself is its only price. It inspires gentleness, sympathy, mutual faith, and confidence. True love also, in a measure, elevates the intellect.

"All love renders wise in a degree," says the poet Browning, and the most gifted minds have been the sincerest lovers. Great souls make all affections great; they elevate and consecrate all true delights. The sentiment even brings to light qualities before lying dormant and unsuspected. It elevates the aspirations, expands the soul, and stimulates the mental powers. One of the finest compliments ever paid to a woman was that of Steele, when he said of Lady Elizabeth Hastings, "that to have loved her was a liberal education." Viewed in this light, woman is an educator in the highest sense, because, above all other educators, she educates humanly and lovingly.

It has been said that no man and no woman can be regarded as complete in their experience of life until they have been subdued into a union with the world through their affections. As woman is not woman until she has known love, neither is man man. Both are requisite to each other's completeness. Plato entertained the idea that lovers each sought a likeness in the other, and that love was only the divorced half of the original human being entering into union with its counterpart. But philosophy would here seem to be at fault, for affection quite as often springs from unlikeness as from likeness in its object.

The true union must needs be one of mind as well as of heart, and based on mutual esteem as well as mutual affection. "No true and enduring love," says Fichte, "can exist without esteem; every other draws regret after it, and is unworthy of any noble human soul." One cannot really love the bad, but always something that we esteem and respect as well as admire. In short, true union must rest on qualities of character, which rule in domestic as in public life.

But there is something far more than mere respect and esteem in the union between man and wife. The feeling on which it rests is far deeper and tenderer—such, indeed, as never exists between men or between women. "In matters of affection," says Nathaniel Hawthorne, "there is always an impassable gulf between man and man. They can never quite grasp each other's hands, and therefore man never derives any intimate help, any heart-sustenance, from his brother man, but from woman—his mother, his sister, or his wife."

Man enters a new world of joy, and sympathy, and human interest, through the porch of love. He enters a new world in his home—the home of his own making—altogether different from the home of his boyhood, where each day brings with it a succession of new joys and experiences. He enters also, it may be, a new world of trials arid sorrows, in which he often gathers his best culture and discipline. "Family life," says Sainte-Beuve, "may be full of thorns and cares, but they are fruitful; all others are dry thorns." And again, "If a man's home, at a certain period of his life, does not contain children, it will probably be found filled with follies or with vices."

A life exclusively occupied in affairs of business insensibly tends to narrow and harden the character. It is mainly occupied with self—watching for advantages, and guarding against sharp practice on the part of others. Thus the character unconsciously tends to grow suspicious and ungenerous. The best corrective of such influences is always the domestic—by withdrawing the mind from thoughts that are wholly gainful, by taking it out of its daily rut, and bringing it back to the sanctuary of home for refreshment and rest.

A man's real character will always be more visible in his household than anywhere else; and his practical wisdom will be better exhibited by the manner in which he bears rule there than even in the larger affairs of business or public life, His whole mind may be in his business; but, if he would be happy, his whole heart must be in his home. It is there that his genuine qualities most surely display themselves—there that he shows his truthfulness, his love, his sympathy, his consideration for others, his uprightness, his manliness—in a word, his character. If affection be not the governing principle in a household, domestic life may be the most intolerable of despotisms. Without justice, also, there can be neither love, confidence, nor respect, on which all true domestic rule is founded.

Erasmus speaks of Sir Thomas Moore's home as "a school and exercise of the Christian religion." "No wrangling, no angry word was heard in it; no one was idle; everyone did his duty with alacrity, and not without a temperate cheerfulness." Sir Thomas won all hearts to obedience by his gentleness. He was a man clothed in household goodness; and he ruled so gently and wisely that his home was pervaded by an atmosphere of love and duty. He himself spoke of the hourly interchange of the smaller acts of kindness with the several members of his family, as having a claim upon his time as strong as those other public occupations of his life which seemed to others so much more serious and important.

But the man whose affections are quickened by home-life does not confine his sympathies within that comparatively narrow sphere. His love enlarges in the family, and through the family it expands into the world. "Love," says Emerson, "is a fire that, kindling its first embers in the narrow nook of a private bosom, caught from a wandering spark out of another private heart, glows and enlarges until it warms and beams upon multitudes of men and women, upon the universal heart of all, and so lights up the whole world and nature with its generous flames."

It is by the regimen of domestic affection that the heart of man is best composed and regulated. The home is the woman's kingdom, her state, her world—where she governs by affection, by kindness, by the power of gentleness. There is nothing which so settles the turbulence of a man's nature as his union in life with a high-minded woman. There he finds rest, contentment, and happiness—rest of brain and peace of spirit. He will also often find in her his best counsellor, for her instinctive tact will usually lead him right when his own unaided reason might be apt to go wrong. The true wife is a staff to lean upon in times of trial and difficulty; and she is never wanting in sympathy and solace when distress occurs or fortune frowns. In the time of youth, she is a comfort and an ornament of man's life; and she remains a faithful helpmate in maturer years, when life has ceased to be an anticipation, and we live in its realities.

What a happy man must Edmund Burke have been, when he could say of his home, "Every care vanishes the moment I enter under my own roof!"

And Luther, a man full of human affection, speaking of his wife, said, "I would not exchange my poverty *with* her for all the riches of Croesus *without* her!" Of marriage he observed: "The utmost blessing that God can confer on a man is the possession of a good and pious wife, with whom he may live in peace and tranquility—to whom he may confide his whole possessions, even his life and welfare." And again he said, "To rise betimes, and to marry young, are what no man ever repents of doing."

A woman's best qualities do not reside in her intellect but in her affections. She gives refreshment by her sympathies, rather than by her knowledge. "The brain-women," says Oliver Wendell Holmes, "never interest us like the heart-women." Men are often so wearied with themselves that they are rather predisposed to admire qualities and tastes in others different from their own. "If I were suddenly asked," says Mr. Helps, "to give a proof of the goodness of God to us, I think I should say that it is the most manifest in the exquisite difference He has made between the souls of men and women, so as to create the possibility of the most comforting and charming companionship that the mind of man can imagine."

It is this characteristic sympathy of woman which gives to home its charm, and to home and childhood reminiscences a sacredness which causes such songs as "Home Sweet Home" and "The Old Oaken Bucket" to be the favorites of all classes. When Samuel Woodworth wrote "The Old Oaken Bucket," he was living with his family in New York City. One hot day he came into the house and pouring out a glass of water, drained it eagerly. As he set it down he exclaimed, "That is very refreshing, but how much more refreshing would it be to take a good long draught from the old oaken bucket I left hanging in my father's well at home!" "Selim," said his wife, "wouldn't that be a pretty subject for a poem?" At this suggestion Woodworth seized his pen, and as the home of his childhood rose vividly to his fancy, he wrote the now familiar words.

There are few men who have written so wisely on the subject of marriage as Sir Henry Taylor. What he says about the influence of a happy union in its relation to successful statesmanship applies to all conditions of life. The true wife, he says, should possess such qualities as will tend to make home as much as may be a place of repose. To this end, she should have sense enough or worth enough to exempt her husband as much as possible from the troubles of family management, and more especially from all possibility of debt. "She should be pleasing to his eyes and to his taste; the taste goes deep into the nature of all men—love is hardly apart from it; and in a life of care and excitement, that home which is not the seat of love can not be a place of repose—rest for the brain, and peace for the spirit, being only to be had through the softening of the affections."

The true wife takes a sympathy in her husband's pursuits. She cheers him, encourages him, and helps him. She enjoys his successes and his pleasures, and makes as little as possible over his vexations. In his seventy-second year, Faraday, after a long and happy marriage, wrote to his wife: "I long to see you, dearest and to talk over things together, and call to mind al the kindnesses I have received. My head is full, and my heart also, but my recollection rapidly fails, even as regards the friends that are in the room with me. You will have to resume your old function of being pillow to my mind, and a rest—a happy-making wife."

Some persons are disappointed in marriage, because they expect too much from it; but many more, because they do not bring into the co-partnership their fair share of cheerfulness, kindness, forbearance and common sense. Their imagination has perhaps pictured a condition never experienced on this side heaven, and when real life comes with its troubles and cares, there is a sudden waking-up as from a dream. Or they look for something approaching perfection in their chosen companion, and discover by experience that the fairest of characters have their weaknesses. The golden rule of married life is, "bear and forbear." Marriage, like government, is a series of compromises. One must give and take, refrain and restrain, endure and be patient. One may not be blind to another's failings, but they may at least be borne with good-natured forbearance. Of all qualities, good temper is the one that wears and works the best in married life. Conjoined with self-control, it gives patience—the patience to bear and forbear, to listen without retort, to refrain until the angry flash has passed. How true it is in marriage that "the soft answer turneth away wrath."

It has been said that girls are very good at making nets, but that it would be better still if they would learn to make cages. Men are often as easily caught as birds, but as difficult to keep. If the wife cannot make her home bright and happy, so that it shall be the cleanest, sweetest, cheerfulest place that her husband can find refuge in—a retreat from the toils and troubles of the outer world—then God help the poor man, for he is virtually homeless!

No wise person will marry for beauty mainly. It may exercise a powerful attraction in the first place, but it is found to be of comparatively little consequence afterwards. Not that beauty of person is to le underestimated, for, other things being equal, handsomeness of form and beauty of features are the outward manifestations of health. But to marry a handsome figure without character, fine features unbeautified by sentiment or good nature, is the most deplorable of mistakes. As even the finest landscape, seen daily, becomes monotonous, so does the most beautiful face, unless a beautiful nature shines through it. The beauty of today becomes commonplace tomorrow; whereas goodness, displayed through the most ordinary features, is perennially lovely. Moreover this kind of beauty improves with age, and time ripens rather than destroys it. After the first year, married people rarely think of each other's features, and whether they be classically beautiful or otherwise. But they never fail to be cognizant of each other's temper. "When I see a man," says Addison, "with a sour, riveled face, I cannot forbear pitying his wife; and when I meet with an open, ingenuous countenance, I think of the happiness of his friends, his family and his relations."

A man's moral character is, necessarily, powerfully influenced by his wife. A lower nature will drag him down, as a higher will lift him up. The former will deaden his sympathies, dissipate his energies and distort his life; while the latter, by satisfying his affections, will strengthen his moral nature, and, by giving him repose, tend to energize his intellect. Not only so, but a woman of high principles will insensibly elevate the aims and purposes of her husband, as one of low principles will unconsciously degrade them. De Tocqueville was profoundly impressed by this truth. He entertained the opinion that man could have no such mainstay in life as the companionship of a wife of good temper and high principle. He says that, in the course of his life, he had seen even weak men display real public virtue, because they had by their side a woman of noble character, who sustained them in their career, and exercised a fortifying influence on their views of public duty; while, on the contrary, he had still oftener seen men of great and generous instincts transformed into vulgar self-seekers, by contact with women of narrow natures, devoted to an imbecile love of pleasure, and from whose minds the grand motive of Duty was altogether absent. De Tocqueville himself had the good fortune to be blessed with an admirable wife; and in his letters to his intimate friends he spoke most gratefully of the comfort and support he derived from her sustaining courage, her equanimity of temper, and her nobility of character. The more, indeed, that De Tocqueville saw of the world and of practical life, the more convinced he became of the necessity of healthy domestic conditions for a man's growth in virtue and goodness. Especially did he regard marriage as of inestimable importance in regard to man and woman's true happiness; and he was accustomed to speak of his own as the wisest action of his life. Writing to his bosom friend, De Kergorlay, he said: "Of all the blessings which God has given me, the greatest of all, in my eyes, is to have lighted on Marie. You can not imagine what she is in great trials. Usually so gentle, she then becomes strong and energetic. She watches me without my knowing it; she softens, calms, and strengthens me in difficulties which disturb *me* but leave her serene." In another letter he says: "I can not describe to you the happiness yielded in the long run by the habitual society of a woman in whose soul all that is good in your own is reflected naturally, and even improved. When I say or do a thing which seems to me to be perfectly right, I read in Marie's countenance an expression of proud satisfaction which elevates me. And so, when my conscience reproaches me, her face instantly clouds over. Although I have great power over her mind, I see with pleasure that she awes me; and so long as I love her as I do now, I am sure that I shall never allow myself to be drawn into any thing that is wrong."

M. Guizot was in like manner sustained and encouraged, amidst his many vicissitudes and disappointments, by his noble wife. If he was treated with harshness by his political enemies, his consolation was in the tender affection which filled his home with sunshine. Though his public life was bracing and stimulating, he felt, nevertheless, that it was cold and calculating, and neither filled the soul nor elevated the character. "Man longs for a happiness," he says in his "Memoires," "more complete and more tender than that which all the labors and triumphs of active exertion and public importance can bestow. What I know today, at the end of my race, I have felt when it began, and during its continuance. Even in the midst of great undertakings, domestic affections form the basis of life; and the most brilliant career has only superficial and incomplete enjoyments, if a stranger to the happy ties of family and friendship." We have spoken of the influence of a wife upon a man's character. There are few men strong enough to resist the influence of a lower character in a wife. If she do not sustain and elevate what is highest in his nature, she will speedily reduce him to her own level. Thus a wife may be the making or the unmaking of the best of men.

Sir Samuel Romilly left behind him, in his Autobiography, a touching picture of his wife, to whom he attributed no small measure of the success and happiness that accompanied him through life. "For the last fifteen years," he said, "my happiness has been the constant study of the most excellent of wives—a woman in whom a strong understanding, the noblest and most elevated sentiments, and the most courageous virtue, are united to the warmest affection and to the utmost delicacy of mind and heart; and all these intellectual perfections are graced by the most splendid beauty that human eyes ever beheld." Romilly's affection and admiration for this noble woman endured to the end; and when she died the shock proved greater than his sensitive nature could bear. Sleep left his eyelids, his mind became unhinged, and three days after her death the sad event occurred which brought his own valued life to a close. Sir Francis Burdett, to whom Romilly had been often politically opposed, fell into such a state of profound melancholy on the death of his wife that he persistently refused nourishment of any kind, and died before the removal of her remains from the house; and husband and wife were laid side by side in the same grave. Not only have women been the best companions, friends, and counselors, but they have in many cases been the most effective helpers of their husbands in special lines of work. Galvani was especially happy in his wife. It is said to have been through her quick observation of the circumstance of the leg of a frog, placed near an electrical machine, becoming convulsed when touched by a knife, that her husband was first led to investigate the science which has since become identified with his name. Lavoisier's wife also was a woman of real scientific ability, who not only shared in her husband's pursuits, but even undertook the task of engraving the plates that accompanied his "Elements."

The late Dr. Buckland had another true helper in his wife, who assisted him with her pen, prepared and mended his fossils, and furnished many of the drawings and illustrations of his published works. "Not with standing her devotion to her husband's pursuits," says her son, Frank Buckland, in the preface to one of his father's works, "she did not neglect the education of her children, but occupied her mornings in superintending their instruction in sound and useful knowledge. The sterling value of her labors they now in after-life fully appreciate, and feel most thankful that they were blessed with so good a mother."

A still more remarkable instance of helpfulness in a wife is presented in the case of Huber the Geneva naturalist. Huber was blind from his seventeenth year, and yet he found means to study and master a branch of natural history demanding the closest observation and the keenest eyesight. It was through the eyes of his wife that his mind worked as if they had been his own. She encouraged her husband's studies as a means of alleviating his privation, which at length he came to forget; and his life was as prolonged and happy as is usual with naturalists. He even went so far as to declare that he should be miserable were he to regain his eyesight. "I should not know," he said, "to what extent a person in my situation could be beloved; besides, to me my wife is always young, fresh, and pretty, which is no light matter." Huber's great work on "Bees" is still regarded as a masterpiece, embodying a vast amount of original observation on their habits and natural history. Indeed, while reading his descriptions, one would suppose that they were the work of a singularly keen-sighted man, rather than of one who had been entirely blind for twenty-five years at the time at which he wrote them.

Not less touching was the devotion of Lady Hamilton to the service of her husband, the late Sir William Hamilton. After he had been stricken by paralysis through overwork at the age of fifty-six, she became hands, eyes, mind and everything to him. She identified herself with his work, read and consulted books for him, copied out and corrected his lectures, and relieved him of all business which she felt herself competent to undertake. Indeed, her conduct as a wife was nothing short of heroic, and it is probable that but for her devoted and more than wifely help, and her rare practical ability, the greatest of her husband's works would never have seen the light. He was by nature unmethodical and disorderly, and she supplied him with method and order. His temperament was studious but indolent, while she was active and energetic. She abounded in the qualities which he most lacked. He had the genius, to which her vigorous nature gave the force and impulse.

When Sir William Hamilton was elected to his professorship, after a severe and even bitter contest, his opponents, professing to regard him as a visionary, predicted that he could never teach a class of students, and that his appointment would prove a total failure. He determined, with the help of his wife, to justify the choice of his supporters, and to prove that his enemies were false prophets. Having no stock of lectures on hand, each lecture of the first course was written out day by day, as it was to be delivered on the following morning. His wife sat up with him night after night, to write out a fair copy of the lectures from the rough sheets, which he drafted in the adjoining room. "On some occasions," says his biographer, "the subject of the lecture would prove less easily managed than on others, and then Sir William would be found writing as late as nine o'clock in the morning, while his faithful but wearied amanuensis had fallen asleep on a sofa." Sometimes the finishing touches to the lecture were left to be given just before the class-hour. Thus helped, Sir William completed his course; his reputation as a lecturer was established, and he eventually became recognized throughout Europe as one of the leading intellects of his time.

The woman who soothes anxiety by her presence, who charms and allays irritability by her sweetness of temper, is a consoler as well as a true helper. Niebuhr always spoke of his wife as a fellow-worker with him in this sense. Without the peace and consolation which he found in her society, his nature would have fretted in comparative uselessness. "Her sweetness of temper and her love," said he, "raise me above the earth, and in a manner separate me from this life." But she was a helper in another and more direct way. Niebuhr was accustomed to discuss with his wife every historical discovery, every political event, every novelty in literature; and it was mainly for her pleasure and approbation, in the first instance, that he labored while preparing himself for the instruction of the world at large.

The wife of John Stuart Mill was another worthy helper of her husband, though in a more abstruse department of study, as we learn from his touching dedication of the treatise "On Liberty." "To the beloved and deplored memory of her who was the inspirer, and in part the author, of all that is best in my writings—the friend and wife, whose exalted sense of truth and right was my strongest incitement, and whose approbation was my chief reward, I dedicate this volume."

Not less touching is the testimony borne by another great living writer to the character of his wife, in the inscription upon the tombstone of Mrs. Carlyle, where are inscribed these words: "In her bright existence she had more sorrows than are common, but also a soft amiability, a capacity of discernment, and a noble loyalty of heart, which are rare. For forty years she was the true and loving helpmate of her husband, and by act and word unweariedly forwarded him as none else could in all of worth that he did or attempted."

Besides being a helper, woman is emphatically a consoler. Her sympathy is unfailing. She soothes, cheers, and comforts. Never was this more true than in the case of the wife of Tom Hood, whose tender devotions to him, during a life that was a prolonged illness, is one of the most affecting things in biography. A woman of excellent good sense, she appreciated her husband's genius, and, by encouragement and sympathy, cheered and heartened him to renewed efforts in many a weary struggle for life. She created about him an atmosphere of hope and cheerfulness, and no where did the sunshine of her love seem so bright as when lighting up the couch of her invalid husband. Nor was he unconscious of her worth In one of his letters to her, when absent from his side, Hood said: "I never was any thing, dearest, till I knew you; and I have been a better, happier, and more prosperous man ever since. Lay by that truth in lavender, sweetest, and remind me of it when I fail. I am writing warmly and fondly, but not without good cause. First, your own affectionate letter, lately received; next, the remembrance of our dear children, pledges—what darling ones!—of our old familiar love; then, a delicious impulse to pour out the overflowings of my heart into yours; and last, not least, the knowledge that your dear eyes will read what my hand is now writing. Perhaps there is an afterthought that, whatever may befall me, the wife of my bosom will have the acknowledgment of her tenderness, worth, excellence—all that is wifely or womanly—from my pen."

Many other similar true-hearted wives rise up in the memory, to recite whose praises would more than fill up our remaining space—such as Flaxman's wife, Ann Denham, who cheered and encouraged her husband through life in the prosecution of his art, accompanying him to Rome, sharing in his labors and anxieties, and finally in his triumphs, and to whom Flaxman, in the fortieth year of their married life, dedicated his beautiful designs illustrative of Faith, Hope, and Charity, in token of his deep and undimmed affection—such as Katherine Boutcher "dark-eyed Kate," the wife of William Blake, who believed her husband to be the first genius on earth, worked off the impressions of his plates and colored them beautifully with her own hand, bore with him in all his erratic ways, sympathized with him in his sorrows and joys for forty-five years, and comforted him until his dying hour—his last sketch, made in his seventy-first year, being a likeness of himself, before making which, seeing his wife crying by his side, he said, "Stay, Kate! just keep as you are; I will draw your portrait, for you have ever been an angel to me."

Trial and sufferings are the tests of married life. They bring out the real character, and often tend to produce the closest union. They may even be the spring of the purest happiness. Uninterrupted joy, like uninterrupted success, is not good for either man or woman. When Heine's wife died, he began to reflect upon the loss he had sustained. They had both known poverty, and struggled through it hand in hand, and it was his greatest sorrow that she was taken from him at the moment when fortune was beginning to smile upon him, but too late for her to share in his prosperity. "Alas," said he, "among my griefs must I reckon even her love—the strongest, truest, that ever inspired the heart of woman—which made me the happiest of mortals, and yet was to me a fountain of a thousand distresses, inquietudes and cares? To entire cheerfulness, perhaps, she never attained, but for what unspeakable sweetness, what exalted enrapturing joys, is not love indebted to sorrow! Amidst growing anxieties, with the torture of anguish in my heart, I have been made, even by the loss which caused me this anguish and these anxieties, inexpressibly happy! When tears flowed over our cheeks, did not a nameless, seldom-felt delight stream through my breast, oppressed equally by joy and sorrow!"

There is a degree of sentiment in German love which seems strange to English readers. The German betrothal is a ceremony of almost equal importance to the marriage itself, and in that state the sentiments are allowed free play, while English lovers are restrained, shy, and as if ashamed of their feelings. Take, for instance, the case of Herder, whom his future wife first saw in the pulpit. "I heard," she says, "the voice of an angel, and soul's words such as I had never heard before. In the afternoon I saw him, and stammered out my thanks to him; from this time forth our souls were one." They were betrothed long before their means would permit them to marry, but at length they were united. "We were married," says Caroline, the wife, "by the rose-light of a beautiful evening, We were one heart, one soul." Herder was equally ecstatic in his language. "I have a wife," he wrote, "that is the tree, the consolation, and the happiness of my life. Even in flying, transient thoughts (which often surprise us), we are one."

Take, again, the case of Fichte, in whose history his courtship and marriage form a beautiful episode. He was a poor German student, living with a family at Zurich in the capacity of tutor, when he first made the acquaintance of Johanna Maria Rahn. Her position in life was higher than that of Fichte; nevertheless she regarded him with sincere admiration. When Fichte was about to leave Zurich, his troth plighted to her, she, knowing him to be very poor, offered him a gift of money before setting out. He was inexpressibly hurt by the offer, and, at first, even doubted whether she could really love him, but, on second thought, he wrote to her expressing his deep thanks, but at the same time, the impossibility of him accepting such a gift from her. He succeeded in reaching his destination, though entirely destitute of means. After a long and hard struggle with the world, extending over many years, Fichte was at length earning money enough to enable him to marry. In one of his charming letters to his betrothed he said: "And so, dearest, I solemnly devote myself to thee, and thank thee that thou hast thought me not unworthy to be thy companion on the journey of life. There is no land of happiness here below, I know it now, but a land of toil, where every joy but strengthens us for greater labor. Hand in hand we shall traverse it, and encourage and strengthen each other, until our spirits—oh, may it be together!—shall rise to the eternal fountain of all peace."

What a contrast does the courtship and married life of the blunt and practical William Cobbett present to the esthetical and sentimental love of these highly refined Germans! When he first set eyes upon the girl that was afterwards to become his wife, she was only thirteen years old, and he was twenty-one—a sergeant-major in a foot regiment stationed at St. John's, in New Brunswick. He was passing the door of her father's house one day in winter, and saw the girl out in the snow, scrubbing a washing-tub. He said at once to himself, "that's the girl for me." He made her acquaintance, and resolved that she should be his wife so soon as he could get discharged from the army. On the eve of the girl's return to Woolwich with her father, who was a sergeant-major in the artillery, Cobbett sent her a hundred and fifty guineas which he had saved, in order that she might be able to live without hard work until his return to England. The girl departed, taking with her the money, and five years later Cobbett obtained his discharge. On reaching London, he made haste to call upon the sergeant-major's daughter. "I found," he says, "my little girl a servant-of-all-work (and hard work it was), at five pounds a year, in the house of a Captain Brisac, and, without hardly saying a word about the matter, she put into my hands the whole of my hundred and fifty guineas, unbroken." Admiration of her conduct was now added to love of her person, and Cobbett shortly after married the girl, who proved an excellent wife. He was, indeed, never tired of speaking her praises, and it was his pride to attribute to her all the comfort and much of the success of his after-life.

Chapter 25

Example—Models

"Children may be strangled, but Deeds never; they have an indestructible life, both in and out of our consciousness." —George Eliot.

"There is no action of man in this life, which is not the beginning of so long a chain of consequences, as that no human providence is high enough to give us a prospect to the end." —Thomas of Malmesbury.

EXAMPLE IS ONE of the most potent of instructors, though it teaches without a tongue. It is the practical school of mankind, working by action, which is always more forcible than words. Precept may point to us the way, but it is silent, continuous example, conveyed to us by habits, and living with us in fact, that carries us along. Good advice has its weight; but without the accompaniment of a good example it is of comparatively small influence; and it will be found that the common saying of "Do as I say, not as I do" is usually reversed in the actual experience of life.

All persons are more or less apt to learn through the eye rather than the ear; and, whatever is seen in fact, makes a far deeper impression than any thing that is merely read or heard. This is especially the case in early youth, when the eye is the chief inlet of knowledge. Whatever children see they unconsciously imitate.

They insensibly come to resemble those who are about them—as insects take the color of the leaves they feed on. Hence the vast importance of domestic training. For whatever may be the efficiency of schools, the examples set in our homes must always be *Of* vastly greater influence in forming the characters *Of* our future men and women. The home is the crystal of society—the nucleus of national character; and from that source, be it pure or tainted, issue the habits, principles, and maxims which govern public as well as private life. The nation comes from the nursery.

Example in conduct, therefore, even in apparently trivial matters, is of no light moment, inasmuch as it is constantly becoming inwoven with the lives of others, and contributing to form their natures for better or for worse. The characters of parents are thus constantly repeated in their children; and the acts of affection, discipline, industry, and self-control, which they daily exemplify, live and act when all else which may have been learned through the ear has long been forgotten. Hence a wise man was accustomed to speak of his children as his "future state." Even the mute action and unconscious look of a parent may give a stamp to the character which is never effaced; and who can tell how much evil action has been stayed by the thought of some good parent, whose memory their children may not sully by the commission of an unworthy deed, or the indulgence of an impure thought? The veriest trifles thus become of importance in influencing the characters of men. "A kiss from my mother," said West, "made me a painter." It is on the direction of such seeming trifles when children that the future happiness and success of men mainly depend. Fowell Buxton, when occupying an eminent and influential station in life, wrote to his mother, "I constantly feel, especially in action and exertion for others, the effects of principles early implanted by you in my mind." Buxton was also accustomed to remember with gratitude the obligations which he owed to an illiterate man, a game-keeper, named Abraham Plastow, with whom he played, and rode, and sported—a man who could neither read nor write, but was full of natural good sense and mother wit. "What made him particularly valuable," says Buxton, "were his principles of integrity and honor. He never said or did a Ming in the absence of my mother of which she would have disapproved. He always held up the highest standard of integrity, and filled our youthful minds with sentiments as pure and as generous as could be found in the writings of Seneca or Cicero. Such was my first instructor and, I must add, my best."

Early impressions are most lasting, and hence it is that parents cannot be too guarded in the example set before children. The Rev. John Newton's career is a striking example of the permanency of early impressions. His devout mother died when he was but six years of age. Although this event practically ended his moral education, the instruction received in those early years was not lost. Though apparently forgotten amid the dissipation of his sea-faring life, the impressions received were never wholly dismissed. Though the immediate cause of his reform was a dream at sea, yet the efficient cause was the quiet and apparently uneventful years of earliest childhood spent in a humble cottage home.

A curious circumstance is related by a survivor of the wreck of the "Central America," which sailed from Havana in 1847, and sunk in mid-ocean.

He had been some hours in the water, and had floated away from the rest, when the voice of his mother sounded in his ears. Years had passed away since he, a thoughtless child, had stolen one evening into the room of a dying sister, and devoured some grapes which had been placed beside her bed for her refreshment during the night. Terrified at his selfishness, he had slunk off to his chamber, but his mother, guessing who was the guilty intruder, had come to him and said. "Johnny, did you eat sister's grapes?" And now those words, uttered in a reproachful tone, again sounded distinctly in his ear, and he saw the pale face and tearful eyes of his mother as she turned away and left him. The act had wounded his conscience, but had long since been forgotten. Now, however, it rose upon his mind with a clearness and force which were appalling

Lord Langdale, looking back upon the admirable ex ample set him by his mother, declared, "If the whole world were put into one scale, and my mother into the other, the world would kick the beam." Mrs. Pennick, in her old age, was accustomed to call to mind the personal influence exercised by her mother upon the society amidst which she moved. When she entered a room it had the effect of immediately raising the tone of the conversation, and as if purifying the moral atmosphere—all seeming to breathe more freely and stand more erectly. "In her presence," says the daughter, "I became for the time transformed into another person." So much does the moral health depend upon the moral atmosphere that is breathed, and so great is the influence daily exercised by parents over their children by living a life before their eyes, that perhaps the best system of parental instruction might be summed up in these two words: "Improve thyself."

There is, indeed, an essence of immortality in the life of man, even in this world. No individual in the universe stands alone; he is a component part of a system of mutual dependencies; and by his several acts he either increases or diminishes the sum of human good now and forever. As the present is rooted in the past, and the lives and examples of our forefathers still to a great extent influence us, so are we by our daily acts contributing to form the condition and character of the future. Man is a fruit formed and ripened by the culture of all the foregoing centuries; and the living generation continues the magnetic current of action and example destined to bind the remotest past with the most distant future. No man's acts die utterly; and though his body may resolve into dust and air, his good or his bad deeds will still he bringing forth fruit after their kind, and influencing future generations for all time to come. It is in this momentous and solemn fact that the great peril and responsibility of human existence lies.

Thus, every act we do or word we utter, as well as every act we witness or word we hear, carries with it an influence which extends over, and gives a color, not only to the whole of our future life, but makes itself felt upon the whole frame of society. We may not, and indeed can not, possibly, trace the influence working itself into action in its various ramifications amongst our children, our friends, or associates; yet there it is assuredly, working on forever. And herein lies the great significance of setting forth a good example—a silent teaching which even the poorest and least significant person can practice in his daily life. There is no one so humble, but that he owes to others this simple but priceless instruction. Even the meanest condition may thus be made useful; for the light set in a low place shines as faithfully as that set upon a hill. Everywhere, and under almost all circumstances, however externally adverse—in moorland districts, in cottage hamlets, in the close alleys of great towns—the true man may grow. He who tills a space of earth scarce bigger than is needed for his grave, may work as faithfully, and to as good purpose, as the heir of thousands. The commonest workshop may thus be a school of industry, science, and good morals, on the one hand; or of idleness, folly, and depravity, on the other. It all depends on the individual men, and the use they make of the opportunities for good which offer themselves.

A life well spent, a character uprightly sustained, is no slight legacy to leave to one's children, and to the world; for it is the most eloquent lesson of virtue and the severest reproof of vice, while it continues an enduring source of the best kind of riches. Well for those who can say, as Pope did, in rejoinder to the sarcasm of Lord Hervey, "I think it enough that my parents, such as they were, never cost me a blush, and that their son, such as he is, never cost them a tear."

True-hearted persons, even in the humblest station in life, who are energetic doers, may give an impulse to good works out of all proportion, apparently, to their actual station in society. Thomas Wright might have talked about the reclamation of criminals, and John Pounds about the necessity for Ragged Schools, and yet done nothing; instead of which they simply set to work without any other idea in their minds than that of doing, not talking. And how the example of even the poorest man may tell upon society, hear what Dr. Guthrie, the apostle of the Ragged School movement, says of the influence which the example of John Pounds, the humble Portsmouth cobbler, exercised upon his own working career:

"The interest I have been led to take in this cause is an example of how a man's destiny—his course of life, like that of a river—may be determined and affected by very trivial circumstances. It is rather curious—at least it is interesting to me to remember—that it was by a picture I was first led to take an interest in ragged schools—by a picture in an old, obscure, decaying burgh that stands on the shores of the Frith of Forth, the birth-place of Thomas Chalmers. I went to see this place many years ago; and, going into an inn for refreshment, I found the room covered with pictures of shepherdesses with their crooks, and sailors in holiday attire, not particularly interesting. But above the chimney-piece there was a large print, more respectable than its neighbors, which represented a cobbler's room. The cobbler was there himself, spectacles on nose, an old shoe between his knees—the massive forehead and firm mouth indicating great determination of character, and beneath his bushy eyebrows, benevolence gleamed out on a number of poor fagged boys and girls who stood at their lessons round the busy cobbler. My curiosity was awakened; and in the inscription I read how this man, John Pounds, a cobbler in Portsmouth, taking pity on the multitude of poor ragged children left by ministers and magistrates, and ladies and gentlemen, to go to ruin on the streets—how, like a good shepherd, he gathered in these wretched outcasts—how he had trained them to God and to the world—and how, while earning his daily bread by the sweat of his brow, he had rescued from misery and saved to society not less than five hundred of these children. I felt ashamed of myself. I felt reproved for the little I had done. My feelings were touched. I was astonished at this man's achievements; and I well remember, in the enthusiasm of the moment, saying to my companion—'That man is an honor to humanity, and deserves the tallest monument ever raised within the shores of Britain.' I took up that man's history, and I found it animated by the spirit of Him who had compassion on the multitude. John Pounds was a man of tact besides; and, like Paul, if he could not win a poor boy any other way, he won him by art. He would be seen chasing a ragged boy along the quays, and compelling him to come to school, not by the power of a policeman, but by the power of a hot potato. He knew the love an Irishman had for a potato; and John Pounds might be seen running holding under the boy's nose a potato, like an Irishman, very hot, and with a coat as ragged as himself. When the day comes when honor will be done to whom honor is due, I can fancy the crowd of those whose fame poets have sung, and to whose memory monuments have been raised, dividing like the wave, and, passing the great, and the noble, and the mighty of the land, this poor, obscure, old man stepping forward and receiving the especial notice of Him who said, Inasmuch as ye did it to one of the least of these, ye did it also to Me."

The education of character is very much a question of models; we mould ourselves so unconsciously after the characters, manners, habits and opinions of those who are about us. Good rules may do much, but good models far more; for in the latter we have instruction in action—wisdom at work. Good admonition and bad example only build with one hand and pull down with the other. Hence the vast importance of exercising great care in the selection of companions, especially in youth. There is a magnetic affinity in young persons which insensibly tends to assimilate them to each other's likeness. Mr. Edgeworth was so strongly convinced that from sympathy they involuntarily imitated or caught the tone of the company they frequented, that he held it to be of the most essential importance that they should be taught to select the very best models. "No company, or good company," was his motto. Lord Collingwood, writing to a young friend, said, "Hold it as a maxim, that you had better be alone than in mean company. Let your companions be such as yourself or superior; for the worth of a man will always be ruled by that of his company." It was a remark of the famous Dr. Sydenham that every body some time or other would be the better or the worse for having but spoken to a good or a bad man. As Sir Peter Lely made it a rule never to look at a bad picture if he could help it, believing that whenever he did so his pencil caught a taint from it, so, whoever chooses to gaze often upon a debased specimen of humanity and to frequent his society, can not help gradually assimilating himself to that sort of model. It is therefore advisable for young men to seek the fellowship of the good, and always to aim at a higher standard than themselves. Francis Horner, speaking of the advantages to himself of direct personal intercourse with high-minded, intelligent men, said, "I can not hesitate to decide that I have derived more intellectual improvement from them than from all the books I have turned over."

Contact with the good never fails to impart good, and we carry away with us some of the blessing; as travellers' garments retain the odor of the flowers and shrubs through which they have passed. Those who knew the late John Sterling intimately, have spoken of the beneficial influence which he exercised on all with whom he came into personal contact. Many owed to him their first awakening to a higher being; from him they learnt what they were, and what they ought to be. Mr. Trench says of him: "It was impossible to come in contact with his noble nature without feeling one's self in some measure *ennobled* and *lifted up,* as I ever felt when I left him, into a higher region of objects and aims than that in which one is tempted habitually to dwell." It is thus that the noble character always acts; we become insensibly elevated by him, and can not help feeling as he does, and acquiring the habit of looking at things in the same light. Such is the magical action and reaction of minds upon each other.

The chief use of biography consists in the noble models of character in which it abounds. Our great forefathers still live among us in the records of their lives, as well as in the acts they have done, which live also; still sit by us at table, and hold us by the hand; furnishing examples for our benefit, which we may still study, admire, and imitate. Indeed, whoever has left behind him the record of a noble life, has bequeathed to posterity an enduring source of good, for it serves as a model for others to form themselves by in all time to come; still breathing fresh life into men, helping them to reproduce his life anew, and to illustrate his character in other forms. Hence a book containing the life of a true man is full of precious seed. It is a still living voice; it is an intellect. To use Milton's words, "It is the precious life-blood of a master-spirit, embalmed and treasured up on purpose to a life beyond life."

Franklin was accustomed to attribute his usefulness and eminence to his having early read Cotton Mather's "Essays to do good," a book which grew out of Mather's own life. And see how good example draws other men after it, and propagates itself through future generations in all lands, for Samuel Drew avers that he framed his own life, and especially his business habits, after the model left on record by Benjamin Franklin. Thus it is impossible to say where a good example may not reach, or where it will end, if indeed it have an end. Hence the advantage, in literature as in life, of keeping the best society, reading the best books, and wisely admiring and imitating the best things we find in them. "In literature," said Lord Dudley, "I am fond of confining myself to the best company which consists chiefly of my old acquaintance, with whom I am desirous of becoming more intimate; and I suspect that nine times out of ten it is more profitable, if not more agreeable to read an old book over again, than to read a new one for the first time."

Sometimes a book containing a noble exemplar of life, taken up at random, merely with the object of reading it as a pastime, has been known to call forth energies whose existence had not before been suspected. Loyola, when a soldier serving at the siege of Pampcluna, and laid up by a dangerous wound in his leg, asked for a book to divert his thoughts: the "Lives of the Saints" was brought to him, and its perusal so inflamed his mind, that he determined thenceforth to devote himself to the founding of a religious order. Luther, in like manner, was inspired to undertake the great labors of his life by a perusal of the "Life and Writings of John Huss." Dr. Wolff was stimulated to enter upon his missionary career by reading the "Life of Francis Xavier," and the book fired his youthful bosom with a passion the most sincere and ardent to devote himself to the enterprise of his life. William Carey also got the first idea of entering upon his sublime labors as a missionary from a perusal of the voyages of Captain Cook.

Of Condorcet's "Eloge of Haller," Horner said: "I never rise from the account of such men without a sort of thrilling palpitation about me, which I know not whether I should call admiration, ambition or despair." And speaking of the "Discourses" of Sir Joshua Reynolds, he said: "Next to the writings of Bacon, there is no book which has more powerfully impelled me to self-culture. He is one of the first men of genius who has condescended to inform the world of the steps by which greatness is attained. The confidence with which he asserts the omnipotence of human labor has the effect of familiarizing his reader with the idea that genius is an acquisition rather than a gift; whilst with all there is blended so naturally and eloquently the most elevated and passionate admiration of excellence, that upon the whole there is no book of a more *inflammatory* effect." It is remarkable that Reynolds himself attributed his first passionate impulse towards the study of art, to reading Richardson's account of a great painter; and Haydon was in like manner afterwards inflamed to follow the same pursuit by reading of the career of Reynolds. Thus the brave and inspiring life of one man lights a flame in the minds of others of like faculties and impulse; and where there is equally vigorous effort, like distinction and success will almost surely follow. Thus the chain of example is carried down through time in an endless succession of links—admiration exciting imitation, and perpetuating the true aristocracy of genius.

Dr. Arnold was a noble and a cheerful worker, throwing himself, into the great business of his life, the training and teaching of young men, with his whole heart and soul. It is stated in his admirable biography that "the most remarkable thing in the Laleham circle was the wonderful healthiness of tone which prevailed there, It was a place where a new corner at once felt that a great and earnest work was going forward. Every pupil was made to feel that there was a work for him to do; that his happiness, as well as his duty, lay in doing that work well. Hence an indescribable zest was communicated to a young man's feeling about life; a strange joy came over him on discerning that he had the means of being useful, and thus of being happy; and a deep respect and ardent attachment sprang up towards him who had taught him thus to value life and his own self, and his work and mission in the world. All this was founded on the breadth and comprehensiveness of Arnold's character, as well as his striking truth and reality; on the unfeigned regard he had for work of all kinds, and the sense he had of its, value, both for the complex aggregate of society and the growth and protection of the individual. In all this there was no excitement; no predilection for one class of work above another; no enthusiasm for any one-sided object, but a humble, profound and most religious consciousness that work is the appointed calling of man on earth; the end for which his various faculties were given; the element in which his nature is ordained to develop itself, and in which his progressive advance towards heaven is to lie."

Chapter 26

Character—the True Gentleman

"That which raises a country, that which strengthens a country, and that which dignifies a country—that which spreads her power, creates her moral influence, and makes her respected and submitted to, bends the heart of millions, and bows down the pride of nations to her—the instrument of obedience, the fountain of supremacy, the true throne, crown, and sceptre of a nation;this aristocracy is not an aristocracy of blood, not an aristocracy of fashion, not an aristocracy of talent only; it is an aristocracy of Character. That is the true heraldry of man." —The London Times

THE CROWN AND GLORY of life is Character. It is the noblest possession of a man, constituting a rank in itself, and an estate in the general goodwill; dignifying every station, and exalting every position in society. It exercises a greater power than wealth, and secures all the honor without the jealousies of fame. It carries with it an influence which always tells; for it is the result of proved honor, rectitude, and consistency—qualities which, perhaps more than any other, command the general confidence and respect of mankind.

Character is human nature in its best form. It is moral order embodied in the individual. Men of character are not only the conscience of society, but in every well-governed State they are its best motive power; for it is moral qualities in the main which rule the world. Even in war, Napoleon said, the moral is to the physical as ten to one. The strength, the industry, and the civilization of nations—all depend upon individual character; and the very foundations of civil security rest upon it. Laws and institutions are but its outgrowth. In the just balance of nature, individuals, nations, and races, will obtain just so much as they deserve, and no more. And as effect finds its cause, so surely does quality of character amongst a people produce its befitting results.

Though a man have comparatively little culture, slender abilities, and but small wealth, yet, if his character be of sterling worth, he will always command an influence, whether it be in the workshop, the counting house, the mart, or the senate. Canning wisely wrote in 1801, "My road must be through Character to Power; I will try no other course; and I am sanguine enough to believe that this course, though not perhaps the quickest, is the surest." You may admire men of intellect; but something more is necessary before you will trust them. Hence Lord John Russell once observed in a sentence full of truth, "It is the nature of party in England to ask the assistance of men of genius, but to follow the guidance of men of character," This was strikingly illustrated in the career of the late Francis Horner—a man of whom Sidney Smith said that the Ten Commandments were stamped upon his countenance. "The valuable and peculiar light," says Lord Cockburn, "in which his history is calculated to inspire every right-minded youth, is this. He died at the age of thirty-eight; possessed of greater public influence than any other private man, and admired, beloved, trusted, and deplored by all, except the heartless or the base. No greater homage was ever paid in Parliament to any deceased member. Now let every young man ask—how was this attained? By rank? He was the son of an Edinburgh merchant. By wealth? Neither he, nor any of his relations, ever had a superfluous sixpence. By office? He held but one, and only for a few years, of no influence, and with very little pay. By talents? His were not splendid, and he had no genius. Cautious and slow, his only ambition was to be right. By eloquence? He spoke in a calm, good taste, without any of the oratory that either terrifies or seduces. By any fascination of manner? His was only correct and agreeable. By what, then, was it? Merely by sense, industry, good principles, and a good heart—qualities which no well-constituted mind need ever despair of attaining. It was the force of his character that raised him; and this character not impressed upon him by nature, but formed, out of no peculiarly fine elements, by himself. There were many in the House of Commons of far greater ability and eloquence. But no one surpassed him in the combination of an adequate portion of these with moral worth. Horner was born to show what moderate powers, unaided by any thing whatever except culture and goodness, may achieve, even when these powers are displayed amidst the competition and jealousy of public life."

Franklin, also, attributed his success as a public man, not to his talents or his powers of speaking—for these were but moderate—but to his known integrity of character. Hence it was, he says, "that I had so much weight with my fellow-citizens. I was but a bad speaker, never eloquent, subject to much hesitation in my choice of words, hardly correct in language, and yet I generally carried my point."

The rules of conduct followed by Lord Erskine—a man of sterling independence of principle and scrupulous adherence to truth—are worthy of being engraven on every young man's heart. "It was a first command and counsel of my earliest youth," he said, "always to do what my conscience told me to be a duty, and to leave the consequences to God. I shall carry with me the memory, and I trust the practice, of this parental lesson to the grave. I have hitherto followed it, and I have no reason to complain that my obedience to it has been a temporal sacrifice. I have found it, on the contrary, the road to prosperity and wealth, and I shall point out the same path to my children for their pursuit."

Every man is bound to aim at the possession of a good character as one of the highest objects of life. The very effort to secure it by worthy means will furnish him with a motive of exertion; and his idea of manhood, in proportion as it is elevated, will steady and animate his motive. It is well to have a high standard of life, even though we may not be able altogether to realize it. "The youth," says Mr. Disraeli, "who does not look up will look down; and the spirit that does not soar is destined perhaps to grovel." He who has a high standard of living and thinking will certainly do better than he who has none at all. "Pluck at a gown of gold," says the Scotch proverb, "and you may get a sleeve o't." Whoever tries for the highest results can not fail to reach a point far in advance of that from which he started; and though the end attained may fall short of that proposed, still, the very effort to rise of itself can not fail to prove permanently beneficial.

There is a truthfulness in action as well as in words, which is essential to uprightness of character. A man must really be what he seems or proposes to be. When a gentleman wrote to Granville Sharp, that from respect for his great virtues he had named one of his sons after him, Sharp replied: "I must request you to teach him a favorite maxim of the family whose name you have given him—*Always endeavor to be really what you would wish to appear.* This maxim, as my father informed me, was carefully and humbly practiced by *his* father, whose sincerity, as a plain and honest man, thereby became the principal feature of his character, both in public and private life." Every man who respects himself, and values the respect of others, will carry out the maxim in act—doing honestly what he proposes to do—putting the highest character into his work, slighting nothing, but priding himself upon his integrity and conscientiousness.

The true character acts rightly, whether in secret or in the sight of men. That boy was well trained who, when asked why he did not pocket some pears, for nobody was there to see, replied, "Yes, there was: I was there to see myself; and I don't intend ever to see myself do a dishonest thing." This is a simple but not inappropriate illustration of principle, or conscience, dominating in the character, and exercising a noble protectorate over it; not merely a passive influence, but an active power regulating the life. Such a principle goes on moulding the character hourly and daily, growing with a force that operates every moment. Without this dominating influence, character has no protection, but is constantly liable to fall away before temptation; and every such temptation succumbed to, every act of meanness or dishonesty, however slight, causes self degradation.

And here it may be observed how greatly the character may be strengthened and supported by the cultivation of good habits. Man, it has been said, is a bundle of habits, and habit is second nature. Metastasio entertained so strong an opinion as to the power of repetition in act and thought, that he said, "All is habit in mankind, even virtue itself." Butler, in his "Analogy," impresses the importance of careful self-discipline and firm resistance to temptation, as tending to make virtue habitual, so that at length it may become more easy to do good than to give way to sin. "As habits belonging to the body," he said, "are produced by external acts, so habits of the mind are produced by the execution of inward practical purposes, *i.e.*, carrying them into act, or acting upon them—the principles of obedience, veracity, justice and charity." And again, Lord Brougham says, when enforcing the immense importance of training and example in youth, "I trust everything, under God, to habit, on which, in all ages, the lawgiver as well as the schoolmaster, has mainly placed his reliance; habit, which makes everything easy, and casts the difficulties upon the deviation from a wonted course." Thus making sobriety a habit, and intemperance will be hateful; make prudence a habit, and reckless profligacy will become revolting to every principle of conduct which regulates the life of the individual. Hence the necessity for the greatest care and watchfulness against the inroad of any evil habit; for the character is always weakest at that point at which it has once given way, and it is long before a principle restored can become so firm as one that has never been moved. It is a fine remark of a Russian writer, that "Habits are a necklace of pearls; untie the knot, and the whole unthreads."

Wherever formed, habit acts involuntarily, and without effort, and it is only when you oppose it that you find how powerful it has become. What is done once and again, soon gives facility and proneness. The habit at first may seem to have no more strength than a spider's web, but once formed, it binds as with a chain of iron. The small events of life, taken singly, may seem exceedingly unimportant, like snow that falls silently, flake by flake, yet accumulated, these snowflakes form the avalanche.

Self-respect, self-help, application, industry, integrity—all are of the nature of habits, not beliefs. Principles, in fact, are but the names which we assign to habits; for the principles are words, but the habits are the things themselves; benefactors or tyrants, according as they are good or evil. It thus happens as we grow older, a portion of our free activity and individuality becomes suspended in habit, our actions become of the nature of fate, and we are bound by the chains which we have woven around ourselves.

It is indeed scarcely possible to over-estimate the importance of training the young to virtuous habits. In them they are the easiest formed, and when formed, they last for life; like letters cut on the bark of a tree, they grow and widen with age. "Train up a child in the way he should go, and when he is old he will not depart from it." "Remember," said Lord Collingwood to a young man whom he loved, "before you are five-and-twenty you must establish a character that will serve you all your life." As habit strengthens with age, and character becomes formed, any turning into a new path becomes more and more difficult. Hence, it is often harder to unlearn than to learn, and for this reason the Grecian flute-player was justified who charged double fees to those pupils who had been taught by an inferior master. To uproot an old habit is sometimes a more painful thing, and vastly more difficult than to wrench out a tooth. Try and reform a habitually indolent, or improvident, or drunken person, and in a large majority of cases you will fail. For the habit in each case has wound itself in and through life until it has become an integral part of it, and cannot be uprooted.

As daylight can be seen through very small holes, so little things will illustrate a person's character. Indeed, character consists in little acts, well and honorably performed; daily life being the quarry from which we build it up, and rough-hew the habits which form it. One of the most marked tests of character is the manner in which we conduct ourselves towards others. A graceful behavior towards superiors, inferiors, and equals, is a constant source of pleasure. It pleases others because it indicates respect for their personality; but it gives tenfold more pleasure to ourselves. Every man may, to a large extent, be a self-educator in good behavior, as in every thing else; he can be civil and kind, if he will, though he have not a penny in his purse. Gentleness in society is like the silent influence of light, which gives color to all nature; it is far more powerful than loudness or force, and far more fruitful. It pushes its way quietly and persistently, like the tiniest daffodil in spring, which raises the clod and thrusts it aside by the simple persistency of growing.

Morals and manners, which give color to life, are of much greater importance than laws, which are but their manifestations. The law touches us here and there, but manners are about us everywhere, pervading society like the air we breathe. Good manners, as we call them, are neither more nor less than good behavior; consisting of courtesy and kindness; benevolence being the preponderating element in all kinds of mutually beneficial and pleasant intercourse amongst human beings. "Civility," said Lady Montague, "costs nothing and buys every thing." The cheapest of all things is kindness, its exercise requiring the least possible trouble and self-sacrifice. "Win hearts," said Burleigh to Queen Elizabeth, "and you have all men's hearts and purses." If we would only let nature act kindly, free from affectation and artifice, the results on social good humor and happiness would be incalculable. The little courtesies which form the small change of life, may separately appear of little intrinsic value, but they acquire their importance from repetition and accumulation. They are like the spare minutes, or the groat a day, which proverbially produce such momentous results in the course of a year or in a lifetime.

Manners are the ornament of action; and there is a way of speaking a kind word, or of doing a kind thing, which greatly enhances their value. What seems to be done with a grudge, or as an act of condescension, is scarcely accepted as a favor. Yet there are men who pride themselves upon their gruffness; and though they may possess virtue and capacity, their manner is often such as to render them almost insupportable. It is difficult to like a man who, though he may not pull your nose, habitually wounds your self-respect, and takes a pride in saying disagreeable things to you. There are others who are dreadfully condescending, and can not avoid seizing upon every small opportunity of making their greatness felt. When Abernethy was canvassing for the office of surgeon to St. Bartholomew Hospital, he called upon such a person—a rich grocer, one of the governors. The great man behind the counter seeing the great surgeon enter, immediately assumed the grand air towards the supposed suppliant for his vote. "I presume, sir, you want my vote and interest at this momentous epoch of your life." Abernethy, who hated humbugs, and felt nettled at the tone, replied: "No, I don't: I want a pennyworth of figs: come look sharp and wrap them up; I want to be off." The cultivation of manner—though in excess it is foppish and foolish—is highly necessary in a person who has occasion to negotiate with others in matters of business. Affability and good breeding may even be regarded as essential to the success of a man in any eminent station and enlarged sphere of life; for the want of it has not infrequently been found in a great measure to neutralize the results of much industry, integrity, and honesty of character. There are, no doubt, a few strong tolerant minds which can bear with defects and angularities of manner, and look only to the more genuine qualities; but the world at large is not so forbearant, and can not help forming its judgments and likings mainly according to outward conduct.

Another mode of displaying true politeness is consideration for the opinions of others. It has been said of dogmatism, that it is only puppyism come to its full growth; and certainly the worst form this quality can assume, is that of opinionativeness and arrogance. Let men agree to differ, and, when they do differ, bear and forbear. Principles and opinions may be maintained with perfect suavity, without coming to blows or uttering hard words; and there are circumstances in which words are blows, and inflict wounds far less easy to heal. As bearing upon this point, we quote an instructive little parable spoken some time since by an itinerant preacher of the Evangelical Alliance on the borders of Wales:—"As I was going to the hills," said he, "early one misty morning, I saw something moving on a mountain side, so strange-looking that I took it for a monster. When I came nearer to it I found it was a man. When I came up to him I found he was my brother."

 The inbred politeness which springs from right-heartedness and kindly feelings, is of no exclusive rank or station. The mechanic who works at the bench may possess it, as well as the clergyman or the peer. It *is* by no means a necessary condition of labor that it should, in any respect, be either rough or coarse. The politeness and refinement which distinguish all classes of the people in many continental countries show that those qualities might become ours too—as doubtless they will become with increased culture and more general social intercourse—without sacrificing any of our more genuine qualities as men. From the highest to the lowest, the richest to the poorest, to no rank or condition in life has nature denied her highest boon—the great heart. There never yet existed a gentleman but was lord of a great heart. And this may exhibit itself under the hodden gray of the peasant as well as under the laced coat of the noble. Robert Burns was once taken to task by a young Edinburgh blood, with whom he was walking, for recognizing an honest farmer in the open street. "Why, you fantastic gomeral!" exclaimed Burns, "it was not the great coat, the scone bonnet, and the saunders-boot hose that I spoke to, but *the man* that was in them; and the man, sir, for true worth, would weigh down you and me, and ten more such, any day." There may be a homeliness in externals, which may seem vulgar to those who can not discern the heart beneath; but, to the right-minded, character will always have its clear insignia. William and Charles Grant were the sons of a farmer in Inverness-shire, whom a sudden flood stripped of every thing, even to the very soil which he tilled. The farmer and his sons, with the world before them where to choose, made their way southward in search of employment until they arrived in the neighborhood of Bury in Lancashire. From the crown of the hill near Wahnesley they surveyed the wide extent of country which lay before them, the river Irwell making its circuitous course through the valley. They were utter strangers in the neighborhood, and knew not which way to turn. To decide their course they put up a stick, and agreed to pursue the direction in which it fell. Thus their decision was made, and they journeyed on accordingly until they reached the village of Ramsbotham, not far distant. They found employment in a print-work, in which William served his apprenticeship; and they commended themselves to their employers by their diligence, sobriety, and strict integrity. They plodded on, rising from one station to another, until at length the two men themselves became employers, and after many long years of industry, enterprise, and benevolence, they became rich, honored and respected by all who knew them. Their cotton-mills and print-works gave employment to a large population. Their well-directed diligence made the valley teem with activity, joy, health, and opulence. Out of their abundant wealth they gave liberally to all worthy objects, erecting churches, founding schools, and in all ways promoting the well-being of the class of working-men from which they had sprung. They afterwards erected, on the top of the hill above Walmesley, a lofty tower in commemoration of the early event of their history which had determined the place of their settlement. The brothers Grant became widely celebrated for their benevolence and their various goodness, and it is said that Mr. Dickens had them in his mind's eye when delineating the character of the brothers Cheeryble. One amongst many anecdotes of a similar kind may be cited to show that the character was by no means exaggerated. A Manchester warehouseman published an exceedingly scurrilous pamphlet against the firm of Grant Brothers, holding up the elder partner to ridicule as "Billy Button." William was informed by some one of the nature of the pamphlet, and his observation was that the man would live to repent of it. "Oh!" said the libeller, when informed of the remark, "he thinks that some time or other I shall be in his debt; but I will take good care of that." It happens, however, that men in business do not always foresee who shall be their creditor, and it so turned out that the Grants' libeller became a bankrupt, and could not complete his certificate and begin business again without obtaining their signature. It seemed to him a hopeless case to call upon that firm for any favor, but the pressing claims of his family forced him to make the application. He appeared before the man whom he had ridiculed as "Billy Button" accordingly. He told his tale and produced his certificate. "You wrote a pamphlet against us once?" said Mr. Grant. The supplicant expected to see his document thrown into the fire; instead of which Grant signed the name of the firm, and thus completed the necessary certificate. "We make it a rule," said he, handing it back, "never to refuse signing the certificate of an honest tradesman, and we have never heard that you were any thing else." The tears started into the man's eyes. "Ah," continued Mr. Grant, "you see my saying was true, that you would live to repent writing that pamphlet. I did not mean it as a threat—I only meant that some day you would know us better, and repent having tried to injure us." "I do, I do, indeed, repent it." "Well, well, you know us now. But how do you get on—what are you going to do?" The poor man stated that he had friends who would assist him when his certificate was obtained. "But how are you off in the meantime?" The answer was, that, having given up every farthing to his creditors, he had been compelled to stint his family in even the common necessaries of life, that he might be enabled to pay for his certificate. "My good fellow, this will never do; your wife and family must not suffer in this way; be kind enough to take this ten-pound note to your wife from me; there, there, now—don't cry, it will be all well with you yet; keep up your spirits, set to work like a man, and you will raise your head among the best of us." The overpowered man endeavored with choking utterance to express his gratitude, but in vain; and putting his hand to his face, he went out of the room sobbing like a child.

The true gentleman is one whose nature has been fashioned after the highest models. It is a grand old name, that of gentleman, and has been recognized as a rank and power in all stages of society. "The gentleman is always a gentleman," said the old French general to his regiment of Scottish gentry at Rousillon, "and invariably proves himself such in need and in danger." To possess this character is a dignity of itself, commanding the instinctive homage of every generous mind, and those who will not bow to titular rank, will yet do homage to the gentleman. His qualities depend not upon fashion or manners, but upon moral worth—not on personal possessions, but on personal qualities.

Riches and rank have no necessary connection with genuine gentlemanly qualities. The poor man may be a true gentleman, in spirit and in daily life. He may be honest, truthful, upright, polite, temperate, courageous, self-respecting and self-helping—that is, be a true gentleman. The poor man with a rich spirit is in all ways superior to the rich man with a poor spirit. The brave and gentle character may be found under the humblest garb. Here is an old illustration, but a fine one. Once on a time, when the Adige suddenly overflowed its banks, the bridge of Verona was carried away with the exception of the center arch, on which stood a house, whose inhabitants supplicated help from the windows, while the foundations were visibly giving way. "I will give a hundred French louis," said the Count Spolverini, who stood by, "to any, person who will venture to deliver these poor unfortunate people." A young peasant came forth from the crowd, seized a boat, and pushed into the stream. He gained the pier, received the whole family into the boat, and made for the shore, where he landed them in safety. "Here is your money, my brave young fellow," said the count. "No," was the answer of the young man, "I do not sell my life; give the money to this poor family, who have need of it." Here spoke the true spirit of the gentleman, though he was in the garb of a peasant.

Not less touching was the heroic conduct of a party of Deal boatmen in rescuing the crew of a collier-brig in the Downs but a short time ago. A sudden storm which set in from the northeast drove several ships from their anchors, and it being low water, one of them struck the ground at a considerable distance from the shore, when the sea made a clean breach over her. There was not a vestige of hope for the vessel, such was the fury of the wind and the violence of the waves. There was nothing to tempt the boatmen on shore to risk their lives in saving either ship or crew, for not a farthing of salvage was to be looked for. But the daring intrepidity of the Deal boatmen was not wanting at this critical moment. No sooner had the brig grounded than Simon Pritchard, one of the many persons assembled along the beach, threw off his coat and called out, "Who will come with me and try to save that crew?" Instantly twenty men sprang forward with "I will," "and I." But seven only were wanted; and running down a galley-punt into the surf, they leaped in and dashed through the breakers, amidst the cheers of those on shore. How the boat lived in such a sea seemed a miracle; but in a few minutes, impelled by the strong arms of these gallant men, she flew on and reached the stranded ship, "catching her on the top of a wave"; and in less than a quarter of an hour from the time the boat left the shore, the six men who composed the crew of the collier were landed safe on Walmer Beach. A nobler instance of indomitable courage and disinterested heroism on the part of the Deal boatmen—brave though they are always known to be—perhaps can not be cited; and we have pleasure in here placing it on record.

There are many tests by which a gentleman may be known; but there is one that never fails—How does he exercise power over those subordinate to him? How does he conduct himself towards women and children? How does the officer treat his men, the employer his servants, the master his pupils, and man in every station those who are weaker than himself? The discretion, forbearance, and kindliness with which power in such cases is used, may indeed be regarded as the crucial test of gentlemanly character. When La Motte was one day passing through a crowd, he accidentally trod upon the foot of a young fellow, who forthwith struck him on the face: "Ah, sir," said La Motte, "you will surely be sorry for what you have done, when you know that *I am blind.*" He who bullies those who are not in a position to resist may be a snob, but can not be a gentleman. He who tyrannizes over the weak and helpless may be a coward, but no true man. The tyrant, it has been said is but a slave turned inside out.

Gentleness is indeed the best test of gentlemanliness. A consideration for the feelings of others, for his inferiors and dependents as well as his equals, and respect for their self-respect, will pervade the true gentleman's whole conduct. He will rather himself suffer a small injury, than by an uncharitable construction of another's behavior, incur the risk of committing a great wrong. He will be forbearant of the weaknesses, the failings, and the errors, of those whose advantages in life have not been equal to his own. He will be merciful even to his beast. He will not boast of his wealth, or his strength, or his gifts. He will not be puffed up by success, or unduly depressed by failure. He will not obtrude his views upon others, but speak his mind freely when occasion calls for it. He will not confer favors with a patronizing air. Sir Walter Scott once said of Lord Lothian, "He is a man from whom one may receive a favor, and that's saying a great deal in these days."

Lord Chatham has said that the gentleman is characterized by his sacrifice of self and preference of others to himself in the little daily occurrences of life. In illustration of this ruling spirit of considerateness in a noble character, we may cite the anecdote of the gallant Sir Ralph Abercrombie, of whom it is related, that when mortally wounded in the battle of Aboukir, he was carried in a litter on board the ship; and, to ease his pain, a soldier's blanket was placed under his head, from which he experienced considerable relief. He asked what it was. "It's only a soldier's blanket," was the reply. "*Whose* blanket is it?" said he, half lifting himself up. "Only one of the men's." "I wish to know the name of the man whose blanket it is." "It is Duncan Roy's of the 42d, Sir Ralph." "Then see that Duncan Roy gets his blanket this very night." Even to ease his dying agony the general would not deprive the private soldier of his blanket for one night. The incident is as good, in its way, as that of the dying Sydney handing his cup of water to the private soldier on the field of Zutphen.

Chapter 27

The Discipline of Experience

"Be the day weary, or be the day long,
At length it ringeth to evensong."
—Ancient Couplet.

PRACTICAL WISDOM is only to be learned in the school of experience. Precepts and instructions are useful so far as they go, but, without the discipline of real life, they remain of the nature of theory only. The hard facts of existence have to be faced, to give that touch of truth to character which can never be imparted by reading or tuition, but only by contact with the broad instincts of common men and women.

To be worth any thing, character must be capable of standing firm upon its feet in the world of daily work, temptation and trial; and able to bear the wear-and-tear of actual life. Cloistered virtues do not count for much. The life that rejoices in solitude may be only rejoicing in selfishness. Seclusion may indicate contempt for others; though more usually it means indolence, cowardice, or self-indulgence. To every human being belongs his fair share of manful toil and human duty; and it can not be shirked without loss to the individual himself, as well as to the community to which he belongs. It is only by mixing in the daily life of the world, and taking part in its affairs, that practical knowledge can be acquired and wisdom learned. It is there that we find our chief sphere of duty, that we learn the discipline of work, and that we educate ourselves in that patience, diligence, and endurance which shape and consolidate the character. There we encounter the difficulties, trials, and temptations which, according as we deal with them, give a color to our entire after-life; and there, too, we become subject to the great discipline of suffering, from which we learn far more than from the safe seclusion of the study or the cloister. Contact with others is also requisite to enable a man to know himself. It is only by mixing freely in the world that one can form a proper estimate of his own capacity. Without such experience, one is apt to become conceited, puffed up, and arrogant; at all events, he will remain ignorant of himself, though he may heretofore have enjoyed no other company.

Any one who would profit by experience will never be above asking help. He who thinks himself already too wise to learn of others, will never succeed in doing any thing either good or great. We have to keep our minds and hearts open, and never be ashamed to learn, with the assistance of those who are wiser and more experienced than ourselves.

The man made wise by experience endeavors to judge correctly of the things which come under his observation, and form the subject of his daily life. What we call common sense is, for the most part, but the result of common experience wisely improved. Nor is great ability necessary to acquire it, so much as patience, accuracy, and watchfulness. Hazlitt thought the most sensible people to be met with are intelligent men of business and of the world, who argue from what they see and know, instead of spinning cobweb distinctions of what things ought to be.

For the same reason, women often display more good sense than men, having fewer pretentions, and judging of things naturally, by the involuntary impression they make on the mind. Their intuitive powers are quicker, their perceptions more acute, their sympathies more lively, and their manners more adaptive to particular ends. Hence their greater tact as displayed in the management of others, women of apparently slender intellectual powers often contriving to control and regulate the conduct of men of even the most impracticable nature. Pope paid a high compliment to the tact and good sense of Mary, Queen of William III, when he described her as possessing, not a science, but (what was worth all else) prudence.

The whole of life may be regarded as a great school of experience, in which men and women are the pupils. As in a school, many of the lessons learned there must needs be taken on trust. We may not understand them, and may possibly think it hard that we have to learn them, especially where the teachers are trials, sorrows, temptations, and difficulties; and yet we must not only accept their lessons, but recognize them as being divinely appointed.

The results of experience are, of course, only to be achieved by living; and living is a question of time. The man of experience learns to rely upon Time as his helper. "Time and I against any two," was a maxim of Cardinal Mazarin. Time has been described as a beautifier and as a consoler; but it is also a teacher. It is the food of experience, the soil of wisdom. It may be the friend or the enemy of youth; and Time will sit beside the old as a consoler or as a tormentor, according as it has been used or misused, and the past life has been well or ill spent.

"Time," says George Herbert, "is the rider that breaks youth." To the young, how bright the new world looks!—how full of novelty, of enjoyment, of pleasure! But as years pass, we find the world to be a place of sorrow as well as of joy. As we proceed through life, many dark vistas open upon us—of toil, suffering, difficulty, perhaps misfortune and failure. Happy they who can pass through and amidst such trials with a firm mind and pure heart, encountering trials with cheerfulness, and standing erect beneath even the heaviest burden!

A little youthful ardor is a great help in life, and is useful as an energetic motive-power. It is gradually cooled down by Time, no matter how glowing it has been, while it is trained and subdued by experience. But it is a healthy and hopeful indication of character—to be encouraged in a right direction, and not to be sneered down and repressed. It is a sign of a vigorous, unselfish nature, as egotism is of a narrow and selfish one; and to begin life with egotism and self-sufficiency is fatal to all breadth and vigor of character. Life, in such a case, would be like a year in which there was no spring. Without a generous seed-time, there will be an unflowering summer and an unproductive harvest. And youth is the spring-time of life, in which, if there be not a fair share of enthusiasm, little will be attempted, and still less done. It also considerably helps the working quality, inspiring confidence and hope, and carrying one through the dry details of business and duty with cheerfulness and joy.

"It is the due admixture of romance and reality," said Sir Henry Lawrence, "that best carries a man through life. . . . The quality of romance or enthusiasm is to be valued as an energy imparted to the human mind to prompt and sustain its noblest efforts." Sir Henry always urged upon young men, not that they should repress enthusiasm, but sedulously cultivate and direct the feeling, as one implanted for wise and noble purposes. "When the two faculties of romance and reality," he said, "are duly blended, reality pursues a straight, rough path to a desirable and practicable result; while romance beguiles the road by pointing out its beauties—by bestowing a deep and practical conviction that, even in this dark and material existence, there may be found a joy with which a stranger intermeddleth not—a light that shineth more and more into the perfect day."

The apprenticeship of difficulty is one which the greatest of men have had to serve. It is usually the best stimulus and discipline of character. It often evokes powers of action that, but for it, would have remained dormant. As comets are sometimes revealed by eclipses, so heroes are brought to light by sudden calamity. It seems as if, in certain cases, genius, like iron struck by the flint, needed the sharp and sudden blow of adversity to bring out the divine spark. There are natures which blossom and ripen amidst trials, which would only wither and decay in an atmosphere of ease and comfort. Thus it is good for men to be roused into action and stiffened into self-reliance by difficulty, rather than to slumber away their lives in useless apathy and indolence. It is the struggle that is the condition of victory. If there were no difficulties, there would be no need of efforts; if there were no temptations, there would be no training in self-control, and but little merit in virtue; if there were no trial and suffering, there would be no education in patience and resignation. Thus difficulty, adversity, and suffering are not all evil, but often the best source of strength, discipline and virtue.

The Spaniards are even said to have meanly rejoiced in the poverty of Cervantes, but for which they supposed the production of his great works might have been prevented. When the Archbishop of Toledo visited the French ambassador at Madrid, the gentlemen in the suite of the latter expressed their high admiration of the writings of the author of "Don Quixote," and intimated their desire of becoming acquainted with one who had given them so much pleasure. The answer they received was, that Cervantes had borne arms in the service of his country, and was now old and poor. "What!" exclaimed one of the Frenchmen "is not Senor Cervantes in good circumstances? Why is he not maintained, then, out of the public treasury?" "Heaven forbid!" was the reply, "that his necessities should be ever relieved, if it is those which make him write; since it is his poverty that makes the world rich!"

"I remember," says Northcote, "when Mr. Locke, of Newbury Park, first came over from Italy, and old Dr. Moore, who had a very high opinion of him, was crying up his drawings and asked me if I did not think he would make a great painter. I said, 'No, never!' 'Why not?' 'Because he has six thousand a year!'"

No doubt Thomas Gray would have given us many other literary productions equal or superior to his "Elegy" had he been persecuted by "the stings and arrows of an outrageous fortune," instead of being possessed of a patrimony which enabled him to follow a life of retirement, devoting most of his time to literary acquisition. He possessed one of the best stored minds of his age. His "Elegy, written in a country churchyard," is of itself sufficient to immortalize his name. It was written immediately after his return from a long journey abroad, in which he wandered over much of Europe. The changes which his few years of absence wrought among those he had been accustomed to meet, flushed with life's hopes and "busy cares"—the reminiscences called up by the newly made inscriptions in the old familiar church-yard—no doubt gave inspiration to the now familiar lines.

It is a mistake to suppose that men succeed through success; they much oftener succeed through failure. By far the best experience of men is made up of their remembered failures in dealing with others in the affairs of life. Such failures, in sensible men, incite to better self-management, and greater tact and self-control, as a means of avoiding them in the future. Ask the diplomatist, and he will tell you that he has learned his art through being baffled, defeated, thwarted, and circumvented, far more than from having succeeded. Precept, study, advice, and example could never have taught them so well as failure has done. It has disciplined them experimentally, and taught them what to do as well as what *not* to do—which is often still more important in diplomacy.

Many have to make up their minds to encounter failure again and again before they succeed; but if they have pluck, the failure will only serve to rouse their courage, and stimulate them to renewed efforts. Talma, the greatest of actors, was hissed off the stage when he first appeared on it. Lacordaire, one of the greatest preachers of modern times, only acquired celebrity after repeated failures. Montalembert said of his first public appearance in the Church of St. Roche: "He failed completely, and, on coming out, everyone said, 'Though he may be a man of talent, he will never be a preacher.'" Again and again he tried, until he succeeded; and only two years after his *debut,* Lacordaire was preaching in Notre Dame to audiences such as few French orators have addressed since the time of Bossuet and Masillon.

Thus, it is not ease and facility that tries men and brings out the good that is in them, so much as trial and difficulty. Adversity is the touch-stone of character. As some herbs need to be crushed to give forth their sweetest odor, so some natures must be tried by suffering to evoke the excellence that is in them. Hence trials often unmask virtues, and bring to light hidden graces. Men apparently useless and purposeless, when placed in positions of difficulty and responsibility, have exhibited powers of character before unsuspected; and where we before saw only pliancy and self-indulgence, we now see strength, valor, and self-denial.

As there are no blessings which may not be perverted into evils, so there are no trials which may not be converted into blessings. All depends on the manner in which we profit by them or otherwise. Perfect happiness is not to be looked for in this world. If it could be secured, it would be found profitless. The hollowest of all gospels is the gospel of ease and come fort. Difficulty, and even failure, are far better teachers. Sir Humphrey Davy said: "Even in private life, too, much prosperity either injures the moral man, and occasions conduct which ends in suffering, or it is accompanied by the workings of envy, calumny, and malevolence of others."

Life, all sunshine without shade, all happiness without sorrow, all pleasure without pain, were not life at all—at least not human life. Take the lot of the happiest—it is a tangled yarn. It is made up of sorrows and joys; and the joys are all the sweeter because of the sorrows; bereavements and blessings, one following another, making us sad and blessed by turns. Even death itself makes life more loving; it binds us more closely together while here. Dr. Thomas Browne has argued that death is one of the necessary conditions of human happiness, and he supports his argument with great force and eloquence. But when death comes into a household, we do not philosophize—we only feel. The eyes that are full of tears do not see; though in course of time they come to see more clearly and brightly than those that have never known sorrow. The wise person gradually learns not to expect too much from life. While he strives for success by worthy methods, he will be prepared for failures. He will keep his mind open to enjoyment, but submit patiently to suffering. Wailings and complainings of life are never of any use; only cheerful and continuous working in right paths are of real avail.

Nor will the wise man expect too much from those about him. If he would live at peace with others, he will bear and forbear. And even the best have often foibles of character which have to be endured, sympathized with, and perhaps pitied. Who is perfect? Who does not suffer from some thorn in the flesh? Who does not stand in need of toleration, of forbearance, of forgiveness? What the poor imprisoned Queen Caroline Matilda, of Denmark, wrote on her chapel-window ought to be the prayer of all—"Oh! keep me innocent! make others great."

Then, how much does the disposition of every human being depend upon their innate constitution and their early surroundings; the comfort or discomfort of the homes in which they have been brought up; their inherited characteristics; and the examples, good or bad, to which they have been exposed through life! Regard for such considerations should teach charity and forbearance to all men. At the same time, life will always be to a large extent what we ourselves make it. Each mind makes its own little world. The cheerful mind makes it pleasant, and the discontented mind makes it miserable. "My mind to me a kingdom is," applies alike to the peasant as to the monarch. The one may be in his heart a king, as the other may be a slave. Life is for the most part but the mirror of our own individual selves. Our mind gives to all situations, to, all fortunes, high or low, their real characters. To the good, the world is good; to the bad, it is bad. If our views of life be elevated—if we regard it as a sphere of useful effort, of high living and high thinking, of working for others' good as well as our own—it will be joyful, hopeful, and blessed. If, on the contrary, we regard it merely as affording opportunities for self-seeking, pleasure, and aggrandizement, it will be full of toil, anxiety, and disappointment.

There is much in life that, while in this state, we can never comprehend. There is, indeed, a great deal of mystery in life—much that we see "as in a glass darkly." But though we may not apprehend the full meaning of the discipline of trial through which the best have to pass, we must have faith in the completeness of the design of which our little individual lives form a part. We have each to do our duty in that sphere of life in which we have been placed. Duty alone is true; there is no true action but in its accomplishment. Duty is the end and aim of the highest life; the truest pleasure of all is that derived from the consciousness of its fulfillment. Of all others, it is the one that is most thoroughly satisfying, and the least accompanied by regret and disappointment. In the words of George Herbert, the consciousness of duty performed "gives us music at midnight."

> "This above all—to thine own self be true;
> And it must follow, as the night the day,
> Thou canst not then be false to any man."
> —*Shakespeare.*

> "Might I give counsel to any young man, I would say to him, try to frequent the company of your betters. In books and in life, that is the most wholesome society; learn to admire rightly; the great pleasure of life is that. Note what great men admired; they admired great things; narrow spirits admire basely, and worship meanly." —*W. M. Thackeray*

> "Man is his own star, and the soul that can
> Render an honest and a perfect man
> Commands all light, all influence, all fate;
> Nothing to him falls early or too late.
> Our acts our angels are, or good or ill,
> Our fatal shadows that walk by us still."
> —*Beaumont & Fletcher.*